JOURNAL FOR THE STUDY OF THE OLD TESTAMENT SUPPLEMENT SERIES
162

Editors
David J.A. Clines
Philip R. Davies

Editorial Board
Richard J. Coggins, Alan Cooper, Tamara C. Eskenazi,
J. Cheryl Exum, Robert P. Gordon, Norman K. Gottwald,
Andrew D.H. Mayes, Carol Meyers, Patrick D. Miller

JSOT Press
Sheffield

Of Prophets' Visions
and the
Wisdom of Sages

Essays in Honour of
R. Norman Whybray
on his Seventieth Birthday

edited by
Heather A. McKay
and David J.A. Clines

Journal for the Study of the Old Testament
Supplement Series 162

Copyright © 1993 Sheffield Academic Press

Published by JSOT Press
JSOT Press is an imprint of
Sheffield Academic Press Ltd
343 Fulwood Road
Sheffield S10 3BP
England

Typeset by Sheffield Academic Press
and
Printed on acid-free paper in Great Britain
by Biddles Ltd
Guildford

Production Editor	*Typesetter*
J. Webb Mealy	Robert Knight

British Library Cataloguing in Publication Data

Of Prophets' Visions and the Wisdom of
Sages: Essays in Honour of R. Norman
Whybray on his Seventieth Birthday.—(JSOT
Supplement Series, ISSN
0309-0787; No. 162)
I. McKay, Heather A. II. Clines, David
J.A. III. Series
221.6

ISBN 1-85075-423-3

CONTENTS

WISDOM

PENTATEUCH

ABBREVIATIONS

AB	Anchor Bible
AEM	*Archives épistolaires de Mari*
AHw	W. von Soden, *Akkadisches Handwörterbuch*
ANET	J.B. Pritchard (ed.), *Ancient Near Eastern Texts*
ARM	*Archives royales de Mari*
ArOr	*Archiv orientálni*
ATD	Das Alte Testament Deutsch
BA	*Biblical Archaeologist*
BBB	Bonner biblische Beiträge
BDB	F. Brown, S.R. Driver and C.A. Briggs, *Hebrew and English Lexicon of the Old Testament*
BETL	Bibliotheca ephemeridum theologicarum lovaniensium
BHK	R. Kittel (ed.), *Biblia hebraica*
BHS	*Biblia hebraica stuttgartensia*
Bib	*Biblica*
BJRL	*Bulletin of the John Rylands University Library of Manchester*
BK	*Bibel und Kirche*
BKAT	Biblischer Kommentar: Altes Testament
BN	*Biblische Notizen*
BR	*Biblical Research*
BWANT	Beiträge zur Wissenschaft vom Alten und Neuen Testament
BZ	*Biblische Zeitschrift*
BZAW	Beihefte zur *ZAW*
CBQ	*Catholic Biblical Quarterly*
CBQMS	*Catholic Biblical Quarterly*, Monograph Series
ConBOT	Coniectanea biblica, Old Testament
CTA	A. Herdner, *Corpus des tablettes en cunéiformes alphabétiques*
CQR	*Church Quarterly Review*
DBSup	*Dictionnaire de la Bible, Supplément*
EBib	Etudes bibliques
EncJud	*Encyclopedia Judaica*
ETL	*Ephemerides theologicae lovanienses*
ExpTim	*Expository Times*

FOTL	The Forms of the Old Testament Literature
FRLANT	Forschungen zur Religion und Literatur des Alten und Neuen Testaments
HALAT	W. Baumgartner *et al.*, *Hebräisches und aramäisches Lexikon zum Alten Testament*
HBT	Horizons in Biblical Theology
HKAT	Handkommentar zum Alten Testament
HSM	Harvard Semitic Monographs
HUCA	*Hebrew Union College Annual*
HTR	*Harvard Theological Review*
ICC	International Critical Commentary
IDBSup	*IDB, Supplementary Volume*
IEJ	*Israel Exploration Journal*
JAAR	*Journal of the American Academy of Religion*
JAOS	*Journal of the American Oriental Society*
JCS	*Journal of Cuneiform Studies*
JBL	*Journal of Biblical Literature*
JNES	*Journal of Near Eastern Studies*
JQR	*Jewish Quarterly Review*
JSOT	*Journal for the Study of the Old Testament*
JSOTSup	*Journal for the Study of the Old Testament, Supplement Series*
JSP	*Journal for the Study of the Pseudepigrapha*
JSS	*Journal of Semitic Studies*
KAI	H. Donner and W. Röllig, *Kanaanäische und aramäische Inschriften*
KAT	Kommentar zum Alten Testament
KHAT	Kurzer Hand-Commentar zum Alten Testament
MHUC	Monographs of the Hebrew Union College
NABU	*Nouvelles assyriologiques brèves et utilitaires*
NCB	New Century Bible
NICOT	New International Commentary on the Old Testament
NRSV	New Revised Standard Version
OBO	Orbis biblicus et orientalis
Or	*Orientalia*
OrAnt	*Oriens antiquus*
OTG	Old Testament Guides
OTL	Old Testament Library
OTS	*Oudtestamentische Studiën*
PTMS	Pittsburgh Theological Monograph Series
RA	*Revue d'assyriologie et d'archéologie orientale*
RB	*Revue biblique*
ResQ	*Restoration Quarterly*
RV	*Revised Version*
SBLDS	SBL Dissertation Series

SBS	Stuttgarter Bibelstudien
SBT	Studies in Biblical Theology
ScrH	*Scripta Hierosolymitana*
SEÅ	*Svensk exegetisk årsbok*
SJOT	*Scandinavian Journal of the Old Testament*
SJT	*Scottish Journal of Theology*
SOTSMS	Society for Old Testament Study Monograph Series
SR	*Studies in Religion / Sciences religieuses*
SUNT	Studien zur Umwelt des Neuen Testaments
THAT	*Theologisches Handwörterbuch zum Alten Testament*
ThWAT	G.J. Botterweck and H. Ringgren (eds.), *Theologisches Wörterbuch zum Alten Testament*
VF	*Verkündigung und Forschung*
VT	*Vetus Testamentum*
VTSup	*Vetus Testamentum*, Supplements
WMANT	Wissenschaftliche Monographien zum Alten und Neuen Testament
ZAW	*Zeitschrift für die alttestamentliche Wissenschaft*
ZDMG	*Zeitschrift der deutschen morgenländischen Gesellschaft*
ZDPV	*Zeitchrift des deutschen Palästina-Vereins*
ZTK	*Zeitschrift für Theologie und Kirche*

CONTRIBUTORS TO THIS VOLUME

Athalya Brenner is Senior Lecturer in the Department of General Studies at the Technion, Israel Institute of Technology, Haifa, Israel, and Professor of Feminism and Christianity at the Catholic University of Nijmegen, The Netherlands

Walter Brueggemann is Professor of Old Testament, Columbia Theological Seminary, Decatur, Georgia.

Henri Cazelles is Professeur honoraire à l'Institut Catholique, and Directeur d'Etudes à l'Ecole Pratique des Hautes Etudes, Paris.

Ronald Clements was formerly Samuel Davidson Professor of Old Testament Studies, King's College, London, University of London.

David Clines is Professor of Old Testament, University of Sheffield.

Richard Coggins is Senior Lecturer in Old Testament Studies, King's College, London, University of London.

James Crenshaw is Robert L. Flowers Professor of Old Testament, Duke University, Durham, North Carolina.

John Eaton was formerly Reader in Old Testament Studies, University of Birmingham.

Anthony Gelston is Reader in Theology, University of Durham.

Robert Gordon is Lecturer in Divinity, University of Cambridge.

Michael Goulder is Professor of Biblical Studies, University of Birmingham.

Lester Grabbe is Head of Department of Theology and currently Dean of Humanities, University of Hull.

Knud Jeppesen is Lecturer in Old Testament Studies, University of Aarhus, Denmark.

Michael Knibb is Professor of Old Testament Studies, King's College, London, University of London.

Heather McKay is Senior Lecturer in Religious Studies, Edge Hill College, Ormskirk, Lancashire.

Andrew Mayes is Professor of Hebrew, University of Dublin, and Fellow of Trinity College.

Tryggve Mettinger is Professor of Old Testament Studies, Lund University, Sweden.

Alberto Soggin is Professor of Hebrew Language and Literature, University of Rome.

Hugh Williamson is Regius Professor of Hebrew at the University of Oxford and Student of Christ Church.

R. NORMAN WHYBRAY:
A BIOGRAPHICAL SKETCH

Michael A. Knibb

Norman Whybray was born on 26 July 1923 at East Molesey, Surrey, and received his secondary education at Kingston Grammar School. He went up to Oxford on a State Scholarship in 1941 and, under war-time conditions, read French in the Honour School of Modern Languages, Part I, and then transferred to Theology. He underwent ordination training at Lincoln theological College in 1944–45 and was ordained Deacon in the Church of England in 1946, and Priest in 1947. After a curacy at St Michael's, Basingstoke, Norman held teaching posts at the General Theological Seminary, New York, and at the Queen's College, Birmingham, and was then appointed Professor of Old Testament and Hebrew at Central Theological College, Tokyo, in 1952. He remained there until 1965, although he did return to Oxford for a two-year period in 1960 to read for a DPhil under G.R. Driver; the thesis that he wrote was subsequently published under the title *Wisdom in Proverbs: The Concept of Wisdom in Proverbs 1–9* (1965). He returned permanently to England in 1965 to take up a post as Lecturer in the Department of Theology at the University of Hull; he was promoted to Reader in 1969, and was appointed Professor of Hebrew and Old Testament Studies in 1978. In normal circumstances Norman might have been expected to remain in post for some time. But in the stringent and difficult circumstances that affected all British universities in the early eighties Norman took the decision to retire early. He was appointed Emeritus Professor by the University of Hull in 1982, and he and Mary then moved to Ely, where they have remained ever since.

The circumstances of his early career led to the fact that Norman was already in his early forties by the time that his first book (*Wisdom in Proverbs*) appeared. But since then a constant stream of books and articles has issued from him, and in total these represent a remarkable scholarly achievement. A major part of his work has formed a continuation of his early concern with the Old Testament wisdom tradition, and what is perhaps his most important book in this area, *The Intellectual Tradition in the Old Testament* (1974), represented a significant challenge to received views about the role of the 'wise' in Israel. But he has also published two valuable commentaries, on Proverbs (1972), and on Ecclesiastes (1989), while his monograph on the Succession Narrative (1968), in which he emphasized the connections with scribal wisdom literature, should also be mentioned in this context. Norman's other major concern has been with Old Testament prophecy, particularly the book of Isaiah. His important commentary on Isaiah 40–66 (1975) was accompanied by two monographs that were concerned with problems raised by this section of the book. The first, *The Heavenly Counsellor in Isaiah xl 13-14* (1971), which happened to be the first in the unfortunately short-lived Society for Old Testament Study Monograph Series, is a detailed examination of the theological significance of this passage within the context of Second Isaiah. The second, *Thanksgiving for a Liberated Prophet: An Interpretation of Isaiah 53* (1978), offers both radical criticism of traditional interpretations of the meaning of this chapter, and an original interpretation of his own. But Norman's interests have not been confined just to prophecy and wisdom, and reference ought to be made here to his *The Making of the Pentateuch: A Methodological Study* (1987), which forms a valuable contribution to the debate, which has revived over the past two decades, concerning the origin of the Pentateuch.

This is not the place to try to offer a detailed evaluation of Norman Whybray's scholarly achievement, an achievement represented both by the books and monographs mentioned above and by his numerous articles. But perhaps it may be said here that in all his published work Norman has shown originality of thought, a willingness to challenge received opinions, careful attention to detail, clarity of exposition, and—a quality often lacking in scholars—common sense.

Norman Whybray has played a major role in the affairs of the Society for Old Testament Study since his return to this country in 1965. He has regularly attended meetings of the Society, where he has been a source of wise advice and has become a father-figure to many members of the Society. He has served on more than one occasion on the Committee of the Society. He was Editor of the Society's *Book List* from 1974 to 1980, and, although he followed a distinguished line of editors, it is fair to say that under his editorship the coverage received by the *List* and its standing in the scholarly world increased considerably. He is currently Editor of the very helpful series of *Old Testament Guides*, which are published under the joint imprint of JSOT Press and the Society for Old Testament Study, and he has himself written two of these guides. And he was elected President of the Society for 1982 and in that year presided over a memorable Summer meeting at the University of Hull. Those who were present at the meeting will not forget the marvellous tea that he and Mary generously provided on the lawn of their home at Hull. The meeting at Hull happened to coincide with Norman's retirement from his chair and formed a fitting climax to his career at Hull. It also followed a year after the well-deserved award to him by the University of Oxford of the degree of Doctor of Divinity.

In his personal life Norman Whybray has had to bear a double blow, and he has done so with characteristic fortitude. His first wife Hélène died in 1978 after a protracted illness, and then in 1990 his adopted son Peter also died. Those who know Norman are aware how much he was affected by the deaths of Hélène and Peter. But they were also very pleased that after the death of Hélène he met again an old friend, Mary, whom he had first known many years previously, and that they married in 1979.

For the past decade Norman and Mary have made their home in Ely, where they are frequently visited by friends and colleagues and by Mary's daughters. All alike benefit from very generous hospitality, while Old Testament colleagues also benefit from shrewd advice on Old Testament matters. While they have been at Ely, Mary has become steadily more involved in the local community, and Norman has continued with a very productive schedule of writing and editing. It is the earnest wish of all their friends and colleagues that they should both continue to flourish in their life together at Ely for many years to come.

PUBLICATIONS OF R. NORMAN WHYBRAY

Books

The Church Serves Japan (London: Society for the Propagation of the Gospel, 1956).

Gendai no Kyuyakuseisho Kenkyu Gaikan [A Survey of Modern Study of the Old Testament] (Tokyo: Kyobunkwan, 1961).

Wisdom in Proverbs: The Concept of Wisdom in Proverbs 1–9 (SBT, 45; London: SCM Press, 1965).

The Succession Narrative: A Study of II Sam. 9–20 and I Kings 1 and 2 (SBT, 2/9; London: SCM Press, 1968).

The Heavenly Counsellor in Isaiah xl 13-14: A Study of the Sources of the Theology of Deutero-Isaiah (SOTSMS, 1; Cambridge: Cambridge University Press, 1971).

The Book of Proverbs (The Cambridge Bible Commentary; Cambridge: Cambridge University Press, 1972); *Shingen* (trans. H. Matsuura; Tokyo: Shinkyo Shuppansha, 1983).

The Intellectual Tradition in the Old Testament (BZAW, 135; Berlin: de Gruyter, 1974).

Isaiah 40–66 (NCB; London: Oliphants, 1975).

Thanksgiving for a Liberated Prophet: An Interpretation of Isaiah Chapter 53 (JSOTSup, 4: Sheffield: JSOT Press, 1978).

Two Jewish Theologies: An Inaugural Lecture (Hull: University of Hull Press, 1980).

The Second Isaiah (OTG; Sheffield: JSOT Press, 1983).

The Making of the Pentateuch: A Methodological Study (JSOTSup, 53; Sheffield: JSOT Press, 1987).

Ecclesiastes (NCB: Grand Rapids: Eerdmans; London: Marshall, Morgan & Scott, 1989).

Ecclesiastes (OTG; Sheffield: JSOT Press, 1989).

Wealth and Poverty in the Book of Proverbs (JSOTSup, 99; Sheffield: JSOT Press, 1990).

Articles

'The Old Testament Concept of Corporate Personality and its Significance for Christian Doctrine' [Japanese], *Shingaku no Koe* (Tokyo) 2/1 (1956), pp. 1-14.

'The Dead Sea Scrolls and Christianity' [Japanese], *Shingaku no Koe* (Tokyo) 4/3 (1958), pp. 9-16.

'The Church in the Old Testament' [Japanese], *Shingaku no Koe* (Tokyo) 5/2 (1958), pp. 1-9.

'A Guide for Readers of the Book of Genesis' [Japanese], *Shingaku no Koe* (Tokyo) 6/3 (1960), pp. 1-9.

'A Graduate Seminary Library in the Mission Field', *Library Trends* (Illinois) 9/2 (1960), pp. 186-93.

'The Church at the Crossroads', *Worldwide* (London: SPCK) 46 (1961), pp. 1-8.

'Some Historical Limitations of Hebrew Kingship', *CQR* 163 (1961–62), pp. 136-50.

'National And/Or Catholic', in *On the Move to Unity: Cambridge Sermons on the Anglican Approach* (ed. J.E. Fison; London: SCM Press, 1962), pp. 29-34.

'Our Liturgical Heritage: The Psalms' [Japanese], *Shingaku no Koe* (Tokyo) 7/2 (1963), pp. 1-15.

'Canaanite Creation Myth', *ExpTim* 74 (1963), p. 309.

'Ecumenical Prospects in Japan', *Faith and Unity* (London: SPCK) 8/3 (1964), pp. 35-36.

'Proverbs viii 22-31 and its Supposed Prototypes', *VT* 15 (1965), pp. 504-14; repr. in *Studies in Ancient Israelite Wisdom* (ed. J.L. Crenshaw; New York: Ktav, 1976), pp. 390-400.

'Ecumenical Relations in Japan', *Network* (London: SPG), 1966.

'Some Literary Problems in Proverbs i–ix', *VT* 16 (1966), pp. 482-96.

'עֲנּוֹת in Exodus xxxii 18', *VT* 17 (1967), p. 122.

'The Joseph Story and Pentateuchal Criticism', *VT* 18 (1968), pp. 522-28.

'"Their Wrongdoings" in Psalm 99.8', *ZAW* 81 (1969), pp. 237-39.

'The United Monarchy', in *A Source Book of the Bible for Teachers* (ed. R.C. Walton; London: SCM Press, 1970), pp. 121-27; repr. in *A Basic Introduction to the Old Testament* (ed. R.C. Walton; London: SCM Press, 1980), pp. 95-104.

'The Divided Kingdom', in *A Source Book of the Bible for Teachers* (ed. R.C. Walton; London: SCM Press, 1970), pp. 127-33; repr. in *A Basic Introduction to the Old Testament* (ed. R.C. Walton; London: SCM Press, 1980), pp. 105-14.

'Proverbs, Book of', in *The Interpreter's Dictionary of the Bible. Supplementary Volume* (Nashville: Abingdon, 1976), pp. 702-704.

'A Response to Professor Rendtorff's "The 'Yahwist' as Theologian? The Dilemma of Pentateuchal Criticism"', *JSOT* 3 (1977), pp. 11-14.

'Qoheleth the Immoralist? (Qoh 7:16-17)', in *Israelite Wisdom: Theological and Literary Essays in Honor of Samuel Terrien* (ed. J.G. Gammie, W.A. Brueggemann *et al.*; Missoula, MT: Scholars Press, 1978), pp. 191-204.

'2 Samuel 11.1–12.31: King David's Seduction of Bath-Sheba and its Consequences', in *Readings in Biblical Hebrew*, II (ed. J.H. Eaton; Birmingham: Department of Theology, University of Birmingham, 1978), pp. 29-44.

'Slippery Words: IV. Wisdom', *ExpTim* 89 (1977–78), pp. 359-62.

'Conservatisme et radicalisme dans Qohelet', in *Sagesse et religion: Colloque de Strasbourg (octobre 1976)* (ed. E. Jacob; Paris: Presses Universitaires de France, 1979), pp. 65-81.

'Yahweh-Sayings and their Contexts in Proverbs, 10,1–22,16', in *La Sagesse de l'Ancien Testament* (ed. M. Gilbert; BETL, 51; Gembloux: Duculot; Leuven: Leuven University Press, 1979), pp. 153-65 (2nd edn, Leuven: Peeters and Leuven University Press, 1990, with additions on pp. 411-12).

'Reflections on Canonical Criticism', *Theology* 84 (1981), pp. 29-35.

'Ordinary Time: Thirteenth to Twentythird Sundays', in *This is the Word of the Lord: The Year of Mark (Year B)* (ed.

R. Duckworth; Oxford: Bible Reading Fellowship and Oxford University Press, 1981), pp. 114-38.

'The Identification and Use of Quotations in Ecclesiastes', in *Congress Volume, Vienna 1980* (ed. J.A. Emerton; VTSup, 32; Leiden: Brill, 1981), pp. 435-51.

'Qoheleth, Preacher of Joy', *JSOT* 23 (1982), pp. 87-98.

'Prophecy and Wisdom', in *Israel's Prophetic Tradition: Essays in Honour of Peter R. Ackroyd* (ed. R.J. Coggins, A. Phillips and M. Knibb; Cambridge: Cambridge University Press, 1982), pp. 181-99.

'Wisdom Literature in the Reigns of David and Solomon', in *Studies in the Period of David and Solomon and Other Essays: Papers Read at the International Symposium for Biblical Studies, December 1979* (ed. T. Ishida; Tokyo: Yamakawa Shuppansha, 1982), pp. 13-26.

'On Robert Alter's *The Art of Biblical Narrative*', *JSOT* 27 (1983), pp. 75-86.

'Two Recent Studies on Second Isaiah', *JSOT* 34 (1986), pp. 109-17.

'Old Testament Theology—A Non-Existent Beast?', in *Scripture: Meaning and Method. Essays Presented to A.T. Hanson* (ed. B.P. Thompson; Hull: Hull University Press, 1987), pp. 168-80.

'Ecclesiastes 1.5-7 and the Wonders of Nature', *JSOT* 41 (1988), pp. 105-12.

'Poverty, Wealth and Point of View in Proverbs', in *ExpTim* 100 (1988–89), pp. 332-36.

'Today and Tomorrow in Biblical Studies: II. The Old Testament', *ExpTim* 100 (1988–89), pp. 364-68.

'The Social World of the Wisdom Writers', in *The World of Ancient Israel* (ed. R.E. Clements; Cambridge: Cambridge University Press, 1989), pp. 227-50.

'Ecclesiastes', 'Servant Songs', 'Wisdom Literature', in *A Dictionary of Biblical Interpretation* (ed. R.J. Coggins and J.L. Houlden; London: SCM Press; Philadelphia: Trinity Press International, 1990), pp. 183-84, 628-31, 726-29.

'The Sage in the Israelite Royal Court', in *The Sage in Israel and the Ancient Near East* (ed. J.G. Gammie and L.G. Perdue; Winona Lake, IN: Eisenbrauns, 1990), pp. 133-39.

' "A Time to be Born and a Time to Die." Some Observations on Ecclesiastes 3:2-8', in *Near Eastern Studies Dedicated to H.I.H. Prince Takahito Mikasa* (ed. M. Mori, H. Ogawa and M. Yoshikawa; Bulletin of the Middle Eastern Culture Centre in Japan, 5; Wiesbaden: Harrassowitz, 1991), pp. 469-83.

'Sanday (William)', 'Sanders (Henry Arthur)', in *Supplément au Dictionnaire de la Bible*, XI (1991), cols. 1329-31, 1331-32.

'Thoughts on the Composition of Proverbs 10–29', in *Priests, Prophets and Scribes: Essays on the Formation and Heritage of Second Temple Judaism in Honour of Joseph Blenkinsopp* (ed. E. Ulrich *et al.*; JSOTSup, 149; Sheffield: JSOT Press, 1992), pp. 102-14.

Works Edited or Co-Edited

The Japan Christian Yearbook, 1965 (Tokyo: Kyobunkwan) (co-editor)

Book List of the Society for the Study of the Old Testament, 1974–80 (editor).

Old Testament Guides, Sheffield: JSOT Press, editor from 1983.

Forthcoming

'Wisdom Psalms' (J.A. Emerton Festschrift).

Proverbs (NCB; London: Harper–Collins; Grand Rapids: Eerdmans).

The Composition of the Book of Proverbs

PROPHECY AND SOCIETY IN ISRAEL[*]

Andrew Mayes

I

> The element in which the prophets live is the storm of the
> world's history, which sweeps away human institutions... It
> belongs to the notion of prophecy, of true revelation, that
> Jehovah, overlooking all the media of ordinances and institu-
> tions, communicates himself to the *individual*, the called one
> (Wellhausen 1973: 398).

That nineteenth-century characterization of prophecy, which
lifts it out of time and circumstance in a very idealistic way,
has fundamentally shaped our perception of prophecy until
recently. Even when Israelite prophecy was set in the context
of prophecy as a general religious phenomenon, and indeed
also when increasing emphasis came to be placed on the
psychological conditioning of prophetic experience, the basic
picture changed little. So, Lindblom (1962: 46) could write:

> A prophet may be characterized as a person who, because he is
> conscious of having been specially chosen and called, feels forced
> to perform actions and proclaim ideas which, in a mental state
> of intense inspiration or real ecstasy, have been indicated to him
> in the form of divine revelations.

The prophet is an individual who has been called; as the recipient of revelation, the prophet proclaims that revelation to an
audience.

It is no cause for wonder, then, that the study of the prophetic books should have concentrated on the retrieval of the

* It is a privilege to offer this as a tribute to Norman Whybray, both
for his wide-ranging and incisive contribution to the study of Old Testament prophecy and wisdom, and for his friendly encouragement and
thoughtful support for his colleagues.

authentic words of those individual prophets under whose names materials from a variety of backgrounds have been collected. The truth was to be found in the *ipsissima verba* of the great prophetic personalities, and everything else was secondary if not spurious. Gunkel's early studies identified the oldest prophetic forms as brief poems oriented to the future. Foretelling the future always remained their principal purpose, but the prophets also became concerned with giving the ethical reason why what they prophesied had to happen. So they added to their threats reproaches in which they raised accusation against Israel (Gunkel 1969: 48-75). Thus the basic framework of understanding was reached. The original prophetic word is a poetic oracle about the future. This was received by the prophets in a moment of ecstatic inspiration. When they proclaimed that word they added to it their own word of accusation, giving the reason for the doom expressed in the oracle.

The essential contours of this understanding are found also with von Rad:

> The divine word was, of course, primary in point of time: this was what came to the prophet in a moment of inspiration, to be passed on to those whom it concerned. This the prophet did by prefixing to it a diatribe which identified the people addressed (1965: 37).

Even Westermann, who, in reviewing the study of prophetic speech forms, seems to have attempted to break away from the value judgment that is beginning to become clear here, could not in the end do so. In other words, Westermann in the end concluded: 'God's word, in the proper sense, is only the announcement. It is designated as such by the introductory messenger formula...' (1967: 132); that is, it is the prophetic announcement about the future, and it alone, which is 'the real word of God' (149). Finally, Koch's fine and persuasive discussion of the forms of prophetic speech, which even includes the recognition that the formula 'Thus said the Lord...' does not refer to a specific point in time when the messenger received the word of God, cannot avoid distinguishing between the word of the prophet and the real divine word (Koch 1969: 190-92).

These are idealistic presentations of prophecy. They pre-suppose and reflect a model of prophecy that is certainly rooted in the Old Testament: so, in Amos 4.1-3 the prophetic word of accusation in v. 1 introduces, and roots in a particular situation, the divine word about the future that comes to expression in vv. 2-3. This model also, however, clearly expresses particular theological convictions about the way in which God relates to his creation. There is a strong reflection of Protestant rejection of any interruption in the immediate relationship between God and the individual, with an equally strong Protestant emphasis on the calling and duty to which the individual must submit in order to be right with God. On this view, these prophets truly were, in the words of another Old Testament scholar, 'proto-Protestants of an earlier dispensation' (Volz 1949: 30; cf. Berger 1963: 944).

II

Two elements of this idealistic presentation of prophecy stand out as worth closer examination. First, the prophet is one who has been called; secondly, the prophet is the recipient of revelations. Both are basic and essential features of this theo-logical model of prophecy; both serve to maintain and express this idealistic understanding.

In relation to the prophetic *call*, Lindblom (1962: 182) argued:

> In Israel the certainty of being called by Yahweh was one of the most characteristic features of the prophetic consciousness. This certainly was an impelling force in the lives of the prophets and at the same time a source of confidence and fortitude. The legitimacy of the true prophet and the authority of his message are established by his call. He knew that he was properly called by Yahweh to carry out his task. The false prophet is declared to be such, and his visions and messages are rejected as value-less, not because he did not have visions and ecstatic experi-ences, but because he had not been called.

In a similar way, von Rad (1965: 54-55) believed that it was the call that set the prophets apart from their fellow Israelites as individuals 'cut off from the religious capital on which the majority of the people lived', and made them dependent instead on their own inner resources. It was the call of Yahweh that characterized the genuine prophet.

The status of this account must be clarified carefully. It seems to mean, indeed it surely can only mean, that the true prophets of Yahweh knew that they were such because of their own inner conviction that they had received a call from Yahweh. It was on this ground that Jeremiah could declare to Hananiah, 'Hear now, Hananiah! Yahweh has not sent you, but you have made this people trust in a lie' (Jer. 28.15). This was not, however, a judgment open to anyone else to make; there was no objective, external mark that such a call had been given and received; there was no proof by which the prophets could demonstrate to others that they had been marked out by Yahweh.

This would imply that whatever may be the significance of the inner convictions of the prophet (and about that it is difficult for us to say anything), the reference that any prophet makes to a call must have a point other than that of establishing and demonstrating the validity of the claim to be a prophet. The conviction of the call may indeed have functioned to strengthen the prophet (any prophet) in the face of opposition, but it could never demonstrate legitimacy.

A fresh understanding of the purpose of prophetic references to a call begins with the observation that those prophetic passages which record such a call (Isa. 6; Jer. 1; Isa. 40.1-11; Ezek. 1–3) show quite clear formal similarities, at least insofar as they record the commissioning of the prophets, their objection to that commission, the divine reassurance and promise of Yahweh's presence, and a confirming sign. This pattern is, moreover, one that marks also the narrative of the call of Moses in Exod. 3.10-12.[1] The significance of this may be expressed in these terms: in referring to their call in this way the prophets are not so much demonstrating legitimacy as claiming legitimacy, a claim that is later formally reflected

---

1.   The formal structure of the call narrative has been investigated especially by Habel (1965: 297-323), Richter (1970), and Schmidt (1977: 123-30). The fact that some question may exist over the precise relationship of all appearances of the call form does not affect the point being made here.

and recognized in Deut. 18.15. The prophets claim to belong to the authentic Yahwistic religious tradition that, at least in Deuteronomy, is understood to reach back to Moses.

The form by which the prophets express their call also finds a parallel in Genesis 24, which relates the story of Abraham's sending his servant to his home country to seek a wife for Isaac. As the servant recounts this commission to Laban (Gen. 24.34-49), he refers to the commission, his objection, his master's reassurance, and the sign that confirmed the one designated as Isaac's wife. As with the prophetic call narratives, so here the messenger indeed refers to a point of time in the past when he had received his commission, but it is not on this that the emphasis lies. Rather, the purpose of the form is a twofold one: on the one hand, it is to assert that a commission has been given; on the other hand, it is to give expression to the nature and content of that commission. The prophetic call narratives (and it is only those to which we have access) reflect prophetic claims to be true representatives of Yahweh and express the substance of the commission that they have been given. They may also reflect the personal convictions of the prophets that they have been called, a conviction that may have functioned to strengthen and encourage them in the face of disbelief, but there is nothing here that to the outsider could have demonstrated their legitimacy. These call narratives are essentially vehicles of prophetic preaching and prophetic claims.

The *visionary experiences* of the prophets may also be given an idealistic type of interpretation that could be taken to confirm the model of prophecy expressed by Wellhausen and others. Here in these mysterious encounters with Yahweh the prophets received the divine message that they then imparted in the form of poetic oracles about the future.

Yet again, however, it is clear that it is hardly justifiable to stop short with this form of understanding,[2] and that for at least two reasons. In the first place, vision reports in the prophetic books follow a common general pattern consisting of

2. On prophetic visions, cf. especially Long 1976: 353-65; Schmidt 1979: 537-64; Zimmerli 1982: 95-118.

an introductory announcement followed by a brief transitional element and finally by the description of the vision itself. The regularity of this form indicates the possibility of its use as a conventional means of reporting a prophetic message, whether or not an actual vision gave rise to it. Jer. 24.1-10 is a very probable example of the conventional use of the form, for here the prosaic and expansive use of deuteronomistic expressions make it highly unlikely that it is anything other than a deuteronomistic sermon. In some cases, therefore, the conventional form of a visionary report may be used in order to convey a message that is actually rooted elsewhere. Secondly, however, even when actual visions do lie behind these reports, these cannot be understood in a simplistic way as the *fons et origo* of prophetic messages. Visions are states of mind, psychological conditions, to which some individuals are susceptible. Indeed, as 1 Kgs 22.13-23 and 2 Kgs 8.7-15 indicate, they represent states of mind that could be summoned to order. They are within the competence of the prophetic personality, as they divined the future on request, the means by which ideas, impressed on the unconscious mind, were brought to consciousness. The vision is, in other words, a vehicle rather than the source of prophetic understanding, and one cannot appeal to it as the mysterious point of communion between the prophet and Yahweh in which the divine message for Israel was received.

So, neither in the case of the call nor in the case of the visionary experience—both of which are foundational to the idealistic presentation of prophecy—can it be claimed that we have reached what might be called the characteristic essence of prophecy or the essential source of prophecy in unfathomable mystery. In both cases, we have *vehicles* of prophecy rather than foundations of prophecy. In the one case, we have a rhetorical form used to express the substance of the message; in the other, we may have the same thing, or, insofar as visions are actually present here, the record of psychological states of mind that the prophets themselves could induce. In neither case is there a strong support for the view that the prophet is to be understood solely as an individual called by Yahweh, to whom Yahweh gave revelations.

III

In the attempt to develop an understanding of prophecy alternative to the idealistic theological type of model, two terms have come to assume some importance. These are 'charisma' and 'ecstasy'. Neither is a particularly new term in the context of prophecy, but the one has undergone a revival and the other something of a transformation in sense, and these changes of perspective have contributed much to the development of a fresh view of prophecy as a historical and social as well as a religious phenomenon. The terms are by no means unrelated, but for the purposes of clarification they should be first examined separately.

The word *charisma* is associated particularly with the work of Max Weber who used it to denote a type of leadership or authority in society.[3] Whereas traditional authority is that handed down and exercised by the family heads in a traditional society, and legal-rational authority is that typical of a total system in a modern bureaucratic state, charismatic authority is personal, exclusive and entirely independent of traditional or hierarchic structures. Whereas the first two are characterized by permanence and stability, charismatic authority is characterized by instability and transience. Charismatic authority knows no routine, no laws or rules of procedure based on precedent; rather, it breaks open existing structures, introducing something new.

Of the type of charismatic leader, Weber (1964: 358-59) wrote:

> The term 'charisma' will be applied to a certain quality of an individual personality by virtue of which he is set apart from ordinary men and treated as endowed with supernatural, super-human, or at least specifically exceptional powers and qualities.

For Weber, the paradigmatic charismatic figure is, in fact, the

---

3.   For a good treatment of charismatic leadership within the Weber tradition, cf. Malamat 1976: 152-68. For a comprehensive study reference may also be made to Mayes 1989: index, *s.v.* 'charisma'.

prophet who brings a new divine word to challenge the traditional or accepted structures of society:

> We shall understand 'prophet' to mean a purely individual
> bearer of charisma, who by virtue of his mission proclaims a
> religious doctrine or divine commandment... The personal call is
> the decisive element distinguishing the prophet from the priest.
> The latter lays claim to authority by virtue of his service in a
> sacred tradition, while the prophet's claim is based on personal
> revelation and charisma (Weber 1965: 46).

It is clear, however, that Weber was strongly influenced here
by the individualistic understanding of prophecy typical of his
contemporaries such as Wellhausen, and that this stood in
some tension with his use of the relational term 'charisma' to
describe their activities. In fact, Weber did not maintain this
primary association of charisma with prophecy, but came to
use it rather to characterize the leaders of Israel in the pre-
monarchic period. It is to that context that the term was then,
largely under the influence of Alt and Noth, more or less
confined. The charismatic leaders of Israel were the so called
judges, individuals who came forward spontaneously in times
of crisis to lead Israel in victory over its enemies.

   This not altogether helpful restriction upon the application
of the term 'charisma' in the Old Testament context had quite
clear causes and consequences: it reflected a preconceived
understanding of the nature of prophecy along the idealistic
theological lines outlined above, and it tended to distort rather
than to clarify the historical and social significance of prophecy in Israel. Nevertheless, the association of prophecy with
charisma did not altogether disappear, and in fact received a
good theoretical grounding in Rendtorff's 'Reflections on the
Early History of Prophecy in Israel' (1967). Here it was argued
that pre-classical Israelite prophecy was marked by three
dominant concerns: with Israel as the people of Yahweh rather
than as a monarchic state, with the right conduct of war
according to the laws of the holy war, and with the observance
of sacral, covenant law. Insofar as early Israelite prophecy is
identified by these concerns, it can be argued that its real
roots then lie in pre-monarchic charismatic leadership, for

here these same concerns are dominant and characteristic.[4]

The term 'charisma', therefore, is not only appropriate also for early prophecy, but its continued use in this context highlights an essential aspect of prophecy that is otherwise neglected, that is, the relational character of prophecy as a social and historical phenomenon involving prophets with their followers. A prophet is not simply an individual, but an individual exercising a form of leadership over those who acknowledge that prophetic authority.

Weber (1965: 3) made a connection between charisma and *ecstasy* in these terms: ecstasy was a subjective condition through which the prophets' charisma was strengthened and represented to their followers. It is the term 'ecstasy', then, as denoting a personal and subjective condition, that became dominant in the discussion of prophecy. Perhaps its best definition within the context of the theological approach to prophecy was provided by Lindblom (1962: 4-5): ecstasy is

> an abnormal state of consciousness in which one is so intensely absorbed by one single idea or one single feeling, or by a group of ideas or feelings, that the normal stream of psychical life is more or less arrested. The bodily senses cease to function; one becomes impervious to impressions from without; consciousness is exalted above the ordinary level of daily experience; unconscious mental impressions and ideas come to the surface in the form of visions and auditions.

Lindblom went on to distinguish between various degrees of ecstasy, but consistently maintained this understanding of it as a subjective psychological condition. This was an approach perfectly compatible with the dominant, idealistic interest in the nature of Old Testament prophecy as a channel of communication between Yahweh and Israel. Ecstasy is a purely individual experience; it is the condition of the individual

4. For a somewhat similar understanding, cf. van der Toorn 1987: 191-218, where it is argued that the pre-monarchic leaders in Israel exhibited a combination of the functions of *kahin* (soothsayer) and *sayyid* (chief), a combination that was eventually broken, with the chiefly functions coming to be assumed by a non-charismatic dynastic king, while the *kahin* type functions developed into early and then classical prophecy.

prophet in communion with God; in a state of ecstasy the historical and social are transcended, as the prophets empty themselves in order to receive the divine revelation. One can understand how ecstasy, rather than charisma, became then the favoured term in the discussion of the nature of prophecy.

While this understanding retains its validity, it does, however, require supplementing, particularly along the lines suggested by Petersen (1981). Petersen has attempted to use 'role theory' to understand the behaviour and recorded experiences of the prophets, and as a context for understanding ecstasy. That is, he understands ecstasy not simply as a subjective, personal condition of an individual prophet, but rather objectively as one measurable degree of the prophet's involvement in the social role of being a prophet. The presupposition is that the role of the prophet is a socially definable phenomenon, indeed a social given independent of its manifestation in any particular individual, to which belong certain public activities and of which there are certain public expectations. In this respect, the role of the prophet is analogous to the role of the judge, of the king, of the priest and so on. The inclusion of prophecy within the context of social roles institutionalizes prophecy and makes it a phenomenon no more or less individualistic than kingship and priesthood. The individual adopts a role, the role that is appropriate to a particular context. The degree of that individual's commitment to and involvement in the adopted role may, however, vary; ecstasy is one of those degrees. The range of degrees of involvement extends from effective non-involvement to what is called bewitchment, and include: casual role enactment that is automatic and routine; ritual acting, as, for example, the greeting by a waiter in a restaurant; engrossed acting by an actor who, while maintaining an independent identity, is absorbed in a role; classical hypnotic role-taking implying a higher degree of self-involvement; histrionic neurosis, characterized by psychosomatic disorders; ecstasy, in which voluntary action is suspended and which is marked by distinctive physical activity such as speaking in tongues, or walking on coals; bewitchment, the most intensive stage of role involvement, exemplified in the behaviour of those who believe themselves to be the object of sorcery or witchcraft.

Various activities reported of the prophets may be fairly easily located within this spectrum of degrees of involvement in the prophetic role. So, Isaiah's walking naked and barefoot and Jeremiah's wearing a yoke around his neck may be understood as either ritual acting or engrossed acting; Jeremiah's intense experiences, as reported in Jer. 4.19, may be understood as a manifestation of histrionic neurosis. It may also be, as Petersen believes, that none of these prophetic experiences should be described as ecstatic. Whether or not that is the case, however, what is important here is that ecstasy is no longer seen simply as a private, subjective condition, but rather is that by which the individual publicly manifests his or her adoption of a socially given role. It has a very public along with a private dimension, and, along with charisma, may serve as a term very appropriate to the task of trying to locate the prophets and their activities within Israelite history and society.

Both ecstasy and charisma, then, are useful terms in the development of a theoretical understanding of prophecy as a social phenomenon. Both of them have to do with the social dimension of prophecy, and one of them, charisma, has particular value both in giving prophecy a broader diachronic dimension, by rooting prophecy in pre-monarchic charismatic leadership, and in drawing attention to the fact that individual prophets had followers, and that it is in the relationship between the prophet and those followers that prophecy came into existence.

IV

Recent study of Israelite prophecy is very conscious of its social dimension, and, given the role of prophecy in Israelite religion, the accurate delineation of the contours of this dimension will have ramifications for the more general question of the relationship of Israelite religion to Israelite society. Two interrelated questions may serve as a focus for our discussion: the relationship of prophets to the Israelite cult, and the existence of prophetic support groups. In both cases the questions have to do with prophets in their relations to society, so developing what has already been said with regard to the prophets as charismatics, and carrying important implications for our understanding of the origin and nature of prophetic preaching.

The question of *the relationship of the Israelite prophets to the cult of Israel* has not been really directly addressed for some time,[5] but it still contains significant issues that are unresolved. Wellhausen's presentation of the prophet, as an inspired individual standing in a direct and immediate relationship with God independent of human institutions, was little modified by Weber in spite of the latter's sociological approach to prophecy under the definition of charisma. Weber, almost paradoxically, described the prophet as an individual bearer of charisma, marked out from other religious functionaries by his personal call—a free speaker who preached under the influence of spontaneous inspiration, and with complete inner independence, to the public in the market place or to the elders in the city gate (Weber 1965: 46-59).

From a number of points of view this picture of the solitary prophet was open to attack. In the first place, it distorted the prophet's role in relation to other religious functionaries, and was out of keeping with the evidence of the Old Testament itself. The picture of the prophet as an individual communicator of divine messages did not account for the representative function that the prophet also performed. Gen. 20.7 may not be reliable evidence that Abraham was a prophet, but it certainly is reliable evidence of a significant function of prophecy: to intercede with Yahweh. On a number of occasions Jeremiah was commanded by Yahweh not to plead with him for Israel and not to make intercession on its behalf (cf. 7.16; 11.14; 14.11). The prophet was an intermediary who both proclaimed revelation and interceded for Israel.

This immediately suggests an association with the sanctuary and Israel's cult, and in fact that connection is well established. Samuel was a prophet who ministered in the service of Yahweh, under the supervision of Eli, the chief priest at the

5. One of the more recent treatments, reflecting the traditional view, is Williams 1969, which is intended as a response to Berger (1963).

sanctuary of Shiloh (1 Sam. 3.1); the band of prophets whom Saul met were coming down from the high place at Gibeah (1 Sam. 10.5); Elijah set up the altar of Yahweh on Mt Carmel and there too Elisha was to be found for consultation (1 Kgs 18; 2 Kgs 4.25). The duties of prophets at sanctuaries are now no longer very clear to us, but it is reasonable to assume that, as distinct from the priests who proclaimed torah, perhaps through the use of the sacred lot (Deut. 33.8), the prophets gave guidance for extraordinary situations or situations unsuited to the use of the sacred lot, such as times of personal or communal distress. This is perhaps supported by those psalms of lament which either contain prophetic oracles (Ps. 12) or are marked by a remarkable change of mood as the psalmist expresses his certainty that he has been heard (Ps. 6).

These are isolated points derived from the Old Testament itself. The theoretical framework and foundation for them, which is so important for a comprehensively credible description of the cultic role of prophets, was provided by Berger (1963) in his study of the relationship of office and charisma. Berger reviewed the study of prophecy since Weber and Wellhausen, but his most useful contribution lay in his argument that the innovatory power of charisma does not necessarily imply social marginality. Prophecy represented a power for radical change that derived from within Israelite social institutions rather from outside those institutions. With this understanding of the nature of prophecy, it is not impossible that even the classical prophets should be closely related to the institutional cult.

It is this recognition that then allowed for the later attempts of Wilson (1980) and Petersen (1981) to fix more precisely the place of prophets in the cult. Working on the basis of field studies carried out by the anthropologist I.M. Lewis, Wilson and Petersen distinguished between two forms of cult with their corresponding forms of prophecy or intermediation. The two forms are 'central possession religions' or 'main morality possession religions' on the one hand, and 'peripheral possession cults' on the other. These are descriptive terms referring to the setting of the respective phenomena in society: central possession religions are those that are fostered by society in general, that belong to the main or dominant group or groups in society and express the morality and ethos of the dominant social culture; peripheral possession cults may be identified as those fostered on the margins of society, among those who in one way or another are politically, socially and economically disadvantaged.

Possession, intermediation, prophecy, arise in these contexts for different reasons, and the role of the intermediary is correspondingly different. So prophecy arises in the context of the central religion as a result of military, social or economic pressures from outside being exerted on society as a whole; the central intermediary has a strong political role, giving guidance for the army in time of war, regulating the succession at a time of change of ruler, providing supernatural legitimation for the existing social order; the object of worship in the central cult is the god of society as a whole, perceived as a moral god, and the central intermediary is concerned with morality in society. On the other hand, the pressures leading to the rise of peripheral cults are internal to society—discrimination against a minority of a political, social or economic nature. Prophetic activity in this context is a group ecstatic phenomenon, and the major concern is with effecting change in society in order to promote the welfare of the oppressed minority; it is, therefore, the power rather than the moral nature of the god worshipped by the minority group that is distinctive.

This distinction between central and peripheral cults has contributed fruitfully to our understanding of Israelite prophecy, though the results are not always as clear or unambiguous as one might wish.[6] Certainly at least in the case of Elijah the model seems appropriate, for he shows many of the characteristics associated with peripheral status: he was threatened by the central establishment; the worship of Yahweh in the time of Ahab was threatened with displacement from its central position as the religion of the state; the stories about Elijah and Elisha concern as much if not more the power rather than the morality of Yahweh (2 Kgs 2.23-25).

Whatever may be the case about about these problems,

6. Some of the difficulties have been noted by Carroll (1989: 216-18).

however, the discussion has served to highlight what has become a basic recognition in the study of prophecy: that the prophets were not simply messengers of Yahweh, but were also *representative of groups within Israel*, wherever in Israelite society these groups were located. So, Wilson (1980: 51-56) has gone so far as to argue that every prophet had a support group, and that the prophetic message is to be understood as the expression of the internalized values of the support group, behind which may be found sociopolitical and socioeconomic concerns. This is probably a too rigid understanding of a complex situation, too rigid in the sense that it cannot be demonstrated that every prophet had a particular group of disciples who may be identified as a support group, and also in that there is more to religious language and ideas than the covert expression of sociopolitical and socioeconomic concerns.[7]

Wilson is probably right, however, in the general principle behind his argument: prophecy is not to be understood in an idealistic way on the model of a one-way line of communication between God and Israel through the individual prophet. It has an essential relationship to the historical, religious, social, economic and political conditions of Israel that somehow has to be formulated. The traditional model of prophecy is a linear one in which prophet and people are passive recipients of a divine word; this model takes little notice of the context out of which that word came and into which it was spoken, nor does it reckon with the expectations that both prophet and people would already have had about the nature of the divine will for Israel. Moreover, this linear model makes it very difficult to accommodate and comprehend the phenomenon of prophetic conflict, as reflected, for example, in Jeremiah 28. If a prophet is to be understood solely as the mediator of a divine word, how is fundamental disagreement between prophets to be explained? What is required is a model of prophecy in which the prophet interacts with both God and people and in which the people have their own relationship with God apart from the prophetic channel of communication.[8] Both prophet and people are, therefore, active in the coming

7.   See the critical discussion by Herion (1986: 10-14).
8.   For a development of this, cf. especially Overholt 1981: 55-78.

into being of the divine word. The function of the prophet is to realize and to articulate the will of God in the context of his or her (charismatic) relationship with a particular group. The prophet realizes and articulates what is recognized to be the word of God by a particular group, whether a specific group of disciples, as perhaps in the case of Isaiah, or a more diffuse group within society. It is with increasing differentiation within society that different groups originate with different material and ideal interests, within which the Israelite religious tradition would be differently interpreted. It is in these situations of conflict, conflict that reaches beyond political and economic interest to embrace the total self-understanding, that prophetic conflict arises. The word of God, arising out of and addressed to these situations, is part of an evolving Israelite self-understanding that cannot but reflect the tensions inherent in that process.

Within this wider social framework, it is possible to expand, correct and balance the idealistic presentation of prophecy. Prophetic visions, and the call of the prophet, may then be seen as elements of the message of the prophet as a charismatic leader within Israel. This term should be restored to the context of prophecy, for it emphasizes an essential aspect of prophecy—the relationship of the prophets to those who acknowledged them as prophets—that is crucial for our appreciation of the origin and meaning of prophetic preaching.

BIBLIOGRAPHY

Berger, P.
  1963   'Charisma and Religious Innovation: The Social Location of
             Israelite Prophecy', *American Sociological Review* 28: 940-50.
Carroll, R.P.
  1989   'Prophecy and Society', pp. 203-25 in *The World of Ancient
             Israel: Sociological, Anthropological and Political Perspectives*
             (ed. R.E. Clements; Cambridge: Cambridge University Press).
Gunkel, H.
  1969   'The Israelite Prophecy from the Time of Amos', pp. 48-75 in
             Twentieth Century Theology in the Making, I (ed. J. Pelikan;
             London: Collins).
Habel, N.C.
  1965   'The Form and Significance of the Call Narratives', *ZAW* 77:
             297-323.

Herion, G.A.
1986   'The Impact of Modern and Social Science Assumptions on the
            Reconstruction of Israelite History', *JSOT* 34: 3-33.
Koch, K.
1969   *The Growth of the Biblical Tradition* (London: A. & C. Black).
Lindblom, J.
1962   *Prophecy in Ancient Israel* (Oxford: Basil Blackwell).
Long, B.O.
1976   'Reports of Visions among the Prophets', *JBL* 95: 353-65.
Malamat, A.
1976   'Charismatic Leadership in the Book of Judges', pp. 152-68 in
            *Magnalia Dei. The Mighty Acts of God: Essays on the Bible and
            Archaeology in Memory of G. Ernest Wright* (ed. F.M. Cross,
            W.E. Lemke and P.D. Miller; New York: Doubleday).
Mayes, A.D.H.
1989   *The Old Testament in Sociological Perspective* (London:
            Marshall Pickering).
Overholt, T.W.
1981   'Prophecy: The Problem of Cross-Cultural Comparison',
            Semeia 21: 55-78.
Petersen, D.L.
1981   *The Roles of Israel's Prophets* (JSOTSup, 17; Sheffield: JSOT
            Press).
Rad, G. von
1965   *Old Testament Theology*, II (Edinburgh: Oliver & Boyd).
Rendtorff, R.
1967   'Reflections on the Early History of Prophecy in Israel', pp. 14-
            34 in *History and Hermeneutic* (ed. R.W. Funk; New York:
            Harper & Row).
Richter, W.
1970   *Die sogenannten vorprophetischen Berufungsberichte*
            (FRLANT, 101; Göttingen: Vandenhoeck & Ruprecht).
Schmidt, W.H.
1977   *Exodus* (BKAT, II/2;Neukirchen–Vluyn: Neukirchener Verlag).
1979   'Die prophetische Grundgewissheit', pp. 537-64 in *Das Proph-
            etenverständnis in der deutschsprachigen Forschung seit
            Heinrich Ewald* (ed. P.H.A. Neumann; Darmstadt: Wissen-
            schaftliche Buchgesellschaft).
Toorn, K. van der
1987   'From Patriarchs to Prophets. A Reappraisal of Charismatic
            Leadership in Ancient Israel', *Journal of Northwest Semitic
            Languages* 13: 191-218.
Volz, P.
1949   *Prophetengestalten des Alten Testaments* (Stuttgart: Calwer
            Verlag).
Weber, M.
1964   *The Theory of Social and Economic Organization* (New York:
            Free Press).

1965   *The Sociology of Religion* (London: Methuen).
Wellhausen, J.
    1973   *Prolegomena to the History of Ancient Israel* (Gloucester, MA:
                Peter Smith [orig. *Prolegomena to the History of Israel*
                (Edinburgh: A. & C. Black, 1885)]).
Westermann, C.
    1967   *Basic Forms of Prophetic Speech* (London: Lutterworth).
Williams, J.G.
    1969   'The Social Location of Israelite Prophecy', *JAAR* 37: 153-65.
Wilson, R.R.
    1980   *Prophecy and Society in Ancient Israel* (Philadelphia: Fortress
                Press).
Zimmerli, W.
    1982   'Visionary Experience in Jeremiah', pp. 95-118 in *Israel's
                Prophetic Tradition* (ed. R.J. Coggins, A.C.J. Phillips and
                M.A. Knibb; Cambridge: Cambridge University Press).

PROPHETS, PRIESTS, DIVINERS AND SAGES IN ANCIENT ISRAEL

Lester L. Grabbe

From the time of Wellhausen the 'classical prophets' were exalted as a unique phenomenon in history and theology. Not infrequently other religious figures were considered inferior if not even denigrated—priests, 'pre-classical' prophets, the wisdom authors.[1] Such figures as diviners were naturally beyond the pale.

In recent years this sharp dichotomy has been blunted. It is now generally recognized that 'classical' prophecy represents a major continuum with 'pre-classical' prophecy and that prophecy is not necessarily to be divorced from the cult; also, current interest in the wisdom tradition has changed the negative judgment that was once passed upon it. Nevertheless, one still sees a good deal of influence of the old views, even if they operate on a more subtle and perhaps even unconscious level.[2]

Robert Wilson has helped to put the situation in perspective by his use of the term 'intermediary' for prophets, priests, diviners and the like.[3] This seems to be roughly equivalent to the common anthropological category of 'religious specialists'.

---

1. See especially J. Wellhausen, *Prolegomena to the History of Israel* (Edinburgh: A. & C. Black, 1885), pp. 411-15.

2. Cf., e.g., H.M. Orlinsky, 'The Seer-Priest in Ancient Israel', *OrAnt* 4 (1965), pp. 153-74; *idem*, 'The Seer-Priest and the Prophet in Ancient Israel', *Essays in Biblical Culture and Bible Translation* (New York: Ktav, 1974), pp. 39-65 (also in B. Mazar [ed.], *The World History of the Jewish People*. III. *Judges* [New Brunswick, NJ: Rutgers University Press, 1971], ch. 12); G. Fohrer, *History of Israelite Religion* (Nashville: Abingdon Press, 1972; ET of *Geschichte der israelitischen Religion*, 1968), part 2, ch. 3 (pp. 223-91).

3. R.R. Wilson, *Prophecy and Society in Ancient Israel* (Philadelphia: Fortress Press, 1980), pp. 27-28.

While Wilson recognized the existence of other 'intermediaries', however, he focused only on prophets. My purpose is to survey the social roles of the major intermediaries or religious specialists in order to gain a better idea of their relationship to one another and their function in the society of ancient Israel. The role of divine kingship, which rightly falls under 'religious specialists', is omitted here because it is too complex to treat in this context.

Religious Specialists in Anthropological Study

The techniques and methods of social anthropology have a particular place in Old Testament research; for it must never be forgotten that ancient Israel cannot be studied like a contemporary society. No one can or will do anthropological field work on ancient Israelite society. It is accessible only indirectly, through archaeology and literary remains. Social anthropology is extremely useful in allowing us to develop new models and analogues, to ask new questions, to look at the ancient data from new perspectives, but we must never forget the limitations on our knowledge. Some very basic sets of information that any modern field study would gather as a matter of routine are simply closed to us. The excitement of new discovery must not blind us to the severe constraints at times imposed on us by this lack.

Anthropological studies indicate several points about religious specialists that are worth noting and using to interrogate the Old Testament data. These will first be listed, then specific examples will be looked at in order to support these assertions:

1.   While certain basic religious needs are found across a wide variety of pre-industrial societies, the religious specialists who meet these needs and their relationship to each other often vary greatly from society to society. One society may have priests and shamans; another may distinguish prophets, shamans, healers and witch-finders; a third may divide healers into several categories; and so on.

2. The roles of religious specialists are distinctly classified for the sake of research, yet in actual practice it is not always easy to distinguish between them. One individual may exercise more than one role in a particular society; in another society, there may be greater specialization. But in most societies there is usually a certain amount of overlap and blurring of roles. Max Weber's 'ideal types' of priest, prophet and the like have been very influential in anthropological and biblical research, but even he recognized that they actually grade into one another.[4] Indeed, Weber's use of ideal types has sometimes been misunderstood and misused.[5] For the sake of heuristic research he would construct an ideal type, but he always recognized that it was only a research model. The ideal type may not exist everywhere, or even *anywhere* in some cases, but functions as a scholarly construct that must always be measured against the actual living situation in society. Although Weber recognized that the roles of priest and prophet overlapped, some of his statements nevertheless need correcting. For example, contrary to Weber, there are many examples of prophets coming from priestly ranks.[6]

3. The most important dichotomy from a social point of view is often not that between individual specialists (e.g. priest versus prophet) but between level of function, whether at *individual level* or at *state/national* level (i.e. national prophet versus local prophet).[7]

4. See M. Weber, *The Sociology of Religion*; the edition I have used is G. Roth and C. Wittich (ed.), *Economy and Society* (2 vols.; Berkeley: University of California Press, 1978), I, pp. 424-27.

5. See Weber's discussion in Roth and Wittich (eds.), *Economy and Society*, I, pp. 18-22. On the subject generally, see B. Wilson, *Religion in Sociological Perspective* (Oxford: Oxford University Press, 1982), pp. 95-105. For criticism of this usage as it relates to a particular theory, see my 'Social Setting of Early Jewish Apocalypticism', *JSP* 4 (1989), pp. 27-47, especially 32-33.

6. See Weber's statement in Roth and Wittich (eds.), *Economy and Society*, I, pp. 440.

7. Cf. the important distinction between 'peripheral' and 'central' cults

Following are examples of anthropological studies that support the points just made:

The Nuer[8]

The most important ritual expert among these Sudanese people is the 'earth priest' or 'leopard-skin priest'. This is primarily a hereditary office that resides in certain families. The major function of this priest is to purify acts of homicide and other pollutions that arise during feuds, as well as to act as a mediator in such situations. Of perhaps less importance are the cattle-priests who function in regard to all aspects of cattle: fertility, health, feeding, acquiring by raiding, and so on. Another important function is that of prophet. Although Evans-Pritchard downplayed the role of prophets in his later writings, it is now recognized that prophets have probably always functioned in Nuer society, and some have been famous and very important.[9] There are also other lesser ritual experts such as curers and diviners.

The significant fact for our purposes is the extent to which the roles of prophet and priest overlap. First, the most famous prophets have generally come from priestly families. Secondly, there is a tendency for priests to take on prophetic functions and for prophets who are not already of the priestly lines to attempt to take on priestly roles:

and figures made by I.M. Lewis, *Ecstatic Religion: A Study of Shamanism and Spirit Possession* (London: Routledge, 2nd edn, 1989); see also the discussion by R.R. Wilson (*Prophecy and Society in Ancient Israel*, pp. 38-40), who has applied the theory to Israelite prophets. The same division can be found among diviners, healers, and even cultic functionaries.

8.   For information in this section, I am primarily dependent on T.O. Beidelman, 'Nuer Priests and Prophets', in T.O. Beidelman (ed.), *The Translation of Culture: Essays to E.E. Evans-Pritchard* (London: Tavistock, 1971), pp. 375-415. See also E.E. Evans-Pritchard, 'The Nuer: Tribe and Clan', *Sudan Notes and Records* 18 (1935), pp. 37-87, esp. pp. 47-75. It should be noted that some aspects of his later discussion in *Nuer Religion* (Oxford: Oxford University Press, 1956), pp. 287-310, are not as reliable. Cf. Beidelman, 'Nuer Priests', p. 410 n. 28.

9.   See Beidelman, 'Nuer Priests', pp. 395-97, on the question of whether prophets are of recent origin among the Nuer.

> [T]here seems a tendency for Nuer prophets to spring from priestly lineages and sometimes for prophetic and ambitious individuals outside such lineages to try to assume priestly attributes... To put it in Weber's terms, Nuer priests sometimes widen and strengthen their authority by assuming charismatic powers more often associated with prophetic figures; and Nuer prophets try to convert their charismatic powers into a more routinized authority.[10]

Nuer prophets must also be seen as the extreme of a continuum with other spirit-possessed individuals who may be only herbalists and healers. All prophets have some magical attributes relating to healing, warfare and fertility. On the other hand, Nuer priests often seek to augment their authority by charismatic and supernatural powers. Prophets may also attempt to pass on their functions to their sons just as sons inherit the priestly office of fathers.[11] Thus, there is a considerable overlap between the various religious specialists in Nuer society, and a clear distinction between them is not always evident:

> The status of a 'bull' [any prominent person because of wealth, kinship, etc.], a ghoul, a priest, or a prophet is theoretically different but not always readily distinguishable when such labels are applied to actual data, whether case material or ideological formulations... The Nuer data demonstrate similarities between priest and prophets and also, in some respects, parallels between both these and asocial or antisocial witches or ghouls.[12]

The Dinka[13]

The Nuer and Dinka peoples seem to have influenced one another, though the exact relationship is not always clear. The priestly functions of prayer, sacrifice and invocation of the deity for prosperity of the people and success in war are carried out by the 'masters of the fishing spear'. These individuals belong to certain clans with the clan-deity Flesh who is the source of life. By the very existence and vitality of the

---

10. Beidelman, 'Nuer Priests', p. 377.
11. Beidelman, 'Nuer Priests', pp. 388-89, 400.
12. Beidelman, 'Nuer Priests', pp. 404-405.
13. This section is dependent upon G. Lienhardt, *Divinity and Experience: The Religion of the Dinka* (Oxford: Clarendon Press, 1961).

spear masters, the life of the community is maintained.[14]

Divination is widely practised as well. On the simplest level this may be done by practically anyone, by manipulation of mussel shells or similar techniques. Also, the use of fetish bundles is widespread, especially to gain individual help and to curse enemies, though the possession of these is not usually admitted. But as one moves up the scale, the higher ranks of diviners are able to practise their craft because of having one of the free deities (as opposed to clan deities) in their bodies. The highest ranks of diviners are easily assimilated to the prophets who also perform an important function. Since the really great prophets have all been from the ranks of fishing-spear masters, there is no hard-and-fast distinction between priestly, prophetic and divinatory functions.[15]

Kiganda Religion[16]
With regard to the Kiganda religion of Uganda, Peter Rigby has noted that

> the rigid distinctions frequently made in the African context between prophets, diviners, priests, and mediums are not really applicable, and hence do not serve a useful analytical purpose; however, some differences between these roles and offices, and their incumbents, obviously do exist.[17]

There are a variety of priests, prophets, diviners and mediums who mediate between humans and the complex world of spirits. More important than the distinction between these is that between those who operate on the personal level and those who function on the state level, whatever their designation.

The national shrines of the hero-gods and kings have regular priests whose service is primarily on behalf of the king. The common people will not generally go to the national

14. Lienhardt, *Divinity and Experience*, esp. pp. 206-18.
15. Lienhardt, *Divinity and Experience*, esp. pp. 64-80; also pp. 206, 208.
16. For information in this section, I am primarily dependent on P. Rigby, 'Prophets, Diviners, and Prophetism: The Recent History of Kiganda Religion', *Journal of Anthropological Research* 31 (1975), pp. 116-48.
17. Rigby, 'Prophets, Diviners, and Prophetism', p. 117.

shrines for their needs but to the local 'spirit shrines' of the diviners, healers and prophets. Since the national shrines are basically oriented toward the past, prophets (whose concern is with the future) usually operate on the personal level; however, there are prophets associated with the national shrines whose main function is to prophesy for the king and state officials, and some of these prophets have had considerable power over the king and his advisers. Nevertheless, some of the major national prophets began their careers as diviners. As Rigby notes about one famous Kiganda prophet,

> Kigaanira's case also demonstrates the close interdependence of the roles of diviner and prophet, at least for Kiganda religion. Even during the height of his powers as a politically important prophet, Kigaanira remained potentially a diviner, and when his political role was over, he returned to divination and the mediumship of Kibuuka [a Kiganda god]...[18]

The prophets at the national shrines bridge the divide between the past-oriented cult and the future-oriented function of the prophet and diviner. Finally, the fluid state of things is shown by the fact that the same individual may perform more than one role:

> It could even be argued that the very profusion and variety of terminology for Baganda priests, prophets, mediums, diviners, healers, and medicine men... and the constant manipulation of them, is structurally consistent with the ease with which an individual may perform several of these roles simultaneously. It is also consistent with the ability of a person to transform himself from one role to another during the course of his professional life.[19]

Plains Indians of North America[20]

Shamans (medicine men) are widespread among these particular tribes, but some tribes also have priests. For

18. Rigby, 'Prophets, Diviners, and Prophetism', p. 139.
19. Rigby, 'Prophets, Diviners, and Prophetism', p. 132.
20. The information of this section comes from R.H. Lowie, *Indians of the Plains* (American Museum of Natural History; New York: McGraw–Hill, 1954), pp. 161-64; reprinted in W.A. Lessa and E.Z. Vogt (eds.), *Reader in Comparative Religion: An Anthropological Approach* (New York: Harper & Row, 2nd edn, 1965), pp. 452-54.

example, the Pawnee have priests whose official duty it is to learn sacred songs and ritual procedure. They, rather than the chiefs, are the supreme authority of the tribe because of their care of the sacred medicine bundles that underlie the political structure of the tribe.[21] This office is hereditary. The shamans also have features of priests in that they learn their techniques as disciples of great masters. Yet their powers of healing are supposed to derive from a particular animal who acts as the protector and source of power of the individual shaman. Treatment of illness often consists of herbal remedies and other physical means, but serious illness is treated by one who gained his technique from a visionary experience. Such shamans often specialize in one particular type of affliction. Thus, the traditional distinction made between priest and shaman is not so clear-cut in this case.

The Shona[22]
According to the belief of the Shona tribes of Zimbabwe, the traditional diviner-healer is the *n'anga* whose responsibility it is to communicate with the spirit world about the cause of an illness and the means of a cure.[23] The *n'anga* is also consulted about various personal matters for which an answer is sought. While many common people have some elementary divining skills, for serious matters an individual would go only to a diviner of reputation, one who has a healing spirit. Various methods of divining are used, divining dice being especially popular. Some diviners rely entirely on their spirits, however, and receive their messages while in a possession trance. It is possible to become a *n'anga* purely by being tutored by specialists in herbal remedies and the like, but the most

21. 'Each of the thirteen Skidi villages owned a bundle...Four of the bundles were pre-eminent, and a fifth...took absolute precedence; the priests of these bundles rather than the titular chiefs held supreme authority. Normally, the four priests in turn assumed responsibility for the welfare of the people for the period of a year' (Lowie, *Indians*, p. 164 = Lessa and Vogt, *Reader*, p. 454).

22. See especially M. Bourdillon, *The Shona Peoples* (Gweru, Zimbabwe: Mambo, rev. edn, 1982).

23. Bourdillon, *Shona*, pp. 141-61.

respected gain their abilities with the help of a healing spirit. Those who have such a spirit may gain knowledge of herbal cures by tutelage under a master, but many learn them solely by dreams and other forms of communication from their healing spirits.

The spirits possessing various individuals are ancestral spirits. A special category are the 'lion spirits' who are the spirits of dead chiefs.[24] A lion-spirit medium is mainly concerned with public affairs and thus is distinguished from the *n'anga*, but the distinction is not rigid. Sometimes a *n'anga* is consulted about public matters (especially relating to witchcraft, which is not considered in the lion spirit's domain), while some lion-spirit mediums also practise as diviners and healers. It is especially common for *makombwe* spirit mediums to be consulted on private matters. These are possessed by a particular group of lion spirits of the very early inhabitants of the country. While normal lion spirits are considered territorial, the *makombwe* spirits have more widespread influence. Thus, their mediums are not associated with a particular territory and must gain their prestige by the size of their private clientele.

Cultic functions are generally carried out by tribal elders or others within the family and relate to local and family spirits. However, the high god Mwari has an organized cult among the southern Shona.[25] This is administered by a permanent priest and priestess, a keeper of the shrine, and a 'voice'. Delegations from the surrounding chiefdoms often come for oracles from Mwari, usually about public matters. The oracle may occasionally provide advice on private matters but will normally refer such requesters to lesser diviners. Because the function of this cult is similar to that of the lion spirits, lion-spirit cults are not dominant among the southern Shona as in the north.

Under the influence of Christianity, a number of native independent churches have grown up. One influential one is Johane Maranke's African Apostolic Church.[26] Among its

24. Bourdillon, *Shona*, pp. 243-49.
25. Bourdillon, *Shona*, pp. 266-71.
26. Bourdillon, *Shona*, pp. 287-94.

ecclesiastical officers are prophets and healers. The function of
the prophet is primarily to diagnose the cause of an illness,
which the healer then proceeds to cure. While the term
'prophet' is borrowed from the Bible, the function of the individual closely parallels that of the traditional diviner and is
clearly an adaptation of the native religion. Healing also often
takes the form of casting out evil spirits.

The Prophet Smohalla among the Washani Indians[27]
The religion founded by Smohalla among an Indian tribe of
the Pacific Northwest may have been to some extent
influenced by Christianity, but the fundamentals of it were
those of the aboriginal religion in this area. Smohalla arose as
a prophet in the mid-nineteenth century at a time when there
was considerable conflict with the white authorities over the
Indian lands. A concerted effort was made to move the Indian
tribes to particular areas away from their ancestral home and
to induce them to become farmers and homesteaders.

Although there is no evidence that Smohalla ever advocated
violent resistance, he opposed the white plans as contrary to
the divine will. According to him the various Indian groups
were given particular areas by the creator Nami Piap. A 'holy
covenant' (!) existed between humanity and God. One of the
conditions that this placed on the Indians was not to divide up
the land, farm it, sell it or otherwise disturb it after the
customs of the whites. He preached against those of his fellow
countrymen who had abandoned the traditions of the
ancestors and had become farmers. Like Jeremiah (6.16), he
called them back to the 'old paths', to obedience to the god's
laws as laid down from the beginning. His message was to
denounce law-breaking and violation of the divine covenant
as he saw it.

27. See C.E. Trafzer and M.A. Beach, 'Smohalla, the Washani, and
Religion as a Factor in Northwestern Indian History', *American Indian
Quarterly* 9 (1985), pp. 309-24.

Religious Specialists in Israel

Not surprisingly, there are differences between ancient Israel and many of the pre-industrial societies studied by social anthropologists. An important one is that of a monotheistic (or henotheistic) world view rather than one with a multitude of spirits and other deities. However, one must immediately register a qualification here, for this world view represents only the bias of a particular minority group at a particular time, viz. the editors of the tradition and some of the tradents. Israelite popular religion probably did recognize a multitude of deities and/or spirits, which is evidenced not least by the constant complaint that the people 'went after other gods'.[28] Thus, while various sorts of divination, along with the appeal to magic and spirits, are condemned by the Deuteronomist (Deut. 18.9-14), it is evident that such specialists were in considerable demand by some segments of the population (cf. 1 Sam. 28; Ezek. 13). One should also note the expression, the 'spirit of Yahweh', as well as the instances in which the 'angel (*mal'āk*) of Yahweh' does the revealing (1 Kgs 13.18; 19.5, 7; 2 Kgs 1.3, 15). One might see an analogy here with the spirit or spirits of certain intermediaries in anthropological studies. Such an interpretation is also supported by the development of a world of good and evil spirits that became prominent in the post-exilic period.

As is often acknowledged, the 'pre-classical' prophets show a variety of function. Samuel was both a cult functionary ('priest') and a prophet ('seer'). Granted, 1 Samuel 9 is often thought to be the story of an anonymous seer that has been assimilated to the Samuel tradition;[29] nevertheless, even in this event it still demonstrates that the functions of priest and

28. For a recent study of the development of Israelite religion from polytheism to monotheism, see M.S. Smith, *The Early History of God: Yahweh and the Other Deities in Ancient Israel* (San Francisco: Harper, 1990).

29. See A.F. Campbell, *Of Priests and Kings: A Late Ninth Century Document (1 Samuel 1–2 Kings 10)* (CBQMS, 17; Washington, DC: Catholic University of America, 1986), pp. 18-21 and the literature cited there.

prophet were not thought by the tradents to be mutually exclusive.

Several Old Testament passages associate prophets with healing. Ahijah was consulted by the wife of King Jeroboam as to whether their son would recover (1 Kgs 14.2). The Elisha tradition has several stories relating to cures, including Naaman (2 Kgs 5) and the king of Damascus (2 Kgs 8.7-15). According to the Isaiah tradition, the prophet was consulted about Hezekiah's illness and directly participated in its cure (2 Kgs 20.1-11; Isa. 38.1-8, 21). The recovery of lost objects and similar tasks is also a prophetic function in some texts (1 Sam. 9.3-10, 18-20 [Samuel]; 2 Kgs 6.1-7 [Elisha]). The ability to command a drought and then to make it rain is credited to Elijah (1 Kgs 17.1-7; 18.41-46). Elisha in particular has many of the traits associated with shamans in other cultures.[30]

Thus we find that the functions of prophets and diviners in contemporary societies is matched in many ways by the traditions about the 'pre-classical' prophets in the Old Testament: healing and cures; finding lost objects; commanding the rains; providing messages about the future, especially with regard to the right course of action to take. This could operate on a purely individual level, but many examples have to do with the king or other state official asking for help. Nor is there any clear division between prophets, since many of the examples show the same specialist being consulted on both an individual and an official state level.

Some scholars would accept the situation just described with regard to the 'pre-classical' prophets but vehemently deny it to the written prophets. The question is, Can such a variety of function be attributed to the 'classical' prophets? Some of the examples already given involve the 'classical' prophets, such as Isaiah. One might argue that the tradition of Isaiah's involvement in Hezekiah's cure is unhistorical. This may indeed be the case, but this is not necessarily so, and attempts to prove such must guard against the danger of circular reasoning. Certainly, the tradents and editors evidently saw no conflict with the idea that a great prophet such as Isaiah might be involved in healing.

One important point with regard to the written prophets is the number of them who were either themselves priests or in some way associated with the temple and cult. Isaiah seems to have functioned in conjunction with the temple and monarchy at least part of his life (or so the tradition: Isa. 6–7; cf. 2 Kgs 19.20–20.19). Jeremiah was of a priestly family and spent much of his career in close association with the temple, even when some (but not all) of the temple personnel opposed him.[31] Ezekiel was also a priest (Ezek. 1.3). Several of the written prophets have been widely accepted as cult prophets (Nahum, Zechariah, Haggai, perhaps Joel and Habakkuk).[32]

Another fact about the written prophets is the nature of the preserved data. The earlier prophets are known by stories about their activities, but we hear little if anything about their specific prophecies. With prophets such as Hosea, Micah and several others, we have almost no biographical detail, but rather (allegedly) their actual words. Thus, we do not know whether Hosea was consulted about lost asses or whether Joel participated in healing rituals. One might deny such activities to Amos since he was not originally a prophet (Amos 7.14-15).[33] Also, prophets like Isaiah who functioned at the state level might have been above such things, but we should probably be cautious about being too dogmatic, since Elijah

31. Cf. J. Blenkinsopp, *Prophecy in Ancient Israel* (London: SPCK, 1984), p. 175 n. 72. Although Wilson (*Prophecy and Society*, pp. 241-42) places Jeremiah in the category of 'peripheral prophet', R.P. Carroll (in an unpublished paper) has observed that Jeremiah should really be designated as a 'central prophet' according to the categories used by I.M. Lewis (*Ecstatic Religion*). See also the critique of Wilson in D.L. Petersen, *The Roles of Israel's Prophets* (JSOTSup, 17; Sheffield: JSOT Press, 1981), pp. 43-47.

32. See Blenkinsopp, *Prophecy in Ancient Israel*, pp. 32-33. On cult prophecy in general, see the classic study of A.R. Johnson, *The Cult Prophet in Israel* (Cardiff: University of Wales Press, 2nd edn, 1962).

33. There seems to be agreement on this one point. Otherwise, the literature discussing the precise meaning of the phrase, *lō'-nābî' 'ānōkî wᵉlō' ben-nābî' 'ānōkî*, makes a substantial pile.

and Elijah are credited with personal as well as national activities. Attempts to make a distinction between earlier and later prophets purely on *ex silentio* arguments are hazardous.

Another difficulty pertains to the manner in which the written prophets received their messages. They are often distinguished from 'visionaries',[34] but such a distinction is simplistic. Isaiah had at least one vision (Isa. 6), and Ezekiel had them regularly. We often read that the 'word of Yahweh came to' so-and-so. But how did it come? There seems to be a variety of possible ways. For example, on one occasion 'the word of Yahweh' came to Nathan (2 Sam. 7.4), but this message is later referred to as a 'vision' (*ḥizzāyôn*, v. 17). Therefore, the fact that no vision is mentioned is not necessarily a sign that none occurred.

Priests were intermediaries and instruments of God, just as were the prophets. Although this was mainly through the cult, an important duty was that of teaching. This included cultic *torah* but was not limited to it. Ethical instruction was an important duty as well (Hos. 4.4-6; Mic. 3.11; Mal. 2.4-9). Priests were also conceived of as judicial figures, to settle disputes and decide difficult cases (Deut. 17.8-13; 19.17; 21.5).

Although priests primarily communicated to God on behalf of the Israelite, they had one important mode of receiving messages: by the divinatory techniques of the Urim and Thummim and of the ephod. We have a number of examples from the early period of the monarchy (1 Sam. 23.2-12; 30.7-8; Hos. 3.4).[35] In this sphere, the priest was not different from the prophet but only provided another route by which God could communicate, as indicated by 1 Sam. 28.6: 'And when Saul inquired of the Lord, the Lord did not answer him, either by dreams, or by Urim, or by prophets'. In a number of other areas, priests and prophets exercised similar functions: blessings and cursings (Deut. 21.5; Num. 22–24; 2 Kgs 2.24),

---

34. See, e.g., the articles of Orlinsky cited above.

35. Cf. H.B. Huffmon, 'Priestly Divination in Israel', in C.L. Meyers and M. O'Connor (eds.), *The Word of the Lord Shall Go Forth: Essays in Honor of David Noel Freedman in Celebration of his Sixtieth Birthday* (ASOR Special Volume Series, 1; Winona Lake, IN: Eisenbrauns, 1983), pp. 355-59.

encouraging the army and seeking God's assistance before battle (Deut. 20.2; 1 Sam. 14.3, 19, 36-41; 23.9; 1 Kgs 22) and giving guidance in cultic matters (Hag. 2.10-14; Isa. 1.10-17; 8.16, 8.20; 30.9; Zech. 7.2-7). Priests were also to be consulted about the healing of certain sorts of diseases; however, in each case it seems a matter of pronouncing on cultic purity rather than having an actual part in the curing process (Lev. 13–14).

The Position of the 'Wise' in Society

Many questions about the 'wise' of Israelite society still remain. Professor Whybray has argued that wisdom in Israel represented an intellectual tradition but that there was no professional class of sage ('wise men' or 'wise women').[36] Not everyone has been convinced that there was no such professional class,[37] but Whybray has demonstrated that wisdom was by no means confined to this class even if such existed. The words 'wise', 'wisdom' and the like are applied to a range of areas of knowledge and skill, as well illustrated by Professor Whybray. Noteworthy is the fact that the term 'sage' is used in a number of Old Testament passages to apply to a specific skill, that of the diviner (Gen. 41.8; Isa. 44.25; Dan. 2.12). This has led to a widely accepted distinction by modern scholars between 'proverbial wisdom' and 'mantic wisdom'.[38] However, it seems doubtful that such a distinction was generally made in ancient Israel or the Near East. The term 'wisdom' (*ḥokmâ*) was used for this sort of knowledge as well as that gained by the study of nature, society, and so on. Knowledge, whether gained by supernatural or human means, was still knowledge. Sometimes God was credited with giving special skills to workmen even though the same sort of

36. R.N. Whybray, *The Intellectual Tradition in the Old Testament* (BZAW, 135; Berlin: de Gruyter, 1974).

37. See, e.g., the review by G.E. Bryce, *JBL* 94 (1975), pp. 596-98.

38. See the classic articles of H.-P. Müller, 'Magisch-mantische Weisheit und die Gestalt Daniels', *UF* 1 (1969), pp. 79-94; 'Mantische Weisheit und Apokalyptik', in P.A.H. de Boer (ed.), *Congress Volume, Uppsala 1971* (VTSup, 22; Leiden: Brill, 1972), pp. 268-93.

ability could be acquired by practice and natural ability (Exod. 35.30-35).

When we look at modern anthropological studies of religious specialists, we find an interesting parallel. Knowledge of healing is sometimes associated with the study of traditional lore passed down from generation to generation. But it may also (or even *exclusively* in some cultures) be acquired by special revelation through dreams or by spirit possession.[39] Thus, it becomes clear that 'wisdom/sage' overlaps both the supernatural and the mundane spheres. In the same way it overlaps the functions of priests, prophets, diviners and the like.[40] Wisdom might be acquired through lore passed down by priests or by prophets to their disciples or by diviners from their teachers or by diviners on the basis of spirit revelation. The term 'wise' could apply to counsellors and scribes but also to any person with special knowledge or skills above the ordinary. Those able to contact and in some way harness the supernatural, such as priests, prophets and diviners, were in a special position to acquire 'wisdom' and be called 'wise'.

We do not know who wrote the wisdom books or how they or the wisdom tradition of Israel were passed on. It would hardly be surprising if the wisdom tradition was found to be concentrated in the scribal and court circles of Israel during the monarchy. But a study of post-exilic Israel suggests that the circles that studied, catalogued and passed on wisdom were concentrated around the temple. Not all the qualified priests were needed to work in the cult as a full-time job. Priests served as scribes and administrative officials through much of the period of the Second Temple.[41] It seems a reasonable

39. See the section above on the Shona.
40. A recent article pointing out the overlap between prophecy and mantic wisdom is J.C. VanderKam, 'The Prophetic-Sapiential Origins of Apocalyptic Thought', in J.D. Martin and P.R. Davies (eds.), *A Word in Season: Essays in Honour of William McKane* (JSOTSup, 42; Sheffield: JSOT Press, 1986), pp. 163-76.
41. For much of the Second Temple period, the chief administrative official of Judah was the high priest, sometimes under a regional governor appointed by the Persian, Greek or Roman authorities. The term 'theocracy' is sometimes used of this form of state. See further my study, *Judaism from Cyrus to Hadrian* (2 vols.; Minneapolis: Fortress Press,

hypothesis that the study of and speculation about astronomy, astrology, eschatology, God's plan in history, and other sorts of esoteric knowledge would have been concentrated in the priestly circles, where such knowledge could be useful as well as interesting and where there were individuals with leisure to cultivate such interests.[42]

Conclusions and Implications

A number of the older views about priests, prophets and wisdom have been challenged in recent years. The insights gleaned from social anthropology suggest that this revisionism should continue. Views plainly biased by preconceived notions about what an Old Testament prophet must and must not be still find their way into the scholarly literature. It is time that some of these sacred cows were herded to the abattoir.

One of these is the idea that there was something special about the means of inspiration and activities of the 'classical', as opposed to the 'pre-classical', prophets. One may well argue that the message of the canonical prophets is unique. Be that as it may, this does not justify the assumption that the role or function of the 'classical' prophets must be special. On the contrary, much that was once taken to be characteristic of the canonical prophets can be found in many different cultures around the world. This includes the prophetic mode of receiving messages from God and the personal call.[43] The proclamation of repentance and turning back to the old ways is one found widely among prophets in all cultures.[44]

1992), I, pp. 73-75. On the scribes of the temple, many of whom were undoubtedly priests, see pp. 488-91.

42. See M.E. Stone, *Scriptures, Sects and Vision: A Profile of Judaism from Ezra to the Jewish Revolts* (Oxford: Basil Blackwell, 1980), pp. 42-44.

43. Cf. Rigby, 'Prophets, Diviners, and Prophetism', p. 134. For an important discussion on the question, see M.J. Buss, 'An Anthropological Perspective upon Prophetic Call Narratives', *Semeia* 21 (1982), pp. 9-30.

44. For example, the Kiganda prophet Kigaanira called on his people to turn away from foreign religions and carry out proper worship, so that their exiled king would be returned—a message strikingly like that of some of the OT prophets. See Rigby, 'Prophets, Diviners, and Prophetism', p. 136. A similar message was preached by Smohalla (see above).

Another old idea that needs to be laid to rest is the assumption that the 'professions' of priest, prophet and sage were not only clearly distinct but fundamentally opposed to one another. All one can say is that there was enormous variety, especially among the different sorts of prophets, and that the interrelationships were not constant but changed over time and geographical area. The functions of priest, prophet and the like were *sometimes* clearly distinct; also, *some* prophets were opposed to *some* priests as well as to *some* individuals labelled as sages, but this is all that can be said. The complexity and constant readjustment of the relationships must be recognized. Priest, prophet, diviner and wisdom teacher all attempted to find out about various 'hidden' things, such as God's will for the individual, what to expect in the future, what actions would bring success and prosperity, what to avoid for the same results.

Priesthood in Israel was hereditary, and only those of appropriate descent could perform the sacrificial aspects of the cult. But beyond this there were cult functionaries (cult singers and evidently cult prophets) and functions that over-lapped with those of other religious specialists. Priests, prophets and wisdom instructors taught about the religious and ethical demands of God and the types of deeds that would bring success in life. Priests, prophets and diviners all attempted to look into the future in one way or another. The wisdom literature is filled with questions and answers about how to guarantee success in the future and to understand the ways of God and the workings of the cosmos.

What does emerge from a comparison of Israel and contemporary pre-modern societies is the division between religious specialists who act on behalf of the individual and those who perform for the state. Of course, the same individual might carry out activities in both spheres. This is important to keep in mind because in some cases our sources have focused on one or other of these activities to the extent perhaps of suggesting that one individual differed more from another than was actually the case. Thus, Elijah's healings or Elisha's minor miracles may make them appear to be a different sort of prophet from Isaiah or Jeremiah, whereas this impression may simply be traceable to the selective reporting of our limited and heavily edited sources.

When we consider the implications of these findings, two major points stand out:

1. It is necessary to consider more carefully the complex relationships of various religious specialists and their interaction at all levels of society.

2. It is important to note how the relationships of religious specialists have developed and changed with time and especially as a consequence of certain special historical events.

With regard to the last point, Israel's history did not end with the Exile, although some studies seem to operate as if it did. The monarchy ceased, only to be reintroduced in the persons of the Hasmonaean priests and, later, the Herodian dynasty. A tradition also developed that prophecy had died out in the early post-exilic period, but the ironic thing is that Josephus, one of our sources for this tradition (*Apion* 1.8 40-41), himself claimed to be a prophet (*War* 3.8.9 §§399-408)! He also claims to be a priest (*Life* 1.1-6). The Urim and Thummim were evidently no longer available to the priests (Ezra 2.63 // Neh. 7.65). The religious needs remained much the same, but there was a readjustment among religious specialists to meet these needs in the changed and changing situation. With the development of a canonical literature, written scripture became an important source of knowledge about the future and God's will, and thus the biblical interpreter took over in part the former job of the priest, prophet and diviner. Similarly, new 'sciences', such as that of astrology, took over some of the functions of prophet and diviner.

On the other hand, the various practitioners of magic and the miracle workers and exorcists, who emerge in the clear light of day during the post-exilic period, may not be new at all. Some at least, and perhaps most, already existed in pre-exilic times—as is indicated by hints here and there in the biblical text and other sources. The disapproval that the editors and tradents felt toward such practices meant a good deal of suppression of information, but what evidence remains indicates a flourishing popular religion that contained elements known well only from post-exilic sources.[45] The insights from social anthropology can help us to reassess the familiar data from the Old Testament tradition and the new data of archaeology to gain a better picture of Israel's religion in Old Testament times. This has been only a short treatment of a complex subject, but a longer study is in the process of preparation.

It is with great pleasure that I dedicate this paper to Professor Whybray, whose interests have cut across both prophetic and wisdom literature. We are all in his debt, but as his successor as teacher of Old Testament at Hull, I am doubly aware of the long shadow he casts.[46]

45. See J.B. Segal, 'Popular Religion in Ancient Israel', *JJS* 27 (1976), pp. 1-22; Grabbe, *Judaism from Cyrus to Hadrian*, I, ch. 8.

46. An earlier draft of this paper was read at the Society of Biblical Literature International Meeting in Sheffield, August 1988.

FROM MARI TO MOSES:
PROPHECY AT MARI AND IN ANCIENT ISRAEL

Robert P. Gordon

Modern study of near eastern (non-Israelite) prophecy, whether as a subject in its own right or (usually) as background to the more lavishly illustrated Israelite phenomenon, begins with Golénischeff's publication in 1899 of the Egyptian Wen Amon text which relates an occurrence of ecstatic prophesying in a temple at Byblos in the eleventh century BCE.[1] Since 1899 a number of texts illustrative of ancient near eastern prophecy, and confirming that 'prophecy' in some sense is indeed involved, have been forthcoming from a number of near eastern sites, Mari in the mid-Euphrates region being pre-eminent among them. In this study attention will focus on texts from the second millennium that might be regarded as precursors (if not progenitors) of the Israelite phenomenon.

Strangely, the Ugaritic texts, which have shed light on many other features of Israelite religion, have little to say on prophecy.[2] There are a couple of uninformative references to 'seers',[3] and, in a text written in Akkadian, there is a mention

1.   W. Golénischeff, 'Papyrus hiératique de la Collection W. Golénischeff contenant la description du voyage de l'égyptien Ounou-Amon en Phénicie', in *Recueil de travaux relatifs à la philologie et à l'archéologie égyptiennes et assyriennes* 21 (NS 5) (ed. G. Maspero; Paris: Librairie Emile Bouillon, 1899), pp. 74-102 (text and translation into French, pp. 76-102). See also A. Erman, 'Eine Reise nach Phönizien im 11. Jahrhundert v. Chr.', *Zeitschrift für ägyptische Sprache und Altertumskunde* 38 (1900), pp. 1-14 (translation into German, pp. 4-14).

2.   Cf. J. Gray, *The Legacy of Canaan* (VTSup, 5; Leiden: Brill, 2nd edn, 1965), p. 217.

3.   See A.F. Rainey, 'The Kingdom of Ugarit', *BA* 28 (1965), p. 123.

of 'ecstatics' (see below). To relieve some of this dearth, Ringgren quotes, from the Baal epic, a speech by Kothar wa-Ḫasis to Baal, in which he finds prophetic oracular form:

> I tell you, O Prince Baal,
> I repeat, O Rider of the Clouds:
> Behold, your enemy, O Baal,
> Behold, your enemy you shall smite,
> Behold, you shall destroy your foes.
>> You shall take your eternal kingdom,
>> Your dominion for generation after generation.[4]
>>> (*CTA* 2.4.7-10)

This oracle from a god to a god is therefore given the status of a heavenly story with an earthly meaning in a way broadly comparable with Thorkild Jacobsen's transposing of Sumerian mythical references to the gods in council into political reality ('primitive democracy') in the city-states of ancient Sumer.[5]

The Western Hypothesis

There has been a sustained interest in the prophetic texts from Mari since the first publications. Further attention is guaranteed by the appearance in 1988 of volume I/1 of *Archives épistolaires de Mari* (= *ARM* 26/1), which, as well as the new material, includes a number of previously published texts.[6] In addition, an *āpilum* text is included among the letters of *Yarīm-Addu* published in volume I/2 of the same series.[7]

---

4. H. Ringgren, 'Prophecy in the Ancient Near East', in *Israel's Prophetic Tradition. Essays in Honour of Peter R. Ackroyd* (ed. R.J. Coggins, A. Phillips and M.A. Knibb; Cambridge: Cambridge University Press, 1982), p. 9.

5. T. Jacobsen, 'Primitive Democracy in Ancient Mesopotamia', *JNES* 2 (1943), pp. 159-72 (= pp. 157-70 in *Toward the Image of Tammuz and Other Essays on Mesopotamian History and Culture* [ed. W.L. Moran; Cambridge, MA: Harvard University Press, 1970]).

6. J.-M. Durand, *Archives épistolaires de Mari*, I/1 (*ARM*, 26; Paris: Editions Recherche sur les Civilisations, 1988), pp. 375-452 (= *AEM*). The texts discussed in this study follow Durand's numbering, but normally they also carry the older classification.

7. D. Charpin *et al.*, *Archives épistolaires de Mari*, I/2 (*ARM*, 26; Paris:

The most notable feature of the newly published texts is the occurrence of an Akkadian cognate of the Hebrew *nābî'* ('prophet') in text 216 (A. 2209), in which Tebī-gērī-šu reports on his consultation of Ḥanean prophets about the safety of the king of Mari.[8] Tebī-gērī-šu says that he assembled the ^{lú}na-*bi-i*^{meš} *ša* ḫa-na-meš the day after he arrived at Ašmad in order to discover whether it would be safe for the king to engage in a ritual lustration outside the walls of his city. It is only in recent years that such possible cognates of the Hebrew *nābî'* have begun to be canvassed. Apart from the claimed existence of a cognate at Ebla,[9] there are occurrences of a form *munabbītu* in thirteenth-century texts from the Syrian city of Emar. Each of the three occurrences of the word is associated with the goddess Išḫara, and one suggestion (which still requires corroboration) is that the word means 'prophetesses'.[10]

The description of the prophets in text 216 as 'Ḥanaean' seems to link this particular form of prophecy with the West Semites, since the Ḥanaeans are well known as an Amorite element within the population of Mesopotamia.[11] At first sight, therefore, there appears to be evidence of the western origin of at least some elements of Mesopotamian prophecy. This case has already been put by Malamat in relation to what he calls 'intuitive prophecy', and without the benefit of text 216.

Editions Recherche sur les Civilisations, 1988), pp. 177-79 (text 371 [A. 428]).

8. *AEM* I/1, p. 444 (line 7). See also D.E. Fleming, 'LÚ and MEŠ in ^{lú}na-*bi-i*^{meš} and its Mari Brethren', *NABU* (1993/1), pp. 2-4.

9. See G. Pettinato, 'The Royal Archives of Tell Mardikh-Ebla', *BA* 39 (1976), p. 49.

10. See D. Arnaud, *Recherches au pays d'Aštata Emar. VI/3. Textes sumériens et accadiens* (Paris: Editions Recherche sur les Civilisations, 1986), texts 373 (line 97), 379 (line 12), 383 (line 10). Cf. A. Tsukimoto, 'Emar and the Old Testament: Preliminary Remarks', *Annual of the Japanese Biblical Institute* 15 (1989), pp. 4-5.

11. Cf. M. Anbar, *ḥšbtym h'mwryym bm'ry whtnḥlwt bny-yśr'l bkn'n* (Tel Aviv: Tel Aviv University, 1985), pp. 72-74, 149-61; A. Malamat, *Mari and the Early Israelite Experience* (The Schweich Lectures of the British Academy, 1984; Oxford: Oxford University Press, 1989), pp. 38-39, 99, etc.

66 *Of Prophets' Visions and the Wisdom of Sages*

Malamat observed that there are more West Semitic idioms and linguistic forms in the prophecies as compared with the other Mari texts, and he surmised that the original messages may have been in Amorite and subsequently rendered into Akkadian, 'the language of the chancery'.[12]

This Ḫanaean connection was anticipated by J.F. Ross in an article published in 1970 which now deserves a fresh inspection in the light of text 216.[13] Ross sought to establish a common background for prophecy at Hamath and in Israel, with Mari and its satellite tribespeople, the Ḫanaeans, supplying that background. The eighth-century Zakkur inscription from Hamath is crucial for Ross's theory.[14] Ilu-wer in line 1 of the inscription is identified by Ross with the god Itur-mer who was worshipped at Mari and, after the downfall of Mari, at Ḫana. Moreover, Ross thought that Zakkur's reference to himself as an 'š 'nh (side A, line 2) should be understood to mean 'man of Ḫana', thus establishing a link between Mari and Hamath via Amorite Ḫana. However, it remains more likely that 'š 'nh in the Zakkur inscription should be translated by 'humble man': 'I was a humble man, but the lord of heaven [rescued] me'—and this despite Ross's defence of the ḫ / ' equation on the questionable analogy of ḫa-bi-ru = 'pr.

The West Semite hypothesis on the origins of Mari prophecy is, for that matter, not uncontested in recent discussion of the subject. Malamat himself had to acknowledge that four of the *muḫḫûm* prophets who are named in the Mari texts have Akkadian names, though he tried to explain this as the result of assimilation to the dominant language of the region.[15] The hypothesis is seriously questioned by Maria deJong Ellis in a recent article in which she suggests a connection between traditional Babylonian divinatory practices and Old Babylonian prophecy.[16] Such a link is already suggested by the Old

12. Malamat, *Mari and the Early Israelite Experience*, pp. 84-85.
13. J.F. Ross, 'Prophecy in Hamath, Israel, and Mari', *HTR* 63 (1970), pp. 1-28.
14. Text in H. Donner and W. Röllig, *Kanaanäische und aramäische Inschriften*, I (Wiesbaden: Otto Harrassowitz, 1966), p. 37.
15. Malamat, *Mari and the Early Israelite Experience*, p. 86.
16. M. deJong Ellis, 'Observations on Mesopotamian Oracles and

Babylonian *bārûm* text published by Goetze in 1968, which
has the diviner praying to Shamash in the following terms:

> O Shamash, I am placing in my mouth pure cedar...
> Being now clean, I shall draw near to the assembly of the gods
>   for judgment (*a-na pu-ḫu-ur ì-lí e-ṭe-eḫ-ḫi a-na di-nim*)
>   (lines 1, 9-10).[17]

Access to the divine council provides, as we shall see, a point
of substantial contact between divinatory and prophetic
experiences.

DeJong Ellis finds further evidence of the link in an oracular text from Ishchali that is presented in the form of a letter
addressed by the goddess Kititum to King Ibalpiel of Eshnunna.[18] There is no direct mention of the divine council in
the text; nevertheless the goddess's claim that she has been
regularly communicating the secrets of the gods to the king
appears to assume such a background. Thus, whereas
Malamat contrasted the *bārûm* with the prophet, with the
former viewed as an urban phenomenon and the latter as
semi-nomadic tribal in origin,[19] deJong Ellis argues for a
bārûm–prophecy continuum within Babylonia which, if it
involved a West Semitic connection, should at best be associated with West Semitic elements within the Old Babylonian
population.[20]

Prophetic Texts: Literary and Historiographic Considerations', *JCS* 41–
42 (1989), pp. 138-39, 145-46.

17. A. Goetze, 'An Old Babylonian Prayer of the Divination Priest', *JCS*
22 (1968), pp. 25-29 (25). Cf. also text A (HSM 7494) published by
I. Starr in *The Rituals of the Diviner* (Bibliotheca Mesopotamica, 12;
Malibu: Undena Publications, 1983), pp. 30-36, esp. lines 13-19 (pp. 30-31).

18. M. deJong Ellis, 'The Goddess Kititum Speaks to King Ibalpiel.
Oracle Texts from Ishchali', in *Mari. Annales de recherches interdisciplinaires*, V (Paris: Editions Recherche sur les Civilisations, 1987),
pp. 235-57.

19. A. Malamat, 'A Forerunner of Biblical Prophecy: The Mari
Documents', in *Ancient Israelite Religion* (Festschrift F.M. Cross; ed.
P.D. Miller, P.D. Hanson and S.D. McBride; Philadelphia: Fortress Press,
1987), p. 37.

20. *Mari. Annales de recherches interdisciplinaires*, V, p. 257.

Ecstatic Prophecy

The two most frequently mentioned terms for 'prophet' at Mari are, of course, *āpilum* and *muḫḫûm*, and much has been written already about their functional and social significance. The newer texts from Mari shed further light on both categories.[21] As noted above, Ugarit provides one of the most striking references to the *muḫḫûm* type, in an Akkadian text dating approximately to 1300 BCE.

> *aḫu-ú-a ki-ma maḫ-ḫe-e* [*d*]*a-mi-šu-nu ra-am-qu*
>
> 'my brothers like ecstatics (in) their (b)lood washed'
>
> (RS 25.460).

The possibility of comparison with the self-lacerating Baalistic prophets of 1 Kgs 18.28-29 and with the prophet of Zech. 13.5-6 is obvious enough.[22]

Durand thinks that the Mari texts give a further indication of the life-style of the average *muḫḫûm* in the fact that the word *etqum* (basically 'fleece') is used of the hair of a *muḫ-ḫûm* in preference to the more common and less expressive *šārtum* ('hair').[23] However, the matter is not as simple as that. As Durand himself notes, *etqum* is also used by the high official Sūmū-Hadû in reference to his own hair in text 182 (A. 2135). This balances the fact that in the Gilgamesh Epic Enkidu in his uncivilized phase sports an *etqum* (I, ii 37). Moreover, it is only text 215 (A. 455) that uses *etqum* to describe the hair of a *muḫḫûm*.[24] The more usual term *šārtum* occurs in relation to a *muḫḫûm* in texts 200 (M. 6188) and 201 (A. 368), just as it does in connection with an *āpilum* (texts 204 [A. 2264], 219 [M. 13496 + M. 15299]), *assinnum*

---

21. For comment on the *āpilum*, see the concluding section of this article.

22. Cf. J.J.M. Roberts, 'A New Parallel to 1 Kings 18.28-29', *JBL* 89 (1970), pp. 76-77.

23. *AEM* I/1, pp. 387-88.

24. Text 234 (= *ARM* 13.112), which Durand includes in his section on dreams, also uses *etqum*, though, as generally with dream reports, there is no mention of a *muḫḫûm*.

(text 213 [A. 100]) and *qammatum* (text 203 [A. 963]).[25] The occurrence of *etqum* in text 215 should perhaps also be seen in the light of certain 'irregularities' in this text, as Nakata has described them.[26] In particular, text 215 reverses the usual order of 'hair and hem' as compared with other dream reports that deal with the authentication of a prophet through the familiar method of checking a lock of hair and a hem belonging to the individual concerned.[27] The idea of the hirsute prophet also surfaces in Durand's discussion of the *qammatum* in text 203 (A. 963). Durand insists that the usually preferred form *qabbâtum* ('speaker'?) cannot be supported, and that *qammatum* indicates the hairy condition of the 'prophetess'.[28]

More illuminating than any of this crinal curiosity is text 206 (A. 3893) in which a *muḫḫûm* devours a raw (*balṭūssu*) lamb and announces a 'devouring' (*ú-ku-ul-tum*) that threatens the country.[29] The acted parable-cum-wordplay is of a kind familiar in the Hebrew Bible, but the crudity of the action exceeds anything attributed to the Israelite prophets.

Prophecies and Dreams

At this point we have to confront the question of definition raised by Nakata, who has argued that prophecies and dreams in the Mari texts should be sharply distinguished.[30] He makes a number of points chiefly concerned with the identity of the sources and of the recipients of the communications, the presence or absence of patterns of reporting, and the content of the messages reported. An additional reason given for the

25. See also the short list in F. Ellermeier, *Prophetie in Mari und Israel* (Theologische und orientalistische Arbeiten, 1; Herzberg: Verlag Erwin Jungfer, 1968), pp. 98-99.

26. I. Nakata, 'Two Remarks on the So-Called Prophetic Texts from Mari', *Acta Sumerologica* 4 (1982), pp. 144, 147 n. 11.

27. The order 'hem and hair (*etqum*)' also occurs in text 234r. (= *ARM* 13.112), lines 12-13.

28. *AEM* I/1, p. 396. Malamat ('A Forerunner of Biblical Prophecy', p. 38) argues for the older explanation from *qabû* ('speak').

29. *AEM* I/1, pp. 434-35.

30. *Acta Sumerologica* 4 (1982), pp. 143-44.

clear differentiation between the two types of report is the belief that prophecy belongs to the cultural sphere of the West Semites, while communication by dreams and visions is a concept widely diffused throughout the ancient near east.[31]

Durand observes this distinction in *AEM* I/1, except that *ARM* 10.9 (A. 2233) is included in his section on prophetic texts (no. 208). Whether, in the end, the distinction between prophecy and dream/vision is useful is a good question. It is noticeable that Durand thinks that in most cases the second group could be entitled 'dreamed prophecies' (*prophéties rêvées*).[32] Moreover, as we have seen, the assumption of a West Semitic matrix for prophecy is open to question, and it is certainly not a very secure plank in the case for dividing between Mari prophecies and dreams. Furthermore, if we look more closely at the dream reports we shall find that, whatever the differences from the prophecies, there are significant points of parallel and overlap, which is partly why none of Nakata's criteria enjoys absolute status: there are always exceptions and qualifications to be entered.

The closeness of the two categories of prophecy and dream is also suggested by the way in which they are associated in a couple of the texts. Thus Durand's text 227 (M. 9576) recounts a dream experienced by a woman whose name is only partly preserved; in it she sees the *muḫḫûm* prophets Hadnu-El and Iddin-Kubi 'alive' and reports what they said.[33] In text 237 (A. 994 = *ARM* 10.50) Addu-dūrī recounts two disturbing dreams that she had, relating to the fall of Mari, while the same text reports an oracular utterance of a *muḫḫûm* warning Zimri-Lim to remain at Mari.[34] It is all very well to divide a text like this into three sections (10.50 a–c), as does Nakata, but this categorizing should not be allowed to obscure the fact that dreams and prophetic oracle coexist in the one text. It is also the case that the familiar 'hair and hem' authentication of the person mediating the communication applies to the dreamers

31. Cf. A.L. Oppenheim, *Ancient Mesopotamia* (rev. edn; Chicago: University of Chicago Press, 1977), p. 221.

32. *AEM* I/1, p. 459.

33. *AEM* I/1, p. 467.

34. *AEM* I/1, pp. 478-79.

as well as the prophets (texts 226 [M. 9034], 229 [A. 222], 234 [M. 13841], 237 [A. 994]). The mention of the fact that the 'hair and hem' had not been obtained in one instance (text 233 [A. 15]) also attests their importance, even in relation to dreams. Finally, text 240 (A. 3424) appears to conclude with a request for a present, and, as we shall see, there was a practice of giving presents to prophets out of palace resources.

The Divine Council

One of the distinguishing features of Hebrew prophecy in its most developed phase is the sense of prophetic vocation exemplified in, for example, the books of Hosea and Jeremiah— and, we need not doubt, in the individuals whose careers lie behind the books. Some hint of this outlook is found in the first canonical occurrence of 'prophet' in the Hebrew Bible, at Gen. 20.7, where Abraham is so described because of the intercessory function that he is capable of discharging on behalf of the king of Gerar.

This vocational aspect of prophecy comes specially to prominence in the idea of the 'divine council', rejected as part of the polytheistic 'old order' in Psalm 82,[35] but a productive source of imagery for a number of Old Testament texts.[36] In Babylonian parlance this is the *puḫur ilī*, heavenly counterpart of the earthly citizen assembly. The idea of the divine council assumes an important role as regards the authentication of Hebrew prophets (see especially Jer. 23.9-40), but it has become increasingly clear that, far from the idea of prophetic participation in the divine council being unique to Israel,[37] non-Israelite prophecy could be represented within a

35. See, for example, C.H. Gordon, 'History of Religion in Psalm 82', in *Biblical and Near Eastern Studies* (Festschrift W.S. LaSor; ed. G.A. Tuttle; Grand Rapids: Eerdmans, 1978), pp. 129-31.

36. Cf. E.T. Mullen, *The Assembly of the Gods: The Divine Council in Canaanite and Early Hebrew Literature* (HSM, 24; Chico, CA: Scholars Press, 1980).

37. *Pace* Mullen, *The Assembly of the Gods*, p. 218 (esp. n. 181 on Mari, 'no concept of the prophet standing in the assembly of the gods is to be found in this material'); similarly M.E. Polley, 'Hebrew Prophecy within the Council of Yahweh, Examined in its Ancient Near Eastern Setting', in

similar framework. We have already noted the Old Babylonian *bārûm* text published by Goetze as relevant also to
Mesopotamian prophecy. In Mari text 208 (A. 2233) someone—possibly Qišti-Dīrītim, the *āpilum* of the obverse—
reports a discussion among the gods of the circle of Ea. Despite
the fragmentariness of the text, it appears that the prophet is
witnessing a session of a divine council.

Durand's text 196 (A. 3719) also deserves inclusion here.[38]
Again the text is incomplete, but it is evident that what is
being described is a session of a divine council. Dagan
summons Tišpak, the god of Eshnunna, in order to pass
judgment upon him: his day (?) has passed, and he will 'meet
his day' just as had the city of Ekallātum.[39] The god Yakrub-
El is also mentioned, as is the city-god Ḥanat who asks Dagan
not to forget the judgment that he has delivered. Although the
text is deficient at the precise point where the session of the
gods is introduced, the preceding references to Šamaš-naṣir's
waiting for an oracle in Dagan's temple in Terqa make it possible that what follows is a dream report.

This is clearly the case in the much later Balaam text from
Deir 'Alla in Transjordan (c. 700 BCE), according to which the
seer Balaam wept after hearing the decision of the gods
meeting in council.[40] There is no explicit mention of the council

Scripture in Context. Essays on the Comparative Method (ed. C.D. Evans,
W.W. Hallo and J.B. White; PTMS, 34; Pittsburgh: Pickwick Press, 1980),
p. 151.
    38. *AEM* I/1, pp. 422-23.
    39. There is some uncertainty about *ú-ud-ka* (lines 8-9 [rev.]), here
translated 'day', following Durand. Durand (p. 411) also refers to the
occurrence of *u₄-mu-šu qé-er-bu* ('his days are near') in text 212 (A. 3217
= ARM 10.6). Cf. the discussion by J.-G. Heintz, 'Aux origines d'une
expression biblique: *ūmūšū qerbū*, en A.R.M. X/6, 8'?', *VT* 21 (1971),
pp. 528-40.
    40. For the text see J. Hoftijzer and G. van der Kooij, *Aramaic Texts
from Deir 'Allā* (Leiden: Brill, 1976); J.A. Hackett, *The Balaam Text from
Deir 'Allā* (HSM, 31; Chico, CA: Scholars Press, 1984). On the divine
council in the Deir 'Alla text, see M. Weippert, 'The Balaam Text from
Deir 'Allā and the Study of the Old Testament', in *The Balaam Text from
Deir 'Alla Re-evaluated* (ed. J. Hoftijzer and G. van der Kooij; Leiden: Brill,
1991), pp. 151-84 (169-74).

in the Ishchali text published by deJong Ellis, but, as was noted above, the disclosure of the secrets of the gods to Ibalpiel is read by deJong Ellis against such a background. This is probably to go beyond the evidence, even though it may be granted that the concept of prophetic access to the divine council could have been sufficiently familiar not to need spelling out every time it was a factor in prophetic or quasi-prophetic contexts. This may apply particularly to text 233 (A. 15) which reports the dream experience of Malik-Dagan in the Dagan temple at Terqa:

> Now go! I send you (*a-li-ik áš-ta-pa-ar-ka*).
> Thus shall you speak to Zimri-Lim, saying...[41]

There is an obvious parallel with Isa. 6.8 ('Whom shall I send, and who will go for us?'), where also a meeting of the divine council provides the context for Isaiah's commissioning.

It will have been noted that our evidence for the non-Israelite, and especially Mari, prophets' experience of the divine council comes from texts that report *dreams*. If the already discussed distinction between prophecy and dreams/visions were maintained, then, strictly speaking, the admission of *prophets* to the divine council might still have to be regarded as a biblical idea, so far as the present evidence goes. However, it is probably in the nature of things that explicit mention of the divine council—not to speak of descriptions of its proceedings—should come in dream/vision reports. The same applies in the Hebrew Bible where prophetic experience of the divine council is, in the texts most quoted, of the visionary kind (see 1 Kgs 22.19-22; Isa. 6.1-13; cf. Ezek. 1–2; Zech. 3.1-10). It is not surprising, therefore, to find that in the critique of 'false prophecy' in Jer. 23.9-40 the contrast is between standing in the council of Yahweh and experiencing dreams. By implication, Jeremiah lays claim to the former (cf. vv. 18, 22), whereas the opposing prophets take their stand on visions/dreams (vv. 16, 25 ['I have dreamed, I have dreamed'], 27, 28, 32).

In view of the easy association of witnessing the divine council and dream experiences, we might conclude, then, that

41. *AEM* I/1, p. 473 (lines 32-33).

Jeremiah 23 tilts especially against the idea that the 'false prophets' have experience of the divine council in their dreams. The dream/vision may be the normal mechanism by which the experience is gained, but the idea that there is an underlying reality in which these prophets have participated is rejected. So far as the generality of prophetic texts—whether in the Bible or at Mari—is concerned, it would be a reasonable assumption that, in some instances at least, the idea of the divine council is somewhere in the background. Polley suggests that it is so for Amos's visions (Amos 7.1-9; 8.1-2; 9.1), and though this is not explicitly said in the text it remains a possibility.[42]

Messenger Prophets

The messenger function of the prophets, whether at Mari or in Israel, may also presuppose the admission of the prophet to the divine council before the divine/royal message is delivered to its intended recipient. An indication of this messenger function of the Mari prophet may lie in the practice of giving rewards to prophets, just as was the case with the *mār šiprim*. Malamat notes that there are references in Mari administrative texts to 'prophets' as recipients of presents, usually of clothing, from the palace.[43] In one text (*ARM* 9.22.14) an *āpilum* is involved, but usually it is a *muḫḫûm* (*ARM* 21.333. 34; 22.167r.8; 23.446.9, 19; 25.142.3) or *muḫḫûtum* (22.326.6-10). Malamat's interpretation of this is that the Mari prophets 'received material support from the royal court', and that they were to some extent comparable with the so-called 'court prophets' of Israel, or with the Baal and Asherah prophets maintained at the court of Ahab and Jezebel. Durand also comments on the giving of presents to prophets, building on references in three prophetic texts that he presents in *AEM*

42. M.E. Polley, *Amos and the Davidic Empire: A Socio-Historical Approach* (New York: Oxford University Press, 1989), p. 11.
43. Malamat, *Mari and the Early Israelite Experience*, p. 86. See also Malamat's short note, 'Parallels between the New Prophecies from Mari and Biblical Prophecy: II) Material Remuneration for Prophetic Services', *NABU* (1989/4), pp. 63-64.

I/1.[44] A *qammatum* (see above) of Dagan of Terqa delivered herself of a warning message and received a garment and a nose-ring (*ṣerretum*) from the palace as reward (text 199 [A. 925 + A. 2050], lines 51-52). Durand also thinks that the poorly preserved text 203 (A. 963) reflects a similar arrangement with a *qammatum* (lines 13-15), while the savage *muḫ-ḫûm* of text 206 (A. 3893) actually asks for an item of clothing in return for his dramatic contribution (lines 23-24). Durand's texts certainly support the view that the 'prophetic presents' were given as a reward for messages delivered, just as with (other) royal messengers.

The same may also apply to the references in the administrative documents cited by Malamat. Indeed, text A. 4674 (*ARM* 25.142), which is quoted in part by Malamat, points quite convincingly to the 'messenger reward' interpretation. A *muḫḫûm* of Adad received a silver ring 'when he delivered an oracle for the king' (*i-nu-ma te-er-tam a-na* lugal *id-di-nu*). Significantly, this follows a reference to a present given to an individual 'who brought the news' (*š[a] bu-su-ur-tam ub-lam*).[45] The messenger function of the Mari prophets therefore seems to be confirmed by the way in which they received presents for messages delivered. This, rather than a maintained status at court, appears to be indicated by the various texts that we have considered.

Prophecy, Accountability, Ethics

The growing amount of prophetic material coming to light at Mari in particular renders impossible the claim of H.M. Orlinsky that 'it is divination, and not prophecy, that finds its parallels in the Mari and other social structures and documents in the Fertile Crescent of old'.[46] This judgment was

44. See *AEM* I/1, p. 380.
45. This latter clause is given in the form quoted by Durand, *AEM* I/1, p. 380.
46. H.M. Orlinsky, 'The Seer in Ancient Israel', *OrAnt* 4 (1965), pp. 153-74 (170). Such comparisons as Orlinsky allows are between near eastern 'prophets' ('diviners') and Israelite 'seers'—which latter he distinguishes sharply from the classical prophets.

based on a small number of published texts and, for example, was pronounced in advance of the publication of volume 10 of *Archives royales de Mari*.[47] Dismissive accounts of near eastern prophecy that reject it as in no way comparable with the biblical phenomenon become more visibly wide of the mark as the number of available texts increases and as their contents are more thoroughly analysed. Nor should it be forgotten that the multifarious prophecy of ancient Israel was often nationalistic in outlook, sometimes mundane in its preoccupations, and frequently concerned with the royal house.

While the Mari prophets were generally supportive of the national dynasty, it is not true to say that they were completely uncritical of the royal house. The unconditional undertaking of Annunitum to Zimri-Lim in text 214 (A. 671) is balanced by the fact that Zimri-Lim is informed in another (233 [A. 15]) that, if he had been reporting fully to Dagan, the god 'would long ago have delivered the kings of the Yaminites fully into the power of Zimri-Lim' (lines 29-31).

Again, in a letter from Nūr-Sîn to Zimri-Lim (A. 1121) the god Adad declares that, since he had restored Zimri-Lim as national dynastic ruler in Mari, he was entitled to an estate (*niḫlatum*) in return.[48]

> If he does not give (it), I am lord of throne, territory and city, and what I have given I shall take away. If, on the other hand, he fulfils my desire, I shall give him throne upon throne, territory upon territory, city upon city; and I shall give him the land from the east to the west (lines 21-28).

This is reported as a message relayed through *āpilum*-prophets, and its implication as regards the possibility of negative action by Adad is clear. The same is indicated by Nūr-Sîn's expression of anxiety lest, in the event of anything

47. This volume, published in 1978, contains the majority of the Mari prophetic texts published in advance of *AEM* I/1.

48. The text is scheduled to appear in *Archives épistolaires de Mari* I/3. For text and translation see B. Lafont, 'Le roi de Mari et les prophètes du dieu Adad', *RA* 78 (1984), pp. 7-18; for English translation and discussion see A. Malamat, 'A Mari Prophecy and Nathan's Dynastic Oracle', in *Prophecy* (Festschrift G. Fohrer; ed. J.A. Emerton; Berlin: de Gruyter, 1980), pp. 68-82.

untoward ever occurring, he should be blamed for not having communicated important messages to Zimri-Lim (lines 34-45). While text A. 1121 could in no sense be called a 'judgment oracle', its tone is far from that of unconditional commitment or patronal monocularity on the part of the god in question.[49]

It is a familiar charge against near eastern prophecy that it lacks the socio-ethical awareness of its biblical counterpart. So Blenkinsopp turns to Egyptian ethical teaching as a likely source of inspiration for the social protest of the Israelite prophets.[50] This does not mean, however, that Blenkinsopp regards the Egyptian texts as in any sense 'prophetic'— *malgré* the heading 'Egyptian Oracles and Prophecies' that introduces a section including the 'Admonitions of Ipu-wer' and the 'Prophecy of Neferti' in Pritchard's *Ancient Near Eastern Texts*.[51] Moreover, the point that the proper locus of Egyptian 'prophetic' material is within the wisdom genre has been argued in two recent articles by Shupak.[52] Furthermore, if the concept of prophecy is elasticated to include Egyptian ethical texts, may we not just as legitimately appeal to ethical material in, say, Mesopotamian non-prophetic texts (e.g. 'Advice to a Prince')?[53]

There is, in any case, some hint of ethical concern in the Mari prophecies, as a number of writers have noted in connection with text A. 1121. There Zimri-Lim is counselled by Adad through an intermediary prophet: 'When a wronged

49. For a comparison of this text with both the *Heilswort* and the *Unheilswort* in 1 Kgs 9.1-9 see A. Schmitt, *Prophetischer Gottesbescheid in Mari und Israel: Eine Strukturuntersuchung* (BWANT, 114; Stuttgart: Kohlhammer, 1982), pp. 65-87 (81-87).

50. J. Blenkinsopp, *A History of Prophecy in Israel* (London: SPCK, 1984), pp. 55-56.

51. J.B. Pritchard, *Ancient Near Eastern Texts Relating to the Old Testament* (Princeton: Princeton University Press, 3rd edn, 1969), pp. 441-49 (441).

52. N. Shupak, 'Egyptian "Prophetic" Writings and Biblical Wisdom Literature', *BN* 54 (1990), pp. 81-102; *idem*, 'Egyptian "Prophecy" and Biblical Prophecy', *Shnaton* 11 (1990), pp. 1-40. I have not been able to consult this latter study.

53. See W.G. Lambert, *Babylonian Wisdom Literature* (Oxford: Clarendon Press, 1960), pp. 110-15.

man or woman cries out to you, stand and judge their case'.[54]
Text 232 (A. 907) shows how this might apply in practice. A
woman whose servant (?) had been abducted was instructed
by Dagan in a dream to carry a message to Zimri-Lim telling
him that he was held responsible for the girl's safe return.
Since there is no suggestion that Zimri-Lim was implicated in
the abduction, it evidently was as king and law-maker that he
was held responsible. We now also have Durand's text 194
(A. 4260) in which Shamash instructs Zimri-Lim through an
āpilum to declare a remission of debts (*andurārum*) and to
send those who had a legal case to the feet of Shamash (lines
41-46).[55] The text is one of a small number collected in a section headed 'Echange de lettres avec les dieux', but it is no
less significant on that account.

Prophecy Alfresco

The study of the ancient pre-Israelite prophetic texts tends to
confirm the view voiced earlier in this discussion, viz. that the
more we learn about the non-Israelite version the less wide
the gap between it and its Israelite counterpart appears.
Further illustration of this point may be found in the prophetic text 371 (A. 428) published by Charpin in *AEM* I/2.[56] In
the first place, the prophet figure is described as an *āpilum* of
Marduk (*a-pí-lum ša ᵈamar-utu* [line 9]), which, at least on
the surface, associates the phenomenon of prophecy directly
with Babylon and not just with the West Semites. (The text
apparently was written in Babylon.) It may be that a Mari
term has been used for a functionary who bore another title
in Babylon,[57] but there is a danger here of special pleading.

This *āpilum* of Marduk does not deliver his oracle within
the confines of a temple as in various other instances (e.g.
texts 195, 199, 209, 214), but at the door of the royal palace
in Babylon and then at the door of Ishme-Dagan's residence,
and in the hearing of the general populace. He differs in this

---

54. Cf. Lafont, 'Le roi de Mari', pp. 10-11 (lines 53-54).
55. See *AEM* I/1, pp. 405, 418.
56. *AEM* I/2, pp. 177-78.
57. So Charpin, *AEM* I/2, p. 179.

last respect from the *āpilum* who delivered a message at the door of the palace in text 208, and even from the *muḫḫûm* who spoke in the hearing of the elders at Saggarātum (text 206). At the door of Ishme-Dagan the *āpilum* of text 371 addresses him in the second person, using the words of Marduk himself as the god proclaims his displeasure at several of Ishme-Dagan's actions. Here prophecy has come out into the public arena and has, if one may so speak, taken another step in the direction of its biblical counterpart. We may expect that, with further publication of texts and their detailed analysis, the delineation of the Mari prophets will become still clearer. This could even have uncovenanted benefits for those members of the goodly fellowship of biblical prophets who have suffered loss of status amid current preoccupation with prophetic redactors and with prophecy as first and foremost a bookish phenomenon.

* * *

I am delighted to offer this short study for inclusion in the Festschrift for Norman Whybray, among whose major contributions to Old Testament scholarship the study of the prophets has featured prominently.[58]

58. I should like to thank J. Nicholas Postgate for his helpful comments on this paper, and especially for his advice on some of the finer points of Akkadian spelling. Since this article went to press a discussion with a bearing on the concluding paragraphs above has been published by S.B. Parker ('Official Attitudes toward Prophecy at Mari and in Israel', *VT* 43 [1993], pp. 50-68).

PROPHECY—TRUE AND FALSE

Richard J. Coggins

1. The topic of 'false prophecy' has been much discussed; all
the standard treatments of prophecy in ancient Israel devote
some attention to it, and there have been numerous articles,
and even books, with false prophecy, and the rivalry between
different prophets, as their basic theme.[1] Nevertheless, the
feeling remains that many such discussions, valuable though
they are, fail to address some of the issues at stake in the
problem of false prophecy. This essay makes no claim that it
will address all such issues, but it may serve to provoke
further reflection, partially at least by drawing attention to
some aspects of the problem that tend to be overlooked.

2. There is clearly a sense in which any office can be ineffec-
tively discharged, because the holder is incompetent, or inadequately motivated, or has been corrupted by rivals, or for a
host of other reasons. Such limitations are so commonplace as
not to need illustration; it is part of the human condition that
people will from time to time find themselves in, or be chosen
for, offices that subsequent experience shows them to be
incapable of discharging competently. In such cases it may
often be difficult to know where inadequacy ends and falsity
begins, for few will acknowledge openly that they cannot cope
with a task; the temptation to give a false impression that one
is coping is a powerful one, both among the holders of office

---

1. Among the standard surveys see J. Lindblom, *Prophecy in Ancient
Israel* (Oxford: Blackwell, 1962), pp. 210-15; J. Blenkinsopp, *A History of
Prophecy in Israel* (London: SPCK, 1984), pp. 184-88; and, with specific
reference to Jeremiah, R.P. Carroll, *From Chaos to Covenant* (London:
SCM Press, 1981), pp. 192-97. See also n. 11 below.

and among those whose own position is in any way tied up with the successful discharge of that office.

2.1. There is also a different, and no less important, sense in which the holders of an office may be regarded as incompetent. That arises when they are the victims of calumny from their rivals. In the modern West that state of affairs is most common—at least in public—with politicians, so that we should feel that those in opposition were scarcely fulfilling their role unless they were questioning the competence and integrity of those in government (and, of course, a government will raise exactly the equivalent doubts about the opposition). But plenty of examples from the contemporary world show that in other fields too, not least in religion, rival claims to understanding of the truth may excite bitter controversy.

2.2. Our knowledge of the ancient world in general and of Israel in particular suggests that it too could provide plenty of examples in each of these categories. (The British Museum in 1990 mounted an exhibition on 'Fakes', and it is interesting to note that the section of the catalogue dealing with the use of documents to misrepresent reality begins by asserting that in the ancient world 'the perpetrators of such frauds were often priests'.[2])

2.2.1. In the Hebrew Bible, priests and prophets are often condemned for their inadequacy in face of the great responsibilities with which they were entrusted. Thus, it appears as if the condemnation of the 400 court prophets in 1 Kings 22 is of this kind; particularly would this be true if Jehoshaphat's scepticism as to the reliability of their advice ('Is there not another prophet of the LORD of whom we may enquire?', v. 7) is to be understood as anything more than a literary device on the part of the narrator. Similar in kind may well be the dismissal of the prophets, along with other religious figures, in Hos. 4.4-6; Isaiah's scathing denunciation of drunken priests and prophets (Isa. 28.7); the scorn of Jeremiah in the section 'Concerning the Prophets' in 23.9-32; and quite possibly Amos's apparent rejection of any suggestion that he

2. M. Jones (ed.), *Fake? The Art of Deception* (London: British Museum, 1990), p. 59. I am grateful to Professor Alan Millard for supplying me with the details of this reference.

was one of the prophets (Amos 7.14). In all these instances the 'falsity' of the prophets seems to lie primarily in their alleged inadequacy to perform the tasks to which they had been called.

2.2.2. But to some extent in these passages, and still more elsewhere, we find language that makes it appear as if the condemnation is nearer to our second category: vilification on ideological grounds. This may well be the case in all the passages already referred to, but it can most readily be illustrated from the attack upon prophets found in Mic. 3.5 ('the prophets who lead my people astray, who cry "Peace" when they have something to eat, but declare war against him who puts nothing into their mouths'). This is, as we have seen, one of several such condemnations in the texts dealing with prophets; we need note only that they are often taken entirely at their face value by modern scholars, with no serious consideration being given to the possible underlying ideological viewpoint. Thus one of the most highly regarded of recent commentaries on Micah is able to assert of those here condemned: 'Selfish expediency had become their criterion for the content of their oracles, on the principle that he who pays the piper calls the tune. Eventually they were in the prophecy business for what they could get out of it. Corrupted by cupidity, they turned into religious charlatans, dressing with the right prophetic trimmings their bogus oracles'.[3]

2.3. It will be observed that this exegesis is already (and it goes on at greater length) reading a good deal into Micah's own much briefer condemnation. Here surely is a clear example of our second model: calumny of rivals as part of

---

3. L.C. Allen, *The Books of Joel, Obadiah, Jonah and Micah* (NICOT; Grand Rapids: Eerdmans, 1976), p. 311. Broadly similar ways of expressing the matter can be found in many other commentaries; see for example J.L. Mays, *Micah* (OTL; London: SCM Press, 1976), pp. 82-83. More complex is the view of A.S. van der Woude, who maintains that the words of the 'false prophets' can actually be found within our present book of Micah ('Micah in Dispute with the Pseudo-Prophets', *VT* 19 [1969], pp. 244-60), a view that he placed in the larger context of the eighth-century prophets in his essay 'Three Classical Prophets', in *Israel's Prophetic Tradition* (ed. R.J. Coggins *et al.*; Cambridge: Cambridge University Press, 1982), pp. 32-57, esp. pp. 49-50.

one's role expectations. We have no additional information to enable us to know whether Micah's harsh criticism was justified. No doubt his strictures have an internal logic; there will always be those who defy even the most unpromising circumstances with messages that all is going to be well, and indeed in many situations the role of religious spokespeople has been perceived as that of giving messages of encouragement in times of gloom. Micah may well have been right in warning that the situation was more serious than the prophets whom he condemned, or those who gladly listened to them, could really grasp. But it must equally be borne in mind that Micah's words can be understood as part of an ideologically based condemnation of those who differed from himself. (We may in passing note that this condemnation has often been understood to be part of a more general condemnation of groups described as 'official' or 'cultic' prophets; it may be so, but there is no clear indication of this in the text, or adequate grounds for such assertions from our knowledge of the religious structures of ancient Israel. When it is further asserted that the condemnation is of all 'professional' prophets, it seems as if the cult of the amateur is being carried to almost ludicrous extremes, and one is reminded of Groucho Marx's declining the offer of an operation by a gifted amateur brain surgeon.)

2.4. It will be evident, therefore, that in ancient Israel, as in other societies both ancient and modern, different religious interpretations led to conflict, and that such conflict might well have been expressed in harsh and bitter terms. Modern studies that present the pre-exilic prophets, and Hosea in particular, as part of a 'Yahweh-alone movement', making exclusive claims on behalf of Yahweh that were resisted by those whose reading of the religious situation was different, have offered one ground for the bitterness of these divisions.[4] Whether or not that particular historical reconstruction of events is acceptable, it is clear that by the early sixth century BCE the governing orthodoxy was that Yahweh alone was worthy of worship, and all those who proclaimed the worship

4. For the 'Yahweh-alone' reading of Hosea, see B. Lang, *Monotheism and the Prophetic Minority* (Sheffield: Almond Press, 1983), esp. ch. 1.

of other gods, or the worship of Yahweh in a manner that had come to be regarded as unacceptable, were now to be dismissed as false. Here is one element of the theme of 'false prophecy', a condemnation that could be applied equally to priesthood and to any other religious office, merely because it represented a rival view that came to be regarded as not 'politically correct'. It is not by chance that in Isaiah, Hosea and Micah the condemnations of unacceptable prophets are closely bound with those passages which speak harshly against other religious figures.

3. Yet it is clear that 'false prophecy' is a term of condemnation with much more powerful resonances than, for example, 'false priesthood'. In terms of the Hebrew Bible, false priesthood was exercised when those who in the speaker or writer's view had no right to exercise such an office took such privileges upon themselves; one thinks of the chilling stories of the death of Nadab and Abihu in Lev. 10.1-3 or of King Uzziah's 'leprosy' in 2 Chron. 26.16-21. False prophecy, on the other hand, came increasingly to be perceived as a problem inherent in the very exercise of prophecy as such. In other words, the proper exercise and understanding of prophecy came to be inextricably tied to an understanding of prophecy as prediction.

3.1. For many modern students of the Old Testament, perhaps especially those whose origins are in Protestant traditions, there is a further dimension inherent in the notion of 'false prophecy'. In those traditions priesthood has been regarded with suspicion; as recently as 1956 the late H.H. Rowley could write, in a book intended as a popular introduction to the Old Testament and widely used as such, that 'We are accustomed to think of priests as inherently evil'.[5] It is fair to note that Rowley went on to warn against such an automatic assumption, but it remains a revealing aside. Presumably the comment arose from the religious tradition in which he himself was reared, which must have entertained a deep suspicion of 'priestcraft'. Prophets, on the other hand, were figures to be held in honour, with, of course, the inherent

5. H.H. Rowley, *The Faith of Israel* (London: SCM Press, 1956), p. 37.

danger that any falsity in the exercise of prophecy was of so much the greater seriousness. The matter of true prediction was once again of crucial relevance.

3.2. It is neither appropriate nor feasible in a short essay such as this to rehearse in any detail the different views which have been held as to the role of prophets in the monarchical period in Israel. Despite the impressive attempts, particularly by scholars in the USA, to plot the role and development of prophetism in anthropological terms,[6] it is by no means clear that all the figures whom tradition has come to bracket together as *nebi'im* are correctly so described, or would indeed have recognized their kinship with one another.[7] Insofar as any common role can be discerned, it seems to consist of the conveyance of what were claimed to be messages from God to those in authority. Such a role must contain an element of futurity: 'If you pursue *this* course of action, then *that* consequence will follow'; but that is very different from regarding their main task as announcing what the future would bring.

3.3. At some point, however, it is clear that a significant change in perception took place, and prophets came to be regarded, perhaps by themselves, and certainly by others who recorded their words, as having a message essentially concerned with future events. It is common to link this change of perception with the Deuteronomistic movement, and though it is important to avoid charges of 'pan-Deuteronomism'—the Deuteronomists have sometimes been praised or blamed for virtually every significant development within ancient Israel's religious practice—we can at least say that the book of Deuteronomy itself and the Deuteronomistic History afford us

6. See especially R.R. Wilson, *Prophecy and Society in Ancient Israel* (Philadelphia: Fortress Press, 1980); and D.L. Petersen, *The Roles of Israel's Prophets* (JSOTSup, 17; Sheffield: JSOT Press, 1981). Criticisms made by C.S. Rodd ('On Applying a Sociological Theory to Biblical Studies', *JSOT* 19 [1981], pp. 95-106) have been carried further by R.P. Carroll, 'Prophecy and Society', in *The World of Ancient Israel* (ed. R.E. Clements; Cambridge: Cambridge University Press, 1989), pp. 203-25.

7. See the discussion of this issue by A.G. Auld, R.P. Carroll and H.G.M. Williamson in *JSOT* 27 (1983), pp. 3-44, especially Carroll's contribution, 'Poets, not Prophets'.

the first clear indications of such a shift.[8] Alongside this, however, we may note that the process of preserving and adding
to the oracles of individual figures—Amos, Hosea, and so on—
provides additional testimony to the idea that a future element
of 'fulfilment' came to be regarded as an important aspect of
their messages. (Some scholars would of course see much of
this editing and redactional process as providing further indications of Deuteronomistic activity, but that issue need not
concern us here.) It may indeed be that this element was
important in the process by which these figures came to be
regarded as *nebi'im*, a role that in some cases at least (Amos
7.14 once again!) they had vigorously rejected in their lifetime.

3.4. It will at once be perceived that the prominence of the
idea of prediction adds a new dimension to the prophetic role,
and raises the question of falsity in a drastically new sense. A
prophet may be false because he or she is incompetent or
driven by unworthy motives of different kinds, but that, as we
have seen, is a kind of falsity with which holders of every kind
of office may be charged. Now, in addition, a prophecy, and
therefore the one who uttered it, may be false because its contents are not fulfilled. The two groups of condemnation may
often be bracketed together when a particular individual or
group is accused; in principle, however, they are quite
distinct. In a modern capitalist society a financial adviser may
recommend clients to take particular investments, predicting
that they will prosper; if the investments collapse, that might
be connected with malpractice on the part of the adviser, but
might equally be traceable to other circumstances that could
not have been foreseen. The parallel with the prophets of
ancient Israel must not be pushed too far, but need not be
dismissed entirely; in whatever religious language it was
expressed, surely one element of prophetic prediction was
based on an intelligent assessment of the contemporary political situation. There is an uneasy tension in some modern

8.   The very extended discussions of prophecy, true and false, in
the volumes devoted to Hosea and Amos by F.I. Andersen and D.N.
Freedman (AB; New York: Doubleday, 1980, 1989) appear to take the
predictive role of prophecy for granted, without any attention to the
questionings of this understanding widely voiced in recent years.

studies of the prophets: on the one hand there is the desire to praise them as politically shrewd, seeing deeper into the realities of the situation than their short-sighted contemporaries; on the other hand the claim is often made that they were above the sordid details of political life, and concerned only to call their fellow-citizens back to the demands of the service of God.

4. With these considerations in mind, it may be revealing to take a fresh look at the role of prophets as set out in the Deuteronomistic literature. Whereas in Genesis–Numbers there is no section giving any systematic attention to the role of prophets,[9] it is clear that in the society described or envisaged by Deuteronomy 12–26 prophets had a significant place.

4.1. In the key passages, Deut. 13.1-5 and 18.15-22, it appears as if two distinctive roles can be traced. In the first, the prophet appears once again as the messenger between God/the gods and the community, and the warning here is to test the credentials of the prophet by ensuring that his or her messages come from the appropriate God. Here the accuracy of the prophet's words is not the main criterion; even if 'the sign or wonder which he tells you comes to pass', that cannot be any justification for turning to the worship of other gods, regarded as false by the mono-Yahwistic author of Deuteronomy.

4.1.2. In the second passage the emphasis is different. It is in fact twofold. First, whereas in Num. 12.6-8 Moses' office is contrasted with that of the prophets, here he is explicitly presented (for the first time in Deuteronomy) as a prophet; secondly, the role of prophets is very specifically linked with future prediction. These two themes are, of course, much more closely linked together than might at first sight appear. If the Book of Deuteronomy is rightly understood as the

---

9. The references to prophets in Num. 11–12 are only a very partial exception to this generalization. In Num. 11.24-29 prophets are highly esteemed; in 12.6 prophetic inspiration is compared unfavourably with the direct guidance given by God to Moses. It is impossible here to examine possible reasons (source-critical, literary, social, etc.) for this apparent discrepancy.

prelude to the complete Deuteronomistic History, then Moses' predictive role is very strongly emphasized;[10] his predictions of the fate of the people can be seen as being borne out in the whole of its subsequent history. By contrast with the false pretensions of others who claimed to be prophets, Moses' role was one that was substantiated by subsequent events. As has often been noted, such a test of prophetic authenticity is of little value when applied to the community's contemporary and future situation, for by the time that a prophecy was validated by being fulfilled the damage would have been done. But as a means of showing how the community's present situation had come about, having already been announced by the true prophet Moses, it represented a powerful claim.

4.1.3. In the Deuteronomistic History itself the two episodes most obviously relevant to the consideration of true and false prophecy have often been studied.[11] They are to be found in 1 Kings 13 and 22, each in a context concerned with relations between the Southern and Northern kingdoms, a context, that is to say, where the proper understanding of Mosaic prophecy was of special significance. In these passages, too, the picture of the true prophet as the one whose words came to pass and the false prophet(s) being shown as such by their non-fulfilment can readily be seen.

4.2. But the fact that in these stories the establishment of fulfilment/non-fulfilment is so easily achieved raises an issue that has not always been given its true significance. The meaning of the words of the 'old prophet of Bethel', first a liar and then a speaker of the truth, are unambiguous: 'Your body shall not come to the tomb of your fathers' (1 Kgs 13.22). Again, Micaiah's message to the king of Israel is clear: 'If you return in peace, the LORD has not spoken by me' (1 Kgs 22.28). Whatever the historicity of the events described in

10. See R. Polzin, *Moses and the Deuteronomist* (New York: Seabury Press, 1980), particularly the discussion of authorial conventions in ch. 2, pp. 25-72.

11. For 1 Kgs 13, see especially J.L. Crenshaw, *Prophetic Conflict* (BZAW, 124; Berlin: de Gruyter, 1971), esp. ch. 3, pp. 39-61; S.J. De Vries, *Prophet against Prophet* (Grand Rapids: Eerdmans, 1979), is a study devoted to the story in 1 Kgs 22.

these two chapters, the prophets' words are set out in a way that leaves no room for doubt when we wish to establish who is true and who false; what is required for their fulfilment is clear and unambiguous.

4.2.1. The situation in the story of the confrontation between Jeremiah and Hananiah in Jeremiah 28 is essentially similar. (Whether the delay implied in vv. 11 and 12 is a dramatic device to heighten the tension of the story, or a clue to Jeremiah's personality, showing him as liable to uncertainty at times of strain, need not here concern us.) As the story is told, Jeremiah announces that Hananiah will die before the year is out, and 'in that same year, in the seventh month, the prophet Hananiah died' (v. 17). Again the words of the true prophet are unambiguously fulfilled.

4.2.2. Where a prophecy relates to the fate of an individual, particularly if that fate is to be the person's death, the question of truth/falsity can be established in ways that seem to be beyond dispute. Disputes in ancient Israel between rival groups of prophets may have been of this kind, and if so, we are once again in the area of ideological tension between different understandings of the religious situation that we noted at the beginning of this essay. Certainly the element of mockery that is found in the Deuteronomistic stories relating to false prophets comes in this category; the way in which Zedekiah the son of Chenaanah and his colleagues are described in 1 Kings 22 is surely aimed at making them look foolish. In a sense their falsity is not their own fault, for they have been deceived by a lying spirit from God's own council (vv. 22-23), but how different is our reaction from that engendered by, say, the prologue to the story of Job, which also portrays the human victim of a divine conciliar decision. The narrator's skill ensures that Job commands our sympathy; the 400 prophets look ridiculous. The account of Hananiah in Jeremiah 28 is similar; we are again reminded of the powerful element of ideological rivalry that underlies so much religious dispute.

4.2.3. Another situation in which fulfilment is the vital criterion can be noted if we turn once again to Micah, this time with reference to the passage in which he announces the

inevitable downfall of Jerusalem (3.12). This passage provides
the only unambiguous instance in the Hebrew Bible of a
prophetic message being specifically referred to in another
prophetic collection, for it is discussed in Jer. 26.18-19.
Jerusalem had not fallen; but this does not mean that Micah
was dismissed or condemned as a false prophet on the
grounds that his prophecy had not been fulfilled. Rather, the
claim is made that Hezekiah's repentance had led Yahweh to
change his mind and spare the city, and such a claim cannot
readily be refuted. For those accepted as being within the true
prophetic succession ideological support could be provided,
and non-fulfilment of a particular prophecy was not an
insuperable barrier for those who were so accepted.

4.2.4. The problem of truth and falsity is, however, rarely as
straightforward as this. The stories referred to above are told
in such a way as to make it clear what will count as fulfilment
and non-fulfilment. For the most part, however, prophecies
that have been handed down in writing as part of a collection
of words attributed to an individual are rarely of this kind.
This is a problem to which we must now pay attention in the
context of the understanding of prophecy in the period of the
Second Temple.

5. In Second Temple Judaism it seems clear that the understanding of prophets and prophecy had come to be one that
saw them in terms of prediction. In Zech. 1.4-6 traces of what
may well be an older understanding, of prophets as messengers commissioned to give warnings to the people, may still be
detected, but it would be difficult to find such an understanding in any material later than Zechariah. Increasingly
their words came to be understood as 'oracles of God'
revealing to his servants God's unfolding purpose for
his people.[12] How in such a context was the issue of false

12. J. Barton (*Oracles of God: Perceptions of Ancient Prophecy in
Israel after the Exile* [London: Darton, Longman & Todd, 1986]) provides
an admirably clear exposition of the chief ways in which prophecy came
to be understood in this later period. This understanding of prophecy
also provides the rationale underlying the application by R.P. Carroll
and others of the psychological theory of 'cognitive dissonance' to

prophets and false prophecy to be dealt with?

5.1. That it *was* still an issue can perhaps best be illustrated by the well-known but difficult passage in Zech. 13.2-6. There is no agreement among scholars as to the date or social background of this passage, but two points about it may be noted. First, it appears to reflect a strong antipathy to contemporary claimants to the prophetic role;[13] secondly, it shows this antipathy by quoting a passage from an established prophetic collection, for the *lō' nābî' 'ānōkî* ('I am no prophet') of Zech. 13.5 is surely to be understood as an allusion back to the identical words of Amos 7.14. The prophetic texts, that is to say, are coming to be regarded as authoritative; they provided a body of material to which allusion and reference could be made in support of particular claims for the right understanding of God's demands.[14] When a religious community has a stake in the reliability and authority of particular writings, then it is of crucial importance to uphold the reliability and integrity of those writings—the more so when the writings are understood as prophetic in this predictive sense, having reference to events that were to take place at a time long after the lifetime of the prophets themselves.

5.2. A well-known example of this necessity to maintain the 'truth' of a text regarded as prophetic can be found in Dan. 9.2, with its reference to 'the number of years which, according to the word of the LORD to Jeremiah the prophet, must pass before the end of the desolations of Jerusalem, namely, seventy years'. The phrase 'according to the word of the LORD' ensures that the prophecy must be understood as a

prophetic words. The very title of Carroll's book, *When Prophecy Failed* (London: SCM Press, 1979), illustrates the understanding of prophecy as an exercise capable of 'succeeding', by looking forward to being validated through accurate fulfilment.

13. Barton's discussions of individual passages are for the most part very persuasive, but here he may be challenged when he suggests that Zech. 13.2-6 refers only to 'false claimants to prophetic inspiration' (*Oracles of God*, p. 106); the tenor of the biblical passage implies a more basic antipathy to prophetism than that would suggest.

14. The best study of this development is that of M. Fishbane, *Biblical Interpretation in Ancient Israel* (Oxford: Clarendon Press, 1985).

true one. Elsewhere, notably in Haggai and Zechariah 1–8, it seems as if the 'fulfilment' was understood in terms of the peaceful conditions brought about under Persian rule, though there is no explicit reference to Jeremiah. That want is supplied at the end of 2 Chronicles and the beginning of Ezra, where the reference to seventy years of desolation leads naturally to the rededication of the temple just seventy years after its destruction (2 Chron. 36.22; Ezra 5–6).[15] But for the final compiler of Daniel in the time of Antiochus Epiphanes it was only too apparent that the 'desolations of Jerusalem' were far from being over, and there follows in vv. 24-27 the explanation of the prophecy in terms of 'weeks of years'. (Was one reason for the insertion of Daniel's prayer at this point, vv. 4-19, an awareness of the temerity of what was being undertaken, the reshaping of an inspired prophecy from of old?)

5.2.1. If the book of Daniel appears to treat the words of Jeremiah in a somewhat cavalier fashion, that tendency is carried still further in later writings that had also had an important investment in claiming the 'truth' of prophetic words. The obvious examples are, of course, the Dead Sea Scrolls and the New Testament. As is well known, one of the first of the scrolls to be discovered was a commentary on Habakkuk 1–2, a commentary that well illustrates the *pesher* type of exegesis engaged in by the Qumran community. Thus, when we read that Hab. 1.6, 'Lo, I am rousing the Chaldaeans, that bitter and hasty nation', is to be interpreted of the 'Kittim [Romans] who are quick and valiant in war, causing many to perish',[16] it is clear that the idea of 'true prophecy' has now become so flexible as to defy anything that modern westerners would regard as rational criteria of judgment.

15. Strong arguments against regarding Ezra as the continuation of 2 Chronicles have been put forward in recent years by H.G.M. Williamson and others; this is not the place to examine these in detail, but the links between the two books still seem to be sufficiently close to invite their juxtaposition. Nor is it possible here to enter the discussion whether the temple was indeed rededicated in c. 516 BCE, or whether that dating has been shaped by an awareness of Jeremiah's prophecy.

16. M.A. Knibb, *The Qumran Community* (Cambridge: Cambridge University Press, 1987), pp. 223-25. Knibb provides a discussion of this and other biblical commentary texts from Qumran (pp. 207-55).

5.2.2. The same point may readily be seen in the New Testament, not least in the Gospel of Matthew with its frequent use of expressions referring to the fulfilment of words from God spoken through the prophets. Thus, to take just two examples: the return of Joseph, Mary and Jesus from Egypt is presented as fulfilling the words of Hos. 11.1, whereas that passage in Hosea would normally be taken as having a past reference, to the Exodus. At the end of the same chapter of Matthew, Jesus' dwelling in Nazareth is described as taking place 'that what was spoken by the prophets might be fulfilled, "He shall be called a Nazarene"'. It would be an exaggeration to suggest that Matthew actually concocted prophecy to provide a basis for his presentation, but the identity of this particular 'prophecy' continues to baffle commentators.[17] The use of prophetic material to illustrate and shape a particular story has now become so flexible that questions of true and false prophecy barely arise; it has become impossible to envisage criteria that could be laid down to establish whether or not a particular prophecy has or has not been fulfilled.

6. Conclusions of this kind may seem unduly negative, but they may be necessary, for too often the issue of false prophecy has been approached as if it is an issue that could be resolved to everyone's satisfaction if only the right scholarly techniques were applied. To a far greater extent than such an approach allows, there are ideological factors to be taken into account—particularly the recognition of the need within the religious community to legitimate certain voices and to exclude others—factors that make objective assessment extremely elusive. Perhaps also at times one feels the need for more common sense in the discussion of such issues than has sometimes been evident; and that is one reason why it is a particular pleasure to offer this study to Norman Whybray, with whom the quality of common sense has been prominent

17. For a survey of views of this problem, see R.E. Brown, *The Birth of the Messiah* (Garden City, NY: Image, 1977), pp. 207-13, 223-25. At least 15 different OT texts have been proposed as the point of reference in this citation.

(among many others) in his handling of the material. It is a great pleasure to acknowledge his capacity for asking awkward questions and, surely, proposing some lasting solutions in much study related to the prophetic literature in particular and the Hebrew Bible in general.

FIRST AND LAST IN ISAIAH

Hugh G.M. Williamson

In the years since the publication of Norman Whybray's commentary and other works on Deutero-Isaiah,[1] a major focus of study has been on the extent to which the exilic prophet may have been influenced by the earlier part of the book of Isaiah.[2] Of course, as Whybray himself was aware, some isolated examples had long been known,[3] but the accumulation of further suggestions has now reached the point

---

1. R.N. Whybray, *Isaiah 40–66* (NCB; London: Marshall, Morgan & Scott, 1975); cf. *The Heavenly Counsellor in Isaiah xl 13-14: A Study of the Sources of the Theology of Deutero-Isaiah* (SOTSMS, 1; Cambridge: Cambridge University Press, 1971); *Thanksgiving for a Liberated Prophet: An Interpretation of Isaiah Chapter 53* (JSOTSup, 4; Sheffield: JSOT Press, 1978); *The Second Isaiah* (OTG; Sheffield: JSOT Press, 1983).

2. There are useful surveys of research in J. Vermeylen, 'L'unité du livre d'Isaïe', and G.I. Davies, 'The Destiny of the Nations in the Book of Isaiah', both in J. Vermeylen (ed.), *The Book of Isaiah* (BETL, 81; Leuven: Peeters, 1989), pp. 11-53 and 93-120 respectively, and in M.A. Sweeney, *Isaiah 1–4 and the Post-Exilic Understanding of the Isaianic Tradition* (BZAW, 171; Berlin: de Gruyter, 1988), pp. 1-25. There should now be added in particular R. Albertz, 'Das Deuterojesaja-Buch als Fortschreibung der Jesaja-Prophetie', in E. Blum, C. Macholz and E.W. Stegemann (eds.), *Die hebräische Bibel und ihre zweifache Nachgeschichte: Festschrift für Rolf Rendtorff zum 65. Geburtstag* (Neukirchen–Vluyn: Neukirchener Verlag, 1990), pp. 241-56.

3. For instance, the divine title 'The Holy One of Israel' is said to be one that 'he took over from the vocabulary of his predecessor, the eighth-century Isaiah' (*Isaiah 40–66*, p. 65), and the use of *tôrâ* at 42.4 is compared with 8.16 (p. 73), a verse also referred to in the commentary on 50.4 (p. 151). These and other examples are not, however, regarded as in any sense qualitatively different from other influences on the thought and phraseology of Deutero-Isaiah.

where a number of scholars have concluded that Deutero-Isaiah may never have existed as a separate book but that it was conceived from the very first as an integral continuation of the earlier work. The present article proposes that another example should be added to the list. It differs from many that have been advanced, however, in that it goes beyond the realm of an isolated theme or phraseological echo; indeed, it may be said to furnish one of the most fundamental theological concepts that serves to bind together much of Deutero-Isaiah's literary legacy.[4] If it is accepted, therefore, it will provide powerful evidence for the particular influence of the literary deposit of First Isaiah[5] on Deutero-Isaiah.

The main passage for consideration in the first part of the book is 8.23b–9.6 (ET 9.1-7. I shall follow the Hebrew system of chapter and verse division throughout). The authenticity of this passage is by no means certain, though most commentators now reckon with at least a pre-exilic date for its composition, from the Josianic redaction of the work if not from Isaiah himself. (I shall have a little more to say about this later on.) Nor is the translation of the opening of the passage assured. The RSV (9.1b) represents one widely held approach:

> In the former time he brought into contempt the land of Zebulun
> and the land of Naphtali, but in the latter time he will make
> glorious the way of the sea, the land beyond the Jordan, Galilee
> of the nations.

4.   The question of the unity of Deutero-Isaiah, which is currently much debated, may be left to one side for our present purposes, since most, at least, of the passages that will be discussed are widely agreed to constitute part of the core of Deutero-Isaiah's work; cf. recently H.-J. Hermisson, 'Einheit und Komplexität Deuterojesajas: Probleme der Redaktionsgeschichte von Jes 40–55', in Vermeylen (ed.), *The Book of Isaiah*, pp. 287-312, but contrast R.G. Kratz, *Kyros im Deuterojesaja-Buch. Redaktionsgeschichtliche Untersuchungen zu Entstehung und Theologie von Jes 40–55* (Forschungen zum Alten Testament, 1; Tübingen: J.C.B. Mohr [Paul Siebeck], 1991).

5.   I use this term consciously to refer to the form which the book of Isaiah had assumed by the time of Deutero-Isaiah. By general consent, this will have included a good deal more than the actual words of Isaiah himself.

As has been demonstrated by Emerton,[6] this translation slides over several difficulties, including the facts that the two verbs in the verse, *hql* and *hkbyd*, are in the perfect tense, whereas the RSV translates the first as perfect and the second as future, that *'t*, 'time', is normally a feminine noun,[7] whereas it is construed by the RSV as being complemented by two masculine adjectives, *hr'šwn* and *h'ḥrwn*, 'the former' and 'the latter', and that an ellipse of *k't* has awkwardly to be presupposed before the second adjective, 'and (in) the latter (time)'. After a thorough discussion of these and related problems, together with a consideration of the historical background presupposed in the verse, Emerton offers the following translation 'with a certain freedom intended to bring out the suggested meaning':

> Now has everyone, from first to last, treated with contempt and harshness the land of Zebulun and the land of Naphtali, the way of the sea, the region beyond Jordan, Galilee of the nations.

Whatever we decide about the correct translation of the verse,[8] it is clearly divided into two halves by the contrasting pair *hr'šwn* and *h'ḥrwn*, 'the first and the last', or 'the former

6. J.A. Emerton, 'Some Linguistic and Historical Problems in Isaiah viii.23', *JSS* 14 (1969), pp. 151-75.

7. However, cf. P. Wegner, 'Another Look at Isaiah viii 23B', *VT* 41 (1991), pp. 481-84.

8. Emerton has been followed by, for instance, R.E. Clements, *Isaiah 1–39* (NCB; Grand Rapids: Eerdmans; London: Marshall, Morgan & Scott, 1980), p. 104, and to a considerable extent by J.H. Hayes and S.A. Irvine, *Isaiah, the Eighth-Century Prophet: His Times and his Preaching* (Nashville: Abingdon Press, 1987), pp. 176-79. Alternative interpretations, generally closer to the traditional rendering, which at least take account of his work, include H. Wildberger, *Jesaja. I. Teilband. Jesaja 1–12* (BKAT, 10/1; Neukirchen–Vluyn: Neukirchener Verlag, 2nd edn, 1980), pp. 362-64; H. Barth, *Die Jesaja-Worte in der Josiazeit: Israel und Assur als Thema einer produktiven Neuinterpretation der Jesajaüberlieferung* (WMANT, 48; Neukirchen–Vluyn: Neukirchener Verlag, 1977), pp. 143-45; J. Høgenhaven, 'On the Structure and Meaning of Isaiah viii 23b', *VT* 37 (1987), pp. 218-21; H. Eschel, 'Isaiah viii 23: An Historical-Geographical Analogy', *VT* 40 (1990), pp. 104-109; N. Na'aman, 'Literary and Topographical Notes on the Battle of Kishon (Judges iv–v)', *VT* 40 (1990), pp. 423-36 (434-36).

and the latter', and whether correctly or not this has frequently been taken to refer to contrasting periods of time, one
characterized by 'contempt' and the other by 'glory'. No doubt,
this reading has been influenced by the verse's position
between the gloomy conclusion of ch. 8 and the bright future
envisaged at the start of ch. 9, a point that seems to have
been appreciated as early as the inclusion of the redactional
join in 8.23a: 'But there will be no gloom for her that was in
anguish', if that is the right interpretation of an admittedly
obscure text. In addition, it receives a measure of support from
the use elsewhere in Isaiah 1–39 of the two key words. At 1.26
kbr'šnh refers to days in the distant past, before Zion had
gone so disastrously astray (parallel with *kbthlh*), while at
30.8, in particular, *ywm 'hrwn* refers to a future day that
Isaiah anticipates will dawn after the judgment is past. Once
the matter is expressed in these terms, several points of comparison with the work of Deutero-Isaiah suggest themselves.

First, God himself is described as 'the first and the last' at
44.6 and 48.12 ('I am the first and I am the last'), using the
very two words that divide 8.23b into two halves. 41.4 is
similar: 'I, the LORD, am the first; and with the last (*w't-
'hrnym*) I am He'. This title for God appears to be without
parallel; it is distinctive to Deutero-Isaiah. The possibility
should therefore be considered that he took the relevant
words in 8.23b as titles for God—that he read the verse as
signifying that it was 'the First' (with a capital 'F') who
brought the land into contempt and 'the Last' (with a capital
'L') who would eventually glorify it again.[9] It will then have
been this understanding which led him to coin his distinctive
title. It is noteworthy that, so far as I can see, no commentator
has proposed any other possible influence on Deutero-Isaiah

---

9.   If so, he must have taken *h't* as an independent adverb, meaning
'now', which Emerton has shown is certainly possible, and in addition he
may have regarded the use of *hr'šwn* and *h'hrwn* as an example of what
we should now call the breakup of a stereotyped phrase in poetry; cf.
E.Z. Melamed, 'Break-up of Stereotype Phrases as an Artistic Device in
Biblical Poetry', *ScrH* 8 (1961), pp. 115-53. Y. Komlosh (*Bar-Ilan* 4–5
[1967], pp. 42-49) has proposed that Isaiah himself intended the two
adjectives to refer to God, but this seems improbable.

as regards this title,[10] and that in this respect it differs markedly from all the other divine titles that the prophet uses. Since the title appears in passages where the form of the argument suggests that he is appealing to an accepted characteristic of God in order to build his new revelation upon it, it would be surprising if the prophet had here introduced a wholly novel title that might have invited a challenge from his readers or hearers.

Secondly, therefore, and in development of this last point, we should note that at 44.6 the title occurs in a short paragraph (vv. 6-8) which introduces a very characteristic theme of Deutero-Isaiah and one which, moreover, seems certainly to have been developed in association with it. This is the theme of the contrast between the former (or first) things and the new things that are yet to come which is referred to in the context of the ability to prophesy and which makes up an important element in the prophet's anti-idol polemic:

> Who has announced from of old things to come,
> Let them tell him what is yet to be (44.7b).[11]

Only the God who is himself 'the first and the last' is able to do such a thing. The occurrence of the title at 48.12 is in a context that is making a similar point, while at 41.4 the closely related issue is broached of God's control of history both in the remote past ('calling the generations from the beginning') and in the present ('Who has performed and done this?') with reference to the rise of Cyrus.[12]

---

10. P. Volz (*Jesaia II* [KAT; Leipzig: A. Deichert, 1932], p. 16) and P.-E. Bonnard (*Le second Isaïe: Son disciple et leurs éditeurs* [EBib; Paris: Gabalda, 1972], p. 109 n. 4) refer to 'the first and the last' as a description of (Ahura) Mazda in the *Gathas* (31.8), but it is hardly possible to speak of influence at this stage, even by way of polemic.

11. The first line of the MT 'hardly makes sense' (Whybray, *Isaiah 40–66*, p. 97), as attempts to defend it serve only to underline (cf., for instance, P.A.H. de Boer, *OTS* 11 [1956], p. 15). I follow the majority of commentators in making the very slight emendation to *mî hišmîa' mē'ôlām 'ôtiyyôt*; cf. BHS. For *lmw* in the second line, cf. GKC §103f n. 3.

12. From the Targum to C.C. Torrey, 'Isaiah 41', *HTR* 44 (1951), pp. 121-36, there have been those who have referred Isa. 41.2-4 to Abraham alone. This is unconvincing, however; at best, Abraham is

In these expressions of Deutero-Isaiah's familiar theme, the vocabulary with which we are here primarily concerned is used for God himself, and consequently alternative forms of wording are used for the sharp division of history into distinctive periods. Elsewhere, however, where God is not referred to in these terms, the same ideas are expressed by using the language of 8.23b in a manner that suggests that the various forms of wording are virtually interchangeable. We may compare the following examples:

> Tell us the former things (*hr'šnwt*), what they are,
>> that we may consider them,
> that we may know their outcome (*'ḥrytn*);
>> or declare to us the things to come (*hb'wt*).[13]
> Tell us what is to come (*h'tywt*) hereafter,
>> that we may know that you are gods (41.22b-c, 23a).

> Behold, the former things (*hr'šnwt*) have come to pass,
>> and new things (*wḥdšwt*) I now declare;
> before they spring forth
>> I tell you of them (42.9)

> Who among them can declare this,
>> and show us the former things (*wr'šnwt*)? (43.9b).

> Who told this long ago (*mqdm*)?
> Who declared it of old (*m'z*)? (45.21b).

Similar ideas and vocabulary are found throughout the extended passage 48.3-16, starting with 'The former things I declared of old (*hr'šnwt m'z hgdty*)'; cf. especially vv. 5, 6, 7, 8, 12, 14 and 16, and at 41.26.[14]

Thirdly, this polemical theme is closely associated with the

alluded to as a 'type' of Cyrus, as suggested by G.H. Jones, 'Abraham and Cyrus: Type and Anti-Type?', *VT* 22 (1972), pp. 304-19, with further literature.

13. Most commentators conjecturally invert the order of these two lines on the grounds that it results in better parallelism with the order of both the preceding and the following lines and that it is metrically more satisfying. Whether or not this is correct, it is important to recognize, as the order in the MT makes clear, that the suffix on *'ḥrytn* refers to *hr'šnwt*, not to *hb'wt*.

14. At 45.11, however, *h'tywt* is almost certainly the result of textual corruption; cf. Whybray, *Isaiah 40-66*, p. 108, and *BHS*.

related message of encouragement to the exiles to forget the former things because now God is doing something quite new:[15]

> Remember not the former things (*r'šnwt*),
>> nor consider the things of old (*wqdmnywt*).
> Behold, I am doing a new thing (*ḥdšh*);
>> now it springs forth, do you not perceive it? (43.18-19a).

Equally, it is turned to good use in refuting those who query God's propriety in raising up Cyrus as his agent of deliverance, and the continuation of the passage to be cited makes clear that this is the reverse side of the message of encouragement that the prophet is striving to get across to his recalcitrant audience:

> Remember this and consider,
>> recall it to mind, you transgressors,
>> remember the former things of old (*r'šnwt m'wlm*);
> for I am God, and there is no other;
> I am God, and there is none like me,
> declaring the end from the beginning (*mgyd mr'šyt 'ḥryt*)
>> and from ancient times things not yet done (46.8-10a;
>>> cf. 12-13).

15. This theme has, of course, been frequently analysed; earlier work is helpfully summarized by A. Schoors, 'Les choses antérieures et les choses nouvelles dans les oracles deutéro-isaïens', *ETL* 40 (1964), pp. 19-47. Though it is not the primary concern of the present essay, the recent trend to link the 'former things' with the recorded oracles of First Isaiah is fully compatible with the approach adopted here; see, for instance, D. Jones, 'The Traditio of the Oracles of Isaiah of Jerusalem', *ZAW* 67 (1955), pp. 226-46; J. Becker, *Isaias—Der Prophet und sein Buch* (SBS, 30; Stuttgart: Katholisches Bibelwerk, 1968), pp. 37-38; B.S. Childs, *Introduction to the Old Testament as Scripture* (London: SCM Press, 1979), pp. 328-30; D.G. Meade, *Pseudonymity and Canon: An Investigation into the Relationship of Authorship and Authority in Jewish and Earliest Christian Tradition* (Grand Rapids: Eerdmans, 1987), pp. 35-37; Albertz, 'Das Deuterojesaja-Buch' (above, n. 2), pp. 251-53; C.R. Seitz, *Zion's Final Destiny: The Development of the Book of Isaiah: A Reassessment of Isaiah 36–39* (Minneapolis: Fortress Press, 1991), pp. 199-202. An additional argument in favour of this approach, which does not appear to have been previously noted, is that when Isa. 65.16b-17 refers to this aspect of Deutero-Isaiah's thought, it clearly relates 'the former things' to the time of Israel's judgment.

Now, it is important to notice that all three usages are closely related to one another and that sometimes they appear to overlap within a single passage (e.g. at 42.8-9; 44.6-8; 46.9-11; and in ch. 48). Moreover, Deutero-Isaiah uses a wide range of vocabulary to express what is basically the same thought (for the first half of the pair *r'šnwt*; *qdmnywt*, qualified sometimes by *mr'š*; *mlpnym*; *m'wlm*; *mr'šyt*; *m'z*; *mqdm*; and for the second half of the pair *hb'wt*; *h'tywt*; *hdšwt*; *'šr tb'nh*). We should nevertheless observe that in addition to reflecting three times the specific vocabulary of 8.23b in descriptions of God, he also comes very close to it on two other occasions in these wider contexts when God is not himself referred to in these terms—at 41.22 (*hr'šnwt...'hrytn*) and 46.10 (*mr'šyt 'hryt*).

In the light of all this material, it may now be suggested that Deutero-Isaiah could have reflected on and been influenced by 8.23b in at least three ways. First, whether or not Emerton is right about the verse's original meaning, it is probable that Deutero-Isaiah read it in his new historical context as referring to two different periods of time, each characterized by one of the two contrasting verbs.[16] This, of course, is closer to the approach represented by the RSV, though it differs with regard to the understanding of 'the First' and 'the Last'. Specifically, he may have been encouraged in this direction (as many others since have been) by the general tenor of the verses immediately preceding and following with their apparent switch from a period of gloom to one of hope. Thus, for instance, Isa. 9.1—

> The people who walked in darkness (*bhšk*)
>   have seen a great light (*'wr*);
> those who dwelt in a land of deep darkness,
>   on them has light shined—

will have been taken by him as referring forward to his own day, when those in the 'darkness' of exile would now be led back into the bright 'light' of God's salvation:

16. It is worth observing here that 'make glorious' is securely attested as a possible meaning for *hkbyd* by Jer. 30.19.

And I will lead the blind in the way [that they have not known],[17]
in paths that they have not known I will guide them.
I will turn the darkness (*mḥšk*) before them into light (*l'wr*),
the rough places into level ground (42.16).

Of course, the use of such common words as 'light' and
'darkness' could not in themselves serve as evidence for
Deutero-Isaiah's use of earlier Isaianic material, but provided
it is agreed that it has been established that 8.23–9.6 was of
particular significance for him in the framing of his theology
of the turning of the tide from judgment to salvation, then the
allusion gains weight as a supporting argument. There can
certainly be no doubt that he made frequent use of 'light' as
an image of salvation (usually, though not always, in
association with its converse, 'darkness'); cf. (in addition to
42.16) 42.6-7 (and cf. 49.9); 45.7; 49.6; 50.10; and 51.4.
Similarly, the emphasis in 9.2 on 'joy' (the root *śmḥ* is there
used three times and *gyl* twice)[18] is also found several times in
Deutero-Isaiah as an appropriate response to what is
happening (cf. 41.16; 49.13; 51.3, 11; 55.12 and the comparable uses with *rnn* at 42.11; 44.23; 48.20; 52.8, 9; 54.1).
Other links between this passage and Deutero-Isaiah include
the expression *ḥlq šll*, 'to divide spoil', which is found only at
9.2 and 53.12 in the prophetic literature; the emphasis at the
end that 'the zeal of the LORD of hosts will do this (*t'śh z't*)'
may be compared with the similar expression at 41.20 (and cf.
42.16), though it occurs also at Amos 9.12, while the idea of
fire consuming the oppressor (9.4) may be reflected at 47.14
and 50.11. Thus, seeing the contrast between judgment and
salvation in 8.23–9.6 as a whole, he was led to see it also in
what he took to be the contrasting halves of 8.23b itself.

    Second, reflection on this contrast may have influenced him
to adopt his sharp and characteristic juxtaposing of 'the

17. The repetition of the phrase 'that they have not known' in the first
and second halves of the line is suspicious and seems to overload the first
half metrically. It should probably be deleted, and the previous word
vocalized *badderek* in consequence; cf. Whybray, *Isaiah 40–66*, p. 79.
    18. For the standard emendation of *hgwy l'* to *hgylh*, cf. G.B. Gray, *A
Critical and Exegetical Commentary on the Book of Isaiah I–XXVII* (ICC;
Edinburgh: T. & T. Clark, 1912), p. 175.

former things' and 'the new things' in different contexts precisely on the basis of *hr'šwn* and *h'ḥrwn* in 8.23. As we have seen, among the variety of expressions which he used to give expression to this idea, there is evidence that he drew specifically on the language of 8.23 itself.

Finally, as already noted, 8.23 provides the only possible source for one of his characteristic titles for God in a context where we expect him to be appealing to common ground between himself and his audience rather than coining some wholly novel designation.

In the light of this discussion, we may conclude that a connection between Isa. 8.23b and the various passages in Deutero-Isaiah seems to be probable. Certainly, no other text can be adduced that could serve as an independent source of influence in this regard. Attention has sometimes been drawn to Jer. 50.17, where 'First (*hr'šwn*) the king of Assyria devoured him, and now at last (*wzh h'ḥrwn*) Nebuchadrezzar king of Babylon has gnawed his bones'. Several considerations rule out this possibility, however. First, the date of Jer. 50.17 is uncertain, many commentators arguing that it is later than Deutero-Isaiah. This problem is only heightened by the observation that vv. 17b-18 appear to be a prose addition to their poetic context. Second, it is equally uncertain whether the adjectives are to be construed as adverbial accusatives of time, as is usually done, or as personal adjectives; this latter possibility is entertained by S.R. Driver: 'The first one (who) devoured him was the king of A.; and this, the last one (who) gnawed his bones, was, etc.'[19] Thirdly and decisively, however, this verse in Jeremiah lacks the very features of Deutero-Isaiah's interpretation of Isa. 8.23b that have been singled out above as being most significant and characteristic. Whereas Jer. 50.17 may attest the later influence of Isa. 8.23 understood very much along the lines proposed by Emerton (i.e. wholly negative) and reinterpreted in the light of the Babylonian conquest, Deutero-Isaiah appears to have developed a quite different interpretation of 8.23 in the light of his new historical situation. His contrasting of a period of

19. Cf. S.R. Driver, *The Book of the Prophet Jeremiah* (London: Hodder & Stoughton, 1906), p. 370.

oppression with a following period of deliverance is not found in Jer. 50.17, and when the passage in Jeremiah goes on in vv. 18-19 to speak of a future hope, it does so in a quite different way. Finally, as the editors of the present volume have kindly pointed out to me, 'first' and 'last' in the Jeremiah passage refer to different things (whether people or times), whereas in Deutero-Isaiah they refer to the same 'person' (God). It may thus be concluded that Jer. 50.17 cannot have served as the inspiration for those features of Deutero-Isaiah's thought and style which have been examined above.

If this conclusion is sound, it sheds new light on the question of the date of 8.23b–9.6, which was left on one side at the start of this discussion.[20] Naturally, this procedure could be charged with arguing in a circle—from the assumption of a pre-Deutero-Isaianic date to its establishment. Despite this, however, it seems reasonable to frame the issue in another way: if there is a literary connection between two bodies of literature, which can be more easily explained as dependent? The connection may be observed without recourse to any assumption about priority, and the question of dependency may then be resolved on its own merits.

In my judgment, even discounting the specific manner in which the evidence has been set out above, the material can be more easily explained in terms of Deutero-Isaiah being the one who is dependent than the reverse. We have seen that he uses the theme and its associated vocabulary in several slightly different ways, and that there is some uncertainty as to whether any of these exactly represents the meaning of 8.23. It is thus easier to think that he has been led to re-read the material in the light of his changed circumstances than that a later editor of First Isaiah has picked up several distinct, though related, themes in his work, brought them

20. Opinions on this continue to differ radically, and it is not my intention to deal with all aspects of the debate here. For surveys, see, for instance, J. Vollmer, 'Zur Sprache von Jesaja 9_{1-6}', *ZAW* 80 (1968), pp. 343-50; Wildberger, *Jesaja 1–12*, pp. 362-89; Barth, *Die Jesaja-Worte*, pp. 141-77; J. Vermeylen, *Du prophète Isaïe à l'apocalyptique: Isaïe, I–XXXV, miroir d'un demi-millénaire d'expérience religieuse en Israël* (EBib; Paris: Gabalda, 1977), pp. 232-45.

together and incorporated them in a single passage in Isaiah 1–39 in a manner that does not accurately reflect any one of them in particular or all three of them together. There are many other well-known examples of Deutero-Isaiah working creatively with the material he has inherited, and his presumed manner of procedure here fits in well with this.

Of course, if an irrefutable case had been made out for the post-exilic origin of 8.23b–9.6, then we should be obliged to seek other ways of understanding the method of composition here. In the light of recent discussions, however, it may be questioned whether this is so—and in saying that, it is not necessary to decide whether Isaiah himself wrote the passage, or whether, as Barth and Vermeylen have maintained, it is to be attributed to a Josianic redactor; for our present purposes, either position would be sufficient to account for the evidence.

The strongest counter-argument that could be produced would be the presence of linguistic features that could only be explained as deriving from the period of late Biblical Hebrew, but there are none such. The manner in which linguistic evidence has been used in this debate is generally unsatisfactory from the point of view of method—in particular, because some words or phrases are elsewhere used only in passages generally thought to be late, this cannot settle the issue of whether those words or phrases must themselves be regarded as later. As Hurvitz has shown,[21] this line of argument should only be admitted when it is demonstrated that the postulated later element has consistently replaced some earlier alternative; otherwise, the whole thing turns into a weak argument from silence whose dubious nature is made the greater by the heavily restricted quantity of comparative data available to us.[22] This necessary second step in the argument has not, however, been undertaken by proponents of a late date.

21. Cf. A. Hurvitz, *The Transition Period in Biblical Hebrew: A Study in Post-Exilic Hebrew and its Implications for the Dating of Psalms* [Hebrew] (Jerusalem: Bialik Institute, 1972), pp. 20-24.

22. Cf. C. Hardmeier, 'Jesajaforschung im Umbruch', *VF* 31 (1986), pp. 3-31, who is followed in particular by A. Laato, *Who is Immanuel? The Rise and the Foundering of Isaiah's Messianic Expectations* (Åbo: Åbo Academy Press, 1988), pp. 21-23 and 182.

Indeed, it is striking that even Vermeylen,[23] who is generally by no means averse to this type of argument, does not find the evidence at all compelling in this particular case. Conversely, of course, the fact that much of the vocabulary of the passage has parallels elsewhere in the writing of Isaiah of Jerusalem cannot be used to support Isaianic authorship (cf. Wildberger). The most it can do is to demonstrate Isaianic authorship as a possibility. In short, the evidence from language cannot settle the issue either way.

Other arguments for a late date are equally indecisive, and in this connection it is particularly worthy of note that Werner, one of the chief advocates of a post-exilic date in recent years, relies heavily on the argument from vocabulary and then concedes that 'einzeln genommen mögen die Argumente, die dem Text die Herkunft von Jesaja absprechen und ihn in die nachexilische Zeit datieren, nicht durchschlagen'.[24] Thereafter, he concentrates more on seeking to establish that Wildberger has not convincingly proved Isaianic authorship than on presenting positive arguments for his own alternative view. Naturally, his assumption that 9.1 is dependent upon Deutero-Isaiah begs the question raised by our discussion above.

This being so, the new evidence that has been set out here may be allowed its *prima facie* force. The dependence of Deutero-Isaiah on Isa. 8.23b is the best explanation of the data. If that be granted, then we may conclude that this passage is of peculiar importance in view of both its widespread use by Deutero-Isaiah and its centrality to one of his most characteristic themes. As was pointed out at the start of this article, many of the similarities that have been observed in recent years between the first and second parts of Isaiah are somewhat isolated. Since it is clear that Deutero-Isaiah drew on a number of earlier traditions and literary works, many scholars have been reluctant to allow that the literary deposit of First Isaiah enjoyed a privileged position in this regard. The evidence advanced above (to which I hope to add more in a

23. *Isaïe*, p. 240.
24. W. Werner, *Eschatologische Texte in Jesaja 1–39: Messias, heiliger Rest, Völker* (Forschung zur Bibel, 46; Würzburg: Echter Verlag, 1982), p. 46.

forthcoming monograph) significantly strengthens the case in favour of those who have argued that Deutero-Isaiah worked in conscious literary dependence on his predecessor and that he never intended his work to be read without reference to the wider context which the early form of Isaiah 1–39 provides for it.

It gives me particular pleasure to contribute to this volume in honour of Norman Whybray, friend and respected senior scholar.

MOTHER ZION, FATHER SERVANT:
A READING OF ISAIAH 49–55

Knud Jeppesen

Isaiah 53 is a text that scholars will probably continue to work upon to the end of the world. One of the most serious problems is that there are features in the chapter that give the most satisfactory understanding when read as if Yahweh's Servant is a metaphor for the people, while there are other features that seem to show definitely that the Servant is an individual. Professor R.N. Whybray has carried through the individual interpretation of Isaiah 53 in his *Thanksgiving for a Liberated Prophet*,[1] in which he has shown that the historical meaning is not that the Servant died and returned from the dead.

One thing that supports the notion that the Servant did not die is the sentence in v. 10, 'He shall see offspring'.[2] This is the only example in the Old Testament of זרע as the object of the verb, ראה, but the meaning seems to be clear; B. Duhm, for example, in his famous commentary, compared this line with the end of the Book of Job, where Job saw (ראה) 'children and grandchildren in four generations',[3] and in the context of

1. JSOTSup, 4, Sheffield: JSOT Press, 1978; see also his *Isaiah 40–66* (NCB; London: Oliphants, 1975), *ad loc*. Chapter 53 'by itself, though not without problems, makes good sense as a song of thanksgiving for the deliverance of God's servant, Deutero-Isaiah, from mortal danger' (*Isaiah 40–66*, p. 169; cf. *Thanksgiving*, p. 163 n. 1); so 52.13-15 is not treated as an integrated part of the so-called fourth 'Servant-song'.

2. In Whybray's interpretation 'long life' in 53.10 is connected to the offspring (see e.g. *Isaiah 40–66*, p. 179).

3. Job 42.16; B. Duhm, *Das Buch Jesaja* (HAT, 3/1; Göttingen: Vandenhoeck & Ruprecht, 1892), p. 374; see also Gen. 50.23; Ps. 128.6. In Gen. 48.11 זרע is the object of ראה hiph. On the phrase, see *Thanksgiving*, pp. 79-80.

Isaiah 40–66 זרע almost always means human offspring,[4] and
often the people. On the other hand, in commentaries and
monographs so many different aspects are stressed that one
wonders whether it is only on the surface that the meaning is
clear.[5]

However, the Servant is not the only figure in Deutero-
Isaiah who acquires children in a situation where it was not
expected.[6] A few verses later (54.1), we read about 'the desolate one', who shall have more children than a married woman,
and in the following verse her tent is said to be too small for
her offspring; this barren woman's children (זרע) shall inherit
the gentiles and inhabit the desolate towns (v. 3). It is not
stated explicitly who the woman is. But in spite of the fact
that Zion/Jerusalem is not mentioned by name in the pericope,
or for that matter in the rest of Deutero-Isaiah, it is beyond
doubt that we have here an example of Zion-imagery.

Isaiah 53–54 is part of a section in the book that is
connected to both the other Deutero-Isaianic section (chs. 40–
48), and to the so-called Trito-Isaiah section (chs. 56–66).[7]

---

4.   Isa. 41.8; 43.5; 44.3; 45.19, 25; 48.19; 54.3; 57.3, 4; 59.21; 61.9;
65.9, 23; 66.22, with 55.10 as an exception.
5.   I. Engnell, *The 'Ebed Yahweh Songs and the Suffering Messiah in
'Deutero-Isaiah'* (Manchester: The John Rylands Library, 1948), pp. 36-37
(= *BJRL* 31 [1948], pp. 54-93): the sentence is part of the mythical
background, where death and offspring so often are connected to
each other. J. Lindblom, *The Servant Songs in Deutero-Isaiah* (Lund:
C.W.K. Gleerup, 1951), p. 45: the Servant is dead, but shall survive
through his descendants, who are spiritual, not physical. J. de Leeuw, *De
Ebed Jahweh-Profetien* (Assen: van Gorcum, 1956), pp. 249-50: the words
are first and foremost an expression of the Servant's righteousness
contrary to that of the unrighteous, whose children shall be cut off.
O. Kaiser, *Der königliche Knecht* (FRLANT, 70; Göttingen: Vandenhoeck
& Ruprecht, 1959), p. 119: they show the 'innerweltlichen und inner-
geschichtlichen Horizont' of the Servant song.
6.   The name 'Deutero-Isaiah' is used for Isa. 40–55 as a whole, most
of which is in my opinion made up of prophecies from the Babylonian
exile. We cannot know whether the author was a *he* or a *she* or indeed *one
person*, but following the tradition I call the author 'he'.
7.   Cf. K. Jeppesen, 'From "You, My Servant" to "The Hand of the
Lord is with My Servants". A Discussion of Is. 40–66', *SJOT* 1 (1990),
pp. 113-29 (114-18).

Chapters 49–55 may again be divided into at least two smaller sections. 49.1–52.12 begins with a Servant text with a universal scope, and it ends with a call to a group of people to leave the place where they were; the pericopes in between sometimes deal with the Servant, sometimes with Zion/ Jerusalem, and the people are always within the horizon. This summary covers the second part (52.13–55.13) too, and it is hardly a coincidence. On the following pages we shall therefore read the two parts in the light of each other, and especially look for features that can help us understand the difficult statements about parents and offspring.[8]

1.1.1

From the beginning the Servant pericope in 49.1-13 is addressed to people who are far away, and this corresponds with part of the contents. The Servant's original call was related to Israel only, but from the present time on he is also to bring salvation to the ends of the earth (v. 6); he becomes the 'Servant of the rulers', and kings are to praise him (v. 7). From v. 8 the addressee, a 'you' (masc. sing.) will do the Servant's job in relation to the people; he shall restore the country, set some prisoners free, and lead them safely along a road, which Yahweh will construct for them. The prisoners are probably the exiles, and the Servant has consequently taken over the role of Cyrus.[9]

According to v. 12 the prisoners, the exiles, shall come from all directions, and not from Babylon only; this, of course, reflects the universalism of the text, but the way in which it is expressed is a little disturbing for the line of thought. The text

8. To save space I do not note or discuss all the details in the pericopes that are of importance for the overall structure of Deutero-Isaiah. The reader is referred to R.F. Melugin, *The Formation of Isaiah 40–55* (BZAW, 141; Berlin: de Gruyter, 1976). The translation of the Bible used in this article is mainly the AV.

9. See 41.2-4, 25-29; 44.28–45.7; 46.10-13; and probably also 48.12-14; and cf. Whybray, *Isaiah 40–66*, p. 138: 'the tasks of the two men, though entirely different in the methods which they employed, were identical in their divine origin (Yahweh's call) and in his aim' (cf. also p. 131). The theme of the miraculous road home through the desert is known from chs. 40–48 too; see e.g. 40.3-5.

in itself is silent when it comes to the liberated prisoners' goal, and we are not told either about the actual relations between the prisoners and the person who is to free them.[10]

1.1.2

In 49.14 Zion is brought into focus. As the Servant complains that he had 'laboured in vain' (v. 4), Zion laments that 'the Lord has forsaken me, and my Lord has forgotten me' (v. 14). But playing upon the mother–child imagery Yahweh repudiates her lament and tries to convince her that someone shall 'make haste',[11] doing something in relation to her (vv. 15-17a). The conquerors shall depart, the ruins shall be rebuilt, and Zion shall be as happy as a young bride; she shall soon realize that her place will not be big enough for all the children she will have (vv. 17b-21). Her children will be taken home, not by the Servant, but by kings and queens, who will show Zion the same kind of honour as they will show the Servant (vv. 22-23).[12] In the last verses of ch. 49 Yahweh proves that he is able to free prisoners, and again it is stressed that 'your (fem. sing.) sons' shall be brought safely home, and the whole

---

10. 42.1-7 is normally interpreted as an individual Servant-song, and also other texts in Isa. 40–48 have been interpreted that way; cf. H.-J. Hermisson, 'Israel und der Gottesknecht bei Deuterojesaja', *ZTK* 79 (1982), pp. 1-24. Nevertheless, it is possible to understand the Servant as identical with the people in all cases in chs. 40–48; cf. Jeppesen, *SJOT* 1 (1990), pp. 119-22. A kind of identity between the exiles and the servant may also be suggested in his name 'Israel' (49.3), but this text is so disputable that one should not make any decisive conclusions. In my article (*ibid.*, pp. 113-29), I refer to recent literature about the Servant as an individual or a collective, and I shall therefore not go further here.

11. 49.17: בְּנָיִךְ 'your (fem. sing.) sons'; but, following some of the versions, the word is often vocalized to mean 'your builders'; see Whybray, *Isaiah 40–66*, p. 144. Both readings make sense in the context. 'Builders' fit in, because Jerusalem is in ruins and needs rebuilding. 'Sons' could be an interpretation of the prisoners brought by the Servant in the previous pericope. Judging from the parallel clause, where the other part 'go away', בָּנַיִךְ probably make haste to come to Jerusalem (see C. Westermann, *Das Buch Jesaja: Kapitel 40–66* [ATD, 19; Göttingen: Vandenhoeck & Ruprecht, 1976], p. 176); but if 'your builders' is the right interpretation, they might be making haste to carry out their building job.

12. Cf. the verb form יִשְׁתַּחֲווּ (vv. 7, 23).

world shall understand that the saviour is Yahweh (vv. 25-26).

In 49.20 we read that the 'children of your (fem. sing.) bereavement' shall not have space enough in the future. The imagery is the same as in 54.1-3, but here it is obvious that the future mother with a host of children is the personified Zion/Jerusalem. From a Deutero-Isaianic point of view the exile was a period when Jerusalem was bereaved of her children and did not bear any new children; that is, Jerusalem was without inhabitants.

The mother–children imagery, used about Jerusalem and the Jerusalemites, is an aspect of the figurative language of Zion/Jerusalem as a woman. This language was used in the exilic period, probably both in Babylon and Palestine. We know it in an almost vulgar form from texts like Ezekiel 16 and 23, and also in the book of Jeremiah we find a play on aspects of it (e.g. 4.31), but in a form even closer to the way the imagery occurs in Deutero-Isaiah; it appears also in Lamentations, especially in the first verses of the first chapter.

Zion/Jerusalem as a woman is not an unknown metaphor in the traditions in the first part of the Book of Isaiah; the town is called a זונה, 'harlot' (1.21), and Zion has daughters (3.16-17; 4.4; etc.), and also otherwise a play with the imagery is found.[13] But it is not a marked tradition in Isaiah 1–39, and therefore it is more likely that Deutero-Isaiah has elaborated upon and given his touch to an old idea, which became popular in his day, than that it was a specific Isaianic tradition that he took up.[14]

Already in the opening verses of Deutero-Isaiah, Jerusalem

---

13. See Isa. 3.25-26; 37.22. In most cases 'Zion's daughter' is a name only, and not a living part of the imagery; see Isa. 1.8; 10.32; etc.; this name is used only once in chs. 49–55, viz. 52.2. The tradition is found in Trito-Isaiah too, but not as a dominant feature; the last example, which has some connection to the imagery in chs. 49–55, is Isa. 66.7-14; cf. J.F.A. Sawyer, 'Daughter of Zion and Servant of the Lord in Isaiah: A Comparison', *JSOT* 44 (1989), pp. 89-107 (96-98).

14. I have elsewhere developed the idea that 'Deutero-Isaiah' has worked upon and edited the Isaiah tradition in chs. 1–39*, and that Isa. 1–55* is an answer to the problems of the exiles: *Græder ikke saa saare*, I (Aarhus: Aarhus University Press, 1987), pp. 63-84; *Jesajas Bog fortolket* (Copenhagen: Det danske Bibelselskab, 1988).

is a 'she', who, as a representative of Yahweh's people (עמי, 40.1), is told that her misery has come to an end. In the following chapters Zion/Jerusalem is first and foremost a place in Judah; hardly anything of the imagery is left there. In chs. 49–54, however, Zion/Jerusalem is much more in focus. The imagery is used and reused, and our impression is strengthened that the prophet wanted to carry out his own idea of how to speak of his capital city and its holy place far away as a female person.

Isa. 49.21 refers to Zion's lament over her present fate; she says in her heart, 'who has begotten these for me?' The verb (ילד) is masculine; Zion asks for the father of the children of bereavement and does not seem to recognize herself as the mother of these children. Instead she presents herself with four Hebrew words: שׁכולה, 'bereaved', גלמודה, 'sterile', גלה, 'exiled', סורה, 'gone away'.

The first two words reflect her 'historical' situation as a conquered city, left without inhabitants. The last two words take Zion to the Babylonian exile, to the people's place, but have no equivalent in the LXX, and therefore commentators often consider them secondary.[15] But scholars who follow the LXX in this matter, do not normally present the full LXX-text of the verse. For MT's 'sterile', the LXX has χῆρα, 'widow', which makes the imagery much more homogeneous, and in a way the question about the father even more relevant.

It is easy to argue for the originality of the LXX version, but here we shall discuss one matter only. Zion is a kind of counterpart of Babylon. Zion has been stricken by fatal disasters, Babylon believes she will never suffer (ch. 47); furthermore, Zion is in ch. 49 promised that she will arise again from the blow of the disaster, while the idea of ch. 47 is that Babylon shall now suffer the disaster, and probably never rise from it again. This is much clearer in the LXX; the words ἐγὼ δὲ ἄτεκνος καὶ χῆρα reflect directly the LXX wording in 47.8-9.

On the other hand, original or not, the Hebrew text as we find it in the MT seems to correspond to a Deutero-Isaianic

---

15. '[E]ine späte und recht unglückliche Glosse..., denn die Sprecherin selbst ist nicht verbannt und vertrieben' (Duhm, *Jesaja*, p. 348).

way of thinking. The woman-imagery is at least double;[16] Zion/Jerusalem is the people's mother, whose children are taken away, but she is also together with the people in the *golah*, or perhaps is herself the *golah*.[17]

1.1.3

In 49.18 we touched upon the wedding imagery; this is in the beginning of ch. 50 replaced by divorce imagery, and the addressee is a 'you' (masc. plur.), who have 'been sold for your iniquities, and for your transgressions is your mother put away' (v. 1). Here again, it is not stated explicitly that the mother is Zion, but in all probability she is.

Zion cannot claim to be a divorcee, and her sons cannot claim to be children of divorced parents. They ought to have been there, when God—the father?—called them to help; but still he has the power and will to save them. In an almost apocalyptic and somewhat threatening tone God demonstrates this (v. 3); but the style is in more than one respect abrupt, and therefore it is difficult fully to appreciate the passage.

1.2.1

In 50.4-9 someone, who in v. 10 is interpreted as the Servant, asserts in a first-person speech his faithfulness and staying power under physical suffering. We do not know who did the beating; but we know that the speaker's opponent is heading towards a disaster (esp. v. 9). Neither can we see to whom the words were first directed, but in vv. 10-11 the addressee is a bipartite 'you' (masc. plur.). In the one party the 'you' fear God, even if 'you' walk in darkness. In the other group are the bad people, who will be caught in their own fire.

In relation to vv. 1-3 it is worth mentioning that the 'I' stresses his co-operation with Yahweh. The 'sons' did not come

16. Apparently, this is not an innovation in the tradition; already in Hos. 1–3, which in the OT is the starting point for this imagery, it is not always clear whether it is the mother or the children who play Israel's part.

17. Cf. the introduction to ch. 40, where God's people is a very close parallel to Jerusalem, and where it is Jerusalem and not the people that has ended the צבא; see also 51.16 below.

when they were asked to (v. 2), but this Servant does what he is expected to do, even if it hurts, and he underlines twice that Yahweh the Lord is his helper (vv. 7, 9).

1.2.2

In 51.1–52.12 Zion is again in focus, and different themes are dealt with. First the text is addressed to the good 'you' (masc. plur.) (51.1). They are told to look into their history to convince themselves that Yahweh is able to comfort Zion and make her into a garden of Eden, full of song and music. The author of these prophecies, who liked to talk about Zion with this maternal imagery, never forgot, when bringing Yahweh's word of comfort, that it was a geographical place of ruins that in themselves were in need of good tidings (v. 3; cf. 49.19; 52.9).[18]

In the MT of v. 4 the righteous 'you' (masc. plur.) is replaced by 'my people' and 'my nation'.[19] This does not of course mean that God's people as a whole 'follow after righteousness' or 'seek the Lord', but in the ideology it is the whole people who shall be saved. They should know from history that God's 'salvation shall be for ever' (v. 6), and that therefore they should have nothing to fear.

Three times in the following pericopes a call to *wake up* is found. The first one is a call to Yahweh, or rather to his arm, the sign of power in history (cf. 50.2). God is asked to do things like those he did in the past; he 'cut Rahab', that is, he created the world; he 'dried the sea', that is, he saved the people at the exodus (51.9-10). Verse 11 is a statement about the people's return to Zion in gladness and joy;[20] but it is not clear whether it is part of the address to Yahweh reminding him about his promises, or an introduction to his answer in the following verses.

God's answer in vv. 12-16 is first directed to a 'you' in the

18. The intention of the prophecy is not different from 44.26, for example, where Jerusalem is a city, about which the prophet speaks without the metaphorical language.

19. There is no reason to follow the Peshiṭta in reading plural and no suffix, as e.g. Westermann, *Jesaja*, pp. 188, 190.

20. Cf. Isa. 35.10.

masculine plural, which is the people or at least the righteous part of it: 'I, even I, am the one that comforts you!' Then follows in the same verse a question to a 'you' in the feminine singular, who is probably Zion/Jerusalem as it is in the context.[21]

To make the confusion even greater, the text continues (vv. 13-17) by speaking to a 'you' in the masculine singular, who is entrusted to God: 'I have put my words in your mouth, and I have covered you in the shadow of my hand' (v. 16). This sounds like an oracle to the Servant,[22] and in one of the previous verses the subject for freedom and survival is someone who is bowed down, probably just another image for the exiles whom this person was sent to free by the power of God (vv. 14-15). However, what is said to the 'you' in v. 13 is much more like a reproach to the people.

So, in this pericope we find, on the one hand, an oscillation between the people and a female figure, who is probably Zion, and, on the other hand, an oscillation between the people and a male figure, who is probably the Servant. Zion and the Servant are not identical,[23] but as part of the imagery connected to the two figures each of them can be either identical with the people or related to the people in other ways. At the end of the pericope we find an example that shows how the images are twisted into each other: the creator of heaven and earth tells the male figure, who, we think, is the Servant, that

21. Again there is no reason to make the text better than it is in the MT by means of conjectures; see *BHS* on v. 12, where it suggests to read the masculine singular all through the verse. In Isa. 40–66 God's people is the most frequent object of Yahweh's comfort: 40.1; 49.13; 52.9; cf. 61.2, and especially 66.13, which leads to the other object of Yahweh's comfort, Zion: 51.3, 19; according to R. Rendtorff ('Zur Komposition des Jesajabuches', *VT* 34 [1984], pp. 295-320 [298-99]), 'comfort' is one of the ideas that bind together the book of Isaiah.

22. Cf. 'he has made my mouth like a sharp sword; *in the shade of his hand*, he has hid me' (49.2).

23. I cannot agree with L.E. Wilshire ('The Servant City: A New Interpretation of the "Servant of the Lord" in the Servant Songs of Deutero-Isaiah', *JBL* 94 [1975], pp. 356-67), who has called attention to the many similarities in the Servant-imagery and the Zion-imagery and suggests identity between the two bodies.

he will say to Zion, who normally is female: 'You (masc. sing.!) are my people' (v. 16).

In the second call to wake up (51.17-23), the meaning of the verbal form goes in the direction of 'pulling oneself together'. Jerusalem, who is still the subject in the feminine singular, has been intoxicated by drinking Yahweh's cup of wrath. In this text she has sons, but these sons were worth nothing to help and comfort her, when the disasters came. Now, God shall bring help, take the cup of wrath from her and give it to nations who earlier afflicted her. Here, as in 49.21, we realize how Jerusalem and Babylon change roles in the preaching of Deutero-Isaiah.

The third call (52.1-3) uses the same verb form as the first; in 51.9 it is the arm of Yahweh who is told to 'put on power', and here it is Zion/Jerusalem who is told to do the same. She is described as a prisoner,[24] who is told to arise and leave the place where she is. This means that here Zion or Zion's daughter/Jerusalem is the *golah* with her exiles (cf. 49.21), and not so much the town with its ruins. It is therefore quite natural that the figure addressed (v. 3) is a 'you' in the masculine plural.

52.4-6 is a prose text in which Yahweh speaks of 'my people' in both earlier and present salvation history to prove that they shall return. The present state of degradation will be changed, and the people will realize God's name, and they will understand that he is the one who says, 'Here I am!'[25]

This sentence is really one of the lines God should say to Zion/Jerusalem and the cities of Judah.[26] It is therefore no

24. Reading שְׁבִיָּה, 'captive' (fem.), instead of שְׁבִי, 'sit down' (fem. impv.); cf. *BHS* on 52.2; this of course makes the fate of Zion more clearly a parallel to that of the exiles. But on the other hand, MT as it is, 'Shake yourself from the dust, arise, and sit down', makes Zion a better contrast to Babylon (47.1; see Whybray, *Isaiah 40–66*, p. 165).

25. The pericope is 'probably best seen as a series of later additions inspired by reflection on [Deutero-Isaiah's] word' (Whybray, *Isaiah 40–66*, p. 165).

26. Cf. the message of the female messenger, who announces the arrival and presence of God (40.9-10). K. Elliger (*Deuterojesaja 40,1–45,7* [BKAT, 11/1; Neukirchen–Vluyn: Neukirchener Verlag, 1978], p. 31) translates 'Frohbotschafterin Zion' and argues that Zion herself is the

surprise that in the following verses (vv. 7-10) a male messenger is introduced, bringing words of peace and salvation. He announces Yahweh's return as king to Jerusalem, with comfort for the people and freedom for Jerusalem. The ruins of Jerusalem are summoned to rejoice at what happens to the city. It is not an isolated and local event; Yahweh will show his arm in a universal setting, in the sight of all nations, and so the freedom is realistic from a political point of view also.

1.2.3

The last pericope in the section is short (52.11-12). It is a call to a 'you' (masc. plur.) to go away from 'there' (מִשָּׁם).[27] It will be the beginning of a new exodus,[28] which, if we do not interpret it in accordance with the context, could go from anywhere to anywhere; but in the outline of Deutero-Isaiah it goes from Babylon to Zion.

They will be able to bring back the vessels taken by Nebuchadnezzar, and they will be free to move at their own speed. But the most important message to the exiles is the end of the oracle: 'Yahweh will go before you (masc. plur.), the God of Israel will be your rearguard'.

2.1

'Behold, my Servant shall prosper!' (52.13). Now, again God speaks of the Servant, and as in the Servant text in Isaiah 49 he speaks of him in a universal setting (cf. 49.7). The kings

female messenger. It is, however, not probable that it is Zion that says of God that he 'comes in power, and his arm rules for him'; cf. e.g. 52.7.

27. Cf. the root סור in 49.21, which means the other direction, from Judah to Babylon.

28. In the text there are several examples of play upon ideas connected to the first exodus; see Whybray, *Isaiah 40–66*, p. 168. H.M. Barstad (*A Way in the Wilderness* [*JSS* Monographs; Manchester: The University of Manchester, 1989], pp. 102-105) finds that these verses address Zion/ Jerusalem, and that the imagery is that of the holy war, and not the exodus. Barstad is of course right in stressing that ch. 52 provides a Zion context, but in my view it is important in the wider context of chs. 49–55 to separate the 'Zion-you' (fem. sing.) from the 'people-you' (masc. plur.). Moreover, the placing of these verses in the structure of chs. 40–66 makes them a parallel to 48.20-21, which Barstad discusses (pp. 99-101).

will be astonished when they realize to what a degree God
has changed his former poor appearance to an exalted status.

Isa. 52.13-15 is normally treated as the first part of the so-
called fourth Servant song. But it is possible to understand ch.
53 as a closed text (cf. n. 1, above), which deals with the role
of the Servant, not least in relation to the people. By placing
these verses before ch. 53, the Servant's whole work gains an
international context, which was not original.

For the first and only time in Isa. 49–55 we have a 'we', a
group of speakers (53.1-6).[29] The function of the 'we' is to give
voice to a new insight,[30] and probably the 'we' corresponds to
the 'you' (masc. plur.) that we have met with several times
since the beginning of ch. 50.

'We' have come to the conclusion that they had misjudged
the person who is interpreted as God's servant in the context
(52.13; 53.11). Their earlier relations to him were determined
by his appearance, which was poor and pathetic, and by
people's attitude towards him, which was one of contempt; he
was 'despised and rejected by men' (v. 3). But it was not 'he',
but 'we', with whom something was wrong. His misery was
related to their sins, and his punishment was a condition for
their peace; he was 'stricken, smitten of God' (v. 4), but the
reason was that Yahweh had 'laid on him the iniquity of us
all'.

The next section (53.7-9) continues the description and interpretation of the fate of the 'man of sorrows'. The 'we' is not the
speaker any longer: 'for the transgressions of my people he
was stricken' (v. 8). The suffix in עמי points to Yahweh, but one
cannot be sure whether the whole section is in his voice.

In these verses we have what is normally understood as the

---

29. The suffix in אלהינו in Isa. 52.10 and 55.7 does not count in this
connection. See the analysis of the groups and persons and their mutual
interrelations, as expressed in the personal pronouns in Isa. 52.13–53.12,
in D.J.A. Clines, *I, He, We, and They: A Literary Approach to Isaiah 53*
(JSOTSup, 1; Sheffield: Department of Biblical Studies, 1976), pp. 37-40,
and especially the similarities and differences between 'they' and 'we'
(pp. 39-40).

30. Cf. Isa. 42.24, where it is realized that '*we*' had sinned against
Yahweh, and that was why Jacob-Israel was given 'for a spoil'.

proof texts for the notion that the Servant actually died: he was brought 'as a lamb to the slaughter', 'he was cut off out of the land of the living', he made his 'grave with the wicked', and he 'was with the rich in his death'; but the language is not at all unambiguous. The result of R.N. Whybray's investigations is, as already indicated above: 'The mass of statements in the poem about the Servant, taken together, make it quite clear that he was subjected to violence and humiliation, but these stopped short of his death'.[31]

Therefore the next verses cannot be proof texts of his resurrection either. 53.10-12 deal with the happy future of the Servant. It is probably not the same subject who speaks in v. 53.10 and vv. 53.11-12. Verse 10 mentions Yahweh in the third person: it was the will of Yahweh to cause the sufferings of the Servant and to have success through him.[32] This could be a continuation of the new insight of the 'we', and in this case it was 'we' who realized that the Servant would gain offspring.

In the last two verses of ch. 53, the subject is an 'I', who talks about '*my* servant', and who can do that except Yahweh himself? God certifies that the Servant 'bare the sin of many, and made intercession for the transgressors' (v. 53.12), and that is probably the people.

2.2

I have mentioned זרע, 'offspring', as a catchword connecting ch. 54 to ch. 53; רבים, 'many', is probably another one. In 53.11-12 God says that the servant does his saving acts for 'the many', and in 54.1 a group of the same designation will be the future inhabitants of Jerusalem.

31. Whybray, *Thanksgiving*, p. 106. Furthermore, in itself *death* is used metaphorically about the sufferings of the exiles; see Ezek. 37.11, and cf. Jeppesen, *SJOT* 1 (1990), pp. 124-25.

32. The repeated חפץ in v. 10 is another sign that the Servant has taken over the role of Cyrus in the preaching of Deutero-Isaiah. The same word is used for God's will in connection with Cyrus (44.28; 46.10; 48.14). The last sentence in v. 10 may refer to 'Yahweh's plan for the restoration of his people through imminent historical events' (Whybray, *Thanksgiving*, p. 81).

In the imagery, we have met Zion/Jerusalem as a woman who has given birth (ילדה), but her sons were worth nothing to support her in her present poor state (51.18-20). In 54.1 we find another statement: לא ילדה, 'she has *not* given birth'. Logically this nullifies the statement that 'she has given birth', or vice versa. But in the metaphorical language this is not the case; historically Jerusalem has 'given birth', but she has 'not given birth' in the language that pictures Jerusalem as a widow full of sorrow (54.4); this is the background on which the happy future should be seen. The woman who has not given birth is asked to be joyful;[33] she will find herself surrounded by a lot of new children (54.1-3; cf. 49.19-21). A child born by a barren woman is surely always an unexpected child; the mere idea of such a child made a Sarah laugh (Gen. 18.12),[34] the prayer for such a child made a Hannah suffer the accusation of being drunk (1 Sam. 1.13).

Zion/Jerusalem was already, as we have seen, mother to a group of people with whom God could argue (50.1). She has sons and daughters (40.22), of course especially sons (e.g. 49.25), who will be saved for a happy future. But still the situation is dark; then, as trump card, the most impressive part of the mother imagery is played again as in ch. 49. Zion/Jerusalem will be a *mother by surprise*! This is a way in which it is possible to stress that the initiative belongs exclusively to God.

In 49.12 the captives whom the Servant shall bring home will come from all directions; now, the new inhabitants of the mother town shall spread in all directions, and the offspring shall inherit the gentiles (54.3); God has redeemed Jerusalem with consequences for the whole world.

Yahweh will take away the shame of the town: 'your maker is your husband!' She is, after all, God's wife of his youth. For a short period he gave her up, as he for a while gave up

---

33. It is in itself a surprise: 'Wie konnte man eine unfruchtbare zum Jubel rufen?' (Westermann, *Jesaja*, p. 219). By this terminology 54.1-3 is related to 52.9-10, where the ruins of Jerusalem are with the same verbs summoned to break out in joy.

34. This is not the only example of a connection to the stories of the patriarchs in this imagery'; cf. Sawyer, *JSOT* 44 (1989), p. 95.

humanity in the days of Noah, but now he will restore her in a covenant of peace (54.4-10).

The afflicted and sorry town, still addressed in the feminine singular, is promised a glittering future: God himself will rebuild her with precious stones (vv. 11-12), her children will be taught by God, and all causes for fear will disappear. The town will not be threatened any more; she shall not suffer oppression or disaster, because God is her protector; he has made both the enemy and his weapons.

2.3

Most of ch. 55 is addressed to a 'you' in the second-person masculine plural; they are thirsty and poor, probably again a way of describing the exiles. They are told to come to God to get what they need, including life and a new and an everlasting Davidic covenant with consequences for the nations (vv. 1-4).

In v. 5 suddenly another 'you' in the masculine singular turns up,[35] to disappear again in the rest of the chapter, where the addressee is plural. The theme of the following verses is the return to Yahweh. Not only the faithful will be saved, but also the unfaithful[36] have the possibility of returning to Yahweh. God is much better than the Israelites, and his word and promises will always be fulfilled.

This section, too, ends with a call to leave a place in peace, probably again Babylon. Nature will cheer, and the future will be happy and bright, 'and it shall be for Yahweh for a name, for an everlasting sign that shall not be cut off' (55.12-13).

It is impossible to arrive at a clear *conclusion* after this relatively quick reading of Isaiah 49–55; but this is of course not surprising when dealing with metaphorical language. It is not possible in one sentence and without contradictions to develop how Deutero-Isaiah used the metaphors in question, but it would be wrong either to stress the differences in his use of the metaphor too much or to level them—or for that

35. It is impossible to say whether the singular here is a variant way of addressing Israel, or whether it is part of a 'new David' oracle. So far 'you' (masc. sing.) in chs. 49–55 has been the Servant.

36. רשע. The preaching is here related to that of Ezek. 18 and 33.

matter to attribute them to different sources.

I have said above that the imagery that speaks of Zion and the people and the imagery that speaks of the Servant and the people are twisted into each other, but we have also seen that they are not identical. The similarities and the possibilities of mingling are probably caused by the fact that 'Servant' and 'Zion' were both used in the same prophetical tradition as metaphor for the people.

However, as metaphors dealing with the problems they are not even coordinated. The Servant is the one who has the call on Yahweh's behalf to save the people. When he has set the exiles free and sent them on their way back, it is never said that he leads them directly to Zion, and, when the people comes back to Zion, it is never said that they are led there by the Servant. And the people that the Servant has freed is never called by the name Zion.

The two groups of metaphors run parallel and never cross each other's lines. When, for instance, we arrive at the point where the problems of the people's future are dealt with in the parent–child language, it is worth noticing that the two 'parents' are never connected. The husband of mother Zion is not the father Servant, but God.

The marriage aspect is not dominant in Deutero-Isaiah's preaching, but still it is there. The existence of children obviously implies a marriage, but is mentioned only in connection with the mother, who sometimes is said to live in widowhood. In the OT tradition the marriage imagery apparently was a starting point for the preaching of the relation between the woman–people and Yahweh; the relation was a marriage, but a bad one. In the book of Hosea the woman was simply a 'harlot' (Hos. 1.2), and therefore she was sent away. In Ezekiel 16 Jerusalem was Yahweh's foundling girl, whom he took as his wife when she had developed and matured. But she played the harlot, and therefore God judged her according to the law for adulteresses and gave her into the hands of her lovers (Ezek. 16.38-39).

It is probably of importance, then, that in the preaching of Deutero-Isaiah Zion/Jerusalem never played the harlot. 'The shame of youth' refers probably to what happened in history and not to her sins. In Deutero-Isaiah there are no bills of divorcement for the mother; the children are sent away for their own iniquities, and the mother is sent away for the same reason. It is not like the proverb of the sour grapes eaten by parents and causing pain to the teeth of the children (Jer. 31.29; Ezek. 18.2). As Zion/Jerusalem is not a harlot and not a figure who is responsible for the disaster, in Deutero-Isaiah no guilt is placed upon the Servant. In a way it is the guilt-lessness of the mother and the father that forms the background of the salvation, but the children must also recognize their own guilt. But it is also suggested that the parents can gain new offspring, if the present children are worth nothing.

The important insight is that the guilt is placed upon the present generation. We are close to the explanations in the book of Ezekiel: 'A son shall not bear the iniquity of the father, neither shall the father bear the iniquity of the son; the righteousness of the righteous shall be upon him, and the wickedness of the wicked shall be upon him' (Ezek. 18.20).

Zion is Zion, but is used as a female figure in the metaphorical language; she is the counterpart of Babylon. But the persistent question, which these readings have not answered, is, What was the Servant? Was he some kind of a mysterious figure? Sometimes, when he is identical with the people, one is tempted to understand him as a symbol of the same type as Zion. But when he has his job to do for the sake of Israel, one cannot avoid the feeling that Deutero-Isaiah still had a *person* in mind, especially when the Servant takes over the role of Cyrus.

KNOWLEDGE, HUMILIATION OR SUFFERING:
A LEXICAL, TEXTUAL AND EXEGETICAL PROBLEM
IN ISAIAH 53

Anthony Gelston

The lexicography of Biblical Hebrew has been enriched at a
number of points through the application of comparative
philology. James Barr's *Comparative Philology and the Text
of the Old Testament*[1] subjected this methodology to a searching critique, and exposed weaknesses in a number of specific
proposals made in its light. On pp. 19-21 he mentions one of
the best known proposals, that of D. Winton Thomas, who
claimed that the common verb ידע did not always mean 'to
know', but in a number of passages was a different verb,
cognate with the Arabic root *wd'*, meaning 'to become still,
quiet, at rest'. While the meaning 'to know' suits the vast
majority of occurrences of the root ידע in the Hebrew Bible,
Thomas suggested that the proposed second root is to be found
in some 39 passages in all, including one in Ecclesiasticus,
three where the root ידע is a minority reading, and four where
it is obtained only by emendation. Even when allowance was
made for doubtful instances, the proposal seemed to be
sufficiently broadly based to be plausible.

The root ידע occurs twice in the notoriously difficult prophecy
of the Servant in Isaiah 53. In v. 3 וידוע seems to contain the
passive participle qal of ידע, and it is rendered *'acquainted
with grief'* in both RV and RSV. In v. 11 בדעתו incorporates
either the infinitive construct qal of ידע or the cognate verbal
noun דעת, and RV and RSV accordingly render 'by his *knowledge*'. (Italics in these and subsequent renderings are my own,
and are provided to highlight the translation of the root ידע).

1. Oxford: Clarendon Press, 1968.

The fact that both of these renderings pose difficulties for the understanding of the passage will be apparent from the subsequent discussion. Shortly before his death, Thomas delivered a paper to the Society for Old Testament Study, which was subsequently published in two places;[2] in this he presented a detailed study of the text and interpretation of Isaiah 53. His renderings of the two passages in question are respectively '*brought low* by sickness' (v. 3) and 'received his full measure of *humiliation*' (v. 11). These are reflected in the REB, which renders '*afflicted* by disease' and 'by his *humiliation*'.

It cannot be denied that these renderings are apposite to the context. Norman Whybray[3] followed Thomas in rendering '*humbled* by' in v. 3 and '*humiliation*' in v. 11. In a recent article[4] I too followed Thomas, rendering '*laid low* with sickness' in v. 3 and 'by his *humiliation*' in v. 11. It has been a matter of personal satisfaction to me that, although Norman and I have differed over a number of questions in the interpretation of Second Isaiah, we have agreed in our acceptance of Thomas's theory, which seemed to illuminate a difficult passage.

Thomas himself presented the evidence for the second root ידע in a number of publications, but never reviewed the whole of it together. In 1970 John Emerton published a long and searching study[5] of the passages relevant to Thomas's theory, and concluded that 'there were some problems to which it supplied the best solution. On the whole, Thomas's suggestion about the meanings of ידע seemed to be the most satisfactory working hypothesis.'[6] In an important recent article,[7] however,

2. D. Winton Thomas, 'A Consideration of Isaiah LIII in the Light of Recent Textual and Philological Study', *ETL* 44 (1968), pp. 79-86; and in H. Cazelles (ed.), *De Mari à Qumran* (Paris: Lethielleux, 1969), pp. 119-26.

3. R.N. Whybray, *Isaiah 40–66* (NCB; London: Oliphants, 1975).

4. A. Gelston, 'Isaiah 52.13–53.12: An Eclectic Text and a Supplementary Note on the Hebrew Manuscript Kennicott 96', *JSS* 35 (1990), pp. 187-211.

5. J.A. Emerton, 'A Consideration of Some Alleged Meanings of ידע in Hebrew', *JSS* 15 (1970), pp. 145-80.

6. Emerton, 'Some Alleged Meanings of ידע', p. 179.

7. W. Johnstone, '*YD'* II, "Be humbled, humiliated"?', *VT* 41 (1991), pp. 49-62.

William Johnstone has exposed the weakness of the Arabic basis of Thomas's suggestion that ידע can denote 'be humbled, humiliated'. Johnstone fully explored the semantic range of the Arabic root *wd'*, and concluded that, while 19 of the passages in the Hebrew Bible might legitimately be explained in its light, the meanings proposed in the other 20 could not be sustained in the light of the semantic range of the Arabic root. The two passages in Isaiah 53 are among those where the philological basis is shown to be invalid. Emerton himself published 'A Further Consideration of D.W. Thomas's Theories about *yāda*'[8] almost immediately. In this article he agreed with Johnstone that Thomas's theory must be abandoned, but pointed out that the difficulties that Thomas sought to remove by postulating a different root have not disappeared. In the course of a general discussion of this problem Emerton was able to devote only eight lines[9] specifically to the two passages in Isaiah 53. The present study, which I am glad to offer in honour of Norman Whybray's distinguished contribution to the study of the Old Testament, is an attempt to reconsider these two passages in the light of Johnstone's refutation of Thomas's theory.

One of the attractions of Thomas's theory was that בדעתו in Isa. 53.11 could be seen as a deliberate reference back to ידוע in v. 3, which John Day[10] compared to several other examples of verbal repetition in the chapter. It is not necessary, however, that the root should have the same meaning in both passages. Peter Ackroyd[11] suggested that there might have been a conscious intention to convey a different sense in the two passages. Following Johnstone's refutation of Thomas's theory, it is wise to begin by examining the two passages separately, and

8.   J.A. Emerton, 'A Further Consideration of D.W. Thomas's Theories about *yāda*', *VT* 41 (1991), pp. 145-63.

9.   Emerton, 'A Further Consideration', pp. 160-61.

10.   J. Day, *'Da'at* "Humiliation" in Isaiah liii 11 in the Light of Isaiah liii 3 and Daniel xii 4, and the Oldest Known Interpretation of the Suffering Servant', *VT* 30 (1980), pp. 97-103 (98).

11.   P.R. Ackroyd, 'Meaning and Exegesis', in P.R. Ackroyd and B. Lindars (eds.), *Words and Meanings* (Cambridge: Cambridge University Press, 1968), p. 13.

only to interpret them in the light of each other if suitably
convergent or contrasting meanings suggest themselves. It is
also wise to begin in each case by enquiring whether a
meaning suitable to the immediate context can be found
within the normal semantic range of the root ידע = 'to know'.

At first sight 'acquainted with grief' is only a lighter statement of the Servant's condition than 'brought low', 'humbled'
or 'afflicted' by sickness, disease or suffering, and does not
therefore require a radical rethinking of the passage in its
immediate context. For our present purposes we need not concern ourselves with the precise connotation of the noun
rendered variously 'grief', 'sickness' or 'disease'. Its semantic
range covers all these meanings, and if we opt for a more
specific translation like 'pain' or 'sickness' it remains likely
that in this context it is to be understood in a metaphorical
sense. English usage might suggest that the word 'acquainted'
means simply that the Servant was not entirely a stranger to
the experience of suffering, which would be a relatively weak
statement in the general context of this chapter, and distinctly
weaker than Thomas's interpretation. The Hebrew word,
however, has no such overtones of only slight knowledge, and
this nuance must be discounted.

The real difficulty with this word lies in its grammatical form.
It is most probably to be regarded as the passive participle qal,
and as such it denotes 'known' rather than 'knowing'. The
traditional 'acquainted' is again misleading, because its
passive form suggests 'brought into a state of knowledge' and
expresses the Servant's experience of knowing rather than
the content of his knowledge. Such a concept would be more
naturally expressed in Hebrew by the niph'al of ידע as in Jer.
31.19, or, even more naturally, by the pu'al of למד as in Cant.
3.8. The passive qal of ידע suggests more naturally the object or
content of the knowledge rather than the cognitive experience
of the agent. G.R. Driver[12] refers to Deut. 1.13, Deut. 1.15, the
only other instances of the passive participle qal of this verb
in the Old Testament, where the meaning is certainly
'known', and where, as in Isa. 53.3, it describes persons. The

12. G.R. Driver, 'Linguistic and Textual Problems: Isaiah i–xxxix', *JTS*
38 (1937), pp. 36-50 (49).

context refers to the selection by Moses of heads over groups of 10, 50, 100 or 1000, and those selected had to be both wise and 'known'; REB renders 'men of...repute'. Accordingly, Driver states that if the verb ידע in Isa. 53.3 is the verb 'to know', 'the only possible meaning for ידוע חלי is "known, famous for sickness"', a meaning that Emerton dismisses as 'manifestly absurd'.[13] It would seem, however, to fall within the parameters of the semantic range of the passive of ידע to translate here 'notorious for suffering', and to understand the phrase as indicative of the extraordinary degree of suffering experienced by the Servant. This seems to be how the text is interpreted by the later Greek translations of Aquila, Theodotion and Symmachus. It is certainly not necessary to follow North[14] in translating 'known by sickness', where 'sickness' is regarded as a personification.

The traditional rendering 'acquainted with grief', however, despite its passive form, more naturally implies in English an active knowledge or experience on the part of the Servant. Such a sense is reflected in several of the versions: LXX εἰδὼς φέρειν μαλακίαν, Peshitta *yd' ḥš'*, and Vulgate *scientem infirmitatem*. All of these read as if they were translating the active rather than the passive participle. This can be explained in two ways. 1QIs^a reads the active participle יודע, the position of the vocalic *waw* indicating beyond doubt that the active participle is intended. 1QIs^b reads simply ידע, without vocalic *waw* either before or after *daleth*, and is thus ambiguous; since, however, the passive participle is generally written with vocalic *waw*, this MS too may be thought implicitly to support the reading of the active participle. It may, therefore, be the case that the Hebrew *Vorlage* from which the LXX, Peshitta and Vulgate translations were made also read the active participle.

Emerton,[15] however, points out that the traditional text itself need not be interpreted as a passive participle. He refers

13. Emerton, 'Some Alleged Meanings of ידע', p. 175.
14. C.R. North, *The Second Isaiah* (Oxford: Clarendon Press, 1964), p. 238.
15. Emerton, 'Some Alleged Meanings of ידע', pp. 175-76; 'A Further Consideration', p. 160.

to GK §50f for an alternative possibility, that this is a distinct pā'ûl form with an active meaning. Most of the examples given in GK are from intransitive verbs, but three are from transitive verbs, one being the present instance (rendered 'knowing'). The other two are אחז ('handling') in Cant. 3.8, which seems to be a clear case, and זכור ('mindful') in Ps. 103.14, where there is some uncertainty about the text. In view of the slender evidence for this form in transitive verbs it is probably preferable to follow the evidence of the Qumran MSS and the Versions and read the active participle than to retain the traditional text and interpret it as a pā'ûl, although this must remain a possibility.

The traditional rendering 'acquainted with grief' may therefore be regarded as a legitimate translation of either of the known readings of the consonantal Hebrew text. If one gives preference to the reading of the active participle, or understands the traditional text as a pā'ûl form rather than as a passive participle, the basic meaning is 'knowing' sickness or suffering, and it might even be reasonable to paraphrase 'versed' in suffering. This would yield a meaning not much weaker than 'brought low', 'humbled' or 'afflicted' by suffering, which has been shown by Johnstone to lack a secure philological basis. At the same time, if the traditional text is retained but interpreted as a passive participle, a satisfactory sense can again be obtained: 'known' or possibly 'notorious' for suffering. Both the active 'knowing' suffering and the passive 'known' for suffering are thus soundly based in the textual evidence, and both interpretations can be nuanced in translation so as to underline the extraordinary degree of the Servant's suffering.

Targum Jonathan also renders the verb as a passive participle, but uses a verbal root (זמן), whose meaning seems to be to 'designate'. The Servant is thus described as 'designated' or 'destined' for suffering. This meaning would also seem appropriate in the context, and it is just possible that the ordinary Hebrew verb ידע could be understood in this sense. There are a few passages where such a nuance seems appropriate, and Walter Moberly[16] puts the case succinctly when he writes

---

16. R.W.L. Moberly, *At the Mountain of God* (JSOTSup, 22; Sheffield: JSOT Press, 1983), p. 70.

of this verb: 'When used of God's relationship to man it can have the force of "to elect"'. Moberly is discussing Exod. 33.12, 17, of which J.P. Hyatt[17] writes: '"I know you by name" here means virtually to "single out", to "choose"'. Both refer to Gen. 18.19, perhaps the clearest example of all, where RSV renders 'I have chosen him' and REB 'I have singled him out'. Other passages where this meaning is possible are: 2 Sam. 7.20 = 1 Chron. 17.18; Jer. 1.5 (where REB renders 'I chose you'); Hos. 13.5 (where the text is uncertain); Amos 3.2. Moberly refers to the last three of these passages. In some of them the sense 'recognize' or 'acknowledge' as of a vassal by a suzerain may be more appropriate. It is interesting that the Targum recognizes the sense 'choose' in Amos 3.2. It would certainly fit the context for the Servant in Isa. 53.3 to be described as 'singled out' or 'designated' for suffering, and such an interpretation could claim the support of Targum Jonathan. Moberly, however, pointed out that the passages where ידע may have this sense are passages where the verb is used of God's relationship to human beings, and this is not the case in Isa. 53.3. Too much needs to be read into the phrase here to make this a natural interpretation.

A number of Jewish mediaeval commentators interpreted the root ידע in the sense 'break', 'discipline' or 'punish', explaining the word with reference to the verbs שבר and יסר (pi'el). The evidence has been listed succinctly by Emerton,[18] and its significance has been considered by him[19] in the light of Johnstone's refutation of Thomas's theory. He concludes that the explanation of ידע by שבר was influenced, if not entirely caused, by the Targumic rendering of וידע in Judg. 8.16 by ותבר (cognate with Hebrew שבר), and he describes as attractive the theory (suggested by L.J. Liebreich[20] and accepted by Johnstone[21]) that the Targumic rendering in Judg. 8.16

17. J.P. Hyatt, *Exodus* (NCB; London: Oliphants, 1971), p. 316.
18. Emerton, 'Some Alleged Meanings of ידע', pp. 151-52.
19. Emerton, 'A Further Consideration', pp. 153-57.
20. L.J. Liebreich, 'Observations on "Some Rabbinic Evidence for a Hebrew Root ידע = wd‘ (*JQR* XXXVII, 177-8)"', *JQR* NS 37 (1946–47), pp. 337-39.
21. Johnstone, 'yd‘ II', pp. 60-61.

derived from a Hebrew *Vorlage* וירע (from רעע to 'break', ר
having been read in place of ד). Several of the Jewish commentators who interpret the root ידע in Isa. 53.3 in the sense
'break' refer explicitly to Judg. 8.16. What seems to have
happened is that an apparently satisfactory unusual meaning
of ידע had been discovered in the difficult passage Judg. 8.16,
and that it was then found appropriate in other passages as
well, of which Isa. 53.3 was one. There is in that case a curi-
ous parallel to the development of Thomas's theory, in that
Isa. 53.3 was not one of the passages where difficulty in rendering ידע in the sense to 'know' initially inspired the search for a
different meaning, but once the meaning 'humbled' had been
apparently established in other passages Driver[22] suggested
its suitability in this passage too, and Thomas[23] subsequently
accepted the suggestion and applied the new meaning to בדעתו
in v. 11 as well. However suitable in themselves either
'broken' or 'humbled' may be to the context in Isa. 53.3, we
have seen that there are no insuperable difficulties in gaining
a satisfactory interpretation of this passage within the parameters of the ordinary meaning of the root ידע. In view of the
dubious basis of the Jewish mediaeval interpretation of ידע in
terms of שבר, and the absence of any serious difficulty in
translating the root ידע in Isa. 53.3, there is no need to consider this Jewish mediaeval interpretation further here.

The interpretation of ידע with reference to the pi'el of יסר, on
the other hand, Emerton suggests, is most naturally to be
seen as a development from the ordinary sense to 'know', viz.
to 'teach a lesson'. While this might be regarded as a satisfactory explanation of the difficult Judg. 8.16, it is not a natural
way of reading וידוע in Isa. 53.3. We have already seen that the
niph'al of ידע or the pu'al of למד would be the natural way of
expressing in Hebrew the idea that the servant had been
brought into a state of knowledge by suffering, and the same
would apply to the special nuance 'taught' or 'disciplined'. It
has become clear that there are no serious difficulties standing
in the way of interpreting וידוע in Isa. 53.3 within the para-

22. Driver, 'Linguistic and Textual Problems', p. 49.
23. D. Winton Thomas, 'More Notes on the Root ידע in Hebrew', *JTS* 38
(1937), pp. 404-405.

meters of the ordinary semantic range of ידע to 'know'. Several
interpretations have proved possible, and it is unwise as well
as unnecessary to invoke unusual meanings when the usual
meaning affords satisfactory sense in the context.

Before leaving Isa. 53.3 mention should finally be made of
the reading of one mediaeval MS, de Rossi 319, which reads
וירוע (ר for ד). This would presumably be a passive participle of
ירע, which occurs only once in the Old Testament, at Isa. 15.4,
where, however, the LXX implies ד rather than ר. This reading
was proposed by J. Reider[24] as an emendation, and he translated the phrase 'weak from sickness'. He seems to have been
unaware of the presence of this reading in de Rossi 319,
where, however, it is much more likely to have arisen as an
error in copying. Since the proposed meaning of the phrase is
weak, and the existence of the supposed root in Biblical
Hebrew is doubtful, it seems best to ignore this possibility.[25]

The problem of בדעתו in Isa. 53.11 is a good deal more complex. For one thing, this part of the passage bristles with
textual and exegetical problems, and it is impossible to consider this word in isolation. It is, however, impracticable and
unnecessary to review all the problems of this verse in the
present discussion.[26] The main point to notice is that this
particular word can be construed either with what precedes or
(following the traditional accentuation) with what follows. In
both constructions the normal translation 'knowledge' is
problematic. If the word is construed with the preceding word,
the meaning appears to be: 'he will be satisfied with his
knowledge'. Apart from the fact that the context gives no indication of what knowledge in particular affords the Servant
satisfaction, it is difficult to see how the concept of satisfaction
in knowledge affords meaning in the context of the rest of the

24. J. Reider, 'Etymological Studies: ידע or ירע and רעע', *JBL* 66 (1947),
pp. 315-17.

25. See further the comments by Emerton, 'Some Alleged Meanings of
ידע', p. 176.

26. My own position on the other problems in the verse may be seen in
'Some Notes on Second Isaiah', *VT* 21 (1971), pp. 517-27 (524-27), and
'Isaiah 52.13–53.12', pp. 187-204.

verse. T.H. Robinson[27] suggested that the knowledge was that gained through the vision, that is, that implied in the immediately preceding statement, 'he will see light' (following the reading of 1QIs[a], 1QIs[b] and LXX). It is more likely, however, that if this reading is correct its meaning in this context is essentially 'he will live', that is, come to life again after his death in vv. 8-9. If, on the other hand, בדעתו is construed with what follows, the meaning appears to be: 'by his knowledge shall my Servant justify the many' (ignoring the problematic צדיק, which does not bear on the immediate question). Once again it is difficult to determine what particular knowledge is envisaged, and the concept of justification or vindication of others by one's own knowledge is not only without parallel but difficult in any case to comprehend at all. In the light of Johnstone's exposure of the inadequate philological basis of the rendering 'humiliation', we are compelled either to search for some other meaning of דעת within the normal semantic range of the word that will yield a satisfactory meaning in the context, or to resort to emendation of the text.

A further ambiguity resides in the suffix of בדעתו; it may be either subjective or objective. Retaining for the moment the translation 'knowledge', we thus have four theoretical possibilities. If the word is construed with what precedes—'he will be satisfied with his knowledge'—the reference might be either to the Servant's own knowledge of some unspecified object (subjective suffix) or to the knowledge which others, again unspecified, have of him (objective suffix). The second interpretation, however, is tortuous, and this concept would have been much more clearly expressed by a niph'al infinitive: בְּהִוָּדְעוֹ. If the word is construed with what follows—'by his knowledge shall my Servant justify the many'—the presumption must again be in favour of a subjective suffix, since the verb is active and singular. It is difficult to see how it could be construed as an objective suffix at all, since his own action of justifying could hardly be carried out by the knowledge which others have of him. Nor could the reference be to God's knowledge of

27. T.H. Robinson, 'Note on the Text and Interpretation of Isaiah liii. 3.11', *ExpTim* 71 (1959–60), p. 383.

the Servant, since in that case the suffix would have to be in the first person, to agree with 'my Servant' and the Servant himself would have to be denoted by a separate אֹתוֹ, the whole phrase reading בְּדַעְתִּי אֹתוֹ. It seems, therefore, that the suffix must be construed as a subjective one, whatever the meaning of דעת.

Little help is available from the ancient versions. The LXX and other Greek versions translate by σύνεσις or γνῶσις and construe the word with what precedes, as does the Peshiṭta. Targum Jonathan, on the other hand, renders 'by his wisdom' and construes it with the following words, which it paraphrases and expands. The whole clause is thus rendered: 'by his wisdom shall he justify the just, in order to subject many to the law'.[28] This seems to imply an interpretation along the lines of the Servant bringing about the justification of others by teaching them to accept the obligation of obedience to the Torah, but such an interpretation clearly reads a good deal into the Hebrew text, and cannot be said to be a natural exegesis of it. It finds echoes, however, in some of the Jewish mediaeval commentators. David Kimḥi, for instance, explains דעתו as the Servant's knowledge of the Lord, referring to Isa. 11.9 and Jer. 31.34. Construing the word with the following clause, he interprets the whole in terms of Isa. 2.3: 'that he may teach us his ways'. The Vulgate alone among the ancient versions renders the word in such a way that it can be construed with either what precedes or what follows; the translation itself is literal and raises all the problems of interpretation that the Hebrew does. One has to conclude that the ancient versions offer no hint of either an alternative Hebrew *Vorlage* or an unusual meaning of the word דעת; all of them render it with terms like 'knowledge', 'understanding' and 'wisdom'.

In the quest for an alternative meaning of the word דעת we may begin by asking whether anything may yet be salvaged from Thomas's theory. Johnstone has demonstrated beyond doubt the untenability of the interpretation 'humiliation', but his discussion left open the possibility that in 19 of the 39 passages in which Thomas suggested that the Hebrew root ידע

28. The translation is that of J.F. Stenning, *The Targum of Isaiah* (Oxford: Clarendon Press, 1949), p. 180.

might be cognate with the Arabic root *wd'* the semantic range
of the Arabic root might afford justification for the meanings
suggested by Thomas for the Hebrew. On closer examination,
however, six of these passages must be excluded as irrelevant
to the present passage; they all derive from parts of the verb
other than the qal, and three in any case rest on emendations
on the basis of LXX (Jer. 24.1; Amos 3.3; Prov. 10.21). In fact in
only three passages (Ps. 35.15; Job. 9.5; Eccl. 10.20) is a
meaning from ידע II marginally preferable to 'know'. The
range of meaning claimed for the passages in which the qal
occurs is as follows: be still, quiet, at ease; have rest; care for,
keep in mind; lay down; leave alone, have nothing to do with,
let go on, continue; leave alone, neglect.[29] One could not render
'by his stillness' in the sense of patient submission to
undeserved suffering, as in v. 7, because the meaning 'stillness' has the overtones of 'being at ease'. Hugh Williamson[30]
suggests 'he will be satisfied with his rest', but is this not an
anticlimax after the statement that 'he will see light (i.e. live)'?
The only other meaning that might be thought remotely suitable is 'leave alone, neglect', but this would need to be
expressed in the passive to make it clear that it was neglect of
the Servant rather than neglect of others by him. While 'by
his humiliation' would have suited the context well, we are
driven to the conclusion that none of the meanings of a
second root ידע attested by the actual usage of the supposed
cognate Arabic root *wd'* will afford a satisfactory sense in Isa.
53.11.

One of the passages where Thomas suggested the occurrence of the second root ידע was 1 Sam. 6.3: ונודע לכם, where LXX
has the striking rendering: καὶ ἐξιλασθήσεται ὑμῖν. If this
could have been taken as evidence that the niph'al of ידע could
be used to express the passive sense of atonement being
made, and if it could have been assumed that the qal could
express the corresponding active sense of making atonement,
it would have made possible a highly suggestive translation in
Isa. 53.11: 'by his making atonement my Servant will justify

29. See Johnstone, *'yd'* II', pp. 59-60.
30. H.G.M. Williamson, *'Da'aṯ* in Isaiah liii 11', *VT* 28 (1978), pp. 118-
22 (120).

many'. Such a rendering might be linked with אשם in the previous verse (if this itself is indeed a correct reading). It has
become clear, however, as Emerton points out,[31] that the LXX
translation in 1 Sam. 6.3 is of a variant Hebrew *Vorlage* נכפר
now attested in 4QSamᵃ. There is therefore no evidence that
ידע can mean 'to make atonement', and no basis for an interpretation of Isa. 53.11 on such lines.

Are there then any unusual meanings of the ordinary root
ידע that might make sense in Isa. 53.11? In v. 3 we found that
the special sense to 'designate', 'single out' or 'choose' might
possibly be relevant, but it is difficult to see how this could fit
in v. 11, where the active form is found, and would presumably denote the Servant's choice of some other unspecified
person.

Another possibility that is attractive at first sight is the
special sense of the knowledge of God found in a small number
of passages, where the meaning seems to be that knowledge
of God is shown in obedience to his will and commandments.
BDB, p. 395b, under the noun דעת, gives the meaning (§?, h)·
'*knowledge* of God (incl. obedience)'. Perhaps the clearest
example of this meaning is to be found in Jeremiah's eulogy
of Josiah (Jer. 22.15-16): 'he...dealt justly and fairly; all went
well with him. He upheld the cause of the lowly and poor;
then all was well. Did not this show he knew me? says the
LORD' (REB). Other examples may be seen in Hos. 4.1, 6; 6.6;
Isa. 1.3. In the light of this Bo Reicke[32] suggested the translation of our passage: 'Through his obedience my servant
proves to be truly righteous to the advantage of the multitude'. He argued that such an interpretation is appropriate in
the context of the chapter as a whole, which 'indicates that a
practised knowledge of God in the sense of "submission" and
"obedience" is to be expected here'. It is interesting to find the
sense of 'submission' suggested here, without any invoking of
the second root ידע. L.C. Allen,[33] however, when considering a

31. Emerton, 'A Further Consideration', p. 148 and n. 2.

32. B. Reicke, 'The Knowledge of the Suffering Servant', in *Das ferne und
nahe Wort* (BZAW, 105; Giessen: Töpelmann, 1967), pp. 186-92 (188-89).

33. L.C. Allen, 'Isaiah liii. 11 and its Echoes', *Vox Evangelica* 1 (1962),
pp. 24-28 (26).

similar line of interpretation, makes the pertinent comment that 'although the knowledge of God in the Old Testament implies and leads on to obedience, "obedience" is not easily *substituted* for "knowledge"'. In other words, could the single word דעת convey this particular nuance without anything in the immediate context to suggest such a specific meaning? Would it not in any case need to have the divine object expressed to make the sense clear, i.e. בדעתו אֹתִי, 'by his knowledge of me'?

A meaningful translation of בדעתו within the parameters of the normal meaning of the root ידע that will fit the context in Isa. 53.11 has thus proved elusive. We have found no plausible interpretation that does not require a good deal of reading between the lines. Nor, as we have seen, is there any evidence in the ancient versions of a different Hebrew *Vorlage*. We are driven therefore to consider whether resort should be had to conjectural emendation.

The first English edition of the Jerusalem Bible contained the rendering: 'By his sufferings shall my servant justify many', and a footnote explained that 'sufferings' was the reading of one Hebrew MS, while the rest read 'knowledge'. The New Jerusalem Bible has reverted to 'by his knowledge' without any mention of the variant reading. The reading in question is בְּרָעָתוֹ (ר for ד), and is found in MS Kennicott 89. It is recorded in the apparatus of *BHK*, but not in that of *BHS*. The evidence of one mediaeval MS, unsupported by any other Hebrew MSS or by any of the ancient versions, is quite inadequate to substantiate the reading. It is far more likely to have arisen as a simple copyist's error than to represent a genuine survival of an otherwise lost original reading. But the very ease with which such an error might occur raises the possibility that the opposite error may have occurred at a very early stage in the transmission of the Hebrew text. In other words it is possible that MS Kennicott 89, may, paradoxically, contain the original reading after all, even if it came about as the result of a double and therefore self-cancelling error. If L.C. Allen[34] and John Day[35] are right to see in Dan. 12.4 a

34. Allen, 'Isaiah liii. 11', p. 26.
35. Day, '*Da'at* "Humiliation" in Isaiah liii.11', pp. 97-103.

deliberate reference to Isa. 53.11, the reading בדעתו must presumably have already been established in the latter passage by the middle of the second century BCE. The case for a hypothetical original ברעתו must rest almost entirely on the difficulty of finding a satisfactory meaning of the traditional reading in its context, and the appropriateness to that context of the meaning of the alternative reading suggested. The presence of the alternative reading in MS Kennicott 89 can be regarded at most as supporting evidence, showing how easily the letters ד and ר can be interchanged in the process of copying.

The word רעה is the ordinary word for 'evil', with a wide semantic range, and certainly including the kind of evil that consists of suffering or adversity as well as moral evil. The translation 'by his suffering' falls well within the semantic range of the noun, and several passages in the Hebrew Bible can be cited to illustrate its use with a pronominal suffix denoting the person suffering. Three examples with third person suffix are: Obad. 10 ברעתו (RV 'on their affliction'), Jon 4.6 מרעתו (REB 'his discomfort') and Eccl. 5.12 (EVV 5.13) לרעתו (REB 'to his own hurt'). An example with first-person suffix may be found in Ps. 35.4 חשבי רעתי (RV 'that devise my hurt', REB 'who plan my downfall'), while an example of the plural noun with second-person plural suffix may be found in 1 Sam. 10.19 רעותיכם (RV 'your calamities'). A rendering 'by his suffering shall my Servant justify the many' fits the context of Isa. 53.11 as well as Thomas's rendering of דעת by 'humiliation' (although of course Thomas had a different view of the syntax of the verse). The concept of the Servant's suffering as vicarious seems to be clearly expressed at least in 53.4-6, and to afford an appropriate background for understanding the restored ברעתו in v. 11.

We are now in a position to assess the consequences for the interpretation of Isaiah 53 of Johnstone's refutation of Thomas's theory that the root ידע can denote humiliation. In the case of v. 3 it has proved possible to interpret וידוע in several ways within the ordinary meaning of ידע 'to know'. The Servant is represented as either knowing suffering through his own experience, or being known for his suffering. Either interpretation fits the context, and the active interpretation may be obtained from either the traditional text or the reading of 1QIsᵃ. In the case of v. 11, on the other hand, the difficulties of interpreting בדעתו within the semantic range of the ordinary root ידע 'to know' have proved insuperable, and we have had to resort to conjectural emendation of one letter in the consonantal text. This is not the only passage where a similar emendation seems the best solution to the difficulties of rendering the root, as Emerton points out.[36] Hypothetical emendation is always a last resort, but it is preferable to an unintelligible text. In this case not only is the miscopying supposed one of the simplest imaginable; we have the positive evidence that the reverse error in copying actually occurred in MS Kennicott 89. Both passages in Isaiah 53 can now be interpreted meaningfully within the context of the chapter as a whole, and no radical reinterpretation has been necessitated by the withdrawal of Thomas's explanation of the two occurrences of the root ידע. The main casualty is that the reference back from v. 11 to v. 3, which Thomas's explanation made possible, is no longer tenable, since the same root is no longer found in the two passages. The refutation of Thomas's theory has deprived us of an attractive interpretation, but has not left us with any insuperable problems in the interpretation of this chapter, nor has it necessitated a radically different line of interpretation. The many other uncertainties of interpretation of this passage will no doubt continue to exercise the minds of scholars, and it is always possible that fresh manuscript discoveries will bring further readings to light. In the meantime I hope the present study will have helped to clarify the issues in these passages.

---

36. Emerton, 'A Further Consideration', p. 162.

METACOMMENTATING AMOS

David J.A. Clines

The hallmark of Norman Whybray's scholarship, in my
opinion, is its quizzicality. He takes nothing for granted, he
listens to others with a benevolent scepticism, he believes in
demystifying. No egotist, he even turns the same arched eye-
brow towards himself and his earlier work. He is a great
debunker. But he is not a cynic. He believes in the common
scholarly enterprise, and he knows the literature; but he
knows that we will only make progress if we are all the time
bending the searchlight of common sense on our assumptions.
He would make a great metacommentator; or perhaps, one
should say, he is already, but sees no need for the fancy
modern jargon.

Metacommentary, what is that? Let me try this formulation:
When we write commentary, we read what commentators say.
When we write metacommentary, we notice what commen-
tators do.

This plain and symmetrical account of metacommentary
seems to begin immediately to collapse, however, the moment
it has been formulated. For what do commentators *do* apart
from what they *say*? Apart from playing squash or lying late
in bed, which we do not want to know about, what do commentators do other than what they say?

Well, the main thing they do but do not say is not say what
they don't say. Not many say, Of course, I am failing to ask
this question of the text, or, I am hiding from you, dear
reader, my own opinion on the matter, or, I come to this text
with a prejudice about what it ought to mean. So, since we
innocent members of the public, who go on laying out good
money on commentaries, need protection against these

commentators who are failing to tell us what it is they are failing to tell us, it becomes an urgent public duty to create a neighbourhood watch committee of metacommentators who will tell us how we are being shortchanged.

You can search high and low for metacommentary on Amos and Amos commentators, for it is a rare scholar who will step outside the ideology of the text and notice how severely traditional commentary has been constrained by the outlook of the text. But I did find one, whose feminist perspective gave her a vantage point, outside the text, from which the Amos landscape suddenly took on new and surprising contours. Judith Sanderson, in *The Women's Bible Commentary*, noticed, as everyone else has, how the oracles of Amos vigorously condemn the wealthy women of Samaria for oppressing the poor, but also, as no one else has, that they they do not champion the women among those poor. And when Amos condemns the wealthy women of Samaria, because Sanderson is a feminist reader she does not automatically adopt the prophet's standpoint, but suspects that his condemnation is yet another scapegoating of women, who are being blamed now not only for sexual sins (as usual) but for social and economic injustices in society as well.[1] 'A survey of modern commentaries on Amos 4.1 reveals the alacrity with which women are blamed for societies' evils, [and] their relative powerlessness is disregarded', she writes, metacommentatingly.[2] She is quite right; but her feminist critique is only a paradigm for several types of criticism that can be made.[3]

1. These women, we must recall, are 'the pampered darlings of society in Israel's royalist culture...ruling the society of Israel from behind the scenes with sweet petulant nagging for wealth to support their indolent dalliance' (James L. Mays, *Amos: A Commentary* [OTL; London: SCM Press, 1969], p. 72).

2. Judith Sanderson, 'Amos', in *The Women's Bible Commentary* (ed. Carol A. Newsom and Sharon H. Ringe; London: SPCK, 1992), pp. 205-209 (205-206).

3. I am speaking here only of more or less contemporary commentators. Some older commentators, especially when writing from an avowedly Christian perspective, did not feel the same degree of inhibition towards evaluation of their text. Here, for example, is R.S. Cripps: '[T]he Prophet's conception of God is not perfect. One of the mistakes which the Christian

Metacommentating Amos myself, I propose noticing some of the things commentators do. First, they adopt the view of the text regarding the social and economic situation in ancient Israel. Secondly, they adopt the ideology of the text regarding the existence of God and the authenticity of the prophetic vocation. Thirdly, they conceal from their readers that this is what they are doing.

1. *Commentators and the Social Critique of Amos*

I take here the woe against the rich in 6.4-7:

> Alas for those who lie on beds of ivory,
>   and lounge on their couches,
> and eat lambs from the flock,
>   and calves from the stall;
> who sing idle songs to the sound of the harp,
>   and like David improvise on instruments of music;
> who drink wine from bowls,
>   and anoint themselves with the finest oils,
>   but are not grieved over the ruin of Joseph!
> Therefore they shall now be the first to go into exile,
>   and the revelry of the loungers shall pass away (NRSV).

Let me engage first in a little *Sachkritik* as a backdrop to reading some commentators. There is undoubtedly a great deal of anger in this passage against the rich in Samaria, and its spirit of denunciation against idleness and luxury strikes a chord with democratically minded and hard-working readers. But a reader who has not yet opened a commentary pauses, at least long enough to ask, What exactly is the crime of these Samarians for which they are being threatened with exile? Is there some sin in having expensive ivory inlays on your

Church has made, resulting in damage impossible to calculate, has been to standardise as eternal and ultimate truth that which was but a stage—however lofty—in the slow process of its revelation and discovery... If any picture of God found within the O.T. had been perfect, then one of the reasons for the appearing of Jesus would have become unnecessary' (*A Critical and Exegetical Commentary on the Book of Amos* [London: SPCK, 1929], p. 25). However unacceptable today the theory of 'progressive revelation' may be, at least it enabled its adherents to adopt a critical stance toward their texts.

bedframe? (Amos, we presume, is not worried about the fate of elephants.) No doubt meat of any kind was something of a delicacy in ancient Israel, and these people are eating the meat of choice animals prepared for the table; but is that wrong?[4] (Again we can suppose that Amos is not vegetarian and that the text has no fault to find with the farming methods.)[5] And as for singing idle songs, who among the readers of Amos can cast a stone? Has karaoke suddenly become a sin, as well as a social disease?[6] Drinking wine out of bowls instead of cups does

4. Oh yes, say Andersen and Freedman (F.I. Andersen and D.N. Freedman, *Amos: A New Translation with Introduction and Commentary* [Anchor Bible, 24A; New York: Doubleday, 1989], p. 562). 'The details of the menu supplied by v 4b indicate the unconscionable extravagance of the feast... The sumptuous provision of beef and lamb, and young and tender animals as well, points to eating on a scale far beyond the means of the ordinary worker or farmer.' But are we to read a 'menu' in the reference to 'lambs from the flock' and 'calves from the stall'? Can we even say that Amos means that both are eaten at the same feast? In any case, would it be 'unconscionable extravagance' to have two kinds of meat served at the one banquet? How many unconscionably extravagant restaurants have Andersen and Freedman eaten in, I wonder, and shall we say that if Andersen orders lamb and Freedman veal that their 'excessive behavior' is 'its own condemnation' (cf. p. 563)? And, incidentally, exactly how many items are on this 'menu' anyway? Either it is 'beef and lamb' or it is 'young and tender animals', but it is not 'young and tender animals *as well*'. And is there something reprehensible in eating lamb rather than mutton, Wienerschnitzel rather than Hungarian goulash? Or is it perhaps that the reference to 'young and tender' animals—whom we all feel sensitive about—is nothing more than a rhetorical ploy to make the unsuspicious reader take sides uncritically with the prophet against his opponents?

5. The cryptic remark of Hammershaimb, however, gives pause for thought (Erling Hammershaimb, *The Book of Amos: A Commentary* [trans. J. Sturdy; Oxford: Basil Blackwell, 1970], p. 100). 'It hurts the feelings of the shepherd of Tekoa that good animals are used for feasts of this sort', he says, and the reader wonders whether Amos perhaps thinks the rich should serve diseased animals for dinner, or whether he is against them having opulent feasts but would find no fault with, shall we say, humble feasts—or whether, perhaps, the 'shepherd of Tekoa' entertains tender vegetarian feelings toward his charges.

6. The commentators think that the phrase 'like David' is an inauthentic addition to the text; but they *would* say that, wouldn't they,

admittedly sound greedy, and anointing yourself with the finest (and presumably most expensive) oil rather than bargain basement value-for-money oil is certainly self-indulgent. But how serious is self-indulgence? Is it a crime? Is it a sin that deserves a sentence of deportation? Does being wealthy and conspicuously consuming renewable natural resources (wine, oil, mutton and elephant tusks) put you in line for exile, by any reasonable standards? What are the rich supposed to have been doing? If expensive oil is on sale in the market and you have the money in your pocket to buy it, where is the sin?

Ah well, say the commentators, it's more serious than that. The prophetic criticism is that these people have been indulging themselves *and at the same time* not feeling any pain at the ruin of their people (6.7). So, says the metacommentator, if they *had* been worried about the fate of the nation, it would have been all right for them to be self-indulgent? Well, no, not quite. Actually, they are being hit on both counts. Anyway, says the metacommentator, how does the prophet know that they do not feel pain about their nation? He is presumably not invited to their parties—surely he wouldn't have the nerve to complain about the extravagance if he were—so how does he know what they feel and don't feel? Ah well, it's obvious that if they felt any pain they wouldn't be having parties. Is it? If Rome really is burning, what else is there left to do except fiddle?

Would it perhaps be just as true to say, Amos hates the rich because he is not one of them? If he were richer, he would be using more expensive aftershave himself. It's easy to condemn other people's lifestyle and to blame the ills of society on them. But the truth about political and economic disaster and well-being is probably far too complex to be explained by the behaviour of individuals. The fate of nations is determined much more by structural matters, the operation of markets, demographic changes, disease, war and chance. To be sure, the personal behaviour of other people is not a negligible factor in everyday life; we would all like our fellow citizens to behave better, and we know we would feel less envy and less

because otherwise it would be altogether too hard to say what was wrong with it.

fear if they were all more like us. But if you are a little country being targeted for annexation by a big one, as Israel was by Assyria, the highmindedness and moral sensitivity of the average citizen are not going to make a lot of difference.

In short, it would be uncritical of us to accept Amos's analysis of his society, to simply buy the ideology of the text. Somehow we need to distance ourselves from the prophetic voice, and recognize that the prophet's is only one voice in his community. The prophet, and the text, have a corner to fight, a position to uphold, and we for our part need to identify that position, and to relativize it, not so as to discard it but only so as to give it its proper due. But, hardly surprisingly, most of the books about Amos simply take Amos's point of view for granted. Amos is right, his opponents are wrong; Amos is fair; Amos is accurate; Amos is immensely perceptive; Amos is inspired.[7]

---

7.   Here is a striking example of commentators' incapacity to distinguish between the text and themselves. Andersen and Freedman (*Amos*, pp. 88-97) have a section on 'The God of Israel in the Book of Amos'. It opens by saying, 'Our purpose is to present Amos' picture of the deity, not ours, and to keep it within the thought world of the ancient Near East and the Bible rather than to translate it into contemporary theological or philosophical language' (p. 88). That sounds scholarly and objective enough. But the section concludes by saying: 'What it finally comes down to is the nature of the God of the Bible, the person with whom the prophet must deal (and vice versa) and the person around whom everything turns. When all of the superlatives have been exhausted and when all of the authority or majesty have been accorded and the recognition given to the one incomparable deity who stands uniquely alone and against everything that is perishable, vulnerable, corruptible, and the rest, he nevertheless remains a person. That is the fundamental and ultimate category in the Bible, as without it nothing else matters... Once it is agreed that this God—creator and sustainer of heaven and earth, sole and unique—is the God of the Bible and Israel and Amos and the rest of us, then we may draw closer and ask him who he is, what he is like, and how things run in this world' (p. 97). By this point, plainly, we readers are not reading any more about Amos and the ancient world, for Amos had no Bible and thus no God of the Bible. Nor are we reading about Amos's God when we read that God is 'against everything that is perishable, vulnerable, corruptible' —for are those terms not true of humanity, and is Amos's God 'against' humanity in general? And when, at the end, we start to read about what

In order to practise metacommentary, we need to do some close reading of commentaries. Here is my first exhibit:

> In eighth-century Israel the rich got richer and the poor got poorer...Amos sketches the well-being enjoyed by the upper classes in the capital cities, the splendid society that was built upon the misery of the weak and poor...Expensive furniture, indolent ease, succulent food, the sound of music, and extravagant indulgence—so the affluent in Samaria live. Every item represents a luxurious sophistication that had been possible in earlier times only for royalty, and remained a world apart from the life in the villages. The hollowness of it all only becomes apparent in 6c where this heedless hedonism is thrown into relief against the 'ruin of Joseph' from which it is completely insulated.[8]

Such a rich text repays close reading.

In eighth-century Israel the rich got richer and the poor got poorer.[9]

If it is true that the rich got richer, can we be sure that the poor got poorer? The gap between rich and poor can widen even while everyone's standard of living is improving. What about those who were neither rich nor poor (? the majority). And in any case, how can we possibly know whether the poverty portrayed in Amos was widespread; how can we know whether the rich were in some way responsible for the poverty of the poor or whether there was some structural cause, which was really no one individual's fault, for the poverty of a minority?

Amos sketches the well-being enjoyed by the upper classes in the capital cities, the splendid society that was built upon the misery of the weak and poor.[10]

'Splendid' is ironic, is it not? It is not an objective scholarly description, is it? It is actually representing Amos's (ironic)

is 'agreed' and told that 'we' may 'draw closer and ask him who he is' (how?), we can feel sure that the authors' trumpeted scholarly interests in the ancient world have been submerged by their own ideological beliefs.

8.   Mays, *Amos*, pp. 114, 116.
9.   Mays, *Amos*, p. 114.
10.   Mays, *Amos*, p. 114.

point of view in the guise of a scholarly description, is it not?
And does the author literally mean, 'built upon the misery of
the weak'? It is no doubt true enough that in a competitive
and entrepreneurial society the weakest go to the wall if there
are no programmes for social care; but we cannot simply
assume that a prosperous society owes its prosperity to the
deprivation of its poor.[11] You couldn't say that about modern
Switzerland, for example. Should not biblical commentators
have to do a course in economics before they deliver themselves of opinions about Israelite society that they proffer in
their own voice? Certainly, they shouldn't be allowed to parrot
the prophets and pretend they are doing scholarly analysis.

*Expensive furniture, indolent ease, succulent food, the sound
of music, and extravagant indulgence—so the affluent in
Samaria live. Every item represents a luxurious sophistication
that had been possible in earlier times only for royalty, and
remained a world apart from the life in the villages. The
hollowness of it all only becomes apparent in 6c where this
heedless hedonism is thrown into relief against the 'ruin of
Joseph' from which it is completely insulated.*[12]
What authority has the commentator to take this high moral
tone? Would he care to compare his own living standards in,
let's say, Richmond, Virginia, with those of the affluent in
Samaria of the eighth century BCE? Why does he seem to
sneer at the spread of wealth and sophistication from the
court to a wider section of the populace? Why does he not
approve, as a loyal American, of the democratization of privilege that his text attests? Why does he suggest that if the
villages cannot have cable TV no one else should? And what
right has he to talk of 'heedless hedonism' when he himself, if
he is anything like most of us academics, has probably never
contributed to the gross national product, having devoted

11. Mays actually says that 'The economic base of such luxury is
violence... against the poor' (p. 117). What economic theory, we suddenly
wonder, does Mays subscribe to? Can it be perhaps that he is a Marxist?
Or is this not a serious economic and political remark, but only preacher's
rhetoric?
12. Mays, *Amos*, p. 116.

himself to the selfish pursuit of non-practical knowledge, and being parasitic, like most scholars, upon the wealth-creating sectors of the community for his own bread and butter?

And here is my second exhibit:

> The prophet brutally smashes the attraction of these banquets of the chosen few in society which go on long into the night, by a mournful *hoy* ['woe']. He disturbs the fastidious and dubious atmosphere of these ceremonies where the other man's fate is completely disregarded...There are some who profit at the expense of the community; they enjoy life while the rest weep in misery. Amos does not desire a prosperity founded on oppression. That is why this fastidious set will be deported and this refined but rotten society will vanish away.[13]

From whose point of view does Amos 'brutally smash the attraction' of these banquets? Not that of the readers, presumably, since they will not be very attracted to a party where everyone has long since gone home. It will be that of the partygoers themselves; Amos thinks the national situation too serious for people to be enjoying themselves. And so, apparently, does the commentator. Without thinking, without questioning, he assumes that if Amos says it, it must be right. And what is more, it must be effective. So if Amos stands outside the window and shouts *hoy*, 'woe' (remember, he hasn't been invited to the party), everyone inside finds the party entirely spoiled, its attraction smashed and its fastidious atmosphere fatally disturbed. Really?

Amos doesn't desire a prosperity founded on oppression, says the commentator, no doubt quite correctly. But he omits to mention that neither do the wealthy of Samaria, in all probability. No one except the most depraved and cynical people walk around boasting about founding their prosperity on oppression. So the difference between Amos and those he opposes is not that he is evidently in the right and they are evidently in the wrong; it is a difference in conviction about what is and is not fair dealing. Perhaps Amos is in the right,

13. R. Martin-Achard, *A Commentary on the Book of Amos*, in R. Martin-Achard and S. Paul Re'emi, *God's People in Crisis* (International Theological Commentary; Edinburgh: Handsel Press, 1984), pp. 48, 49.

but perhaps he is not. All I am saying is that to jump to the conclusion that he is in the right is not a scholarly procedure; it is simply the reflex of an uncritical religious belief that assumes that what a prophet in the Bible says must be the truth. And yet that very Bible gives us plenty of evidence about the existence of false prophets in ancient Israel, and about the capacity for error even of those who are genuine.

2. *Commentators and the Religious Ideology of Amos*

Amos, or the book of Amos, is full of religious ideology (or theology, as we tend to call it when we are not being critical but giving our implicit assent to it). The question the meta-commentator asks is whether the commentators on Amos recognize ideology when they see it. Here are some ideological statements you find in the book and in the commentaries.

a. *The Prophetic Sense of Vocation*
The book of Amos is founded on the belief that Amos the prophet had actually been spoken to by God. This is what he claims when he says, 'Thus says Yahweh'. It is an amazing claim, and a shocking one. Most of our acquaintances, we ought to recall, think that people who claim to hear voices from the sky should be locked up. Commentators are hardy souls, however, not easily alarmed, and generous of spirit. How else to explain the fact that almost every textbook on Amos accepts Amos's claim, the book's ideology?

Here is the commentary of that learned German, Hans Walter Wolff. Under the heading 'The Man Amos' he tells us, with due scholarly caution:

> When Amos was born and when he died, we do not know. How old he was at the time of his appearance around 760 BC remains hidden from us...Amos was not a native of the northern kingdom, but a Judean come from Tekoa...As a sheep breeder (and as such to be distinguished clearly from a lowly shepherd) he was probably not exactly poor.[14]

14. Hans Walter Wolff, *Joel and Amos: A Commentary on the Books of the Prophets Joel and Amos* (Hermeneia; Philadelphia: Fortress Press, 1977), p. 90.

'Probably not exactly'; it is the very quintessence of scholarly reserve. But then, in the very next paragraph, scholarship is thrown to the winds and pious statements of belief in the intangible and unknowable are paraded as if they belonged to the same world of discourse:

> It was the hand of Yahweh which uprooted him temporarily from his familiar realm and made him break the silence of the wise in evil times (5.13). Whenever he reveals the basis for his prophetic appearance, he points exclusively to Yahweh's irresistible insistence... To those who attribute his appearance to his own brazen self-will, he directs the question whether then terror at the sudden roar of a lion could be self-willed; it is Yahweh's address that has irresistibly impelled him to make proclamation (3.8)... [B]ecause he has been constrained by Yahweh to proclaim his judgment, Amos also exposes Israel's guilt as reason for this judgment.[15]

So there is a God, and his name is Yahweh, and Yahweh did indeed speak to Amos, just as Amos claims, and I am telling you this with all my authority as a German professor.[16] There were those, no doubt, in Amos's own time who 'attributed his appearance to his own brazen self-will'—though the text, if I read it rightly, tells us only of those who demanded that Amos go home and stop prophesying at Bethel; whether they implied that it was not God who brought Amos to Bethel but Amos's own self-will is rather harder to determine. Anyway, says Wolff, Amos has the better of that exchange because he can whip out the lines, 'The lion has roared; who will not fear? The Lord GOD has spoken; who can but prophesy?' (3.8). Somehow that proves that Amos is in the right, that he has been sent by God, that there is a God, and all the rest of it.

---

15. Wolff, *Joel and Amos*, p. 91.

16. American professors are no different, of course. Says Mays, opening his section on 'The Message' of Amos: 'Amos was Yahweh's messenger to Israel' (*Amos*, p. 6)—which six words, being interpreted, mean, Yes, there is a Yahweh, and yes, Amos is his authentic prophet and Amaziah is a fraud; I know, and I am telling you. It has all the critical finesse and scholarly sobriety of the muezzin's call to prayer: There is no god but God and Muhammad is the prophet of God. There is of course nothing wrong about the muezzin's claim, especially if you are a believer (I don't disbelieve it myself, actually); it's just that it's not critical scholarship.

And any modern readers, by the same token, who attribute Amos's appearance at Bethel to his own brazen self-will—or even say, more modestly, that they suppose Amos just thought it was a good idea to go to Bethel and say what he believed— they too stand condemned by the prophet himself. Amos's rhetorical question is unanswerable. No matter that it is only a claim. No matter that you can't prove the validity of one claim by making another. Amos *has* been impelled by God, he *has* been constrained by Yahweh; this is historical fact. No, we do not know when he was born, and no, we cannot be sure whether he was rich or poor, but yes, we do know he was sent by God and that he was in the right and Amaziah was in the wrong.

b. *Inner-Religious Conflict*
There's another thing, the matter of Amaziah. I don't mind admitting that my own antipodean sympathies and prejudices every time are with the rough-hewn prophet from down under by comparison with the smooth authoritarian toady, the priest Amaziah. But I can't help thinking, But this Amaziah wasn't an atheist, he wasn't a pagan, he wasn't an irreligious man. He worshipped the same God as Amos, and he and Amos believed in almost all the same things. From my perspective, from the perspective of an Assyrian, from the perspective of almost anyone who is not caught up in the political and religious situation of the eighth century BCE, the conflict between them was no more than a minor sectarian dispute. And since we only have Amos's side of it—and that, moreover, is couched in the colourful rhetoric of poetry—how can we ever decide where right and wrong lay? and what, for that matter, would right and wrong in matters of this kind actually be?

c. *Knowledge versus Belief*
Let me try a rather more subtle example, this time from the Danish scholar Erling Hammershaimb. The reader is invited to detect the point at which the scholarship stops and the religious assumptions begin:

> Amos not only knows the land of Israel...; he is also familiar
> with his people's history and the accounts of Yahweh's acts of
> kindness to the people. For him Yahweh is the creator God, who
> has led the people out of Egypt and preserved them during the
> forty years of wandering in the wilderness, and then defeated the
> Amorites in the land of Canaan, so that Israel could dwell there
> (2.9ff.; 9.7). He knows too that Yahweh has continuously cared
> for the spiritual well-being of the people, and sent prophets to
> speak to the people and remind them of his commandments
> (2.11). Amos does not therefore regard himself as proclaiming
> something completely new...[17]

Amos is familiar with his people's history—that is an uncontro-
versial inference from the text of the book itself (provided, of
course, that we leave aside the trifling matter of whether the
author of the book is actually the prophet Amos). He knows
the 'accounts' of the national god's deeds; no problem there.
'For him' Yahweh is this and that—which is the scholarly way
of representing the views of others without at the same time
committing oneself to them. But when we read, 'He knows too
that Yahweh has continuously cared for...his people', we are
bound to ask, 'Knows, does he?' How can he *know* something
that is not a fact? He knows the *tradition* that Yahweh has
cared for his people, but Hammershaimb cannot say that Amos
'knows' it unless Hammershaimb believes it. He cannot mean
that Amos knows it but Amos might be wrong; we don't say
someone 'knows' it is four o'clock if we ourselves believe it is
six. Hammershaimb, though he hasn't done anything very
wicked, has let his guard slip nevertheless. He persuaded us
at the beginning of the paragraph that he was speaking purely
as an 'objective' scholar, dispassionately describing the views
of Amos, but by the third sentence he let us see that in fact he
was not a disinterested observer of Amos at all, but an adher-
ent and promoter of Amos's theological ideas. Any reader who
thinks that such an analysis of the scholar's religious commitment is hypercritical might like to consider how the sentences
would sound if we substituted Zeus for Yahweh, and, shall we
say, Aeschylus for Amos. For Aeschylus, Zeus is the creator.
Fine, we say. He knows too that Zeus has continuously

17. Hammershaimb, *Amos*, p. 12.

sustained the Greek people. Has he indeed?, we cannot help
asking.

d. *The Contrast between 'True' and 'False' Prophets*
Take another example, the matter of the terms in which the
contrast between Amos and the 'professional prophets' is cast.
In insisting he is not a prophet nor a prophet's son, Amos,
says Hammershaimb, 'means that he is not a prophet by pro-
fession, does not belong to a band of prophets, and has not
uttered his prophecies for financial gain like the professional
prophets'.[18] Does this mean that *Amos* claims that the
'professional prophets' utter their prophecies for financial
gain, or that *Hammershaimb* believes that the 'professional
prophets' did so? Given that sentence alone, it is hard to tell.
Certainly, when we read that 'Amaziah himself forbids Amos
to prophesy in the Northern Kingdom, and orders him out, as
being a professional prophet who had appeared there for the
sake of gain',[19] we have no doubt that the point of view being
reported is that of Amaziah and not of the modern critic. But
when we read, a few pages on, that Amos 'wishes to protest at
being included in the same class as the professional prophets,
whose preaching was not dictated by Yahweh, but by the
wish to earn money',[20] the relative clause beginning 'whose
preaching' can only be taken as the words of the scholar.[21] It

18. Hammershaimb, *Amos*, p. 11.
19. Hammershaimb, *Amos*, p. 113.
20. Hammershaimb, *Amos*, p. 117.
21. It is the comma after 'professional prophets' that proves it: if there
had been no comma, the 'whose preaching' clause could be understood as
defining the professional prophets, and in that case could be representing
the perspective of Amos; but the comma turns the clause into a descriptive clause, which can only represent the perspective of Hammerschaimb.
The distinction is the same as that between 'that', which introduces a
defining clause, and 'which', which introduces a descriptive clause. If it is
protested that the comma may have been introduced by the translator, I
offer my apologies to Hammerschaimb, and fasten the blame on the
translator. And if is protested that I am making a lot of fuss about a
comma, I will reply that, in this case, on that comma hangs the difference
between giving the impression that one is uncritically adopting the
opinions of Amos or being a critical scholar. Real critical scholars will go

is the scholar who advances the view that the prophets Amos dissociates himself from are false prophets ('not dictated by Yahweh'), and not even sincerely mistaken, but corrupt, and motivated only by the desire for money. Amos himself (the character Amos in the text, I mean) never says that other prophets are false prophets, and never hints that the preaching of prophets and the sons of prophets is dictated by the wish to earn money. He only says that he is not a 'professional' prophet.[22] As far as we know, he may have nothing against professional prophets; the sum and substance of his reply to Amaziah might well be simply his affirmation of the genuineness of his own calling. And we too might do well to think twice before assuming that 'professional' prophets are in the business of prophesying just for the money; Hammershaimb was a professional biblical scholar, but we wouldn't dream of saying that he was motivated by the wish to earn money.

e. Punishment

It is an essential element in the text's ideology that sin should be punished. The book opens with a powerful indictment of the nations that surround Israel for their crimes, and a repeated threat of punishment. As each nation comes into focus, the prophetic message is: 'For three transgressions of X and for four, I will not turn away the punishment thereof' (e.g. 1.3).[23] Any 'departure' from God is visited with punishment, as in

to any lengths to prevent a comma cheating them of their reputation.

22. He may even be saying that he *was* not a professional prophet, but he *is* now. If the LORD has *taken* him from following the flock, he is not being a shepherd any longer, is he? And if he is not earning a living from shepherding, is he perhaps earning it from prophesying?

But where does the idea of 'professional prophet' come from, anyway? Does *nabi* mean that? Was Ezekiel, who was a professional priest, also a professional prophet? And in any case, is Amaziah implying that Amos is prophesying for the sake of income, and is he urging Amos to earn his living from prophesying elsewhere, or does 'eat bread' mean what it means everywhere else, 'eat', not 'earn'? In sum, has the whole idea of 'gain' perhaps been entirely imported into the text?

23. Actually, the Hebrew text does not have a word for 'punishment', but it is obvious—from the ideology of the book as a whole, really—that it can only be punishment that is inevitable after a crime.

the catalogue of disasters in ch. 4 (famine and plague and war) that failed to make Israel 'return' to the Lord. And the repeated 'therefore' is a further sign of the prophetic ideology; the familiar pattern is: an account of a sin, followed by the 'therefore' that introduces the punishment. The denunciation of the rich that we have already looked at, 'Woe to those who lie on beds of ivory', likewise comes to a conclusion with such a 'therefore': 'Therefore they shall be the first of those to go into exile' (6.7). And to the sin of Amaziah in forbidding Amos to prophesy, there is the same 'therefore' of punishment: 'Therefore thus says the LORD, Your wife shall be a prostitute in the city...' (7.17)—which Amos, interestingly enough, thinks of as a punishment of *him*.

What do the commentators make of this ideology? They never discuss it; they only repeat it. They *agree* with Amos that both Israel and the surrounding nations *deserve to be punished*, and that such punishment should be *capital*. Here, for example, is John Bright:

> Amos's message was a devastating attack on the social evils of the day, particularly on the heartlessness and dishonesty with which the rich had ground down the poor..., but also on the immorality and the careless pursuit of luxury which had sapped the national character—all of which he viewed as sins that Yahweh would surely punish.[24]

The metacommentator is bound to ask whether modern scholars are aware of what they are doing. They are adopting the view, and presenting it as their own, that the best way, or perhaps the only way, of dealing with heartlessness, dishonesty, immorality and luxury (to adopt Bright's terms) is to wipe the offenders out of existence. The metacommentator observes (but is not surprised) how, when it is the deity who is punishing, highminded commentators who would not harm a fly themselves suddenly join the hanging and flogging brigade and think no punishment too severe.

Nor do the commentators seem to notice the conflict between the apparent justice of punishing those who deserve it and the

---

24. J. Bright, *A History of Israel* (London: SCM Press, 2nd edn, 1972), p. 259.

obvious injustice of punishing those who do not. Mays, for
example, can write that the 'prophecy of Amos can be heard
as Yahweh's response to their [the poor's] cry, for the weak
and poor are the special objects of Yahweh's compassion and
concern';[25] but at the same time he can say that 'the consis-
tent burden of his [Amos's] oracles is to announce the disaster
that will fulfil Yahweh's decree of an end for his people'.[26] He
doesn't seem to notice that Yahweh can't be very compas-
sionate to the poor if he intends them to be carried into exile
because of the wrongdoing of their leaders, or that the
prophet's demand for justice does not seem to apply to the
deity.[27]

These commentators surely know that they have many
options open to them when they themselves are wronged by
someone else, and that inflicting injury on others is either a
raw instinctive impulse or else a cruel cold-blooded decision
that they come to at the end of their tether, feel guilty about,
but try to justify nevertheless on some rational grounds. But
once they start commentating on Amos they accede to Amos's
simple moral defeatism. Not one of them has the courage—or
the intellectual capacity—to extract himself (they are all
males) from the ideology of the text and to pronounce a moral

25. Mays, *Amos*, p. 10.
26. Mays, *Amos*, p. 9.
27. Here is a typical commentatorial utterance on the subject: 'The
conception of Yahweh which Amos entertains is that of a god of justice...
[Amos] makes the idea the very centre of his conception of God...
Righteousness being a vital element in Yahweh's character, he not only
will demand it in those who profess to be his followers, but will also enforce
the demand...It is a demand for justice, which, in its simplest and most
natural form, includes honesty, integrity, purity, and humanity...It
demands the utmost consideration of the poor and weak,—*moral* justice'
(W.R. Harper, *A Critical and Exegetical Commentary on Amos and Hosea*
[ICC, Edinburgh: T. & T. Clark, 1905], pp. cxvii-cxviii, cxx) It simply does
not occur to this commentator to ask whether in Amos's conception this
moral standard applies to Yahweh, and whether the threats of famine,
fire, exile and the like can be accommodated with 'the utmost consideration of the poor and weak'. At least Harper does not try to argue that the
punishments are 'a token and proof of divine concern and commitment'
(Andersen and Freedman, *Amos*, p. 383), a disingenuous claim if ever
there was one.

judgment upon the prophecy. To be sure, the future *was* very much as the prophecy says—whether it predicted it or wrote it up in hindsight. Things *were* awful, for rich and poor alike. But it is even more awful to ascribe the destruction of a state and the forceable deportation of its citizens to an avenging God. If that is how a believer finds himself or herself impelled to conclude, that it is a terrible thing to fall into the hands of the living God, the metacommentator can respect that. But to affirm it casually, to pretend that it is unproblematic—*that* is not scholarly, it is not even human.

Must the metacommentator be so waspish?, readers are likely to be asking themselves. Does everything have to become so *personal*, and is it truly scholarly to question the motives and interests of our colleagues, as I have been doing throughout this paper?

The answer is yes. It must be, once we admit that we are not all engaged in some objective quest for determinate meanings, and that our ideologies, our locations, our interests and our personalities determine our scholarship—and separate us from one another.[28] Strip away the bonhomie that passes for scholarly interchange in the corridors of the international congresses, and we find that there is a lot we don't like, don't

---

28. I may be permitted to refer to some recent work of my own where the theme of this sentence is further developed, in various directions and in various settings: 'God in the Pentateuch', in *Studies in Old Testament Theology: Historical and Contemporary Images of God and God's People* (Festschrift for David L. Hubbard; ed. Robert L. Hubbard, Jr, Robert K. Johnston and Robert P. Meye; Dallas: Word Books, 1992), pp. 79-98; 'Haggai's Temple, Constructed, Deconstructed and Reconstructed', in *Second Temple Studies* (ed. Tamara C. Eskenazi and Kent H. Richards; JSOTSup, 117; Sheffield: JSOT Press, 1993), and in *SJOT* (1993); 'Possibilities and Priorities in Biblical Interpretation in an International Perspective', *Biblical Interpretation* 1 (1993), pp. 67-87; 'A World Founded on Water (Psalm 24): Reader Response, Deconstruction and Bespoke Interpretation', in *The New Literary Criticism and the Hebrew Bible* (ed. J. Cheryl Exum and David J.A. Clines; JSOTSup, 143; Sheffield: JSOT Press, 1993); 'The Ten Commandments, Reading from Left to Right', in David J.A. Clines, *Interested Parties: The Ideology of Writers and Readers of the Old Testament* (forthcoming).

approve of, and will not stand for, in our colleagues, a lot that
has yet to be brought into the light, taken the measure of,
and fought over. Managing personal conflict within the
academy may well be the new skill, harder still than
Assyriology or deconstruction, that scholars will need to
acquire in this decade.[29]

29. Examples of the 'new brutality', as we might term it, in biblical
scholarship, may be found in the recent pages of the *Journal of Biblical
Literature*; witness the paper of Ben F. Meyer against E.P. Sanders ('A
Caricature of Joachim Jeremias and his Scholarly Work', *JBL* 110
[1991], pp. 451-62), and that of Meir Sternberg against Danna Fewell and
David Gunn ('Biblical Poetics and Sexual Poetics: From Reading to
Counter-Reading', *JBL* 111 [1992], pp. 463-88). I neither welcome it nor
deplore it; the tensions that come to the surface in such acerbic reviews
are already in existence, and no good can come of suppressing them.

WISDOM LITERATURE: RETROSPECT AND PROSPECT

James L. Crenshaw

The publication of the volume entitled *The Sage in Israel and the Ancient Near East*[1] and the updated reprint of *La sagesse de l'Ancien Testament*[2] offer an occasion to reflect on the status of research in wisdom literature.[3] Anyone remotely familiar

1.   John G. Gammie and Leo G. Perdue (eds.), *The Sage in Israel and the Ancient Near East* (Winona Lake, IN: Eisenbrauns, 1990). The imprecise notion of wisdom characterizing many essays in this massive work detracts from its value and threatens to retard the progress of research in this area. Part of the problem derives from the impossible design: the underlying assumption that sapiential influence has permeated the entire Hebrew Bible. A few scholars struggled valiantly to carry out their assigned task, especially in section IV; others approach the ludicrous, e.g. Loren R. Mack-Fisher's concluding remarks about what constitutes a sage; and still others put forth highly dubious interpretations of the facts, e.g. Walter Brueggemann's hypothetical construct drawn from sociology, Leo Perdue's identification of Ezra as a sage (!) and John Gammie's wide-ranging inclusivism.

2.   Maurice Gilbert (ed.), *La sagesse de l'Ancien Testament* (BETL, 51; Leuven: Leuven University Press, 1990). In addition to the authors' updating of their articles and bibliography, the editor has written a brief survey of wisdom research during the decade from 1979 to 1989. He treats (1) introductions and collected works, (2) texts, (3) ancient commentaries, (4) modern commentaries, (5) studies on intertextual relations, and (6) studies devoted to the individual wisdom books.

3.   My own assessment of the past and future of sapiential studies was completed before I read Claus Westermann's *Forschungsgeschichte zur Weisheitsliteratur 1950–1990* (Abhandlungen zur Theologie, 71; Stuttgart: Calwer Verlag, 1991). His focus on the social locus of wisdom and its literary form corresponds to my own isolation of social world and language of discourse as the central issues under discussion in recent publications, although we articulate the matter somewhat differently. For him, the fundamental questions are: 'Did Israelite sages function within the family or in a professional setting such as school or court?' 'Were the earliest proverbial sayings oral or written?' I share his conviction that the

with the subject must surely be amazed at the sheer quantity of publications, all the more surprising because of earlier neglect.[4] Maurice Gilbert's introduction to *La sagesse de l'Ancien Testament*[5] catalogues this vigorous activity over the past decade, so I shall restrict my remarks to analyzing fundamental issues underlying much of the published research.

Mirroring the interpretation of the Hebrew Bible in general, a spate of publications about ancient wisdom addresses two questions: (1) did Israel's sages constitute a professional class,[6]

oldest biblical aphorisms derive from the family and were transmitted orally, and I also have serious doubts about the prominent role attributed to wisdom of the clan by Hans Walter Wolff and others. Incidentally, Westermann is mistaken that his essay, 'Weisheit im Sprichwort', was ignored for many years. I certainly cited it soon after its publication.

Holger Delkurt's analysis of the fundamental issues underlying sapiential scholarship ('Grundprobleme alttestamentlicher Weisheit', *VF* 36 [1991], pp. 38-71) is devoted to the following topics: (1) the definition of wisdom; (2) the place of wisdom; (0) prophecy and wisdom; (4) wisdom as a theology of creation; (5) speech about God in Proverbs; (6) specific themes such as 'the appropriate moment for speech and silence', 'the poor', and 'fate'; (7) Qoheleth.

4. One could hardly find a better example of interpretive bias, the point made so often today by practitioners of literary interpretation. The imperialism of a particular view of theology excluded wisdom literature from consideration. Dissatisfaction with salvation history coincided with revived interest in Israel's wisdom, which had earlier captured the imagination after its intimate connection with Egyptian wisdom literature was recognized.

5. He builds on the survey of S. Pié i Ninot, 'La literatura sapiencial biblica: Una actualidad bibliográfica creciente', *Actualidad Bibliográfica* 44 (1985), pp. 202-11 and 46 (1986), pp. 163-74. To this may be added the long section by J. Vilchez Lindez in *Sapienciales. I. Proverbios* (Madrid: Ediciones Christiandad, 1984), pp. 39-92, preceded by L. Alonso Schökel's analysis (pp. 17-37).

6. R.N. Whybray, *The Intellectual Tradition in the Old Testament* [BZAW, 135; Berlin: de Gruyter, 1974]) has posed the most vigorous challenge to the dominant view, although he appears to moderate his opinion in 'The Sage in the Israelite Royal Court', in *The Sage in Israel and the Ancient Near East*, p. 139 ('It is possible, on the other hand, that some parts of Proverbs, especially parts of chaps. 1–9 and 22.17–24.22, were composed as "text books" for young pupils—though not necessarily at a royal scribal school').

and (2) what characterizes their language of discourse?[7] In
other words, what was the social world of the sages and how
did they express themselves? Although *sociological* and
literary interests have prevailed, occasional voices have echoed
earlier *conceptual* analyses, particularly about the sages' idea
of God.[8]

1. *The Social World of the Sages*

As R. Norman Whybray's recent essay on this topic shows,[9] no
one has succeeded in positioning the sages in any distinct
social group. To be sure, scholars use phrases like 'elite class',
'intellectuals', 'urban owners of landed estates', 'courtiers' and
'professional counselors or teachers'.[10] In addition, interpreters
usually acknowledge an early period when wisdom's origin
and transmission occurred within family units[11] and a late

7.   Walter Bühlmann (*Vom rechten Reden und Schweigen* [OBO, 12;
Göttingen: Vandenhoeck & Ruprecht, 1976]) shows how self-consciously
the ancient sages reflected on speech and its absence.

8.   Johannes Fichtner's synthesis of ancient wisdom literature, *Das
altorientalische Weisheit in ihrer israelitisch-jüdischen Ausprägung*
(BZAW, 62; Giessen: A. Töpelmann, 1933), includes a lengthy section on
the sages' understanding of God (pp. 97-123).

9.   R.N. Whybray, 'The Social World of the Wisdom Writers', in *The
World of Ancient Israel* (ed. R.E. Clements; Cambridge: Cambridge
University Press, 1989), pp. 227-50. Whybray characterizes the dilemma
facing contemporary scholars in this way: (1) Why would royal scribes,
even under foreign influence, have ignored the folk wisdom in Israel
covering the same topics? (2) Yet the literary quality and clear dependence on foreign models of most of the aphorisms in Proverbs cannot be
denied. (3) If education was actually widespread, why limit the authorship
of wisdom literature to professional sages (pp. 234-35)?

10. The book of Job is particularly problematic as a source for
discerning the status of sages, as Whybray recognizes. Why are Job's
three friends not identified as members of a professional class of the wise
('The Social World of the Wisdom Writers', p. 240)? Moreover, why do the
proverbial collections primarily address adults instead of schoolboys?

11. Claus Westermann (*Wurzeln der Weisheit* [Göttingen: Vandenhoeck
& Ruprecht, 1990]) argues forcefully for the prominence of the family in
early wisdom instruction. He notes the concentration on topics of central
interest to rural populations of simple people (p. 75) and their focus on the
'private' life (p. 43). Nevertheless, he rejects the hypothesis of clan

epoch during which teachers administered their own private schools,[12] with a possible intermediate stage associated with the royal court.[13] A noticeable lack of agreement stands out above all else, and the imprecise dating of the wisdom corpus complicates matters even more.[14] Indeed, disagreement over the limits of wisdom literature,[15] reflected in the tendency in some quarters to identify sapiential activity from Genesis through Esther,[16] bears witness to the mingling of various groups in Israelite society.

Ancient Near Eastern parallels throw light on the phe-

wisdom (p. 35) and downplays the cult, asserting that address to God and by God belongs to a wholly different realm of language (p. 142).

12. Ben Sira's allusion to a building devoted to instruction (51.23) is ordinarily taken literally in contrast to the rhetoric attributed to and descriptive of personified wisdom (Prov. 1.20-33; 8.1-36; 9.1-12; Sir. 24; Wis. 6.12-16; cf. Isa. 55.1-3).

13. The strongest evidence for professional sages at the royal court, the superscription in Prov. 25.1, seems to refer to transcriptional activity (*he'tîqû*) rather than to literary composition.

14. The persistence of views that society in general has discarded only exacerbates the difficulty of postulating even relative chronologies for the several wisdom texts. The task becomes impossible when one takes into account the present state of knowledge about Israel's religious pilgrimage, e.g. the beginnings of personal piety, which Franz Josef Steiert (*Die Weisheit Israels—ein Fremdkörper im Alten Testament?* [Freiburger Theologische Studien; Freiburg: Herder, 1990]), following J. Assmann (*Weisheit, Loyalismus, und Frömmigkeit* [Freiburg: Herder, 1979]), takes as a decisive clue for understanding the wisdom corpus. Michael V. Fox astutely comments: 'But he never comes to grips with the fact that whatever their beliefs and assumptions, the Israelite sages never invoke God's law, never reinforce their teachings by appealing to the promises or demands of the covenant, and never draw upon the lessons of Israelite history... Wisdom's avoidance of the particularities of Israelite law and history is a noteworthy and apparently deliberate practice' (Review of Steiert, *Die Weisheit*, in *JBL* 111 [1992], p. 135).

15. I am firmly convinced that the caveat offered in my article on 'Method in Determining Wisdom Influence upon "Historical" Literature' (*JBL* 88 [1969], pp. 129-42) was well placed and that many who cite it approvingly have not really heeded its warning.

16. Donn Morgan (*Wisdom in the Old Testament Traditions* [Atlanta: John Knox Press, 1981]) tries unsuccessfully to legitimate this hermeneutical enterprise.

nomenon of professional sages,[17] while at the same time highlighting distinct differences between Israelite wisdom and Egyptian or Mesopotamian wisdom.[18] From the period of the Old Kingdom learned counselors advised the Pharaoh and his court; the New Kingdom witnessed a growing pietism among the sages responsible for royal instruction and temple ritual,[19] together with a democratizing of the teaching; and the Demotic period saw a ruralization of sages and a growth of skepticism,[20] approaching fatalism. Over the years Mesopotamian wisdom underwent comparable shifts, wisdom's primary locus changing from the tablet house (*edubba*) to the exorcist's

17. Two articles by Ronald J. Williams ('The Sage in Egyptian Literature', pp. 19-30, and 'The Function of the Sage in the Egyptian Royal Court', pp. 95-98, in Gammie and Perdue [eds.], *The Sage in Israel and the Ancient Near East*) update his earlier article, 'The Sages of Ancient Egypt in the Light of Recent Scholarship', *JAOS* 101 (1981), pp. 1-19 (cf. also Helmut Brunner, *Altägyptische Weisheit* [Zürich: Artemis, 1988], and Miriam Lichtheim, *Late Egyptian Wisdom Literature in the International Context* [Göttingen: Vandenhoeck & Ruprecht, 1983]). The Mesopotamian scene is treated by Rivkah Harris, 'The Female "Sage" in Mesopotamian Literature (with an Appendix on Egypt)'; Samuel Noah Kramer, 'The Sage in Sumerian Literature: A Composite Portrait'; Ronald F.G. Sweet, 'The Sage in Akkadian Literature: A Philological Study' and 'The Sage in Mesopotamian Palaces and Royal Courts', in *The Sage in Israel and the Ancient Near East*, pp. 3-18, 31-44, 45-66, 99-108.

18. At least two things about Mesopotamian wisdom points to its similarity with and difference from biblical wisdom respectively: (1) the vigorous skeptical tradition in *Ludlul, The Babylonian Theodicy* and *The Dialogue between a Master and his Slave*; (2) the centrality of magic. In Egypt scribalism and royal courtiers achieved prominence never enjoyed in Israel.

19. Lichtheim, *Late Egyptian Wisdom Literature*, rejects the claim that late Demotic works such as *Ankhsheshonky* and *Papyrus Insinger* represent a failure of intellectual nerve that takes refuge in piety, but the conclusions of Hans Heinrich Schmid (*Wesen und Geschichte der Weisheit* [BZAW, 101; Berlin: Töpelmann, 1966]) cannot easily be set aside.

20. The first claim stands even if Lichtheim is correct that the sayings in *Ankhsheshonky* are not overwhelmingly concerned about rural existence (*Late Egyptian Wisdom Literature*, p. 4), for they certainly differ dramatically from earlier royal authorship or court instructions. The second claim hardly excludes belief in a deity's benevolence, for its absence fuels the skeptic's comments about fate.

place of activity,[21] although some evidence also points to other
loci, e.g. Sumerian folk proverbs and Babylonian counsels to a
prince.[22]

As is well known, wisdom in Egypt and in Mesopotamia was
essentially bureaucratic.[23] Instruction, primarily pragmatic,
sought to ensure success in the exercise of governmental
responsibilities. In the land along the Tigris and Euphrates
rivers, professional scribes zealously guarded their unique
skills with respect to the complex writing system and secret
magical lore, at the same time eroding interest in literature by
their very esotericism.[24] Available evidence does not support
Gerhard von Rad's hypothesis,[25] reiterated by Walter Brueggemann,[26] that intellectual bureaucratism took hold in Israel
during the Solomonic era. Only the eighth century comes close
to such complex organizational securing of royal interests.[27]

21. Kramer, 'The Sage in Sumerian Literature', p. 38, brings together
the two competing emphases, for he thinks exorcists studied in the tablet
house and learned from an *ummia* (cf. Sweet, 'The Sage in Akkadian
Literature', pp. 60-61).

22. Were folk proverbs held in less esteem than literary products of
professional sages, as Lichtheim thinks was true in Egypt (*Late Egyptian
Wisdom Literature*, p. 25)? Perhaps the answer depends on the audience,
whether an ordinary citizen or a trained scribe.

23. In this respect it contrasts sharply with biblical wisdom, which gives
almost no evidence of serving bureaucratic ends—unless its conservative
and anti-revolutionary ethic aimed at preserving the status quo.

24. A. Livingstone, *Mystical and Mythological Explanatory Works of
Assyrian and Babylonian Scholars* (Oxford: Oxford University Press,
1986).

25. G. von Rad, *Wisdom in Israel* (Nashville: Abingdon Press, 1971).
His hypothesis about the sweeping away of pan-sacralism in a virtual
Enlightenment during Solomon's regime has little to recommend it and is
increasingly rejected.

26. 'The Social Significance of Solomon as a Patron of Wisdom', in
Gammie and Perdue (eds.), *The Sage in Israel and the Ancient Near East*,
pp. 117-32. Brueggemann's neat types have rhetorical appeal, but they
run roughshod over historical probabilities.

27. David W. Jamieson-Drake (*Scribes and Schools in Monarchic
Judah: A Socio-Archaeological Approach* [JSOTSup, 109; Sheffield: JSOT
Press, 1991]) has demonstrated the improbability that Solomon had the
sort of bureaucracy assumed by Brueggemann.

As for esoteric knowledge, the simple Hebrew alphabet discouraged any moves to withhold literature from the people at large, and magic played a less sanctioned role in Israelite religion than in Egypt or Mesopotamia.[28] The debate over literacy in ancient Israel has introduced exciting new data into the discussion of the sages' social world.[29] André Lemaire eloquently promotes a complex system of education during the monarchy embracing most cities in Israel and extending to many remote villages. Drawing on inscriptional data, he imagines the existence of schools as the precondition for the biblical canon, for students needed texts. Others have interpreted the data differently, seeing in them decisive proof of illiteracy throughout the land (misspellings, crude drawings, transpositions of letters). William V. Harris's recent study of *Ancient Literacy* puts Lemaire's optimism under a dark cloud,[30] for, if literacy in classical Greece never exceeded 10%, then one is entitled to ask how Israel ever reached the high level of literacy that many, if not most, interpreters assume. J. Baines's estimate that literacy in Egypt rarely exceeded 1% is even more sobering.[31]

Stated simply, mass literacy, a recent phenomenon, is a direct result of the invention of the printing press, of Protestantism's emphasis on private reading of the Bible, of state and religious funding of education, and of the industrial revolution, which

28. Various biblical allusions to magical practices among the populace indicate that the official position regarding magic and divination did not necessarily commend itself to ordinary citizens.

29. André Lemaire, 'The Sage in School and Temple', in Gammie and Perdue (eds.), *The Sage in Israel and the Ancient Near East*, pp. 165-81, argues for widespread schools in Israel from early times, but my 'Education in Ancient Israel', *JBL* 104 [1985], pp. 601-15, and Menahem Haran, 'On the Diffusion of Literacy and Schools in Ancient Israel', in *VTSup* 40 (Congress Volume, Jerusalem) (1988), pp. 81-95, take a much more conservative view.

30. William V. Harris, *Ancient Literacy* (Cambridge, MA: Harvard University Press, 1989).

31. J. Baines, 'Literacy and Ancient Egyptian Society', *Man* NS (1983), pp. 572-99. I am indebted to Rivkah Harris, 'The Female "Sage" in Mesopotamian Literature', p. 15, for this reference.

made available tangible rewards for educated workers.[32] Ancient Israel lacked these inducements to literacy, at the same time possessing several hindrances to the mastering of reading and writing. First, writing materials were either cumbersome or prohibitively expensive. Secondly, acquiring an education was not cost-effective, especially in an agricultural economy where seasonal work determined one's daily activity. Thirdly, nothing in the economy demanded a literate populace, and participation in society at large depended on one's oral skills. Fourthly, no patron of education assumed the cost of private instruction, and one searches in vain for any mention of philanthropic gifts to education comparable to those in third-century Greece. Fifthly, members of crafts and guilds requiring literacy of some sort undoubtedly kept membership to a minimum, thus protecting their earning power.

In short, neither a strong desire for literacy nor an opportunity to become literate existed in ancient Israel, with the possible exception of a few guilds.[33] In all likelihood, some moral instruction took place in the family, probably in the form of oral teaching.[34] The overwhelming sense of oral instruction persists into the third century, if by w^e'izzēn (12.9) Qoheleth's epilogist alludes to the teacher's manner of listening for insights worthy of dissemination.[35] The legend about the seven *apkallus* in Sumer and the claim that Marduk had four ears at birth emphasize the importance of hearing, as

32. Harris, *Ancient Literacy*, p. 12.

33. Economic interests would have led to protectionism with respect to the special knowledge by which guild members earned their wages. Professional pride also encouraged exclusivism, sometimes reinforced by magical rites as in metallurgy. Rivalry resulted from exclusivity, e.g. the struggle for power within priestly circles.

34. The language of Deut. 6.4-9 mentions written signs within an overwhelmingly oral instructional context, and even Prov. 1–9, presumably a product of a literary composition as opposed to folk origin, describes the process of learning as oral instruction. The dominance of the verb 'hear' (e.g. in 4.1, 10; 5.13) stands out, along with the paucity of references to writing (cf. 3.3).

35. C.F. Whitley, *Koheleth* (BZAW, 148; Berlin: de Gruyter, 1979).

does the phrase designating professional sages as 'wide of ears'.[36]

The situation in Alexandria, the probable setting of the *Wisdom of Solomon*, is unique, as Alan Mendelson's *Secular Education in Philo of Alexandria*[37] effectively demonstrates. There mastering the encyclicals was a means of upward mobility, but knowledge of creation enabled students to move beyond sensory data to what Philo called knowledge of God. Small wonder the *Wisdom of Solomon* actually rattles off the subjects in the school curriculum and dramatically emphasizes the importance of correctly interpreting the 'Book of Nature'.

The Hebrew Bible does not even provide sufficient data to enable critics to ascertain the identity of those to whom teaching was addressed. Curiously, the proverbial collection that seems to comprise instruction for students, Proverbs 1–9, actually employs language of family discourse,[38] whereas the oldest collections lack such vocabulary and give the impression of application to adult members of society. In ancient Egyptian and Mesopotamian wisdom, the clientele of proverbs is exclusively masculine. Rivkah Harris has exhaustively documented the exceptions to this masculine hegemony in the ancient Near East.[39] She refers to educated daughters of royalty and to female scribes who ministered solely to women of the harem, serving as a buffer between the wives of rulers and non-kin males. Although goddesses were patrons of the scribal art in both these lands (Nisaba in Mesopotamia and

36. 'Four were his eyes, four were his ears. When he moved his lips, fire blazed forth. Each of his four ears grew large and (his) eyes likewise, to see everything' (Sara Denning Bolle, *Wisdom in Akkadian Literature: Expression, Instruction, Dialogue* [PhD dissertation, University of California, Los Angeles, 1982], p. 58). Erica Reiner, 'The Etiological Myth of the "Seven Sages"', *Or* 30 (1961), pp. 1-11, treats the *apkallus*.

37. Alan Mendelson, *Secular Education in Philo of Alexandria* (MHUC, 7; Cincinnati: Hebrew Union College Press, 1982).

38. An exclusively metaphorical understanding of vocabulary such as 'my son' and 'father' in the sense of student and teacher requires one to ignore clear indications that some of these instructions took place within a family setting (cf. 1.8; 6.20; 4.3-9).

39. Harris, 'The Female "Sage" in Mesopotamian Literature (with an Appendix on Egypt)', pp. 3-18.

Seshat in Egypt), this fact did not translate into widespread literacy for women any more than a comparable phenomenon did in the Middle Ages in Europe. On rare occasions women actually composed literature, for example, Sargon's daughter Enheduanna, who described her literary activity as 'giving birth', and Ninshatapada, the daughter of Sin-Kashib, the founder of the Old Babylonian dynasty of Uruk.[40] Graphic imagery depicting women as literate, such as scenes showing females with writing implements or written texts, may reflect an *ideal* rather than the *actual* state of things. At least one Egyptian text mentions a wise woman, but this expression suffers from the same ambiguity that *ḥākām* does in the Hebrew Bible.[41] Does the word in its various forms ever bear a technical sense, 'the wise'? Most critics think it does, but few agree on which uses belong to this category. Recent research has cast doubt on the supposed technical use of 'counselor' in Mesopotamia,[42] undercutting the claim—already on shaky ground textually—that the biblical expression 'wise woman' refers to a professional sage.[43] Now and again certain remarks reveal the extent to which women suffered from low self-esteem ('Disregard that it is a mere woman who has written and submitted [this] to you') or from calumny (Egyptian graffiti that compare earlier graffiti to the 'work of a woman who has no mind').[44]

40. Not one female name appears in Dandameyev's study of more than three thousand scribes from the Neo-Babylonian period. In Egypt the New Kingdom witnessed the rise to prominence of several remarkable women, among whom were Hatshepsut, Tiy and Nefertiti.
41. Hans-Peter Müller and M. Krause, '*Chākham; chākhām; chokmāh; chokmōth*', *TDOT*, IV, pp. 364-85.
42. Sweet, 'The Sage in Akkadian Literature', p. 64.
43. P. Kyle McCarter, Jr, 'The Sage in the Deuteronomistic History', in Gammie and Perdue (eds.), *The Sage in Israel and the Ancient Near East*, p. 291, characterizes the woman of Tekoa as an actress 'since Joab tells her what to say and do'. Does the adjective 'wise' in this story simply mean 'clever' or 'calculating' (cf. also the adjective describing Jonadab)?
44. The Egyptian *Satire of the Trades* contains an incidental observation more telling than most direct remarks about the status of women ('The weaver in the workshop, he is worse off than a woman...' [Miriam Lichtheim, *Ancient Egyptian Literature*, I (Berkeley: University of

A different method for discovering the social world of the
sages has been applied to Job and Qoheleth, with interesting
results. In the book of Job Rainer Albertz discerns in-fighting
between rival groups of upper-class citizens, which he characterizes as an unscrupulous enclave bent on amassing wealth
at the expense of less fortunate individuals versus a pious
group who cannot condone such harsh treatment of helpless
citizens.[45] How this latter attitude squares with the fact that
the book is written from the standpoint of a wealthy suffering
innocent who expresses contempt for the scum of the earth in
ch. 30 needs to be explained, for only with great reservation
can it be said that this book champions the cause of the poor, a
point overlooked by J. David Pleins and Gustavo Gutiérrez in
their otherwise perceptive studies.[46] With respect to Qoheleth,
Frank Crüsemann has rendered a verdict of 'guilty' on
charges of heartless surrender to the profit motive regardless
of the consequences.[47] Other readers may concur with Elias
Bickerman that Qoheleth lived in an acquisitive society, an
age characterized by economic ventures aimed at making a
fortune,[48] but they recognize that Qoheleth criticized all such
mercenary endeavors as futile or absurd. In my view, Qoheleth's remarks about victims of oppression with none to deliver

California Press, 1973), p. 188]). The washerman also suffers the
indignity of having to clean women's clothes (p. 189).

45. 'Der sozialgeschichtliche Hintergrund des Hiobbuches und der
"Babylonischen Theodizee"', in J. Jeremias und L. Perlitt (eds.), *Die
Botschaft und die Boten: Festschrift H.W. Wolff* (Neukirchen–Vluyn:
Neukirchener Verlag, 1981), pp. 349-72.

46. J. David Pleins, 'Poverty in the Social World of the Wise', *JSOT* 37
(1987), pp. 61-78, and 'Rhetorics of Opposition: Exploring the Diverging
Social Visions of the Hebrew Bible, with Special Reference to the Wisdom
Tradition', unpublished paper presented in Vienna at the Society of
Biblical Literature International Meeting; and Gustavo Gutiérrez, *On Job*
(Maryknoll, NY: Orbis Books, 1987).

47. Frank Crüsemann, 'Die unveränderbare Welt. Überlegungen zur
"Krisis der Weisheit" beim Prediger (Kohelet)', in *Der Gott der kleinen
Leute* (ed. Willi Schottroff and Wolfgang Stegemann; Munich: Gelnhausen,
1979), pp. 80-104 (ET, *The God of the Lowly* [Maryknoll, NY: Orbis Books,
1984]).

48. Elias J. Bickerman, *Four Strange Books of the Bible* (New York:
Schocken Books, 1967), pp. 139-67.

them convey pathos rather than contempt.

Udo Skladny's pioneering efforts to apply a sociological approach to Proverbs did not persuade many critics,[49] but more recent applications of this perspective appear promising. Joseph Blenkinsopp understands the preoccupation with foreign women in Proverbs 1–9 by reference to the struggle under Ezra and Nehemiah to rid the community of a perceived threat posed by non-Jewish wives.[50] Pleins and others have analyzed the vocabulary of poverty in Proverbs, with some surprising results.[51] All these efforts to clarify the social world of the sages underline the necessity of postulating different centers of sapiential teaching from time to time. Such diversity gives rise to still another question: Did the sages in their several locations use rhetoric that set them apart from the rest of society?

2. *The Sages' Language of Discourse*

Carol A. Newsom's penetrating analysis of the discourse in Proverbs 1–9 illustrates the power inherent in a literary study of sapiential texts.[52] Using categories drawn from Mikhail Bakhtin, Emile Benveniste, Jacques Derrida, Mieke Bal, Toril Moi and others, she focuses on the speaking self and the silent addressee, as well as the feminine subject of that talk. In doing so, Newsom highlights the hidden struggle for power in shaping a world view and the subtle appeal to transcendental authority. Under her critical eye these moral teachings take on their character as life and death decisions by competing generations. Aware of the social consequences of

49. Udo Skladny, *Die ältesten Spruchsammlungen in Israel* (Göttingen: Vandenhoeck & Ruprecht, 1962).

50. Joseph Blenkinsopp, 'The Social Context of the "Outsider Woman" in Proverbs 1–9', *Bib* 72 (1991), pp. 457-73.

51. Pleins, 'Poverty in the Social World of the Wise'; R.N. Whybray, *Wealth and Poverty in the Book of Proverbs* (JSOTSup, 99; Sheffield: JSOT Press, 1990); James L. Crenshaw, 'Poverty and Punishment in the Bible', *Quarterly Review* 9 (1989), pp. 30-43.

52. Carol A. Newsom, 'Woman and the Discourse of Patriarchal Wisdom: A Study of Proverbs 1–9', in *Gender and Difference in Ancient Israel* (ed. Peggy L. Day; Minneapolis: Fortress Press, 1989), pp. 142-60.

actions, the teachers use every means at their disposal to place the enemy on the margin of existence. In my view, no other interpreter has succeeded to this degree in clarifying the discourse as it unfolds in Proverbs 1-9.

I have discussed the compositional nature of the sayings of Agur in Prov. 30.1-14 under the title 'Clanging Symbols'.[53] It seems that this entire unit builds on a principle of frustrated expectation, as again and again the anticipated conclusion to a familiar expression does not appear and in its place something wholly unexpected completes the thought. Here both form and content mesh, for the shocking skepticism corresponds to the stylistic iconoclasm.

David Penchansky's *The Betrayal of God* interprets the perceived dissonance in the Book of Job by using categories from Frederic Jameson, Michel Foucault and Pierre Macherey.[54] For Penchansky, dissonance functions to emphasize the real gaps in divine activity and character, and hence it should not be explained away as editorial tampering with a seamless text. Such an approach implies that a cloud of darkness hovers over the book from start to finish, and this cloud heightens the mystery and terror associated with the deity depicted in Job. Robert Alter has traced an intricate connection between Job's initial lament and the subsequent theophany; in exquisite detail the divine speech mirrors the earlier human complaint.[55] Alter's sensitivity to the imagery of the text approximates the powerful thrust of Othmar Keel's discussion of Egyptian symbolism for chaos, the hippopotamus and the crocodile.[56] I have noted an additional feature of the theophany, the clash between form and content.[57] The anticipated

53. James L. Crenshaw, 'Changing Symbols', in *Justice and the Holy: Essays in Honor of Walter Harrelson* (ed. Douglas A. Knight and Peter J. Paris; Atlanta: Scholars Press, 1989), pp. 51-64.

54. David Penchansky, *The Betrayal of God* (Louisville: Westminster/ John Knox Press, 1990).

55. Robert Alter, *The Art of Biblical Poetry* (New York: Basic Books, 1985), pp. 85-110.

56. Othmar Keel, *Jahwes Entgegnung an Ijob: Eine Deutung von Ijob 38–41 vor dem Hintergrund der zeitgenössischen Bildkunst* (Göttingen: Vandenhoeck & Ruprecht, 1978).

57. James L. Crenshaw, 'When Form and Content Clash: The

comforting presence generated by the theophany in context is mitigated by words that ridicule Job and describe a universe virtually devoid of human beings, yet one in which Yahweh takes great pride.

Michael V. Fox has given a new interpretation of multiple voices in Qoheleth, which he understands as various personae of the author.[58] Appealing to a common stylistic device in the ancient world, as well as in more modern works like Joel Chandler Harris's *The Tales of Uncle Remus*, Fox thinks of a single narrator who assumes different personae. The speaker who frames the story then shifts from third person to first person and addresses others as Qoheleth. This approach enables Fox to argue for unity throughout the book, despite contradictions and apparent epilogues.

Two recent dissertations have examined ancient Near Eastern rhetoric in Sumerian and Akkadian wisdom literature. Robert S. Falkowitz claims in *The Sumerian Rhetoric Collections* that so-called proverb collections are misnamed, for they contain many genres besides proverbial sayings—specifically maxims, riddles, enthymemes, fables, tables and incantations—and he insists that the rhetoric collections were used as texts in schools.[59] Their purpose, in his opinion, was to train scribes in the art of persuasion. Falkowitz thinks many of these genres fluctuated; for example, a proverb became familiar, lost its metaphoric essence, and became a maxim. He also insists that the difference between one genre and another was often hardly noticeable, for metaphors meant to be enigmatic identify riddles and metaphors meant to be understood indicate proverbs. Falkowitz denies that these rhetoric collections ever existed outside the school, despite the traditional appearance akin to folk wisdom, and he supposes that rhetoric

Theology of Job 38.1–40.5', in *Creation in the Biblical Tradition* (ed. J.J. Collins and R.J. Clifford; CBQMS, 1992), pp. 70-84.

58. Michael V. Fox, *Qohelet and his Contradictions* (JSOTSup, 71; Bible and Literature Series, 18; Sheffield: JSOT Press; Almond Press, 1989), and 'Frame-Narrative and Composition in the Book of Qohelet', *HUCA* 49 (1977), pp. 83-106.

59. Robert S. Falkowitz, *The Sumerian Rhetoric Collections* (PhD dissertation, University of Pennsylvania, 1980).

collections were learned after basic sign lists, lexical lists, and grammatical texts. If he is correct, two observations will impinge heavily on wisdom research: consistency was not of great importance, and one cannot deduce a society's values from its proverbs alone, for they do not necessarily express commonly held truths.[60]

The other analysis of discourse in Akkadian wisdom, Sara Denning Bolle's 'Wisdom in Akkadian Literature: Expression, Instruction, Dialogue', interprets the texts from the standpoint of dialogue as understood by Plato and Bakhtin.[61] Bolle first looks at dialogue in Akkadian narratives such as *The Gilgamesh Epic*, then turns to cult texts (incantations), instructions, contest literature, and dialogical texts, e.g. *Theodicy, A Dialogue of Pessimism* and *A Dialogue between a Man and God*. Bolle isolates three features of Platonic dialogue: (1) Socratic *elenchus*, or questioning to expose ignorance, (2) *epagoge*, or arriving at a universal from a particular, and (3) Socratic definition, or searching for the essence. Using Bakhtin's emphasis on polyphonic dialogue, one that never ends, Bolle analyzes ancient dialogues, including inner dialogues and dialogues within dialogues. She recognizes the rich potential of rhetorical questions, which effect transitions, communicate philosophical, timeless truth, enhance drama, draw readers into the narrative, emphasize, and startle. Noting that instructions address a fictitious audience, Bolle perceives that, at a deeper level than the monologue, they address the inner worlds of mind and heart. Taking issue with her teacher Giorgio Buccellati, she understands the *Theodicy* to be internal dialogue carried on within the heart of a single person (like Qoheleth and *The Dialogue of a Man with his*

60. If wisdom and law are integrally related, one would expect proverbial prohibitions to express ancient values. I have explored this putative relationship in an essay entitled 'Prohibitions in Proverbs and Qoheleth', in *Priests, Prophets and Scribes* (Festschrift Joseph Blenkinsopp; ed. Eugene Ulrich *et al.*; JSOTSup, 149; Sheffield: JSOT Press, 1992), pp. 115-24.

61. Sara Denning Bolle, 'Wisdom in Akkadian Literature: Expression, Instruction, Dialogue' (PhD dissertation, University of California, Los Angeles, 1982).

Soul). She sums up the importance of dialogue as follows: 'Wisdom is a matter of communication, enlightening, and instructing: dialogue is its vehicle'.[62]

Returning to the question with which we began this discussion of literary analysis, did the sages use distinctive rhetoric? As the preceding comments on dialogue indicate, we cannot claim exclusive use of these literary features by ancient sages, but we can affirm special rhetoric in some instances.[63] Still, we lack conclusive criteria for distinguishing in every case exactly which text derives from a sapiential milieu and which one does not. The continuing debate over the provenance of the Book of Job illustrates the slippage in this regard.[64]

3. *The Concept of God in Wisdom Literature*

Traditional approaches to wisdom literature have by no means vanished from the contemporary scene. Lennart Boström's *The God of the Sages* looks at the view of God in Proverbs, concentrating on the notion of creation and the belief in a personal relationship between believer and High God.[65] Boström replaces the descriptive term 'act–consequence' with 'character–consequence', which he thinks more accurately reflects the ancient teaching about order as subject to Yahweh's activity.[66] Boström also discerns a higher degree of

62. Bolle, 'Wisdom in Akkadian Literature', p. 280.

63. I have attempted to provide some observations on the sages' rhetoric in 'Wisdom and Authority: Sapiential Rhetoric and its Warrants', in *Congress Volume, Vienna 1980* (ed. J.A. Emerton; VTSup, 32; Leiden: Brill, 1981), pp. 10-29.

64. Katharine J. Dell, *The Book of Job as Sceptical Literature* (BZAW, 197; Berlin: de Gruyter, 1991), pp. 57-107; Bruce Zuckerman, *Job the Silent* (New York: Oxford University Press, 1991); Edwin M. Good, *In Turns of Tempest* (Stanford: Stanford University Press, 1990).

65. Lennart Boström, *The God of the Sages* (ConBOT, 29; Stockholm: Almqvist & Wiksell, 1990). T.N.D. Mettinger, *In Search of God* (Philadelphia: Fortress Press, 1988), pp. 175-200, emphasizes the transition in the book of Job from a hidden to a revealed God.

66. On the place of 'order' in current research, see my essay, 'Murphy's Axiom: Every Gnomic Saying Needs a Balancing Corrective', in *The Listening Heart: Essays in Wisdom and the Psalms in Honor of Roland E. Murphy, O. Carm.* (ed. Kenneth G. Hoglund *et al.*; JSOTSup, 58; Sheffield:

readiness in Israel to speak of an intimate relationship with
the creator than in Egypt, even during the period of deep
piety there.[67] In some respects Boström joins hands with Jon
Levenson, whose *Creation and the Persistence of Evil* highlights the resistant force of chaos alluded to in many biblical
texts.[68]

In a paper in memory of John Gammie,[69] I looked once more
at Johannes Fichtner's conclusions concerning Israelite sages'
reluctance to attribute grace to the deity, in contrast with
Egyptian and Mesopotamian wisdom literature. On the basis
of a fresh analysis of key texts, it is possible to nuance
Fichtner's hypothesis somewhat differently without denying
its essential validity.

Conclusion

In this brief survey of recent research, I do not claim to do
justice to the many fine articles on wisdom literature falling
outside the rubrics selected for discussion. Perhaps I shall be
forgiven if I mention one further area of research: the endea-
vor to locate larger units within collections of proverbs.[70] Of
course, such studies deploy the roguish 'reader response' theory
of literary critics,[71] but the supposed connections between
quite diverse sayings also raise the issue that H.-J. Hermisson

JSOT Press, 1987). One can posit the importance of order in the ancient
sapiential worldview without deifying the concept. In Israel Yahweh had
the final word, and the same can probably be said of Egypt's High God.

67. Williams, 'The Sage in Egyptian Literature', p. 22.

68. Jon Levenson, *Creation and the Persistence of Evil* (San Francisco:
Harper & Row, 1988).

69. James L. Crenshaw, 'The Concept of God in Old Testament
Wisdom', in *In Search of Wisdom: Essays in Memory of John G. Gammie*
(ed. Leo G. Perdue and Brandon Scott; Philadelphia: Westminster/John
Knox), forthcoming.

70. Ted Hildebrandt, 'Proverbial Pairs: Compositional Units in Proverbs
10–29', *JBL* 107 (1988), pp. 207-24; Raymond C. Van Leeuwen, *Context
and Meaning in Proverbs 25–27* (SBLDS, 96; Atlanta: Scholars Press,
1988).

71. David W. Cotter, *A Study of Job 4–5 in the Light of Contemporary
Literary Theory* (SBLDS, 124; Atlanta: Scholars Press, 1992), pp. 97-105.

tried to lay to rest,[72] namely the differences between folk and literary proverbs, on which some light has now come from Africa.[73] Michael Fishbane's perceptive studies on inner-biblical midrash relate to this problem,[74] for his approach assumes wide familiarity with a written biblical text by many ancient readers. If my conclusions about literacy in Israel are reasonably accurate, scholars will need to exercise considerably more restraint in regard to citations of biblical texts.[75] In any event, scholarly interest in sociological and literary interpretations of wisdom promises to enrich more conventional approaches. Perhaps all of these endeavors will clarify the manner in which ancient peoples achieved knowledge and explain the esteem in which learning was held.

72. H.-J. Hermisson, *Studien zur israelitischen Spruchweisheit* (Neukirchen–Vluyn: Neukirchener Verlag, 1968).

73. Claus Westermann, 'Weisheit im Sprichwort', in *Schalom: Studien zu Glaube und Geschichte Israels, Alfred Jepsen zum 70. Geburtstag* (ed. K.H. Bernhardt; Arbeiten zur Theologie, 46; Stuttgert: Calwer Verlag (1971), pp. 73-85; F.W. Golka, 'Die israelitische Weisheitsschule oder "des Kaisers neue Kleider"', *VT* 33 (1983), pp. 257-70; 'Die Konigs- und Hofsprüche und der Ursprung der israelitischen Weisheit', *VT* 36 (1986), pp. 13-36; 'Die Flecken des Leoparden. Biblische und afrikanische Weisheit im Sprichwort', in *Schöpfung und Befreiung: für Claus Westermann zum 80. Geburtstag* (ed. R. Albertz; Stuttgart: Calwer Verlag, 1989), pp. 149-65; and Lawrent Naré, *Proverbes salomoniens et proverbes mossi* (Publications Universitaires Européens; Frankfurt am Main: Peter Lang, 1986).

74. Michael Fishbane, *Biblical Interpretation in Ancient Israel* (Oxford: Clarendon Press, 1985).

75. Contrast the monograph on the book of Joel by Siegfried Bergler, *Joel als Schriftinterpret* (Beiträge zur Erforschung des Alten Testaments und des antiken Judentums, 16; Frankfurt am Main: Peter Lang, 1988).

MEMORY AND ENCOUNTER: AN EDUCATIONAL IDEAL

John Eaton

The prevailing educational tradition of our time discourages
memorization and dutiful reproduction. Students from other
traditions are sometimes surprised to find that, having reproduced their lecturer's words exactly, they fail their examination, even though the same lecturer was among the examiners.
How bewildering, after childhood years in the home country
when education was all learning and repeating! How difficult
to develop the required 'critical ability' and 'originality'! But
even more bewildering is the idea that 'teaching' itself may be
frowned on as a handing down from the top! Better, the
theory goes, if nothing positive is imposed! Rather create a
situation in which something may emerge from below!

   Are we here touching on a clash of cultures—new against
old, west against east? At all events, it is likely that not all the
trends presently prevailing in education will be permanent.
Social changes and crises will ensure that educational methods are reconsidered. There may be fresh interest in the practice of former generations. And so this essay, in honour of one
who has written much on the intellectual tradition of biblical
times, will concern some Israelite approaches to the education
and formation of the individual and the society. Where did
the Israelites stand in matters of learning by heart, recitation,
critical ability, originality, teaching with authority, the effort
to form character?

1. *At the Feet of the Sage*

No doubt the characteristic 'wisdom' sayings, brief and poetic,
were well suited for memorization. They were, says the sage

in Prov. 22.18, pleasant to take deep into one's belly, ready to be deployed fluently upon the lips. But the sages stressed the need for critical ability in their use:

> Limp hang the legs of the lame—
> no less a proverb from the mouth of fools (Prov. 26.7).

Wise judgment was needed to match word to situation:

> Apples of gold in silver filigree—
> so the saying said in its right moment (25.11).

The sayings were not to be learnt without being pondered. They were meant to stimulate meditation, to provoke the mind to habits of discernment. The sayings of the wise were like goads (Eccl. 12.11). Their sharpness would hurt the unthinking user like a brier clutched by a drunk (Prov. 26.9).

So the teacher strove to cultivate discernment in the reception and use of proverbs; the aim was to 'discern discerning sayings' (1.2), 'to discern proverb and figure' (1.6). Discernment, *hînâ*, was synonymous with wisdom. It was the fault of Job's counsellors that they trotted out the teachings without discernment. Theirs were sayings not fitted to the occasion, proverbs hanging limp from the mouth of fools. The skill of the dramatist here almost makes us forget the folly of this misapplication, but it is plainly denounced in the end in the speech of God (Job 42.7).

For the development of discernment, the sage considered several things necessary.[1] Important here was a realistic appraisal of the limits of human understanding. One had to be aware that, however much effort was put into thought and planning, it was the divine purpose that would stand (Prov. 19.21). The wisest may attain to wonder at the God who stretches out the sky-vault over the void and hangs the earth on nothing, yet these are but the fringes of his ways, and how small a whisper do we hear of him (Job 26.7-8)!

The worst bar to developing discernment is to think oneself

---

1. We meet here the interrelation of the sage's favourite themes, which I have tried to display in my *The Contemplative Face of Old Testament Wisdom* (London: SCM Press; Philadelphia: Trinity Press International, 1989).

wise (Prov. 26.12). The sage treats with heavy irony the one who speaks as though having mastered the mysteries. Such a know-all might well be called Mr I-am-God (Ithi-el, cf. Aramaic *'yty* 'I am') or I-am-God-and-I-can-do-it (Ithi-el-wa-ukal); perhaps he would kindly explain to us who have not yet attained wisdom all about the divine work in heaven and earth which he seems to have a decisive hand in (30.1-4)![2]

The key to discernment could be expressed as the 'hearing heart'. Such was the one thing in all the world which the ideal young king desired in order to 'discern' (1 Kgs 3.9). This wonderful educational ideal implies a teachable and open mind, the gift of sympathetic attention, the power of observation, and above all an ear for truth, a listening to the divine voice and a readiness to follow it.

Nowhere does the sage speak of his educational aim as being to inculcate a body of knowledge. Little trace has he left of his syllabus. The goal of his course is expressed as his pupil's attainment of 'the fear of the LORD' and 'the knowledge of God', the fruit of much attention, asking and seeking (2.1-5). This fear will be something to 'discern', and this knowledge something to 'find' (as something graciously given). Such is the 'wisdom', 'knowledge' and 'discernment' that are in view (2.6). It would not seem that one could complete the sage's course, unlike some of ours, in an atmosphere of pride, self-congratulation, honours and titles.

2. *Education in the Worshipping Community*

Deuteronomy and several kindred texts attach great importance to the teaching of the history of the nation's dealings with God. At first sight this might well seem to be a case of

---

2. The name Ithiel is found also in Neh. 11.7 and may originally have meant either 'El exists' or 'El is with me' (see L. Koehler, *Hebräisches und aramäisches Lexikon zum Alten Testament* [Leiden: Brill, 3rd edn, 1967], p. 43). The latter meaning would fit my general interpretation here, but the weight of the irony in this passage and the contrast with the preceding 'the man' incline me to think the name is here understood as I have rendered it.

sheer indoctrination, as each generation was taught the heavily interpreted version of history from an early age. But again, we shall see that the undertaking had some aspects worthy of note in a consideration of formative education.[3] For convenience we may distinguish six such aspects as follows.

1. Obligation was laid on the community to perpetuate remembrance of the events of its origin. The events were recounted as purposeful deeds of God that must be rehearsed and taught to each new generation. At their heart was the deliverance from slavery in Egypt, the covenant of God and people established at Mount Sinai, and the leading into a homeland.

Such stress was laid on this obligation to remember that it was even said that the deeds of salvation were done to create the remembrance. The miracles in Egypt, it is said in Exod. 10.2, were done in order that Moses, and indeed every Israelite, might tell in the ears of their children and grand-children what God had done. From the first, according to Deut. 4.0, the Israelites were taught to guard their soul lest they allow what their own eyes had seen at Horeb to slip from their heart; all through their life they must so beware, and be sure to make these things known to their descendants.

2. The story that must be thus taught and kept in the active memory included within it a call to a way of life. For at the heart of the narration is the proclamation of the command-ments, expressing God's will for the shaping of the new life of this rescued people. They have been freed from the service of tyrants into the service of the Lord. Deliverance and command-ments merge in the story of redemption. Thus the Israelite is told in Deut. 6.20-24:

---

3.   An interesting treatment of Israel's narrative recitals has been given by Walter Brueggemann, *Abiding Astonishment: Psalms, Modernity and the Making of History* (Louisville: Westminster/John Knox Press, 1991). His starting point is in Psalms 78, 105, 106 and 136. He finds the recital grating against the 'Establishment' in that it exalts the independent, overruling will of God, while from another point of view it jars with the experience of the innocent oppressed. He gives good extensive bibliography in the area of history and rhetoric, memory and recital.

> When in time to come your child asks you, 'What is the meaning
> of the testimonies, statutes and orders which the LORD our God
> has commanded you?', you shall say to your child, 'We were
> Pharaoh's slaves in Egypt, and the LORD brought us out of
> Egypt with a mighty hand, and the LORD gave signs and
> portents, great and harmful, on Egypt, Pharaoh and all his
> household before our eyes, but he brought us out from there in
> order to bring us in, to give us the land as he had sworn to our
> fathers. And the LORD commanded us to do all these statutes
> to fear the LORD our God for our good always, that he might
> give us new life as we have this day.

Similarly in Ps. 78.3-7 divine works and commandments are woven together.[4] Not without a note of mystery, the singer tells of the deep events,

> which we heard and knew
> for our fathers recounted them to us.
> We will not hide them from their children,
> recounting for a future generation the LORD's praises
> and his strength and the miracles he did.
> And he established a testimony in Jacob
> and appointed a law in Israel,
> commanding our fathers
> to make them known to their children,
> that the coming generation should know them,
> the children yet to be born,
> so that they in turn should tell them to their children
> and set their hope in God,
> and not forget the deeds of God,
> but keep his commandments.

It is not just that salvation is followed by allegiance to the Saviour; rather, it consists in such allegiance. His *tôrâ* and commandments—his guiding words—are thus a necessary feature of the life of salvation, showing how the relationship

---

4. In a carefully argued treatment, Otto Eissfeldt shows the affinity of Psalm 78 with the Song of Moses (Deut. 32), and gives good grounds for dating these recitals back to the Davidic–Solomonic period: *Das Lied Moses Deuteronomium 32.1-43 und das Lehrgedicht Asaphs Psalm 78* (Berlin: Akademie Verlag, 1958). Aubrey R. Johnson also argues for a Solomonic date for Psalm 78, giving a good exposition, in *The Cultic Prophet and Israel's Psalmody* (Cardiff: University of Wales Press, 1979), pp. 45-66.

can be maintained. So Moses concludes his rehearsal of the sacred teaching (Deut. 32.46-47):

> Set your heart on all the words which I testify to you today, which you shall command your children... for it is no empty speech—it is your very life.

3. The work of remembrance, involving learning, reciting and handing down, brings the original experiences into the present. What happened then becomes the experience of those engaged in the remembrance. To them, now, God is disclosing himself with his same 'I am the LORD' (Exod. 10.2).

This aspect is clear in the observances of worship where remembrance was made both by recital and by elements of dramatic re-enactment. The Passover meal, for example, links with the meal of the ancient story. For the participants, down through the generations, the past becomes present; the ancient freedom is known now.[5]

4. But there is an important qualification in such identification that the worshippers make with the first generation. True, the celebrating worshippers easily pass from 'them' to 'us' as the characters in the story. In Ps. 66.5-6 they say:

> Come and see the deeds of God,
> as he shows himself terrible in action over mankind.
> He turns the sea into dry land,
> they cross through the river on foot.
> There let us rejoice in him!

And the speech of the manifest God makes the same transition in Ps. 81.7-8:

> I removed his shoulder from the load,
> his hands went free from the brick-tub.
> In the affliction you called and I delivered you,
> I answered you from the thunder-cloud,
> I tested you beside the waters of Meriba.

---

5. On re-enactments and creative drama a basic discussion is provided by Sigmund Mowinckel in his *Religion und Kultus* (Göttingen: Vandenhoeck & Ruprecht, 1953), pp. 73-80. See also my *The Psalms Come Alive* (Oxford: Mowbray, 1984; Downers Grove, IL: Inter-Varsity Press, 1986), pp. 116-29.

> Hear, my people, as I admonish you!
> If only, Israel, you would listen to me!...
> I am the LORD your God
> who brought you up from the land of Egypt—
> open wide your mouth and I will fill it full!

But such identification of present rememberers with the original generation is not without critical awareness. There is no heroic generation to serve as role models. The aim of the remembrance is to come to the place where the fundamental salvation is given and make the response that the ancestors failed to make. The account handed down had a critical spirit. In remembrance one must discriminate. One must set one's hope in God—unlike the fathers, that stubborn and rebellious generation, devious in heart, fickle in spirit (Ps. 78.7-8).

5. The activity of remembrance, with its work of teaching, receiving and reciting, is a continual work of formation. It is not done just to initiate a new generation, nor to renew the knowledge in great seasonal celebrations. It is to extend through every day, so that society and all its members may be formed in a disposition towards God and maintained in it. In Deuteronomy it is stressed again and again that any generation or individual that neglects the rehearsing and remembering will soon fall away from awareness of the life-giving revelation and so become a slave to human folly:

> Only be watchful regarding yourself, and guard your soul with great care, lest you forget the things your own eyes have seen, and they slip away from your heart all the days of your life (Deut. 4.9).

The healthful, formative words of God are to be remembered so constantly that they become woven with the stuff of daily routine. In 6.6-9 this is expressed in vivid metaphors based on such practices as tattooing and wearing of pendants as a sign of cultic allegiance:

> And these words which I command you today must be upon your heart, and you must impress them upon your children, and speak of them when you sit down in your house and when you walk along the way, when you lie down and when you rise up. And you must bind them for a sign upon your hand, and they shall be as frontlets between your eyes, and you must write them upon the doorposts of your house and upon your gates.

6. The whole undertaking of remembrance is understood to flow from the initiative of God and to be sustained through co-operation with him. It is seen as his chosen means for his historic salvation through all generations, uniting thus all descendants in the community of the freed, the fellowship of those who walk with him, having his words upon their heart.

We have noted the idea that he planned this remembrance in advance of the great deliverance (Exod. 10.2) and we have seen how earnestly his prophet enjoins his will for its maintenance. The priesthood too, the sanctuary, the liturgy, and the sacred observances in family life—all receive their validity from divine ordinance, and all contribute to the remembrance. Strenuous as is the human part in fixing the mind on the will and work of God, it is made possible by the divine power which runs through the whole undertaking. Loving him so 'with all your strength', you are constantly embraced and upheld by him. To take part in this divine work is indeed to receive life from God.[6]

---

6.   A similar analysis can be made of the New Testament's version of remembrance—evidence of the continuing importance of such recital in religion: (1) There was now a careful handing down of the apostolic account of the divine acts in Jesus from which the community had sprung (Lk. 1.1-2; 1 Cor. 15.3-7). (2) With the narratives of Jesus were bound his words. His people are freed into a new obedience (Lk. 1.74-75). They live in a 'pattern of teaching' in which they have been 'traditioned' (Rom. 6.17). (3) Receiving the tradition, they also receive Christ, learn him, are united with him (Col. 2.6-7; Eph. 4.20-24). In baptism and eucharist, along with recital of the original acts, comes experience of the Saviour. (4) The identification of the believer with Christ is not a glib assumption of superior being but an exposure to the creative might of God. The believer shares the fellowship of Christ's death and resurrection through faith in the working of God (Phil. 3.10; Col. 2.6-12). Critical awareness governs regard for the pioneer generation. Their inadequate behaviour is frankly remembered. One joins with them only to come close to the Saviour's presence. (5) The community and its members, through the rehearsal and reliving of the sacred story, are ever in process of formation (Eph. 4.11-16; Gal. 4.19), in opposition to the fashioning influences of a godless world (Rom. 12.2). The process continues until God's final work of conformation (1 Cor. 15.62; Phil. 3.21). (6) The commemorating tradition is 'from the Lord' (1 Cor. 11.23). God's Spirit teaches, brings to remembrance, witnesses of Christ, guides (Jn 14.26; 15.26; 16.13-14). The apostles are

3. *Songs of Devotion to the Lord as Teacher*

Ideas of education and formation through memory, recital and reflection are illumined also by psalms that exalt God as teacher and guide. The most obvious psalms with this theme are Psalms 1, 19, 25 and 119, and we shall now consider these in turn from this point of view.

Psalm 1 pictures the pious person as absorbed day and night in an intoned recital (verb *hāgâ*) of the Lord's teaching (*tôrâ*). Though comparison with Josh. 1.8 suggests that such recital is aided by a scroll, memory must in any case play a big part. Through memorization, fluency is attained, and the words sink deep into the soul, justifying the comparison with the tree. Transplanted beside constant channels of water, the tree draws on the life-source and flourishes continually. So the ardent reciters of the Lord's teachings draw blessing through the roots of their being, as they are held in communion with the will and person of the Lord.

That such recital includes responses in formulas of appreciation and praise is suggested by another occurrence of the root *hāgâ*, Ps. 19.15. The singer has sent up like an offering the words of his mouth and the resounding (*higgāyôn*) of his heart. His words have included thankful appreciation of the Lord's teaching (*tôrâ*)—commandments that bestow new health, wisdom and joy. The manifold terms for this teaching reflect the singer's devotion and his appreciation of the richness of the guidance: it is instruction, testimony, order, command, rule—but every term is always qualified by attachment to the divine name; only as the breath of the living Lord is this teaching valued. The resonant meditation is an offering to this Lord, 'my Rock and my Redeemer' (19.15).

Psalm 25 is interesting in that it does not use the main synonyms for the Lord's teaching and commandments, and so

15.26; 16.13-14). The apostles are ministering assistants of the sacred word (Lk. 1.2), devoted to its service (Acts 6.4). The various teachers and speakers are enabled by God (Eph. 4.11; 1 Cor. 12.28). Apostolic word and proclamation mediate holy power (1 Cor. 2.4). In all this the Holy Spirit is at work as a pledge of the final transformation (2 Cor. 1.22; Eph. 1.1-14; 4.30).

may reflect the piety preceding the *tôrâ* eulogies of Psalms 19 and 119. What is taught is repeatedly designated a 'way'; the teaching conveys a pattern of life, guidance for a daily journey into ever closer relation with God the teacher. It is the verbs for his teaching that abound in this psalm. He 'causes to learn' (*limmēd*, vv. 4, 5, 9), 'causes to know' (*hôdîaʻ*, vv. 4, 14), 'guides' or 'instructs' (*hôrâ*, vv. 8, 12), 'shows the way' (*hidrîk*, vv. 5, 9). The circle round the teacher is a circle of intimates (*sôd*, v. 14), a friendly group where each is well known and trusted.[7] In this circle the teaching Lord leads each one into practical knowledge of the fellowship-bond (v. 14). The disciple's eyes are fixed on him (v. 15).

The figure of teaching and learning is strongly maintained in Psalm 119, where the synonyms for the Lord's teaching and words of direction are lavishly deployed in a huge acrostic.[8] The singer would 'learn' the commandments (*lāmad*, vv. 7, 71, 73). He is keen to remember them (*zākar*, vv. 52, 55) and not 'forget' them (*šākaḥ*, vv. 16, 61, 93, 109, 141, 153, 176). From the mouth of God he repeats aloud (*sippēr*, v. 13) with his lips the divine orders. The Lord imparts the learning (*limmēd*, vv. 26, 64, 68, 108, 124, 135, 171; cf. 99), enables him to 'know' (*yādaʻ*, v. 125; cf. 66), instructs and guides (*hôrâ*, vv. 33, 102). As in Psalms 1 and 25, the teaching amounts to a 'way', giving value and direction to the daily life (vv. 1, 9, 15, 27, 32, 105).

But all this learning, reciting and care not to forget the numerous directions voiced by the divine teacher is but a foundation course. The mature study is a matter of insight, research (verb *dāraš*, v. 94), and discovery with the force of revelation. The recitations involve meditation and contemplation (verbs *śîaḥ* and *hibbîṭ*, v. 15). With love and reverence

---

7.   The context supports Ludwig Koehler's *Hebräisches und aramäisches Lexikon* (Leiden: Brill, 1st edn, 1953), p. 651, in taking *sôd* here as 'Kreis von Vertrauten', against the third edition (1967/1983, pp. 703-704) with 'Plan, Geheimnis (als Folge oder Ergebnis der Besprechung)'.

8.   A good treatment of this psalm has been given by Will Soll, *Psalm 119: Matrix, Form and Setting* (Washington: Catholic Biblical Association of America, 1991). He inclines to see it as a lament of Jehoiachin.

for the subject-matter, the path of constant meditation is opened (vv. 48, 97, 148; cf. 99).

Through such meditation comes experience of deeper regions of meaning; discernment is graciously given, and wonder awakened (v. 27; cf. 99). Frequently the student-psalmist asks for this gift of discernment, for only with this can he accord with the commandments wholeheartedly (v. 34), only then indeed can he meaningfully learn and know them (vv. 73, 125). And he rejoices that discernment has been given (vv. 95, 100, 104).

This is to reach the point where the Lord's words are opened; light breaks from them, giving insight to the simplest (v. 130). With such insight, the soul truly comes alive (v. 144). It is an experience of revelation, when the Lord uncovers the inner eye and it beholds in or through the commandments marvellous things (*niplā'ôt*, v. 18). Previously the commandments were 'hidden' (v. 19), and the soul was crushed with longing for them in their revealed beauty (v. 20). For these marvels (*pᵉlā'ôt*, v. 129) one yearned and panted with mouth agape (v. 131). At their disclosure, the body trembled and hair bristled (v. 120).

Bernhard Duhm, who treated this psalm with scorn in his commentary, *Die Psalmen*,[9] remarked that it was a pity the psalmist had not thought to share with us some of the wonders he had discovered in the *tôrâ* and helped us understand the joy derived from his research into the food laws, and so forth. But the psalm is referring to an experience of passing through the recited material to an apprehension of the divine. The Lord's teaching has become a flood of grace, answering the prayer 'Grace me your teaching' (*tôrātᵉkā ḥonnēnî*, v. 29).

Conclusion

From Section 1 it is apparent that the value of critical judgment was well understood in ancient Israel. The material handed down by the sages for learning and reciting had to be

9. Bernhard Duhm, *Die Psalmen* (KHAT, 14; Freiburg: J.C.B. Mohr, 1899; 2nd edn, 1922).

used with discernment and discrimination. They regarded the critical faculty as essential, but they cultivated it within a total spiritual disposition that included humility, awe and openness of the whole person to the truth.

Though the education given by the sages may seem rather distinct from the Deuteronomic type of teaching, it is generally recognized that they share some common ground.[10] The sage's value of critical judgment, 'discernment', has some counterpart in all the materials we have surveyed. Forefathers, customarily honoured, were criticized sharply in a way that also challenged the consciences of the rememberers. The teaching handed down was described as thought-provoking—'proverb' (*māšāl*) and 'riddles' (*ḥîdôt*) needing much attention and pondering (Ps. 78.2).

In Section 2 we noted in the worshipping community the ideal of a great story handed down, and kept ever in mind by recitation and other acts of remembrance. It spoke to community and individual of their origins, the purpose and pattern of their living, and of the Good that they should ever love and embrace. The constant remembrance of the story was to fill their lives with its values and with the One who gave the values. It was maintained that neglect of the remembrance would bring enslavement to false values.

From Section 3 we gain the impression that the life of remembrance was like living inside a poem. The poem, created and refined in tradition, was an interpretation of the world, of history and existence. It embodied profound insights, and those who lived in it by remembering it continually were embraced, guided and nourished by it. Our psalms showed how those who lived in the poem could become poets themselves. They respond poetically, singing to their Poet-teacher of his grace as a way, as water of life, as light and sweetness, as counsel of friendship, as revelation of divine beauty.

Modern seekers of God should find much that is meaningful

10. See, for example, Moshe Weinfeld, *Deuteronomy and the Deuteronomic School* (Oxford: Clarendon Press, 1971); and, with reference to Wisdom psalms, Leo G. Perdue, *Wisdom and Cult* (Missoula, MT: Scholars Press, 1977), and Robert Davidson, *Wisdom and Worship* (London: SCM Press; Philadelphia: Trinity Press International, 1990).

in the ideals and practices we have considered—the listening heart dear to the sage, the Deuteronomic living in a story, the poetic communion of the psalmists. The modern seekers may recognize that they too need the means to keep their soul alert and open to God, defended from false values and seductions, and they too will find the means in a great memory, narrative and poetic, that they receive, interpret and hand on.

But even our secular education could beneficially engage with the convictions underlying the Israelite ideals. Here were people who through generations were sure they had something vital to hand down, something worth learning, reciting and pondering. It took the form of a story, in effect a great poem that encompassed and interpreted life, distinguished true values and moulded conduct. It was a story of the Good and gave experience of the Good, leaving no vacuum for poisonous things to fill. It nourished a healthful formation. All the effort of imparting it was met and borne along by a force of rightness, as though the educators had struck on something deep in the purpose of life. Critical ability, discernment, lively response, creativity—all found their place in hearts that could listen in patience and humility, hearts that had no greater ambition than wholly to love the Good that first loved them.

SOME OBSERVATIONS ON THE FIGURATIONS OF WOMAN IN
WISDOM LITERATURE

Athalya Brenner

> This study is presented with admiration and gratitude to
> Professor Norman Whybray, a wise scholar; and to Ms Mary
> Whybray, a wise woman.

When I choose to consider figurations of woman in Wisdom
and Wisdom-related texts from a feminist perspective, two
questions keep insinuating themselves into my mind. 1. What
are the figurations women are imaged (projected) into in this
literary genre? 2. Do these figurations reflect male (M) interests, male perspectives, as conceded by feminist and non-
feminist critics alike?[1] Or do they also, in some or a number of
cases, reflect female (F) interests and perspectives?[2] In short,
whose gender ideologies might these images of woman serve?
This survey is addressed to these two closely bound issues in
the hope of contributing some guidelines towards rereading
Wisdom-type biblical texts.

For the purpose of this survey, the descriptive title 'Wisdom
texts' will refer to the Books of Proverbs, Job and Qoheleth, as
customary in Bible research. In addition, it will include Wisdom-

---

1. For instance, in C.V. Camp, *Wisdom and the Feminine in the Book
of Proverbs* (Sheffield: Almond Press, 1985), and in C. Newsom, 'Woman
and the Discourse of Patriarchal Wisdom: A Study of Proverbs 1–9', in
P.L. Day (ed.), *Gender and Difference in Ancient Israel* (Minneapolis:
Fortress Press, 1989), pp. 142-60—both in reference to Proverbs.

2. My terminology is M for male/masculine, F for female/feminine. See
further, for the terminology and for the gender definition of a text by its
perspective or 'signature', 'Introduction', in A. Brenner and F. van Dijk-
Hemmes, *On Gendering Texts: Female and Male Voices in the Hebrew
Bible* (Leiden: Brill, 1993), pp. 1-11.

related textual blocs that contain the 'inferior stranger
achieves success' Wisdom paradigm—passages from the Joseph
story, the book of Esther, and Daniel. In all these texts, apart
from Job (which belongs to the same genre by scholarly consent), there obtains a preoccupation with women, femininity
and gender relations. This preoccupation with F matters is
especially manifest within two loci of these literary discourses:

1. Rhetorical devices: metaphors, hyperboles, similes and
   repeated idioms.
2. Narrational focalization.[3]

We shall now proceed to examine the material pertaining to
F figurations in each of the text blocs listed, bearing in mind
that the alleged M discourse in which the figurations feature
might perhaps turn out to contain instances of suppressed,
misquoted or misread F discourses.

Female Figurations in Proverbs

Biblical scholarship has traditionally defined Proverbs as an
M document, presented as recorded speech acts, delivered by
M [elder] teachers to M [younger] recipients for the latter's
educational benefit. This seems to be strongly implied by the
'father's teaching of son' convention recurrent in it. The curi-
ous fact that the book is enveloped at each end by F
figurations and metaphors—the זרה[4] woman, Woman Wisdom,
and Woman Folly at its beginning, chs. 1–9; the sayings and
images of ch. 30, culminating in the instruction of King
Lemuel's mother and the Worthy Woman acrostic poem of ch.
31—is almost universally attributed to ambivalent male
fascination with females and sex and the utilization of that

---

3. For the concept of 'focalization', the perspectives through which a
discourse is delivered by its narrator(s) and figures, see M. Bal, *Narratology:
An Introduction to the Theory of Narrative* (Toronto: Toronto University
Press, 1985).
4. The Hebrew term strongly defies translation. It may denote
'foreign' ethnically or, in a more limited sense, socially; 'strange'; 'liminal';
or, much more simply, an 'other'. In order to avoid an attempt to clarify
the term, which is not an easy task, I prefer to retain the Hebrew term.

fascination for didactic purposes. This working hypothesis has heretofore informed all readings of the text, non-feminist and feminist alike. Even Carol Newsom, who illuminates the numerous instances of F discourse in Proverbs 1–9 with great insight, insists that these discourses are 'quoted' within the dominant frame of M discourse.[5] A study made by Fokkelien van Dijk-Hemmes and myself[6] indicates that, on the contrary, a few grounds can be found in the text for reading at least this 'envelope' or parts thereof as echoes of direct (in contra-distinction to 'quoted')[7] F voices or discourses. I shall here summarize some of these grounds, or pointers.

A preoccupation with female figures can cut both ways. Whether we interpret this textual attitude as signifying male interest or female interest is a moot point. If it seems simpler, on this count, to dismiss the attempt to gender texts as insignificant or unfeasible, such a critical move would exclude some specific interests that motivate womanly readers of both sexes. Therefore, wherever applicable, both suggestions for gender reading should be offered and presented as possessing equally valid status for the reading procedure.

Attaching gender motivation to positive or negative evalua-tions of femaleness/femininity, both in evidence in Proverbs 1–9, is not always helpful. I adopt the Hegelian position that stipulates that, within the pattern of master–slave dynamics, collaboration with and defence of the dominant (in this case, M) socio-ethical ideology is often undertaken by the inferior partner (in this case women) even when not beneficial for the latter. F voices can be as critical of their own kind as—and conceivably even more so than—M voices emanating from a text. The passages about the זרה woman and Woman Folly are instructive in this regard. They can be read as an example of the internalization of cultural stereotypes by members of both

---

5. Newsom, 'Woman and the Discourse of Patriarchal Wisdom', pp. 142-60.

6. Brenner and van Dijk-Hemmes, *On Gendering Texts*.

7. Admittedly, written literature is, strictly speaking, always 'quoted'. By 'direct' I here imply a focalizing narrator using a F voice, to be distin-guished from a narrating M voice that reports F speech and describes F phenomena.

genders. The attribution of a gendered 'signature' to a text through an analysis of the seemingly stereotypic role-casting in it may not yield unequivocal results. A loaded attitude can, once again, be interpreted both ways. By itself, a value judgment inherent in the presentations of F figurations cannot serve as a reliable criterion for gendering a text or its focalizer(s).

The warnings against the זרה woman in Proverbs 1–9 (2.16-19; 5.3-14, 20-23; 6.24-26) reach a climax in the dramatic 'story' of ch. 7. This passage is ostensibly a report delivered by an onlooker sitting 'at the window'. That onlooking speaker-in-the-text is commonly identified as a male teacher. Since, apart from Abimelech (Gen. 26.8), in other biblical instances the person at the (latticed) window is always a woman depicted as a wife or mother (Sisera's mother, Judg. 5.28; Michal, 2 Sam. 6.16; Jezebel, 2 Kgs 9.30), there is no reason to assume here that the literary voice of the (maternal) onlooker belongs to a M textual speaker.[8] The attribution of this warning to a F voice is at least as feasible as the usual (M attributed) choice; and it may entail considerable significance for the comprehension of some, or all, of the passages dealing with the זרה. It so happens that the vexing problematic of the זרה woman/women is far from being satisfactorily resolved by attributing the image to M voices expressing M fears and a sense of threat.[9] F fears of an Other, an attractive woman, an outsider, might supply as strong, if not a stronger, motivation for this textual figuration.

Other considerations for gendering Proverbs texts link up with the problem of these texts' placement in a conjectured life

8. See van Dijk-Hemmes, 'The I Persona in Proverbs 7', in *On Gendering Texts*, pp. 57-62; and Brenner, *ibid.*, p. 120. It must be stated, however, that all the female onlookers outside Proverbs are depicted negatively in the texts cited, whereas in Proverbs, according to my interpretation, the proposed F figuration epitomizes positive (maternal, moralistic and moralizing) traits.

9. But cf. Camp's illuminating analyses: 'Wise and Strange: An Interpretation of the Female Imagery in Proverbs in Light of Trickster Mythology', *Semeia* 42 (1988), pp. 14-36; 'What's so Strange about the Strange Woman?', in P.L. Day *et al.* (eds.), *The Bible and the Politics of Exegesis* (New York: Pilgrim Press, 1991).

situation that is perhaps reflected in them to a greater or lesser extent. There is no scholarly consensus about the educational situation invoked in Proverbs 1–9 and elsewhere in this Book, beyond the observation of its configuration as a parent/child relationship.[10] Should this conventionalized description be understood as a metaphorical reference to a 'school' situation? Institutional 'schools' for elite male youth might be conjectured, but ultimately remain within the realm of informed speculation. If the natural locus of education is the home, as reflected in the parent-to-child address, then it stands to reason that references to maternal as well as paternal authority have to be looked for in the text.[11]

In fact, 'mother's instruction' is referred to in numerous passages. Admittedly, within the bound phrase 'father and mother', 'mother' comes second. However, her instruction is certainly invoked. Moreover, the description of Woman Wisdom includes maternal traits,[12] and that of the Worthy Woman, a wife and mother, contains a reference to her 'wisdom' and 'teaching' (תורה, חכמה, Prov. 31.26). It seems that in Proverbs, in addition to the father–son teaching convention, there is also a mother–son (Lemuel's mother, 31.1), perhaps also a mother–daughter, convention.[13] This interpretative

10. See, for instance, M. Haran, 'On the Diffusion of Literacy and Schools in Ancient Israel', in *Congress Volume, Jerusalem 1986* (ed. J.A. Emerton; VTSup, 40; Leiden: Brill, 1988); J. Crenshaw, 'Education in Ancient Israel', *JBL* 104 (1985), pp. 601-15.

11. Camp, *Wisdom and the Feminine*. So also C. Meyers, *Discovering Eve* (New York: Oxford University Press, 1988), pp. 152-64. She hypothesizes that both parents were responsible for their children's acquirement of basic learning skills, and that this responsibility extended to children of both genders.

12. Such as feeding, training, primary education and general care. Cf. Camp, *Wisdom and the Feminine*, and her 'Woman Wisdom as Root Metaphor: A Theological Consideration', in K.G. Hoglund *et al.* (eds.), *The Listening Heart: Essays in Wisdom and the Psalms Presented to Roland E. Murphy* (JSOTSup, 58; Sheffield: JSOT Press, 1987), pp. 56-76. Also see Brenner, in *On Gendering Texts*, pp. 117-19.

13. The Worthy Woman poem (Prov. 31.10-31) is traditionally understood as M praise for a female paragon of virtue, that is, a good wife and mother by M standards. The collaboration paradigm as well as other literary (and historical) considerations raise the possibility of 'a woman's

option has previously not been given serious consideration in either ancient or modern biblical scholarship by anyone apart from Claudia Camp.

The imaging of Wisdom as daughter is another pointer in the same direction. It is worth noting how the literary construct of Wisdom as a divine daughter (8.22-31) is contextualized: it is embedded inside the more usual construct of Wisdom as a teacher/mother (8.1-21, 32-36). The 'daughter' construct might be read as an oblique reference to a divinely approved daughterly wisdom (and wisdom in Proverbs is for the most part the product of education). In order to be meaningful for its addressees, the figuration of Wisdom as a heavenly 'daughter' must have evoked an extratextual social context to which they could have related. Whose gender-motivated vested interest is at stake here—especially when viewed against the predominantly disparaging postbiblical, Jewish attitudes toward female learning? The answer is obvious. If we recognize traces of polemics in favour of F education in 8.22-31, with its attribution of divine origin/authority to Daughter Wisdom, this recognition might, for instance, enable us to understand better the process of composition that ultimately produced ch. 8 in its present form.

Inside Proverbs (that is, beyond the boundaries of the Book's 'envelope'), the situation is not much different. Woman's domestic roles—wife and mother—are discussed in numerous passages. Exhortations to listen to mother's instruction as well as to father's (for instance, 23.22-25); warnings against the זרה woman (23.27-28); ostensibly misogynistic sayings about women's domestic behaviour (27.15; cf. 19.13b; 21.9); evaluations of F married conduct and instructions aimed at women (14.1)—these and other motifs recur. A worthy woman is her husband's pride and joy (as in 31.10-31), but an unworthy one is his disgrace (11.16a, 22; 12.4). The perspective is always a M perspective; the happiness of finding a suitable spouse is gender-specific; to obtain a good woman/wife is to acquire M happiness (18.22). There are no references to a woman's marital bliss or lack of it, or to a husband's execution of his marital obligations and its consequences for the woman

instruction to daughter' as the genre membership of this poem.

in his life. Once more, defining the voice behind these androcentric statements as a F voice is as feasible as defining it as a
M one for, in order to secure a tenuous position in the male
order of society (from which they are by definition excluded),
women have to adapt to its value system and perspectives.

To conclude: in view of our reconsideration of Proverbs texts
which figure woman, it is proposed that they be re-read with
the dual option of M/F voices, M/F readerly attention, in mind.
Although the textual object (addressee) is almost always male,
this identification cannot be automatically inferred for textual
speaking subjects and/or their narrating voices. The alternative
option of reading a Proverbs text as a F text should be
examined alongside the more traditional mode of a M reading.
Both modes are equally legitimized by different readerly
agendas and concerns. Such a procedure will doubtless prove
beneficial for the comprehension of many texts. In particular,
it might explain the figuration of Wisdom as woman in all
three of the conventional, male-related roles open to her in
patriarchal society: a legitimate and loving spouse (4.8), a
mother, and a daughter; and it might thus enhance our comprehension of the זרה figuration.

Female Figurations in Job

The female figures in Job have no independent status; their
function is to relate to Job as wife and daughters. The wife is
nameless, and so, to begin with (1.2, 4, 18), are the daughters.
In the Epilogue, however, the new daughters are given
names and surprising legal rights (42.13-15).

In the Prologue, Job's wife is given the unfortunate task of
suggesting that he ends his misfortune by cursing (or blessing)
God and then dying (2.9-10).[14] Job's retort is aggressively

---

14. Commentators differ as to the meaning of her suggestion. Does she
suggest that Job curse God (understanding the Hebrew ברך as 'curse'),
thus provoking God to kill Job? Alternatively, does she suggest that Job
bless God, then commit suicide? Since both polarized significations of the
Hebrew ברך are used within the Prologue, it is difficult to decide which
interpretative option is preferable. The response made by the textual Job
facilitates both interpretations.

vehement: he rejects her suggestion on ideo-religious grounds. She appears, therefore, a foolish and negative foil to her husband in his total trust in God. Her earthy, materialistic, commonsense attitude is diametrically opposed to Job's spirituality. She emblematizes impatience and emotion; he is an embodiment of pure idealism.[15] In that sense, their confrontation is a repeat performance of the Garden of Eden scene (Gen. 2–3) with a 'therapeutic' twist introduced into it. Contrary to the 'original' scene, here the male is not convinced by the female's initiative. Thereafter the wife ceases to be a speaking subject and is transformed into a spoken-of object. Within Job's great confession (chs. 29–31), she becomes an object for verbal barter. He swears that if he has committed adultery in deed or in fantasy then, *mutatis mutandis*, his wife should become the sexual property of another, even others (31.9-12).[16] The horror of transgressing patriarchal socio-sexual mores attributed to the textual Job is highlighted by the two classes of taboo females mentioned: virgins (31.1) and married women (v. 9). Thus the nonconformity of the Poetic Job in other matters does not pervade his conventionalized and conventional attitudes toward women and sex. It is worth noting that Job's wife is not mentioned again in the Epilogue, although the birth of a compensatory set of offspring might lead us to expect that.[17]

As for Job's daughters, the situation is different. Unnamed in the Prologue, they partake in family occasions like their brothers (1.4, 18). In the Epilogue (42.13-15), the new set of

15. For the double equation of F = materialism and nature, M = idealism and religion, see V.L. Erikson, 'Back to Basics: Feminist Social Theory, Durkheim and Religion', *Journal of Feminist Studies in Religion* 8 (1992), pp. 35-46.

16. For the sexual connotations of the 'grinding woman' metaphor, cf. Brenner, in *On Gendering Texts*, pp. 143-46. Not surprisingly, Job barters his wife off rather than his own self as punishment/expiation for his denied transgressions.

17. Hence, Jewish commentators and other ancient authorities speculate on her identity, to the point of doing away with Job's original wife (as punishment for her sinful, doubting conduct) and supplying him with another.

daughters receives names,[18] their physical beauty is singled out,[19] and finally, what is even more surprising, their 'inheritance among their brothers' (v. 15) is established by their father.

Why are the daughters' namelessness and relative invisibility reversed, so much so that now we know about them and their status much more than we know about their brothers? This is one of the changes introduced by the Epilogue vis-à-vis the Prologue.[20] We encounter a narrational gap here, to be filled by readers' inferences. The reading of a narrational gap often facilitates more than a single interpretation. For instance, Job the pious (of the frame story) might have become a social reformer. Or, the daughters are juxtaposed with Job's wife, whose absence (justified in terms of her previous behavior according to the story's ideocontents) thus becomes more conspicuous. Or, viewed against the obvious patriarchal background of the narrative, wherein daughters' inheritance is uncommon if not altogether impossible, the detailing of and emphasis on the daughters' inheritance hint at the implicitly deconstructive nature of the Epilogue. I prefer the latter reading for, in my view, Job the pious of the frame narrative (chs. 1–2; 42.7-17) is ironically presented as a parody/satire on the 'true believer' figure.[21] Finally, it is not clear what the daughters' inheritance consists of. In the Hebrew Bible mate-

---

18. Two of them—קציעה and קרן הפוך—are names for cosmetics, while the third—ימימה—has another connotation and is perhaps related to Ugaritic *yb / mmt limm*, 'mistress of peoples'.

19. This feature is, simultaneously, conventional and redundant. Conventional, for women are often praised for their good looks—hence attractiveness—in biblical literature, yet ordinarily the description serves a narrational purpose. Here the description is in a sense redundant, for it serves no overt (descriptive/motivational) narrational purpose.

20. Other changes are the disappearance of the satan and of Job's wife.

21. Cf. A. Brenner, 'Job the Pious? The Characterization of Job in the Narrative Framework of the Book', *JSOT* 43 (1989), pp. 37-52. In my opinion Job's description in the frame story—the cluster of adjectives used, the stereotypical numbers 3 and 7, his unparalleled cultic practice, the prose style—all point to a Job who is an ironical reversal of his counterpart in the poetic sections of the Book.

rial inheritance for daughters is a rare exception, the case of Zelophehad's daughters (Num. 27.1-11; 36.1-12) notwithstanding.[22] It remains to postbiblical literature to adapt these details to the prevailing social norm. By insisting on the daughters' *spiritual* rather than *material* inheritance, conformity is re-achieved and social order restored.[23]

Female Figurations in Qoheleth

The worldview advanced in Qoheleth, be it essentially either pragmatic-optimistic or else pragmatic-pessimistic/realistic, or both,[24] is plainly androcentric. The stylistic conventions—the speaking voice is a M voice; the speech is addressed to a M target audience—exclude the possibility of a different reading. Messages (possibly with one exception; see below) are not directed at a mixed or F audience, although many are relevant for the life and thinking of members of both genders.

Androcentrism does not automatically imply misogyny. Yet, the figuration of woman as more 'bitter than death' and as a tempting trap (Qoh. 7.26), presented as a sweeping conclusion from personal experience,[25] is hardly complimentary to a generalized womankind. A further statement, again delivered through the rhetorical convention of first-hand experience,

22. Even if we accept this story as a precedent for historical (when?) juridical practice, it is hardly applicable in the present case, since the textual Job has sons as well as daughters.

23. So, very clearly, in the *Testament of Job*; cf. P.W. van der Horst, *Essays on the Jewish World of Early Christianity* (Freiburg: Universität Verlag, 1990), pp. 94-110. This text also fills the gaps concerning the disappeared satan and the dismissed wife.

24. See, for instance, R.N. Whybray, *Ecclesiastes* (OTG; Sheffield: JSOT Press, 1989), pp. 61-83, with literature cited.

25. F. Zimmermann, *The Inner World of Qohelet* (New York, 1973), claims that this and other warnings and views found in Qoheleth stem from the author's unhappy marital experience expressed by the speaker in the first-person mode. It seems that Zimmermann assumes a relatively uncomplex relationship between textual 'reality' and the 'reality' of human (whose?) experience. Interestingly (albeit indirectly), his interpretation admits to an M gendered reading and constitutive gendering of the Qoheleth text.

comments that whereas a 'real' man is one in a thousand, 'a woman' (presumably one who is reliable/worthy) is not to be found among those few choice individuals.[26] Even if both sayings are quotations incorporated into the Qoheleth text (v. 29 reads like a comment on its predecessors; unfortunately, it is not transparent),[27] their misogynistic impact as a component of the Qoheleth text is unmistakable. The recommendation to enjoy life 'with the woman you love' as long as this is feasible (9.9)[28] hardly offsets the previous comments; if anything, it underlines an ambiguity toward woman who, in the Qoheleth discourse, is allowed an object position (both grammatically and topically) but not a subject position. Furthermore, within the textual speaker's declared experience of sexual enjoyment,[29] women are related to as objects. Throughout

26. My rendering for the non-specific Hebrew text. While it is not clear what the reference is to—human integrity in general? loyalty? trustworthiness? other virtues?—a reading of less (unspecified) than a 1:1000 ratio for female human integrity, perhaps even no human integrity rating for women, makes sense. See further for 7.26-29 in M.V. Fox, *Qohelet and his Contradictions* (Sheffield: Almond Press, 1989), pp. 241-43. Fox, who emphasizes the rhetorical device of 'Qohelet' speaking as if to summarize 'his' experience, does not regard this text as misogynistic. To quote: 'There is bathos in these words: the result of his search in the lofty realms of intellect is just this: a woman is dangerous' (p. 241). Fox apparently means that 'Qohelet' deconstructs 'his' own discourse through this remark. I would submit that at this point Fox's interpretation is in danger of deconstructing itself. Is the result of 'Qoheleth's' quest—the attempt to derive comfort from gender relations—so ludicrous by comparison to 'his' lofty intellectual ideas? Or does Fox mean that finding women *dangerous* is the deconstructive component? If the latter obtains, then I concur.

27. For the practice of quoting in Qoheleth, see R.N. Whybray, 'The Identification and Use of Quotations in Ecclesiastes', in *Congress Volume, Vienna 1980* (ed. J.A. Emerton; VTSup, 32; Leiden: Brill, 1981), pp. 435-51; R. Gordis, *Koheleth: The Man and his World* (New York: Schocken Books, 1969), pp. 95-108.

28. The Hebrew beyond v. 9a is repetitive and corrupt. Does it condone a monogamic attachment to one woman throughout a man's life? Does it advocate love for a suitable woman as an ideal, the only worthwhile thing in life (so if we follow some versions of the *k*tîb* and read כי היא חלקך בחיים [v. 9b], '*she* [the woman] is your lot in life')?

29. If indeed the obscure phrases in 2.8c onwards refer to that; and cf. the commentaries for this passage, especially the Hebrew שׁדה ושׁדוח.

Qoheleth and 'his' contradictions, this state of affairs never varies.

I have tried to show elsewhere[30] that Qoh. 3.2-8 is a poem (framed by 3.1 and 3.9) whose primary, albeit covert, subject matter is desire, sex and gender relations rather than human time (as it is traditionally interpreted). I also argue that the poem is one of the few biblical instances of M love lyrics, possibly aimed at F recipients. Whybray views the passage differently. He sees it as a list—rather than a poem—which developed gradually, hence the variations in the style and in the significations of some key phrases it contains. He rejects a 'sexual' interpretation for the passage's central verse (3.5), and hence for the whole of it.[31] I am not convinced by some of Whybray's critical decisions concerning the passage. Poetry need not necessarily be precise—variations in significations of the same words or phrases need neither detract from poetic impact nor motivate an ascription to another genre. Repetition is a characteristic feature shared by ancient poetry and lists; therefore its existence within a passage cannot be construed as evidence for genre membership this way or the other. Finally, poetry can be the product of gradual evolvement as much as a list can. In spite of these objections, I accept Whybray's analysis of the passage's composition and structure as a model of erudite and balanced application of scholarly principles.

Female Figurations in the Joseph Narrative, Esther and Daniel 1–6

The Joseph narrative, Esther and Daniel 1–6 are constructed along an almost identical paradigm. This paradigm encompasses the following recurrent motifs. Against initial odds, a

---

30. Brenner, in *On Gendering Texts*, pp. 133-53.

31. R.N. Whybray, '"A Time to be Born and a Time to Die." Some Observations on Ecclesiastes 3.2-8', in *Near Eastern Studies Dedicated to H.I.M. Prince Takahito Mikasa on the Occasion of his Seventy-Fifth Birthday* (ed. M. Mari, H. Ogawa and M. Yoshikawa; Bulletin of the Middle Eastern Culture in Japan, 5; Wiesbaden: Harrassowitz, 1991), pp. 469-83. The typescript of this essay was made available to me by Professor Whybray.

Jew/Hebrew rises to political power in a foreign king's court; he is a god-fearing individual; his talents, wisdom and divine inspiration enable a dramatic change in his personal circumstances; he is thus able to help others.[32] These motifs connect with sayings in Proverbs and Qoheleth. Instructions on interaction with a king (Prov. 16.10-15; Qoh. 8.2-4) and the ideals of conventional wisdom (Prov. 1.2-7) are central to these narratives. Curiously, all three contain figurations of woman as 'foreign'/Other (זרה), from the viewpoint of the narrator and/or one of the characters. I therefore feel that including these narratives in the present survey is relevant.

There are three F figurations in the Joseph narrative: a mother, a זרה temptress and a wife. The mother is absent though present, dead but influential: Jacob's love for his son Joseph, the love that initiates and motivates the plot, is defined as an offshoot of his love for the dead Rachel. Nothing is reported about Joseph's wife Asenath beyond her name and a statement about her lineage and status as daughter, wife and mother (Gen. 41.45, 50); it remains for extrabiblical literature to develop this male-dependent skeleton of a F figuration into a fuller literary figure.[33] By contrast to the brevity accorded to the mother and wife figurations, a whole chapter depicts the F temptation embodied in the figure of Potiphar's nameless wife.

When we read Proverbs 7 and Genesis 39 as *intertexts*, each of the two texts acquires additional dimensions. Differences exist, of course. For instance, Potiphar's wife fails in her project while the זרה woman apparently succeeds in implementing hers; cultic overtones may be present in Proverbs 7 (v. 17) but are totally lacking in Genesis 39. The basic paradigm is nevertheless similar. A nameless married woman desires a young man. The husband is absent. The woman initiates action. She tries to seduce the young man. She does so by speech acts rather than by reliance on her looks—her physical

32. This paradigm underlines Dan. 1–6. Here, however, I shall limit myself to dealing exclusively with ch. 5, since there are no female figurations in the other chapters.

33. In *Joseph and Asenath* she is accorded subject status: her emotions are fictionalized and her own 'story', totally absent from the biblical text, is created.

appearance is not reported.[34] She has lust, to be distinguished from love, in mind. There is a seduction scene of sorts. Be the male victim willing (Proverbs) or reluctant (Genesis), his interacting with the woman is detrimental to his well-being: the young fool's fate is a certain death; he will descend to the Sheol that awaits him (Prov. 7.23-27); and Joseph finds himself descending into prison (Gen. 39.20). In both passages, the woman's narrated behaviour and speech acts are construed as an affront to the societal norms prescribed by M marital/moral/religious/sexual codes (Prov. 7.10-13; Gen. 39.8-10). Significantly, the figuration of the זרה seductress is similar in both passages. Significantly, the desired male's conduct is the narrated variable factor that effects a different outcome in each text. Unlike his intertextual counterpart, Joseph does not succumb to the woman's advances. The reward for this restraint as well as for his other virtues is great indeed.[35] Joseph's apparent descent (into prison) is the beginning of his ascent (to fame and influence). Prudence, a virtue much extolled in Proverbs, is wisdom. Genesis 39 reads, then, as a counterfoil to Proverbs 9. Both texts are equally didactic. The latter provides a negative lesson, the former a positive one. The two texts, each with a male protagonist compromised by

34. Apart from in Prov. 6.25. As for Potiphar's wife, we are free to fill in the missing details—attractiveness, appearance, age, motivation—according to our personal inclinations. This process of filling in is an integral part of the reading process; our interpretation of the story as it unfolds depends on our decision regarding the woman's age. Is she older than Joseph, thus taking double advantage of his inferior social position? Younger, which would make for a totally different reading? Of the same age, which has other repercussions altogether? And so on, inasmuch as other 'missing' details are concerned.

35. The Joseph story may be considered a Wisdom-type narrative also because in chs. 37, 39–41 it charts the internal and external journeys travelled by a young, indiscreet 'fool' toward the maturity, selfhood and 'wisdom' that are the prerequisites for his future success (as in Proverbs). The encounter with the temptress looks like an integral stage of this mythic/mythological journey—as in many other myths, and as recognized by rabbinic Midrash for ch. 39. Cf., for instance, *Bereshit Rabbah, Midrash Tanhuma, Midrash Ha-Gadol*, and *Yalkut Shim'oni* for this chapter, and also Joseph's Testament in the *Testaments of the Twelve Patriarchs*.

an intrusive, uncontrolled and uncontrollable F Other at their centre, are true companion pieces.[36]

In the Book of Esther there are three figurations of woman. All three depict woman as wife: Vashti, a 'bad' wife, Esther, a 'good' wife, and Zeresh, a model wife, a wise and knowing companion to a bad husband.

Vashti and Esther are configured as opposites. Vashti is a disobedient wife.[37] Her punishment is to lose all and be dismissed from the story. Chapter 1 emphasizes that Vashti's fate is to serve as warning for all women to obey their husbands. Although not a central theme, this warning betrays a deeply rooted patriarchal worry. Ironically, Vashti's substitute Esther disobeys the king in coming to see him unbidden (4.11; 5.1-2). Esther exploits her sexuality in order to manipulate the king into giving her what she is after. Mordecai virtually pushes her into the foreign king's bed by forbidding her to disclose her national origin (2.10, 20).[38]

And yet, neither Mordecai nor Esther is criticized for his and her obvious disregard for morality and sexual norms.

36. For a feminist counterreading of Genesis 39 and some extrabiblical sources that refer to it, see A. Bach, 'Breaking Free of the Biblical Frame-Up: Uncovering the Woman in Genesis 39', in A. Brenner (ed.), *A Feminist Companion to Genesis* (Sheffield: JSOT Press, 1993), pp. 318-42.

37. For an early feminist reading of Vashti's refusal to heed the king's bidding and come to him, cf. E. Cady Stanton (ed.), *The Woman's Bible* (New York: European Publishing House, 1898), Part II, pp. 85-88. To quote: 'Vashti stands out a sublime representative of self-centred womanhood. Rising to the heights of self-consciousness and of self-respect, she takes her soul into her own keeping, and though her position both as wife and as queen are jeopardized, she remains true...' (p. 88).

No reason for Vashti's refusal is supplied by the MT. Hence, her disobedience seems all the more arbitrary. This narrational gap (omission?) serves the patriarchal concern underlying the story well. In the case of a wife's disobedience, no reasons are relevant. Vashti's refusal, within the ideocontents of the story, is sufficient reason for her dismissal in favour of a more suitable successor. The rabbinic speculations on the reasons for Vashti's refusal are amusingly fanciful but have no basis in the biblical text. Furthermore, they miss the point. Gap-filling at this juncture would obscure the story's concern.

38. Esther's daughterly obedience to Mordecai, her adoptive 'father', is throughout one of her sterling virtues.

Why, then, does Esther—certainly a זרה woman in the king's court, and evidently a skilled manipulator of male sexuality and judgment—receive a better treatment than Vashti and their F counterparts in Proverbs and Genesis? Perhaps because she practises her sexual manipulations discreetly rather than publicly, and on her husband only; or because of her obedience to Mordecai and loyalty to her ethnic source group. Ultimately Esther too disappears from the story when her task is accomplished. Having been used by men to cater to their ambitions and plans and to realize them, she exits the stage after her mission is accomplished, leaving Mordecai and Ahasuerus to run the kingdom (ch. 10). Thus are M proprieties observed. Whether Esther is a role model for F readers, feminist or otherwise, to emulate remains a matter of personal sensibility.

In Daniel 5 the foreign king commits sacrilege by using the Jerusalem Temple utensils during a feast (vv. 1-4).[39] Nobody understands the writing on the wall. Everybody, including the king, is horrified, frightened, powerless to do anything (vv. 6-9). The unnamed[40] queen is the only intelligent person around. She quietly and tactfully suggests that Daniel be sent for in order to solve the mystery, and her counsel proves sound (vv. 10-12). Her conduct stands in stark contrast to that of the males around her, her royal spouse included. Is she given the gift of unhysterical counsel in order to highlight the stupidity of her fictive husband and his companions, who—to their shame—behave like stereotypic frightened women, and therefore need a woman's wisdom to reorient them? Be that as it may, the queen's figure is reminiscent of the Wisdom figure in Proverbs and the 'wise woman' figures of 2 Samuel 14 and 20. Thus, at the end of our survey we once more encounter two figurations of woman that are central to Proverbs—

39. Is there a hint for something more sinister than a regular banquet or feast, with a strong element of sexual licence? The presence of 'women and concubines' (Aramaic: שגלתה ולחנתה), which is emphasized by repetition (vv. 2, 3), is suggestive for such an interpretation.

40. Once more a 'foreign' woman remains unnamed, although her fictive husband is named. It is worth recalling that this convention of unnaming recurs also in Prov. 7 and Gen. 39.

Woman Wisdom and the זרה woman. This time, however, the two figurations are fused. A זרה woman is depicted as a true marital helpmate, 'wise' in the Proverbs sense. And this leads us back to the discussion (not undertaken here) about the wisdom traits ascribed—unwittingly? but certainly ambivalently—to the זרה woman, and the potential of these traits for clarifying the (gender) motivation and sense that underline this important F figuration.[41]

41. Cf. Camp, 'Wise and Strange'. The present study was written in Utrecht, The Netherlands, where I spent six months as Belle van Zuylen Professor in the Faculty of Theology, The University of Utrecht. My thanks to the staff and faculty members, who made my stay pleasant and conducive to work.

THE GOOD NEIGHBOUR IN THE BOOK OF PROVERBS

Ronald E. Clements

It is a marked feature of the Book of Proverbs that it portrays a noticeably different kind of social and community structure among those it addresses from that which pertains to the long narrative units of the Hebrew Bible. Whereas in the latter the genealogies and forms of address emphasize the large extended families of the *bêt 'ābôt* and its tribal affiliations,[1] the proverbial teaching focuses its attention upon the household and the city. When cities flourish, then their inhabitants prosper, and when the city is well and justly governed, then its citizens rejoice (Prov. 11.10-11). Similarly the household is the primary sphere of blessing.[2] It forms a largely self-contained economic unit in which all stand to prosper or fall to ruin together. Geography, rather than kinship affiliation, appears to be the controlling factor in social relationships and the household does not normally lift its horizons temporally beyond the welfare of grandchildren (cf. Prov. 13.22; 17.6), nor laterally beyond those of brothers and sisters (Prov. 17.17; etc.).

Yet social relationships form a major area of preoccupation for the wisdom teachers, since it is in this sphere that the moral dictates of wise conduct display their immense importance for the quality of life enjoyed by any community. Accordingly, the internal dynamics of family life, governing

---

1. For the social structure of ancient Israel and the importance of the *bêt 'ābôt* I am especially indebted to J.W. Rogerson's study of 'Social Organization', in J.W. Rogerson and P.R. Davies, *The World of the Old Testament* (Cambridge: Cambridge University Press, 1989), pp. 45-62.

2. Cf. my study of the importance of the household as a central locus for the operation of wisdom in *Wisdom in Theology* (Grand Rapids: Eerdmans, 1993), pp. 123-50.

relationships between husband, wife and their offspring, provide a primary focus for wisdom's admonitions to address. Thereafter the immediate first consequence of this life within the household of the family unit concerns behaviour towards the adjoining community of the immediate neighbourhood. It is not surprising therefore that the concept of the 'neighbour' appears in a very prominent measure in the Book of Proverbs. The question of how the individual should behave towards his or her neighbours provides a topic on which a great deal of advice is given.

However, much of the moral force of this intense concern with relationships with the anonymous 'neighbour' becomes lost in most English versions of the Bible in view of the wide-spread practice of translating the Hebrew *rēaʿ* as 'friend'. The context is allowed to determine which noun best fits the situation envisaged. In some instances this is undoubtedly appropriate, since the ideal of the close and supportive 'neighbour' does elevate such a person to the status of a true friend. In many instances, however, it seems clear that the goal of the wisdom teachers lay beyond commenting upon the virtue of making and preserving friendships. They were rather striving to arouse a strong community spirit and code of behaviour, in which 'neighbours' would become 'friends'.

Friends, in the fullest sense, may be few in number, and to show love towards them may be easy. In any case they are usually established through personal choice. Neighbours are more numerous and intrude their presence through geography and the chance encounters of work and travel.[3] To learn to love them may be more difficult and demanding. It is our concern therefore to note that the convention of translating *rēaʿ* by the English noun 'friend', in many of its occurrences in the Book of Proverbs, has served to weaken substantially the moral relevance of what the ancient wisdom teachers were arguing for.

There is a further reason why the teaching of the wisdom

3. J. Fichtner, 'Der Begriff des "Nächsten" im Alten Testament', in *Gottes Weisheit: Gesammelte Studien zum Alten Testament* (ed. K.D. Fricke; Arbeiten zur Theologie, II/3; Stuttgart: Calwer Verlag, 1965), pp. 88-114; cf. also D. Kellermann, *ʾrēaʿ*, *ThWAT*, VII, cols. 545-55.

teachers regarding conduct towards a neighbour deserves careful attention in the context of the study of biblical ethics. In the New Testament the command 'to love one's neighbour as oneself' is elevated in the teaching of Jesus to the highest and most comprehensive level as a summary of the goal of Jewish *tôrâ*, second only in importance to the command to love God (Lk. 10.27). The exposition in the Parable of the Good Samaritan, which follows this (Lk. 10.29-37), proceeds to expound the purport of this command by demonstrating that relationships between 'neighbours' should include those between Jews and Samaritans. The Samaritan recognized the distressed Jewish traveller to be a 'neighbour', although he was certainly not a 'friend'! We should also note that, in the Book of Proverbs, the narrower ideal of a friend is more precisely revealed by the term *'ôhēb*, 'one who loves', besides which the notion of a 'companion' (*'allûp*) is also found.

That the Old Testament background to this New Testament commandment is to be sought in the admonition set out in Lev. 19.18 is clearly correct, so far as the verbal composition of the New Testament text is concerned.[4] However, the contribution made by the Old Testament wisdom tradition should not be overlooked to the extent that it has been. Nowhere in the Hebrew Bible is the issue of conduct towards a neighbour more fully explored than in the Book of Proverbs. This undoubtedly reflects the kind of social environment in which the wisdom teachers found themselves. The influence of the extended family in the form of the *bêt 'ābôt* was greatly diminished, whereas urban life and work patterns made the ideal of good community relationships in a neighbourhood of prime importance. Consequently it mattered greatly to define a standard of good conduct towards a neighbour.

In the light of this it seems clear that much of what the advocates of wisdom were commending in behaviour towards neighbours achieved its greatest moral force when such persons were not narrowly recognized as close friends. The

---

4. Cf. H.-P. Mathys, *Liebe deinen Nächsten wie dich selbst: Untersuchungen zum alttestamentlichen Gebot der Nächstenliebe (Lev. 19,18)* (OBO, 71; Freiburg: Universitätsverlag; Göttingen: Vandenhoeck & Ruprecht, 1986).

New Testament's extension of this definition of 'neighbour', to apply it in a very wide sense, moves firmly along a path already marked out in Proverbs.

Clearly it is impossible for the modern scholar to define, either in regard to Lev. 19.18 or to the teaching of the Book of Proverbs, how far the concept of 'the neighbour' was originally intended to apply, since it is so evidently left open.[5] It is not made clear whether it could embrace members of the community who stood outside a fundamental religious loyalty to Jewish tradition, as the Samaritan of the Lukan parable so obviously did. Nor is it explicit whether some element of reciprocal warmth and friendship was required before a truly neighbourly obligation was established. However, it is the very indeterminacy and openness of the concept that makes the extensive range of advice concerning the neighbour such an interesting feature of the Book of Proverbs. The book raises, even if it does not answer, the question raised by the lawyer in the parable, 'And who is my neighbour?' (Lk. 10.27).

We find that, in the edited collection of the book, there are no less than 39 instances where conduct towards a neighbour is either made a subject for comment and reflection, or is focused upon as a topic requiring positive advice. Apart from the relatively obvious and properly expected warning not to sleep with a neighbour's wife in Prov. 6.29, the remaining admonitions fall fairly clearly into three categories.

The first of these concerns the situation of a neighbour in need and serves most fully to identify why it is that being a 'neighbour' is so important to the community at large. The second category concerns wealth, or the lack of it, and serves richly to demonstrate that, among all the factors in the structure of society that brought stress and served to undermine the concept of neighbourliness, that of the difference between

5.   M. Buber (*Two Types of Faith* [trans. N.P. Goldhawk; London: Routledge & Kegan Paul, 1951], p. 70) took it in a very wide sense to apply to those 'with whom thou hast to to do at any time in the course of thy life'. No doubt this imposes a very broad sense upon the command, but, as also in the Book of Proverbs, much of the moral strength of what is advocated arises from the fact that the concept of neighbour cannot be circumscribed by an arbitrarily narrow definition.

wealth and poverty was the most markedly intractable and insurmountable. Possessing wealth made neighbourliness easy, whereas lacking it made it very difficult. Within the horizons of the wisdom teachers this fact provided a central point of attention. The third category of advice and warning concerns speech. What was said to, or more often apparently about, one's neighbours could have the most long-lived and far-reaching consequences. Foolish talk could prevent the possibility of making neighbours into friends.

There is a further reason for making the wisdom teachers' interest in the ideal of 'the good neighbour' a topic of particular attention. It is their approval of the existence of a juridical legal system alongside their strong support for a self-motivated and voluntaristic 'private' morality that lay outside this. In regard to the former, the necessary existence of such a system is fully endorsed and approved in the sapiential tradition, and is occasionally commented upon. In regard to the latter, the limitations of this legal system are frankly recognized: its susceptibility to manipulation is conceded, and the true student of wisdom is advised to avoid becoming entangled in its web. On this front the teaching of Proverbs very much falls into line with the admonitory injunction of Lev. 19.18. A loving attitude towards one's fellow citizens is regarded as vital towards enabling the law to operate justly and constructively.

From the perspective of wisdom, this concern to reach beyond the morality of the official legal processes is noteworthy in view of the emphatic presentation given to the ideal of King Solomon's wisdom as supremely manifested in his juridical insight. The order of wisdom is built upon a concept of law. Furthermore, the role of the king, so heartily commended and supported by the earliest wisdom, is presented as fundamental to this system of legal justice. Yet, alongside this, the wisdom teachers' efforts to inculcate a proper neighbourly attitude strive to reach well beyond the minimal morality that is the best that the law could hope to offer.

The Neighbour in Need

A short 'Charter of Neighbourly Conduct' is set out in Prov. 3.27-30, in which the fundamental attitudes to be adopted are described:

> Do not withhold good from those in need of it,
>> when you are able to do so.
> Do not say to your neighbour, 'Go away and come back another
>> time,
>> I will give it to you tomorrow'—although you have it with
>> you.
> Do not plan harm against your neighbour
>> who is living trustingly beside you.
> Do not pick a quarrel with anyone without cause,
>> when no harm has been done to you (3.27-30).

Perhaps even worse than bringing needless trouble to a neighbour is the possibility of leading them astray into following one's own perverse and misguided behaviour:

> A violent person deceives his neighbour,
>> and leads him on a path that is not good (16.29).[6]

It is then a characteristic of wicked persons that they show no such scruples about respect for a neighbour, but instead set out to make trouble and show no restraint in doing so:

> The wicked like to cause trouble;
>> their neighbours receive no mercy from them (21.10).

The converse of this is firmly endorsed by the teachers of wisdom: the advice of the righteous is a boon to their neighbours:

> A righteous person shows his neighbour the way,[7]
>> but the path of wrongdoers leads astray (12.26).

---

6.   W. McKane (*Proverbs: A New Approach* [OTL; SCM Press, 1970], p. 494) comments: 'He employs deceit in order to achieve his destructive ends'. The main point, however, would appear to lie in the fact that such a violent person hides his true nature under a cloak of neighbourliness.

7.   The Hebrew verb is uncertain and this translation follows that of McKane, *Proverbs*, pp. 447-78. J.A. Emerton, 'A Note on Proverbs xii. 26', *ZAW* 76 (1964), pp. 191-92, takes as 'is delivered from harm'. NRSV has 'gives good advice to friends', which follows the interpretation of McKane.

It reveals much about the social and moral context in which wisdom expected to operate that it raises the concept of the neighbour to a level equivalent to, and sometimes even more important than, that of the closest kin relative:

> A neighbour loves at all times,
>> and a brother is born to share adversity (17.17).

The point of the saying would appear to be to raise the status of the neighbour to the level of a brother, traditionally regarded as the highest and most supportive of all human kinship ties.[8]

A good summarizing admonition regarding the importance of maintaining loyalty to neighbours of long standing is set out in Prov. 27.10:

> Do not forsake your neighbour or your father's neighbour,
>> and do not go to your brother's house in the day of your
>> misfortune.
> A neighbour who is nearby is better
>> than a brother who is far away (27.10).

Clearly there appears to be little connection at first between the injunction not to abandon a long-standing family neighbour and the advice not to burden a brother at a time of misfortune. McKane comments: 'The injunction not to neglect an old friend of the family has no intrinsic connection with the observation that a neighbour who is on the doorstep is a bigger help than a brother who is at a distance'.[9] C.H. Toy feels the dismissive attitude towards a brother's help even more acutely.[10] Yet once the importance within the wisdom tradition of attaching the highest level of significance to a good neighbourly relationship is recognized, the connection becomes clear and is precisely as stated in the concluding line.

---

8. So B. Gemser, *Sprüche Salomos* (HAT, 16; Tübingen: J.C.B. Mohr, 2nd edn, 1963), p. 73. McKane's rendering, 'A companion is always good company', is simply a tautology and leaves little moral force in what is affirmed (*Proverbs*, pp. 237, 505-506).

9. McKane, *Proverbs*, p. 614.

10. Toy, *Proverbs*, p. 486: 'The text must be regarded as defective, or the clause must be taken as a gloss inserted by some scribe whose experience had made him bitter against brothers...'(!).

With a good neighbour who is nearby, and who can be relied upon for support, even the help of a brother will not be needed in a time of adversity. The intention then is not to be dismissive of a brother's responsibility and ability to help, but rather to suggest that, even at a time of personal misfortune, a good neighbour can be as supportive as a brother. The help at hand is greater than the potential help from a distance, provided the neighbour who lives close by lives up to the ideal.

If we have correctly grasped the sense of Prov. 27.10, it further strengthens the contention that it is the value of the spiritual support of a true neighbour that is extolled in 27.9:

> Perfume and incense soothe the mind;
> and the sweetness of a neighbour is better than one's own counsel (27.9).[11]

The teachers of wisdom have striven hard to elevate the responsibilities and role of 'the good neighbour', in recognizing that circumstances will often limit the support-potential of the immediate family kin-group. This must surely have arisen on the basis of the greatly changed patterns of social structure and domicile in the society to which such instructions were addressed. This altered social structure—in which the kin-group was much smaller and the extended family no longer a primary reference for economic, moral and spiritual support—has encouraged a greatly enhanced 'neighbour awareness'.

This changed social awareness is very distinctive of the wisdom teaching, since it recognizes the relativizing, and partial atrophy, of a system of moral values in which feelings of kinship and family obligation were paramount. The concept of kinship loyalty undoubtedly lies at the heart of the older Israelite family and tribal structure. Mutual support through the notion of *gᵉ'ullâ*, protection,[12] and where necessary the exaction of vengeance, had made the extended family the most

---

11. Cf. NRSV margin; McKane (*Proverbs*, pp. 612-13) suggests: 'and the sweetness of a friendship strengthens the spirit'. Similarly also O. Plöger, *Sprüche Salomos (Proverbia)* (BKAT, 17; Neukirchen–Vluyn: Neukirchener Verlag, 1983), pp. 317, 322-23.

12. For this notion of family protection and vengeance, cf. Rogerson, in *The World of the Old Testament*, pp. 47-49.

influential unit of moral and economic life. The Deuteronomic legislation, with its fundamentally urbanizing and centralizing tendencies,[13] sought to deal with this reduction in the power of the older clans and tribes in another way. It aimed to extend the concept of 'brotherhood' to every fellow-Israelite.[14] The wisdom teaching, however, moves in a different direction by envisaging the notion that 'neighbourliness' could be more important than the protection and support of even a person's most immediate kin:

Some neighbours play at friendship,[15]
but there is a friend ('ōhēb) who sticks closer than a
brother (18.24).

The Hebrew verb of the first line is of uncertain meaning and derivation, but the sense given here appears to be on the right lines (cf. NRSV). RSV has 'who pretend to be friends'. Hence the contrast is made between those who give only the outward appearance of friendship and neighbourliness and those who display the full depth of support that such a relationship demands. The instruction urges recognition that true neighbourliness establishes bonds of loyalty and support exceeding what might be expected even of a brother. This is precisely what I have suggested is the deeper intent of Prov. 27.10.

From the perspective of the Christian development of the Hebrew wisdom tradition, it is doubly unfortunate that the meaning of Prov. 22.11 is very uncertain. The rendering adopted by NRSV accords with a wide tradition, and has the support of many commentators:

13. Cf. my comments in *Deuteronomy* (OTG; Sheffield: JSOT Press, 1988), pp. 85-93.
14. Cf. Deut. 15.3, 7, 9; etc., and see L. Perlitt, 'Ein einzig Volk von Brüdern', in *Kirche: Festschrift G. Bornkamm zum 75. Geburtstag* (ed. D. Lührmann and G. Strecker; Tübingen: J.C.B. Mohr, 1980), pp. 7-52.
15. McKane (*Proverbs*, pp. 239, 518-20) renders: 'There is a companion who does nothing but chatter', recognizing the difficulty with the Hebrew verb. This follows G.R. Driver, 'Problems in the Hebrew Text of Proverbs', *Bib* 32 (1951), pp. 173-97 (196), but such a translation appears to trivialize what is affirmed. Toy's '...they seek only society' (*Proverbs*, p. 367) is more plausible in that it suggests the idea that some friends enjoy the friendship, but do not really help in time of need.

> Those who love a pure heart and are gracious in speech
> will have the king as a friend (22.11, NRSV).

The use of the concept of 'a pure heart' connects the saying with the beatitude of Mt. 5.8, where those who display such a character are accorded the ultimate assurance—'they will see God'. Such 'purity of heart' must refer to a complete integrity of purpose and consistency of conduct, rejecting all deviousness and hiddenness of motive, which the wisdom teachers deplored.

The link with the Matthaean tradition becomes all the closer when we note that the Septuagint translates: 'The Lord loves the pure in heart; all who are blameless in their ways are acceptable to him'. It seems likely that the ancient translator's introduction of 'Lord' is an interpretation of 'king', rather than being based on a different reading in the Hebrew.[16] However, in the process, the link with the New Testament beatitude becomes all the closer. The meaning of the original Hebrew is in any case difficult, and, if the NRSV's rendering is adopted, the sense must be: those who display true integrity of attitude and graciousness of speech are worthy of the most honoured neighbours. McKane, however, prefers to see in the saying a commendation of the kind of person that a king would regard with favour (as a servant?).[17] Yet surely the larger context of such sayings points us toward the recognition that this is another saying about good neighbourly behaviour, rather than about royal preferences.

When we seek to summarize what is said in Proverbs about what constitutes appropriate behaviour towards a neighbour in need, it strongly points in the direction of understanding that 'neighbour' is to be construed in a wider, rather than a narrower, sense. The situation of need, rather than ties of friendship, determines the appropriate mode of behaviour.

Wealth and Neighbourliness

If being a neighbour could be established by the purely chance factor of living together in a small community, or of

16. Cf. McKane, *Proverbs*, pp. 567-68.
17. McKane (*Proverbs*, pp. 245, 567-68) translates: 'A king loves a man with a pure mind, the grace of his speech (meets) his approval'.

working with other persons, or even through the unforeseen events of daily life, then clearly many eventualities could obtrude to make neighbourliness difficult.[18] In this regard it is noteworthy that the wisdom teachers drew special attention to the stress imposed on neighbourly conduct by the social contrasts of wealth and poverty:

> Wealth brings many neighbours,
>> but a poor man is separated from his neighbour (19.4).
>
> Many seek the favour of a nobleman,
>> and everyone is a neighbour to someone who gives gifts (19.6).
>
> A poor man is hated even by his brothers,
>> how much more do his neighbours shun him! (19.7).

The negative implications in Prov. 19.4 and 19.7 take on further emphasis with the rendering of *rēa'* as 'friend', rather than 'neighbour' (so NRSV), since this reinforces the sense of social alienation that poverty brings upon any members of the community who are unfortunate enough to become its victims. Even erstwhile friends and kinsfolk found it hard to remain supportive and neighbourly towards one who had lost economic independence and influence in the community. All the more would this have been the case for someone who fell suddenly upon hard times through a commercial misadventure or through acceptance of an unwise financial commitment. It is not surprising, therefore, to discover that the wise had much to say about the social consequences of economic activity, especially if such activity were undertaken recklessly or deceitfully (cf. Prov. 13.11; 28.22).

Like the sentences of Prov. 14.31 and 17.5, the comments regarding poor neighbours contain an implied rebuke of those who take advantage of such misfortune, or who indulge in a degree of *Schadenfreude* (cf. Prov. 22.7, 22-23)! In a society where misfortune and unpremeditated ruin could happen to even the hard-working and upright members, a degree of empathy with the poor was at least demanded.

18. The prominent role given to matters of wealth and poverty in Proverbs is shown in R.N. Whybray, *Wealth and Poverty in the Book of Proverbs* (JSOTSup, 115; Sheffield: JSOT Press, 1991), *passim.*

220   *Of Prophets' Visions and the Wisdom of Sages*

In this regard it is evident that the wisdom teachers were intent upon reporting the kind of conduct that was usually displayed towards such social contrasts in order to urge a more deeply considered alternative:

> A poor person is disliked even by his neighbour,
> but there are many friends for the rich (14.20).

The following verse of sentence instruction spells out in a clearly admonitory fashion what the wisdom teachers regarded as the right and wrong ways of dealing with such a situation:

> Whoever despises his neighbour goes astray,
> but those who are kind to the afflicted are blessed (14.21).

A sympathetic attitude towards the needs of poor neighbours quite evidently required a measure of courage and independence, as well as a willingness to make sacrifices oneself. There were, however, clearly limits to neighbourliness, particularly where economic matters were concerned. With wealth at one's own disposal it was evidently not difficult to make friends out of neighbours. But there were also serious risks to one's own household, if anxiety to help a neighbour led one to take on unwise commitments on his or her behalf.

The wisdom teachers went to considerable trouble to draw attention to these risks and to dissuade the well-intentioned neighbour from undertaking any major financial commitment on behalf of another. Accordingly they set themselves firmly against the policy of becoming surety for a neighbour:

> Only one who lacks sense strikes hands,
> and goes surety on behalf of a neighbour (17.18).

So strongly was this matter felt to be that it is made the subject of a much longer, and even more forcibly worded, warning in Prov. 6.1-3:

> My son, if you have given surety to your neighbour,
> and have made agreement on behalf of a stranger,
> you are snared by your own words,
> trapped by what you yourself have said.

Do this, then, my son, and save yourself,
    for you have fallen into your neighbour's power.
Go, swallow your pride[19] and importune your neighbour.

To escape the consequences of an unwise, or insufficiently thought through, commitment of this nature, the pupil of wisdom is urged to hasten immediately and withdraw from such an obligation:

Give your eyes no sleep
    and your eyelids no rest;
save yourself like a gazelle from its pursuer,
    like a bird from the hand of the trapper! (6.4-5).

If it was unwise to put one's own household economy at risk on behalf of a neighbour, then clearly it was even more fool-hardy and dangerous to do so on behalf of a stranger to the community:

Whoever goes surety for a stranger will suffer for it,
    but the one who hates pledges will be secure (Prov. 11.15;
        cf. 20.16).

Probably the fervent nature of such warnings reveals more about the harsh economic realities of life in ancient Israel and its precarious foundations, than about the goodwill required for neighbourly behaviour. With usury rife, mercantile enter-prise uncertain at best, and daily life inevitably posing unforeseen hazards, to say nothing of the possible risk of unneighbourly deceitfulness, staking one's own wealth upon the uncertainties of another's was deemed to be not worth the risk. It is then a marked characteristic of the way in which the wise viewed economic matters that risks attendant upon these were felt to be best kept within one's own household.

The forceful way in which this caution is urged must surely indicate that it was founded on widespread experience. Perhaps this arose because, in giving surety on behalf of another, the degree of risk to one's own property was often not fully appreciated. More probably, however, it seems likely that the interaction of economic pressures in the biblical world was very inadequately grasped. When one family was put

19. Cf. McKane, *Proverbs*, pp. 218, 322.

under economic strain, it is likely that others were faced with similar risks. Consequently it was better to limit the risk to one household, rather than for others to make public commitments that could all too easily spread the disaster, rather than contain it!

Neighbourliness and Talkativeness

If wealth and poverty are singled out as an area in which the ideal of 'the good neighbour' could easily be placed under strain, then speech and talkativeness are highlighted even more forcibly as an area requiring the greatest caution. Already Prov. 14.21 strongly hints in the direction that finding oneself faced with a poor neighbour could provide an occasion for despising him or her. It was then but a step to proceed to make such feelings public by belittling such a person:

> Whoever belittles a neighbour lacks sense,
>> but a person of intelligence keeps quiet (11.12).

Of course the temptation to belittle another could arise over matters other than economic ones, and a whole range of bad relationships could be sparked off by malicious whisperings or unwise gossip (Prov. 11.13). There was, indeed, no easier way to separate close friends than by spreading malicious talk about them (Prov. 16.28). In this area a strong resilience and a willingness to forgive become very important:

> Whoever forgives an offence seeks love,
>> but the person who dwells on a matter will alienate a
>> companion (*'allûp*) (17.9).

Displaying wisdom required a measure of considerate circumspection. Accordingly, it was foolish to go too often into a neighbour's house, so as to become a nuisance and an intruder:

> Hold back your foot from your neighbour's house,
>> lest your neighbour become weary of you and hate you
>> (25.17).

Equally in other ways it was possible, by unwise conduct, to offend a neighbour and so forfeit the possibility of establishing a satisfactory relationship:

Whoever blesses his neighbour with a loud voice
(rising early in the morning)
will be counted as cursing (27.14).

Although the sentence instruction here addresses a very specific pattern of conduct, it was no doubt intended to apply more generally to related behaviour patterns. With several commentators, we should probably delete the clause in parenthesis as a gloss, since it adds a second reason for the unwisdom of the action that is condemned. It is not that the praise is spoken at the wrong time, but rather that it is spoken for others to hear, and with the obvious intent of impressing them, so that it lacks sincerity. Similar kinds of ill-considered conduct are rebuked with the warning:

Like a madman who shoots deadly firebrands and arrows,
so is the person who deceives a neighbour
and says, 'It is only a joke!' (26.18-19).

It is not made clear in this whether the situation envisaged was one in which the deceit was intentional, but was unmasked so that the perpetrator attempted to pass off such bad conduct as a joke, or whether what was intended from the outset as a joke was very ill considered and inappropriate. In either case, the admonition appears aimed at insincerity in relationships with a neighbour. It seeks to discourage any conduct that fails to treat neighbourly relationships with the seriousness and respect that they deserve.

This is certainly the purport of the warning against flattery:

Whoever speaks smooth words to his neighbour
is spreading a net about his feet (29.5).

NRSV is careful here to spell out explicitly that the net is placed around the feet of the person who is the subject of the flattery. It is a warning that such smooth words are not meant sincerely and are designed to trap the victim.

The overall impact of these instructions, couched in the form of statements defining various community situations, is to urge a constant degree of awareness that good relationships with neighbours mattered greatly. What was said between, and about, neighbours, was considered to lie at the very heart of good neighbourly relationships. To treat them lightly, or to

attempt to belittle or manipulate a neighbour, was to endanger
the fundamental trust and goodwill between those who lived
in close proximity to one another. Without such trust, a healthy
social environment could not be established, and where there
was no such feeling of interdependence and solidarity (*ḥesed*)[20]
the very foundations of morality would be undermined.

It is in this respect that the conventional translation of *rēa'*
as 'friend' falls short of expressing the full range of moral
concern that the wisdom teachers were advocating. Such a
translation suggests that what is set out here in regard to
speech belongs properly in the category of counsel on 'how to
win friends'. Yet it is very evident from the attention focused
on the idea of 'the neighbour' that the wise were anxious for
more than the encouragement of healthy friendships. They
wanted a stable and mutually supportive community!

The wise were anxious to re-establish, on the basis of a code
of neighbourly conduct, the mutual commitment and support
that old Israel had found in the extended family and its
network of protection. Against such a background we may
look for a deeper meaning behind the rhetorical question of
Prov. 20.6:

> Many proclaim themselves loyal,
>   but who can find one worthy of trust? (20.6).[21]

If, in its origins, the notion of 'loyalty' did not necessarily
imply a nationwide commitment to the entire covenant community, but rather suggested no more than loyalty to one's
immediate family and kin, then the rhetoric is very meaningful. Loyalty, when narrowly conceived and focused on the
family, could appear morally virtuous, but yet fail to motivate
a larger and more practical community ethic. It might even

20. The importance of such a feeling of group loyalty as a basic ethical
requirement is set out in K. Doob Sakenfeld, *Faithfulness in Action: Loyalty
in Biblical Perspective* (Overtures to Biblical Theology; Philadelphia:
Fortress Press, 1985), cf. especially 'Loyalty: The Calling of the People of
God', pp. 101-30.

21. Cf. McKane, *Proverbs*, pp. 241, 545: 'Many a man proclaims his
loyalty, but who can find a faithful friend!' However, it would appear that
the instruction is not primarily about the quality of friendship, but about
the lack of real earnestness and commitment in community relationships.

undermine it! Only by questioning such traditionally conceived values, as the wisdom teachers appear to have been attempting, was it possible to establish a set of moral values appropriate to society *as it was actually experienced.*

Accordingly, good neighbourly relationships were not simply about 'making friends', but were directly concerned with the larger realm of moral obligations to society as a whole. It is against such a background that we can understand the desire of the wisdom teachers to keep matters out of court when neighbours quarrelled. However just the process of law endeavoured to be, founded as it was upon the notion of royal justice, such a system clearly had its limitations:

> What your eyes have seen
> > do not hastily bring into court;
> for what will you do in the end
> > when your neighbour puts you to shame (25.8)?

Admittedly the precise reasoning here is not easy to follow, but the implication seems clear. Do not rush to bring a charge against a neighbour; it may well rebound upon you! The problem of 'vexatious litigation', and the temptation to resort to the law in order to resolve neighbourly disputes, could come back onto the head of the over-hasty complainant. This attitude of great caution towards lawsuits and their consequences also appears in the admonition that follows in Prov. 25.9-10:

> Argue out your own dispute with your neighbour,
> > and do not reveal another's secret;
> or else someone who hears you will put you to shame,
> > and your bad reputation will have no end (25.9-10).[22]

22. Earlier commentators such as C.H. Toy and B. Gemser follow the interpretation suggested by the translation of Symmachus which does not envisage a reference here to the taking of legal action, but only to the spreading of gossip and rumour among the community. Cf. Toy, *Proverbs*, pp. 460-61: 'Instead of a warning against lawsuits or quarrels we thus have a caution against gossip'. However, McKane (*Proverbs*, pp. 250, 580-81) is surely correct in seeing here either over-hasty recourse to a court of law, or at least foolish talking about what takes place in legal proceedings. Cf. Driver, 'Problems', p. 190, and NRSV's rendering, 'Do not hastily bring into court'.

It is certainly worthy of note in regard to these admonitions urging a reluctance to press a lawsuit, that the ill-judged consequences of doing so are defined in terms of public humiliation. Although the penalties of suffering disgrace and shame are widely prominent elsewhere in the Old Testament as a major social threat, especially in the psalms and prophetic literature, they provide only a very limited sanction for the wise. Of the relatively few occurrences of the threats of shame in Proverbs, almost all of them refer either to the son or the wife who brings shame (cf. Prov. 10.5; 12.4 [wife]; 17.2; 19.26; 29.15 [children]).

It is therefore particularly noteworthy that hasty resort to press a lawsuit against a neighbour is resisted by the teachers of wisdom on the grounds that such action may well bring humiliation to the complainant. Two concerns appear to have fostered such advice. Any formal appeal to legal proceedings necessarily widened the dispute and magnified its seriousness. Furthermore, even those who 'won' their case would afterwards have to live with the bad feelings it had aroused. In such a situation normal relationships with neighbours involved in the dispute would become impossible.

However, alongside these anxieties there also appears to have been a deep consciousness that it was often very difficult to get at the truth when neighbours quarrelled:

> With their mouths the godless would destroy their neighbours,
>   but by knowledge the righteous are delivered (11.9).

There was, in any case, a further problem with trying to settle neighbourly disputes in a formal way. Even when justice was wholly on one side the ill temper and foolishness of the person accused could easily lead to the entire proceedings getting nowhere:

> When a wise person goes to law with fools,
>   there is ranting and ridicule and no let up (29.9).

The point that is made here would appear to be that the law court is no place to sort out most private disputes, even when the cause is valid, since it will inevitably generate further bad feelings and actions.

Even the gossip who told truths that were meant to remain

confidential did a great deal of harm (Prov. 11.13). Overall, the wise advocated a strong reluctance to bring quarrels between neighbours into more formal court proceedings, and also cautioned against acting as witness against a neighbour:

> Do not be a witness against your neighbour without cause,
>   and do not deceive with your lips (24.28).

The admonition here would seem to counsel not only reticence to bring a charge oneself, but also caution in acting as witness in support of another. The ease with which a witness could mislead, not necessarily with the intent of doing so, is well brought out in Prov. 18.17:

> The person who puts a case first seems right,
>   until another comes and cross-examines [him] (18.17).

Bearing in mind this warning against hasty judgments and a gullible attitude, the caution expressed by the wise against using formal legal procedures to settle quarrels between neighbours makes eminent sense. There was in any case a simpler, if more arbitrary, way of handling such problems:

> Casting the lot puts an end to disputes
>   and decides between strong-willed opponents (18.18).[23]

Overall, the advice that is proffered about dealing with difficult neighbours follows a clear-cut pattern. That such problems should arise in any community is taken as more or less inevitable. The person who experiences such tensions must not therefore feel too aggrieved. Some grievances could simply be overlooked and forgotten, while in other situations a word of rebuke could be sufficient to resolve the difficulty (Prov. 27.5). To carry the grievance further than this, by trying to involve other neighbours, or even to seek a formal legal settlement of the issue, should only be undertaken with the very greatest caution. If the situation goes this far, say the wise, it may become very difficult to settle the matter, and permanent damage may be done to the community.

The teachers of wisdom do appear to have nurtured a very

23. The Hebrew ʿṣûmîm must point either to powerful and influential opponents in a lawsuit (cf. NRSV), or more probably to those who are very confident and assured of their case, and so unwilling to give way.

clear and comprehensive understanding of what constitutes good neighbourly conduct. Moreover, they appear to have striven hard to generate what we can only describe as a 'good neighbour' awareness.

Neither the given bonds and responsibilities of the extended family, nor yet the natural and supportive human ties of friendship, constituted an adequate foundation upon which to build a true community. Only by establishing a more inclusive concern to support and protect all those who were neighbours in a given social context could a truly righteous society be built up. Poverty, quarrelsomeness, and sometimes downright malevolence and irresponsibility, could all put stresses on healthy community relationships. Nevertheless, the wise person was to strive and work for a strong and supportive community by becoming conscious of where the difficulties lay, and by countering evil with resilient and patient goodwill. Standing second only to the command to love God, the injunction 'to love one's neighbour' was singled out in the New Testament as summarising the full meaning of the biblical *torah*, and this is certainly significant. However, it cannot be regarded as a uniquely Christian development, since much of the language and moral awareness on which it rests is already deeply expressed in the Book of Proverbs.

PSALM 37: CONFLICT OF INTERPRETATION*

Walter Brueggemann

In two decades of energetic activity, wisdom studies have reached something of a plateau.[1] As a result of the work of Professor Whybray, along with Gerhard von Rad, James L. Crenshaw, and Roland E. Murphy (to name the most prominent), we are now able to take as a consensus a great deal concerning Israelite wisdom literature, e.g. its modes of disclosure, its assumptions about authority, its probable social contexts, its general theological intentionality, its tensions with more dominant modes of faith, and its paradoxical relation to broader wisdom traditions in the Near East.[2] The dominant wisdom literature, which functions as a normative reference point for scholarly forays concerning wisdom in other places, is found in Proverbs and Job, respectively a

*   I am delighted to join in congratulations to Professor Whybray. I am grateful not only for his scholarship that has impacted my own, but also for his recurring, gracious hospitality.
    1.   See the recent, comprehensive review of the state of scholarship in *The Sage in Israel and the Ancient Near East* (ed. John G. Gammie and Leo G. Perdue; Winona Lake: Eisenbrauns, 1990).
    2.   R. Norman Whybray, *The Intellectual Tradition in the Old Testament* (BZAW, 135; Berlin: de Gruyter, 1974), *Wisdom in Proverbs: The Concept of Wisdom in Proverbs 1–9* (SBT, 45; London: SCM Press, 1965), and his survey, 'The Social World of the Wisdom Writers', in *The World of Ancient Israel: Sociological, Anthropological and Political Perspectives* (ed. Ronald E. Clements; Cambridge: Cambridge University Press, 1989), pp. 227-50; Gerhard von Rad, *Wisdom in Israel* (Nashville: Abingdon Press, 1972); James L. Crenshaw, *Old Testament Wisdom: An Introduction* (Atlanta: John Knox, 1981); and Roland E. Murphy, *Wisdom Literature: Job, Proverbs, Ruth, Canticles, Ecclesiastes and Esther* (FOTL, 13; Grand Rapids: Eerdmans, 1981).

literature of social stability and a literature of dissonant protest.[3] Among other pieces of literature more or less related to this normative corpus, scholars have identified a fairly standard list of sapiential or instructional Psalms.[4]

In this paper, in the context of the scholarly consensus to which I have referred, I will consider Psalm 37, the most easily identified of the list of sapiential Psalms. I will consider it in terms of its socio-theological intentionality, and the effect of its discourse as an act of social power.[5] I will seek to show that the intention of the Psalm is (perhaps deliberately) much less clear than has been most often assumed. This indeterminate quality makes the Psalm surprisingly supple for interpretation, and invites conflicting readings in the face of contextual requirements, interests and possibilities.[6]

3.   On the dialectic, see Leo G. Perdue, 'Cosmology and the Social Order in the Wisdom Tradition', in *The Sage in Israel and the Ancient Near East*, pp. 457-78.

4.   See E. Gerstenberger, 'Psalms', in *Old Testament and Form Criticism* (ed. John H. Hayes; San Antonio: Trinity University Press, 1974), pp. 218-20; Kenneth Kuntz, 'The Canonical Wisdom Psalms of Ancient Israel', in *Rhetorical Criticism: Festschrift for James Muilenburg* (ed. J.J. Jackson and Martin Kessler; Pittsburgh: Pickwick Press, 1974), pp. 186-222; Sigmund Mowinckel, 'Psalms and Wisdom', *VTS* 3 (1955), pp. 204-24; and Roland Murphy, 'A Consideration of the Classification "Wisdom Psalms"', in *Congress Volume, Bonn 1962* (ed. J.A. Emerton *et al.*; VTSup, 9; Leiden Brill, 1963), pp. 156-67.

5.   On the notion of socio-theology, see Marie Augusta Neal, *A Socio-Theology of Letting Go: The Role of a First World Church Facing Third World Peoples* (New York: Paulist Press, 1977). More comprehensively on discourse as power, see Rebecca Chopp, *The Power to Speak: Feminism, Language, God* (New York: Crossroad, 1989).

6.   The programmatic notion of conflict of interpretations is, of course, that of Paul Ricoeur, *The Conflict of Interpretations* (ed. Don Ihde; Evanston, IL: Northwestern University Press, 1974). Ricoeur's juxtaposition of a 'hermeneutics of suspicion' and a 'hermeneutics of retrieval' is closely correlated to Perdue's nice pairing of 'The Paradigm of Order' and 'The Paradigm of Conflict'. See also Leo G. Perdue, 'The Social Character of Paragenesis and Paragenetic Literature', *Semeia* 50 (1990), especially pp. 8-12.

I

The Psalm shares the literary and theological assumptions
that are regularly assigned to the earlier collections of sayings
(sentences and instructions) in the book of Proverbs. That is,
the Psalm in its acrostic form could well be situated in the
book of Proverbs itself, for it relies upon the range of claims
that Zimmerli related to 'creation theology',[7] and which Koch
identified as a 'theory of retribution',[8] so decisive for the oldest
Proverbial wisdom. Of the many interesting and important
rhetorical features of the Psalm, I will consider four:

1. Within the context of the most general sapiential theme
that faithful living results in well-being (i.e. 'deeds–consequence'), the most recurrent accent in this Psalm is concern
for land (vv. 3, 9, 11, 22, 29, 34, plus v. 18 on 'inheritance').
The Psalm is an instruction about how to keep the land and
how to lose the land. The Psalm plunges the reader immediately into practical, public, disputed matters of property,
security and wealth, and therefore power. The statements
about land, as we expect in such discourse, draw issues of
property, security, wealth and power into the moral, theological world of faith, with specific though guarded reference to
Yahweh. The Psalm utilizes rhetoric that holds together
material interests and transcendental claims.[9] Thus the Psalm

7. Walther Zimmerli, 'The Place and Limit of the Wisdom in the
Framework of the Old Testament Theology', *SJT* 17 (1964), pp. 146-58.
8. Klaus Koch, 'Is There a Doctrine of Retribution in the Old
Testament?', in *Theodicy in the Old Testament* (ed. James L. Crenshaw;
Issues in Religion and Theology, 4; Philadelphia: Fortress Press, 1983),
pp. 57-87. See the critique of Koch by Michael V. Fox, *Qoheleth and his
Contradictions* (Sheffield: Almond Press, 1989), p. 125 n. 5.
9. On the interrelatedness of material interest and transcendental
claim, see Norman K. Gottwald, *The Tribes of Yahweh* (Maryknoll, NY:
Orbis Books, 1979), especially ch. 48 on the mutual reinforcement of
'Yahwism' and 'Social Egalitarianism'. See Gottwald, *Tribes*, pp. 592-607,
on his strictures against religious idealism which lacks self-conscious
connection to material interest. Hans-Joachim Kraus (*Psalms 1–59: A
Commentary* [Minneapolis: Augsburg, 1988], p. 408) wants to resist an
'idealist' interpretation of the Psalm by insisting that the Psalm is about
a relation to Yahweh, and not an 'idea' about retribution. Kraus, however,

repeatedly asserts that land (and its derivative blessings and security) are not elements in sheer economic transactions, but belong to the larger fabric of communal relationships with a moral dimension, where righteousness and/or wickedness is enacted, and where Yahweh's power to give or withhold blessing is operative.[10]

This emphasis upon land is expressed in a word pair that is of peculiar interest, *yrš/krt*. While the instructional theme of this Psalm is hardly remarkable in a sapiential context, the use of this word pair is noteworthy. The term *yrš* is regularly and most often used in the land traditions that focus upon or are derived from Deuteronomy. That is, the word is most used in the 'conquest traditions' which concern the seizure of land and the fulfillment of the ancestral promises.[11] Such a usage is quite remote from what seems to be the more domestic horizon of the Psalm concerning the administration of property in a local community, and the difficulties of acquiring and managing landed estates.[12] The term *yrš* is used five times in our Psalm (vv. 9, 11, 22, 29, 34). Remarkably, it is used only four times in all of Proverbs (20.13; 23.21; 30.9; 30.23).[13] In the first two uses of this latter list, the verb is used passively and negatively, 'come to poverty'; that is, these uses are quite unlike the positive uses in our Psalm which have the righteous

stays largely in the area of piety, and does not let material interests impinge upon his reading.

10. On the interface of the economy to the larger social fabric, see Karl Polanyi, *The Great Transformation* (Boston: Beacon Press, 1957), and more recently M. Douglas Meeks, *God the Economist: The Doctrine of God and Political Economy* (Minneapolis: Fortress Press, 1989).

11. For an exploration of other terms in the same semantic field, see Friedrich Horst, 'Zwei Begriffe für Eigentum (Besitz): נַחֲלָה und אֲחֻזָּה', in *Verbannung und Heimkehr: Beiträge zur Geschichte und Theologie Israels im 6. und 5. Jahrhundert v. Chr.* (ed. Arnulf Kuschke; Tübingen: J.C.B. Mohr [Paul Siebeck], 1961), pp. 135-56.

12. That is, this Psalm seems to reflect a settled economy, and does not have in purview military action, either aggressive or defensive. See below on the hypothesis of Frank Crüsemann.

13. The last of these texts has a textual problem at the point of our term. Pertaining to our term, see William McKane, *Proverbs: A New Approach* (OTL; Philadelphia: Westminster Press, 1970), p. 659.

person as an active subject. The verb, moreover, is not used at all in Job.

The second verb of the pair, *krt*, is used five times in our Psalm (vv. 9, 22, 28, 34, 38), four times in juxtaposition to *yrš*. (Only in v. 11 is *yrš* used without *krt* and only in v. 37 is *krt* used without *yrš*.) In all five uses of *krt*, the verb is passive, thus refusing to identify an active agent of 'cutting off'. The usage of *krt* is of interest for two reasons. First, it is quite uncommon to have the passive, negative verb used for such a local denial of property, for the term is most often used either for cultic excommunication (in the Priestly traditions), or as an outcome of war where the enemy is destroyed. Second, it is astonishing that the verb is used so rarely in the core sapiential literature. It occurs four times in Proverbs (2.22; 10.31; 23.18; 24.14) and not at all in Job.[14] In the uses in Proverbs, 2.22 most closely parallels the usage of our Psalm, and has the most noticeable similarity between the Psalm and Proverbs.[15] In 10.31 the verb is used for the 'cutting off' of a perverse tongue; in 10.30, the theme of our Psalm is used, but without the verb. In 23.18 and 24.14 the usage is not without linkage to the subject of our Psalm (see below on *'aḥᵃrît*), but the precise use of the verbs is not the same.

Thus, while 2.22 is a close parallel, in fact we have no other examples in the core wisdom material of the word pair, which occurs five times in our Psalm, plus two incidental uses not in a pair. I suggest that the Psalm, in a most imaginative way, has taken terms from quite different language worlds to formulate a new, taut argument. The term *yrš* is most at home in the world of large land conquest and the term *krt* is most used in terms of cultic exclusion or military defeat. Set in relation to each other, these powerful verbs make the possession of land of enormous moment, both as threat and as possibility. The repeated word pair forces the issue of land as property and security to be intimately linked to larger communal, socio-moral issues. The Psalm redefines and recontextualizes land,

14. The root *krt* occurs in Job 31.1 and 40.28, but not in a way related to our usages.
15. Whybray (*Wisdom in Proverbs*, pp. 40-41) regards these verses as an intrusion here, of a quite generalizing nature.

and that intimate linkage is the central question in reading the Psalm. Note well that connecting *land* and *Yahweh's righteousness* is not the same as 'deeds–consequence', which is a more reductionist category.

Moreover, the two verbs are each time used in an odd asymmetry. The negative verb *krt* is used passively, which conforms to Koch's notion of a 'sphere of destiny' in which land loss simply eventuates directly (automatically?) from wickedness.[16] By contrast, the positive verb *yrš* is an active verb, so that the righteous person is the active agent of acquiring land and generating. The Psalm might have used a hiphil form or a verb like *ntn* in a positive way, in order to make Yahweh's agency in giving land more visible.[17] The Psalm, however, prefers to portray the positive acquiring of land as an active accomplishment wrought through faithful living. Perhaps this contrast that correlates *positive / negative* with *active / passive* is a pedagogical strategy to emphasize that the acquisition or ownership of the land can be actively and intentionally pursued through faithful living. There is indeed something one can do to secure land, whereas the loss of land is not quite so direct.

2. The most startling statement in the Psalm is the assertion of vv. 25-26, the *nun* formulation of the acrostic. As we shall see below, these two verses lend most weight to the common judgment that this Psalm is the voice of a self-assured property-owning class which believes 'the system works', and which is prepared to deny any evidence that might tell against this settled, stable, reliable, controllable view of social reality. The statement that 'deeds–consequences' works is here flat and without nuance, entertaining no exception or slippage. Crüsemann takes v. 25 'as typifying the older wisdom in its entirety'.[18]

16. Koch, 'Is There a Doctrine of Retribution?', pp. 78-83 and *passim*.

17. In v. 34, the role of Yahweh is made more active and explicit, but only in this one instance.

18. Frank Crüsemann, 'The Unchangeable World: The "Crisis of Wisdom" in Koheleth', in *God of the Lowly: Socio-Historical Interpretations of the Bible* (ed. Willy Schottroff and Wolfgang Stegemann; Maryknoll, NY: Orbis Books, 1984), p. 61, takes v. 25 'as typifying the older wisdom

Such a view might be useful as an educational ploy in a very protected environment, or in the context of the very young and the very innocent (or the very devout). Such a view might even be sound piety, the kind that pervades the most innocent sapiential teaching that has as yet experienced no failure of nerve, and has not encountered any cognitive dissonance.[19] Clearly the affirmation of these verses cannot be sustained in the face of any critical social observation, but it is possible to avoid critical social observation in a protected social context.[20]

To his credit, John Calvin, who passionately embraces the truth of scripture, finds this claim at face value too much to defend. He concedes: 'It is certain that many righteous men have been reduced to beggary', and he alludes to the figure of Lazarus in Lk. 16.20 as an acknowledgment of that awareness.[21] Moreover, Calvin asserts that there is 'no certain rule with respect to temporal blessing'. Thus Calvin deftly and tersely erodes the reliability of 'deeds–consequences' as an adequate socio-theological claim, as it is undone for all of us by social reality. Calvin's acknowledgement is unflinching. His solution, however, is less daring, for he takes the affirmation of vv. 25-26 to refer to spiritual blessing, thus requiring the

in its entirety'. See also von Rad, *Wisdom in Israel*, pp. 124-37. Lawrence E. Johnson, *A Morally Deep World* (Cambridge: Cambridge University Press, 1991), pp. 11-12, who finds the same elemental conviction in the world of Socrates, when it is asserted that 'No evil can come to a good man', or can 'befall the soul'.

19. On cognitive dissonance, see Leon Festinger, *A Theory of Cognitive Dissonance* (Stanford: Stanford University Press, 1962), and the use made of the idea by Robert P. Carroll, *When Prophecy Failed: Reactions and Responses to Failure in the Old Testament Prophetic Traditions* (London: SCM Press, 1979).

20. See echoes of the same social posture in Ps. 112. Note well that such a sheltered view of reality is not merely ideological, i.e. holding to a notion, evidence notwithstanding. Such a view also requires a material arrangement, i.e. a deployment of economic-political power which assures that there will be no direct or visible contact with those who embody counter-evidence. The theory depends upon concrete social solutions and the power to sustain them.

21. John Calvin, *Commentary on the Book of Psalms: Second Volume* (Grand Rapids: Baker Book House, 1979), p. 39.

detachment of these verses from the materiality of the rest of the Psalm. Calvin's obvious discomfort with the verses leaves him, as it leaves any interpreter, a problem that requires comment (on which see below).

3. This Psalm celebrates 'the blameless' (*tāmîm*, v. 18, *tam*, v. 27), i.e. those who have solidarity, who bring well-being upon the community.[22] This two-fold usage of the same term is important because it brings this Psalm more fully (than does *yrš/krt*) into the orbit of sapiential vocabulary, and specifically into the problematic of Job. In v. 37 the word pair *tm/ysr* is the same one used to characterize the innocent, unperturbed Job of 1.1, 1.8 and 2.2. (See the same word pair in Prov. 2.7, 21; 29.10; Ps. 25.21.) The one who is 'blameless and upright' is the model person of faith and righteousness, and, according to innocent wisdom, the one sure to be blessed. Thus the word pair (and the use in our Psalm) points to the problem that occupies the poem of Job.

The poem of Job comes to be a battle over the actual blamelessness of Job, and over the significance of that blamelessness, once it is established. While Job is taunted by his wife for his treasured blamelessness (2.9), and is reminded that God does not care about his blamelessness (22.3), what counts most for the dramatic power of the poem is that Job refuses to give up his claim of blamelessness (cf. 12.4; 27.5; 31.6). Until the very end, Job will not relent, even though his claim requires a frontal attack on God's own 'blamelessness' (9.20-22).

Thus our Psalm is unflinchingly allied with and supportive of Joban claims. To be sure, neither the rhetoric nor the courage of this Psalm is as far developed or as intense as is the Joban argument. But the premise is the same, and the implied struggle for moral coherence is the same. Moreover, Prov. 28.10 asserts that the blameless do inherit (*nḥl*), the same verb used in Ps. 37.18 with the term *tāmîm*. It is clear that our Psalm is not as innocent as it first appears, but is willing to take a strong—and what turns out to be a contentious and difficult— stance as the core sapiential argument of theodicy.[23]

22. On the term, see Walter Brueggemann, 'A Neglected Sapiental Word Pair', *ZAW* 89 (1977), pp. 234-58.
23. While Crenshaw shows that later, more developed wisdom teaching

4. The Psalm concludes with a bold assertion that, in the end, matters will be sorted out according to moral distinctions (vv. 37-40). In important ways, these verses simply reiterate the teaching of the entire Psalm. The Psalm does, however, look to a resolution not yet obvious or in hand. It is as though the Psalm in the end concedes that the claim of vv. 25-26 is not obviously established, and so it must provide a faithful way around the problem. We may distinguish between two important concluding assertions.

First, in vv. 39-40, the rhetoric of the Psalm is escalated to witness to the active, decisive intrusion of Yahweh who 'helps, rescues, rescues, saves'. While there have heretofore been hints of divine activity, this is a bold departure from 'deeds–consequences' rhetoric; the verses stand in some tension with the rest of the Psalm and more nearly cohere with Israel's 'confessional' traditions. In an emergency, the Psalm is pushed beyond its excessive innocence to a more vigorous theological affirmation.

Second, and for our purposes more important, vv. 37-38 twice use the term 'posterity (*'ah^arît*) to sort out the future of the blameless and the wicked. Three rhetorical points may be noted. First, the word pair 'blameless, upright' is used as in Job 1.1, 8 and 2.3. This blameless-upright one is the quintessential wise person. Second, the negative passive verb, *krt*, is again used, this time without being paired with *yrš*. Third, in these two verses, unlike vv. 39-40, there are no active verbs and no agent. Yahweh is not mentioned. These verses seem to affirm fully that the righteous person does indeed create a reliable 'sphere of destiny' into the future.

What interests us most here, however, is the double use of *'ah^arît*. The Psalm is willing and able to look beyond a simple moral calculation to a full, climactic reckoning ultimately wrought by God.[24] The book of Proverbs had already concluded

must address the issue of theodicy more boldly and directly, I suggest that the core options concerning theodicy are already present in the old sayings.

24. The fullest content to 'ultimate reckoning' in this Psalm is given by Mitchell Dahood, *Psalms II, 51–100: Introduction, Translation and Notes* (AB, 17; Garden City, NY: Doubleday, 1968), pp. 192-15. Dahood takes

that those who act wickedly have no future, or a sad, lifeless future (Prov. 14.12; 16.25; 20.21; 24.20). Two other uses of *'aḥᵃrît* in Proverbs are of particular interest. In 23.18 and 24.14, it is affirmed that the wise and righteous do indeed have a 'future and hope', i.e. something yet to be received that is beyond present circumstance. Moreover, this positive affirmation in both cases makes use of the niphal of *krt*, the same verb used negatively in our Psalm. Thus our Psalm in its conclusion is a statement of enormous confidence, well beyond the careful calculations and symmetries more easily associated with the earlier part of the Psalm. It is perhaps too much to take these verses 'eschatologically', but the formula of 'yet a little while' in v. 10 encourages such a reading.[25]

There is of course much more to be said about the rhetoric and intentionality of this Psalm. These four elements—*yrš/krt* concerning land, old/young, blameless, posterity—are enough to suggest that this teaching is not a bland summary of an innocuous, optimistic prudentialism. It is, rather, alert to an important intellectual dispute that admits of no easy resolution. Moreover, it is evident that the Psalm is not one long, flat instruction marked by sameness and consistency. There is a variety of markers concerning abrupt rhetorical and substantive turns. These markers raise up issues, evidence tensions, lack of resolution and urgency in the ongoing conversation of practical faith. We are now ready to ask about the mode of discourse and the socio-theological intentionality of the Psalm.

II

Our first reading of this Psalm concerns its 'ideological' support of an economic, social *status quo*. The preoccupation with land in this Psalm assures us that the Psalm is deeply

the negative judgment of v. 17 as 'eschatological destiny', and the positive statement of v. 24 as 'the final reward of the righteous after death'. Dahood's view has not commanded very much scholarly support.

25. While avoiding the specific affirmation of Dahood, Calvin (*Psalms 36–92*, p. 51) nicely says, 'It behooves us to give God time to restore to order the confused state of things'.

embedded in and concerned for social interest. It is not neutral, disinterested or transcendental. In order to explicate this Psalm in relation to its social interest, I shall appeal to Karl Mannheim's much criticized but still useful categories of 'ideology and utopia'.[26]

Psalm 37 is *a powerful practice of social ideology* in the service of landed interests. The term 'ideology' of course admits to two quite different readings. The earlier Marxist usage of the term, operative in Mannheim, is pejorative. Thus ideology is an attempt to articulate one's social interest as social reality, or to present a part of the truth of social reality as though it were the whole. Ideology in this sense consists in deliberate deception in order to present a false, self-serving, self-justifying portrayal of reality. Mannheim uses 'ideology' in this way to describe acts of social legitimation taken by those who hold power. Such legitimating acts defend and justify the *status quo*, so that unequal social arrangements are offered as social 'givens'.

A more neutral use of the term 'ideology', carefully articulated by Clifford Geertz, is that it is simply a foundational articulation of the world which gives sense to experience and which permits the community to share in legitimated assumptions that permit social function.[27] In this sense, the term serves as a near synonym for theology, and contains no pejorative dimension.[28] In one usage or the other, Psalm 37 is 'ideology',

26. In Old Testament studies, the categories of Mannheim have been most programmatically employed by Paul D. Hanson, *The Dawn of Apocalyptic: The Historical and Sociological Roots of Jewish Apocalyptic Eschatology* (Philadelphia: Fortress Press, 1975), p. 72 n. 45, and *passim*. On Mannheim, see Paul Ricoeur, *Lectures on Ideology and Utopia* (New York: Columbia University Press, 1986), ch. 10.

27. Clifford Geertz, 'Ideology as a Cultural System', in his *The Interpretation of Cultures: Selected Essays* (New York: Basic Books, 1973), pp. 193-233. See Ricoeur, *Lectures on Ideology and Utopia*, especially pp. 137-43, and W.J.T. Mitchell, *Iconology: Image, Text, Ideology* (Chicago: University of Chicago Press, 1986), especially Part Three. The issue of the meaning or intention of ideology turns on the issue of whether a truth claim is distortive or integrative.

28. My impression is that when used in this way by 'neutral' social scientists, i.e. positivists, even the so-called neutral usage is in fact

either legitimating inequality, or simply establishing 'deeds–consequence' as a way of understanding public moral coherence.

The use of the category 'ideology' for Psalm 37 was suggested to me by Otto Kaiser, in his helpful study of Job.[29] Kaiser understands ideology to be

> human attempts to explain the whole or important parts of the world or life, and so to gain compelling firm guidelines.[30]

Kaiser further holds that in the early part of the sixth century BCE there was a systematic 'ideologization' of faith in Judah, which produced an ethical rigorism.[31] He describes that effort in this way:

> The ancient religious connection of righteousness and life was elevated to a law that allows no exceptions, and consequently the sufferings of the innocent were understood either as necessary test and purification, or must be categorically denied.[32]

Kaiser then proceeds to cite Psalm 1, Prov. 11.21, 13.9, Gen. 18.16-25 and a confession of Jeremiah as examples of the emergence of this ideology.

Kaiser's argument interests me specifically because he suggests that Psalm 37 is a primary example of this ideology.[33] (He dates the Psalm to the Maccabean period, but the argument would pertain even with a somewhat earlier dating of the Psalm.) Kaiser's argument concerning this Psalm and others like it is that it prepares the way for the literature of

---

latently pejorative. Ricoeur, *Lectures on Ideology and Utopia*, p. 161, writes: 'Because of ideology's origin in the disparaging labeling used by Napoleon against his adversaries, we must keep in mind the possibility that it is never a purely descriptive concept'.

29. Otto Kaiser, *Ideologie und Glaube: Eine Gefahrdung christlichen Glaubens am alttestamentlichen Beispiel aufgezeigt* (Stuttgart: Radius, 1984).

30. Kaiser, *Ideologie und Glaube*, p. 27.

31. Kaiser, *Ideologie und Glaube*, p. 29.

32. Kaiser, *Ideologie und Glaube*, p. 30.

33. Kaiser, *Ideologie und Glaube*, pp. 36-39. On the burden of teaching as 'order', see Raymond C. Van Leeuwen, 'Immorality and Worldview in Proverbs 1–9', *Semeia* 50 (1991), pp. 111-44.

Job and Ecclesiastes as it struggles precisely with this formidable ideology.[34]

Kaiser's argument is richly suggestive, though two preliminary reservations may be noted. First, Kaiser's definition of ideology makes it difficult to determine if his usage is pejorative or not. Second, his willingness to identify the time and historical context of the process of 'ideologization' is not without problem, because it may indeed reflect the old (largely Christian) bias about the 'decline into Judaism'. My own propensity is to take a sociological rather than historical-chronological view of the process. That is, the emergence of ideology is not to be understood as a decision taken at a certain moment in Judaism, but as a characteristic tendency in every time, of those who believe they can sustain the *status quo* by careful attention to moral conduct, and by those who legitimate their privilege by an appeal to 'transcendence'.[35] While there may have been such an intense tendency in post-exilic Judaism, the texts are too difficult to date and the dating largely contains a circular argument in the service of an old hypothesis about 'degenerate Judaism'.

That modest criticism notwithstanding, Kaiser's reading of Psalm 37 seems to me to be correct. The Psalm is a bold and confident articulation of a 'deeds–consequence' view of moral coherence that entertains no doubt, has no failure of nerve, and will host no exceptions.

The statements that contain our two words, *yrš/krt*, make the point with clarity and without ambiguity:

> For the wicked shall be *cut off*,
> but those who wait for the Lord shall *inherit* the land (v. 9).

---

34. Bertil Albrektson, *Studies in the Text and Theology of the Book of Lamentations with a Critical Edition of the Peshitta Text* (Lund: Gleerup, 1963), pp. 214-39, has set up the same problem concerning 'theodic settlement' and 'theodic crisis' with reference to Deuteronomy and Lamentations.

35. On this appeal to transcendence and a critique of it, see Walter Brueggemann, 'A Shape for Old Testament Theology, I: Structure Legitimation', *CBQ* 47 (1985), pp. 28-46, and 'A Shape for Old Testament Theology, II: Embrace of Pain', *CBQ* 47 (1985), pp. 395-415.

The use of *qwh* suggests this is not confidence for what is in hand, but the reception of land is regarded as certain in time to come.[36]

> ...those blessed by the Lord shall *inherit* the land,
>> but those cursed by him shall be *cut off* (v. 22).

Unlike vv. 9 and 10-11, this statement allows a modest place for Yahweh who is the power of blessing and of curse. But the power of blessing and curse attributed to Yahweh, in v. 21, is referred back to wickedness and righteousness, which here concern economic practices of borrowing and generosity. Thus the cause of *yrš/krt* is not the work of Yahweh, but one's own economic performance.

> ...the children of the wicked shall be *cut off*.
> The righteous shall *inherit* the land,
>> and live in it forever (vv. 28b-29).

The statement lacks specificity, but vv. 27-28 which precede refer to evil, good and justice. Gerstenberger, in his comment on Prov. 3.7, identifies this admonition as an epitome of the general perspective of wisdom.[37] It is the embrace of justice or injustice that leads to land or to land loss.

> Wait for the Lord, and keep to his way,
>> and he will exalt you to *inherit* the land;
>> you will look on the *destruction* (*krt*) of the wicked (v. 34).

In this text, Yahweh has an active verb, 'exalt', but again it is 'hoping' and 'keeping' that produce material results.

To these texts that have the word pair may be added vv. 3, 10-11, 18 and 37-38, all of which derive an assured future from a properly practiced present.

Three matters are evident in these assertions. First, they admit of no exceptions or ambiguity. The linkage of act and

---

36. On the concreteness of such waiting-hope, see Hans Walter Wolff, *Anthropology of the Old Testament* (Philadelphia: Fortress Press, 1974), pp. 149-55, and Walther Zimmerli, *Man and his Hope in the Old Testament* (SBT, 2/20; Naperville, IL: Allenson, 1968), ch. 3, especially p. 29.

37. Erhard Gerstenberger, *Wesen und Herkunft des 'apodiktischen Rechts'* (WMANT, 20; Neukirchen–Vluyn: Neukirchener Verlag, 1965), p. 49.

outcome is one-to-one. Second, the grammatical construction characteristically says nothing about how the act and the outcome are related to each other.[38] It is simply so, taken as a premise and as a given, established through the observation of endless cases. The claim which has become 'ideological' is based upon a deposit of trusted experience that is not specified or explained. What was an experienced conclusion has become a non-negotiable premise. Third, while there is no visible or explicit linkage, Yahweh hovers around these assertions in a variety of ways.

We may identify four ways in which Yahweh is regarded in these sayings on land as an outcome of conduct:

1. Only in v. 34 is Yahweh the explicit agent of inheritance.
2. In vv. 28, 29, Yahweh is the implicit subject of the acts.
3. In vv. 3 (cf. v. 4) and 9, Yahweh is the referent of the saying, but only as object, not as subject.
4. In vv. 11, 28b-29 and 37-38, Yahweh is absent, not mentioned at all.

While Yahweh is never far from the process, Yahweh's actual involvement in the process of inheriting and disinheriting is less than direct and frontal. This gingerly way with Yahweh suggests that the guaranteeing presence of *Yahweh* is indispensable for the teaching, even though the teaching is primarily preoccupied with the *land process* itself, and only then, belatedly, with its ethical-theological precondition. It is no stretch of the imagination to conclude that where Yahweh is minimally involved, the moral-theological requirements do indeed seem to be instrumental to the goal of land, precisely what an ideological statement might entail. That is, Yahweh is *useful* to the real concern.[39]

---

38. On the function of such parataxis, see Walter Brueggemann, 'The Uninflected "Therefore" of Hos. 4.1-3', in *Reading from This Place: Social Location and Biblical Interpretation* (ed. Fernando F. Segovia and Mary Ann Tolbert; forthcoming from Westminster/John Knox).

39. I have in mind the notion of 'function' as Norman Gottwald has utilized it (*The Tribes of Yahweh*, pp. 608-21). I am of course aware of the problem of utilitarian faith. But of course this Psalm and its Job-like claim are concerned precisely with the 'usefulness' of Yahweh for the

The identification of the social context and intentionality of such an ideology inevitably are to some extent circular. Though scholars are not fully agreed about the institutional context of such sayings, it is surely not too much to see that this saying reflects the perception of interest of the landed who construe and advocate certain moral-social prerequisites for acquiring and holding land.[40] The Psalm reflects a conviction that the holding of land is itself a sign of *virtue* as well as blessing. The presumption of virtue as well as blessing is the decisive ideological turn in the argument, for it introduces the category of *merit*.

The Psalm not only affirms social stability and continuity, but assumes the virtue of those who enact sound stability, and seeks by its teaching to fend off the loss of property which would be tantamount to the coming of chaos. This reading of the Psalm as a socially interested statement is specifically suggested by Robert Gordis and less directly by Brian Kovacs.[41] Gordis's analysis is especially important because it is prior to and largely innocent of any theoretical, sociological reference, which was taken up in Old Testament studies well after Gordis's publication. That is, Gordis has no social theory to impose upon the text, as have later scholars (including Kovacs and Gottwald) who have become methodologically more intentional. Without appeal to any such grand theory, Gordis sees that the Psalm reflects the affluent land-owner class, as

legitimacy and sustenance of its moral concern. On the question of the 'usefulness' of faith, see Job 1.9.

40. Perdue, 'Cosmology and the Social Order', pp. 476-78, has most helpfully summarized the discussion concerning the social location of the sages.

41. R. Gordis, 'The Social Background of Wisdom Literature', in *Poets, Prophets, and Sages: Essays in Biblical Interpretation* (Bloomington: Indiana University Press, 1971), pp. 160-97; Brian W. Kovacs, 'Is There a Class-Ethic in Proverbs?', in *Essays in Old Testament Ethics* (ed. James L. Crenshaw and John T. Willis; New York: Ktav, 1974), pp. 171-89. Less directly, see also J. David Pleins, 'Poverty in the Social World of the Wise', *JSOT* 37 (1987), pp. 61-78; R.N. Whybray, *Wealth and Poverty in the Book of Proverbs* (JSOTSup, 99; Sheffield: JSOT Press, 1990), and the review article by Whybray, 'Poverty, Wealth, and Point of View in Proverbs', *ExpTim* 100 (1989), pp. 332-36.

does proverbial wisdom more generally. Kovacs with more methodological awareness concludes that the literature (of this proverbial kind) has a strong ideological cast.[42] In my own terms, Psalm 37 as ideology is 'structure legitimating' and serves to sustain a socio-theological 'orientation'.[43] Verses 25-26 provide the ultimate expression of this self-assured claim which unashamedly overrides, denies and ignores social reality to the contrary. The Psalm seems to have arrived at self-confidence for the owner class that this teaching is more reliable than any observable data to the contrary.[44]

III

What interests me, however, is the fact that this Psalm seems to receive a second, very different reading in a second, very different context. In some more contemporary liberation literature, the sorts of claims made in this Psalm are taken not as congratulations for the landed, but as *a ground for hope for the landless*.[45] Moreover, the usage of v. 11 in the Sermon on the Mount (Mt. 5.5) suggests a reading of the Psalm very different from any socially ideological reading—a profound act of determined hope.[46] This reading takes the Psalm (a) as a

42. Kovacs, 'Is There a Class-Ethic?', carefully nuances the class interest in the sayings, but sees that it is not blatant, but somewhat open to new experience that may cause revision in social interest.

43. On my use of these terms, see Brueggemann, 'A Shape for Old Testament Theology I', and *The Message of the Psalms: A Theological Commentary* (Minneapolis: Augsburg, 1984), pp. 25-49.

44. This is then what I term a 'theodic settlement', i.e. an established balance between cost and benefit in terms of social power which legitimates a particular arrangement of power, and which shapes and limits social expectations. While it is usual to employ the term 'theodicy' only in a crisis when social norms seem dysfunctional, in fact there can be no theodic crisis unless there is a previous consensus settlement. I take Ps. 37 to function in powerful and persuasive ways as such a settlement.

45. On this reading, the promise of land becomes something like a 'preferential option for the poor'. See Jose Miranda, *Marx and the Bible: A Critique of the Philosophy of Oppression* (Maryknoll, NY: Orbis Books, 1974), p. 97.

46. See Sharon H. Ringe, *Jesus, Liberation, and the Biblical Jubilee: Images for Ethics and Christology* (Overtures to Biblical Theology;

promise and guarantee of land for those who seem to have no means (except the claims of morality) whereby to acquire land, and therefore (b) as a critical assault on present land arrangements which are unjust and which cannot be sustained. That is, the Psalm is turned against the 'wicked' who now possess the very land that has been promised to 'the meek' and will indeed be given to them. In a word, what is evidently an 'ideological' program of the Psalm to legitimate the *status quo* becomes a practice of 'utopia', an assurance of well-being which is certain if not yet in hand, an assurance of well-being which subverts present ideological claims and their base in social arrangements. Frederic Jameson has subtly observed that the practice of ideology itself has inherent within it a utopian element, a yearning that the hard claims of ideology will eventuate in a well-being that is better than present, legitimate, defended, experienced reality.[47]

Thus, in a second reading, Psalm 37 is an act of utopian hope, i.e. an affirmation about the future, even though the voice of the Psalm gives no hint about how to get from here to

Philadelphia: Fortress Press, 1985), pp. 51-54, and Robert A. Guelich, *The Sermon on the Mount: A Foundation for Understanding* (Waco, TX: Word Books, 1982), pp. 81-83, 101-102, 114. Both Ringe and Guelich link the text to Isa. 61 and its echoes of the Jubilee, and refer to the context of Qumran. While Guelich resists a purely materialist interpretation to which Ringe is more inclined, he says of the promise of v. 11 (p. 101), 'The hope of inheriting the earth is but another Old Testament expression for the initiative of God's sovereign rule in history on behalf of his own (e.g., Isa. 61:7)'. This latter accent is also sounded by Ulrich Luz, *Matthew 1–7: A Commentary* (Edinburgh: T. & T. Clark, 1989), p. 236: 'The promise of the earth makes clear that the Kingdom of Heaven also comprises a new "this world"'.

47. Fredric Jameson, *The Political Unconscious: Narrative as a Socially Symbolic Act* (London: Methuen, 1981), p. 289, writes, '...*all* class consciousness—or in other words, all ideology in the strongest sense, including the most exclusive forms of ruling class consciousness just as much as that of the oppositional or oppressed classes—is in its very nature Utopian'. In speaking of the dialectic of ideology and utopia, Ricoeur, *Lectures on Ideology and Utopia*, p. 251, echoes Jameson: 'As for myself, I assume completely the inextricable role of this utopian element, because I think that it is ultimately constitutive of any theory of ideology. It is always from the depth of a utopia that we may speak of an ideology.'

BRUEGGEMANN *Psalm 37* 247
there. That is, it is not known how the wicked will lose the
land and the righteous will receive it.[48] It is only stated that it
will be so. In this reading, the Psalm is not a defense of
present social reality, but it is an 'eschatological' anticipation
that things will assuredly be different.[49] The transformation of
'ideology' into 'utopia' in this Psalm clearly requires a different
reading of the text which finds in the text very different
points of accent.[50]

We may identify some of the points that authorize and legitimate a second reading, and which seem to be freshly noted in
this second discernment.

— The verbs to which we have referred (*yrš/krt*) are
characteristically imperfect and admit of a future
reading. They describe what is assured, but not in
hand. The word pair is anticipatory, not descriptive.
— In v. 10, the phrase *'ôd mᵉ'aṭ*, if not 'apocalyptic', in
any case anticipates a significant social inversion that
is about to happen.

48. The rhetorical elusiveness of the Psalm about how the wicked will
be dispossessed, in something like a *parataxis*, is strategically important
for the affirmation of the Psalm. The revolutionary hope of the Psalm
knows and trusts that more is assured than is logically or technically
explainable. This elusiveness is part of the subversive rhetorical strategy
for avoiding socio-economic-political details to the hope, details that are
bound to reduce the power of the hope and end in the 'explanations' of the
'ruling class'.
49. 'Eschatology' is admittedly a poor word for the hope of this Psalm.
By the term we can only mean the resolution of social conflict in the
social process, never anything 'beyond' the social process, which would
detract from the socio-economic force of the hope.
50. This is a telling and important case of 'reader-response'. It is
important that in the 'conflict of interpretations' and the freedom of
'reader response', we are not concerned with aesthetic options but with
power struggles driven by competing vested interests. John Goldingay,
'The Dynamic Cycle of Praise and Prayer in the Psalms', *JSOT* 20 (1981),
pp. 85-90, has rightly seen that the same Psalm can perform more than
one such function and yield more than one reading. See my response:
Walter Brueggemann, 'Response to John Goldingay's "The Dynamic
Cycle of Praise and Prayer"', *JSOT* 22 (1982), pp. 141-42.

— The double use of *'aḥªrît* in vv. 37-38 anticipates a
   time to come, quite in contrast to the present, a usage
   of *'aḥªrît* echoed in Ps. 73.17.

— The pervasive assault on the 'wicked' suggests a present-tense time of speaking that is distressing, if not
   unbearable. The wicked, i.e. those who are quite unlike
   and in conflict with the voice of the Psalm, apparently
   now control the land. Thus the anticipatory stance of
   the Psalm is not simply an act of pious trust, though it
   is in part.[51] It is also an act of social criticism and
   social assault that means to expose present realities,
   and to provide the ground for questioning and dis-
   mantling the legitimacy of those who now wrongly
   hold the land.

— The conditions for properly and securely holding the
   land are serious social practices and not simply pious
   postures. These conditions include trust in Yahweh,
   doing good (v. 3), waiting for Yahweh (vv. 9, 34),
   meekness (v. 11), being blameless (vv. 18, 37), righteousness expressed as generosity (v. 21), and righteousness (vv. 29, 39). This entire list, when taken as
   a whole, proposes a radical counter-ethic, counter to
   those who are exploitative, greedy land-grabbers.

The Psalm advocates and proposes, according to
this second reading, a radically different communal
practice. These conditions are not 'ideas', but are concrete social practices. Of course the mere saying of this
hope for land does not turn the hope into reality. The
Psalm nonetheless invites and insists upon a serious
adjudication of two ways in which social power is
secured and in which social stability is developed and
maintained. If the practice of righteousness concerns
the maintenance of a viable social fabric, then the
hope relates to the specifics of socio-economic practice.
These real and serious preconditions for property

51. Kraus, *Psalms 1–59*, p. 408, while recognizing a warm piety in the
Psalm, also notes the 'this-worldly hope for God's intervention' that he
sees resurfacing in Mt. 5.5, in a way congruent with Guelich's comment
on the Beatitude.

mean that the property must be managed with reference to Yahweh and with reference to the community
intended by Yahweh, clearly reference points sys-
tematically disregarded by the detached market-
economy practice of the wicked who believe gain is
unrelated to social fabric.

— We have seen that Yahweh is only softly articulated
in these affirmations. There is no doubt, however, that
the reference to Yahweh, even if subdued, is decisive,
as in the concluding verses (vv. 39-40). It is the inter-
ventionist, side-taking God who is decisive in the
adjudication of land, property, and finally peace.

— The reference to 'blamelessness' (vv. 18, 37) brings
this Psalm into the world of Job. There is no doubt
that Job's 'blamelessness' is deeply under assault in
the poem of Job. Nonetheless, in more recent readings
of Job, the restoration of Job (42.10-17) is taken as
integral to the art form and to the theological intention of the final form of the text.[52] 'Blamelessness' in
the end is not mocked: Job may indeed serve God 'for
nought' (Job 1.9), but in the end he *is* rewarded. Thus
I suggest that Psalm 37, read as social anticipation
(and therefore as social criticism), is not naive and
innocent about real social conflict and frustration, but
in fact traces the same socio-theological dispute that is
more explicit and vigorous in Job. It is the conviction

52. On the role and function of these last verses in the book of Job, see
J. Gerald Janzen, *Job* (Interpretation; Atlanta: John Knox, 1985),
pp. 261-69, and especially David J.A. Clines, 'Deconstructing the Book of
Job', in *What Does Eve Do to Help? and Other Readerly Questions to the
Old Testament* (JSOTSup, 94; Sheffield: JSOT Press, 1990), pp. 106-23.
On pp. 113-14, Clines writes: '[I]t is even more disconcerting that what
one hardly ever sees argued is the view that in fact the epilogue under-
mines the rest of the Book of Job...It tells us, and not at all implicitly,
that the most righteous man on earth is the most wealthy...[B]y ch. 42,
no one, not even in heaven, is left in any doubt that it is the piety of Job,
somewhat eccentrically expressed to be sure, that has led to his ultimate
superlative prosperity. What the book has been doing its best to
demolish, the doctrine of retribution, is on its last page triumphantly
affirmed.'

of the 'righteous' that they live in a world where wicked land practices cannot prevail.[53] In the meantime, the righteous (meek) must wait (vv. 9, 34). In their waiting, they must act in and for the community in ways quite contrasted with the modes of the wicked who act against the community.

I do not suggest that a *utopian reading* is a better or final reading that trumps the *ideological reading*. I suggest only that it is a second possible reading. This reading does not resolve the oddness of vv. 25-26, but surrounds and perhaps overwhelms those verses with counter claims. Even the utopian, anticipatory practice of the Psalm in the end, however, will not break with the claims of vv. 25-26, which are a clear insistence upon a righteously ordered creation.[54] The anticipatory note, however, resists any chance of self-congratulations that an ideological reading of vv. 25-26 might host. That is, the anticipatory reading offers no congratulations because the gift of land is not yet in hand, and will not ever be in hand because of any virtue or merit. These verses have nothing in hand, but are a passionate hope without any hint of a failure of nerve. It is the deep expectation of these verses that the children of the righteous will not in the end be hungry or reduced to begging. In a world currently wicked,

53. On this conviction, see my analysis of Psalm 9–10: Walter Brueggemann, 'Psalms 9–10: A Counter to Conventional Social Reality', in *The Bible and the Politics of Exegesis: Essays in Honor of Norman K. Gottwald on his Sixty-Fifth Birthday* (ed. David Jobling *et al.*; Cleveland: Pilgrim Press, 1991), pp. 3-15, 297-301. I have urged that in these two Psalms, (a) Yahweh is an advocate for the poor against the rich, and (b) the Psalms are themselves an act of rhetorical, and therefore socio-political, transformation.

54. On the order of creation as an horizon for anticipatory faith, see H.H. Schmid, 'Creation, Righteousness and Salvation: "Creation Theology" as the Broad Horizon of Biblical Theology', in *Creation in the Old Testament* (ed. Bernhard W. Anderson; Philadelphia: Fortress Press, 1984), pp. 102-17, and Rolf P. Knierim, 'On the Task of Old Testament Theology', *HBT* 6 (1984), pp. 91-128.

however, the promise and assurance are not yet kept. Thus
the children of the righteous are vigorous, determined, unde-
terred waiting ones.[55]

IV

The first, i.e. the ideological, reading of the Psalm assumes
and affirms a tight connection of deed and outcome, reflective
of a stable, affluent society, as Gordis has shown.[56] In the first
reading, the Psalm 'reproduces' a stable economic order that
maintains economic advantage for a certain element in the
community. Crüsemann concludes: 'Where ownership of land
is uncontested and at the same time a segmentary solidarity
reigns, it will be normal to expect a correspondence between
what one does and how one fares'.[57]

We must now ask about a second context which has
produced a second, i.e. utopian, reading of the Psalm. The proposal of a social context is always inevitably somewhat hypothetical and circular, but we may at least entertain a cogent
social possibility. In his shrewd analysis of the world of
Koheleth, Crüsemann has suggested that, in the Hellenistic
period, an alien state intruded upon the economy of well-
established small landowners, i.e. the ones who readily trusted
the ideology of 'deed and consequences'.[58] Thus, according to
Crüsemann, the ideological crisis of Koheleth is situated in the
quite concrete social situation of small landowners. As the

55. Notice that the affirmations are thoroughly material in their focus,
not 'spiritual' as in Calvin, and not pious as in Kraus.
56. Crüsemann, 'The Unchangeable World', accepts the verdict of
Gordis as the base line for his own conclusions. He characterizes Gordis's
argument as leading to a conclusion on social location that is
'unquestionably' true (p. 58) and 'irrefutable' (p. 61). In a much earlier
context, P.A. Munch, 'Das Problem des Reichtums in den Psalmen 37, 49,
73', *ZAW* 55 (1937), pp. 37-40, reached the parallel conclusion that this
Psalm reflects a future for a *Bauernideal*.
57. Crüsemann, 'The Unchangeable World', p. 62.
58. Crüsemann's argument is in part based on H.G. Kippenberg,
Religion und Klassenbildung im antiken Judäa (SUNT, 14; Göttingen,
Vandenhoeck & Ruprecht, 1978), to which I have not had access. See the
critical comment of Fox, *Qoheleth and his Contradictions*, pp. 142-46.

state pre-empted property and the capacity to make one's own economic decisions, the society became less and less amenable to management and control, and became increasingly an uncritical, acquisitive, currency-based society. As a result, such threatening experience made appeal to the Yahwistic tradition problematic, economic gain became primary, and despair issued in a somber reflection upon death.[59] In Crüsemann's analysis, Koheleth reflects a growing helplessness and cynicism that seeks only 'to avoid conflict', withdraw from stress, and is determined not to 'get involved'.[60] The urging of Koheleth is, 'One is not to be too much a *tsaddiq*!'[61]

The experience of Koheleth, reflected in the literature, is part of a context that made the old theological confidence in 'deed–consequence' impossible. With the abandonment of the ideology that no longer resonated with experience, Koheleth ends in despair.

Accepting the proposal of Kippenberg and Crüsemann,[62] I suggest that the resignation of Koheleth marks a transition that in the end eventuated in a second, utopian reading of Psalm 37, just as the resignation of Koheleth destroyed the first, ideological reading. In a situation of powerlessness and inability to manage or even to understand one's social setting, the new readers of the Psalm will never reiterate the old ideology, but they also will not accept the resignation of Koheleth. They will instead take the Psalm as a bold anticipation that no longer trusts naively, but that moves past the sense of

59. While he does not attend much to the material dimension of the teaching, James L. Crenshaw has probed the way in which Koheleth finally ends in the despair of death. See Crenshaw, 'The Shadow of Death in Qoheleth', in *Israelite Wisdom: Theological and Literary Essays in Honor of Samuel Terrien* (ed. John G. Gammie *et al.*; Missoula, MT: Scholars Press, 1978), pp. 205-16, and *Ecclesiastes: A Commentary* (OTL; Philadelphia: Fortress Press, 1987), pp. 23-28.

60. Crüsemann, 'The Unchangeable World', pp. 70-73.

61. Crüsemann, 'The Unchangeable World', p. 73.

62. See Rainer Albertz, 'Der sozialgeschichtliche Hintergrund und der "Babylonischen Theodizee"', in *Die Botschaft und die Boten: Festschrift für Hans Walter Wolff zum 70. Geburtstag* (ed. Jörg Jeremias and Lothar Perlitt; Neukirchen–Vluyn: Neukirchener Verlag, 1981), pp. 349-72, for a social analysis of theodicy which is congruent with that of Crüsemann.

fatedness given in Koheleth. In that anticipation, the reading
of the Psalm is no longer easily content with the *status quo*
(how could it be!), nor resigned to the *status quo* (why should
it be?).

Restlessness and hope are grounded in the conviction that
the Psalm still rings true *for the very long haul,* because of the
undoubted promises of Yahweh. The grip of the wicked upon
the land will soon (v. 3), in a little while (v. 10), in the end (vv.
37-38), be turned so that there will be 'inheriting' and 'cutting
off', because the deeds–consequence linkage is not simply
practical common sense, but a passionate conviction that
Yahweh has ordained that the waiting, righteous ones will
have the land that is rightly theirs, which has of late been
seized from them. That is, the affirmation of faith that in a
better time had been an easy legitimation of present-tense
reality now becomes a passionate refusal to accept the fated,
present-tense world of Koheleth. In the first reading, the
'meek', in their righteousness, held the land, and so could be
calmly affirmative. In the second reading, however, the meek
no longer have the land, or do not yet have the land, but
believe that righteousness is so intrinsic to the land process
that the meek will, late if not soon, receive what is rightly and
surely theirs. Thus the 'conflict of interpretation' yields a
hermeneutical process as follows:[63]

First reading of the Psalm	loss of nerve, and	*Second reading* of the Psalm
First reading	loss of nerve, and	*Second reading*
of the Psalm →	resignation →	*of the Psalm*
Ideological description	Koheleth abandons the Psalm	Utopian redescription

This sequence is closely parallel to the dramatic sequence of
the final form of the text of Job:

A first reading of Job's blamelessness (Job 1.1–2.13)	A dispute about Job's blamelessness (Job 3.1–42.6)	A restoration of Job in his blamelessness (Job 42.7-17)
A first reading of Job's	A dispute about Job's	A restoration of Job
blamelessness →	blamelessness →	in his blamelessness
(Job 1.1–2.13)	(Job 3.1–42.6)	(Job 42.7-17)

63. This interpretative grid in its many formulations is especially
shaped by the work of Ricoeur. See Mark I. Wallace, *The Second Naivete:
Barth, Ricoeur, and the New Yale Theology* (Studies in American Biblical
Hermeneutics, 6; Macon, GA: Mercer University Press, 1990).

Moreover, this sequence closely parallels my interpretive grid for the Psalms:

orientation   →   disorientation   →   new orientation[64]

Thus I suggest that a second reading of the Psalm is generated in the same context that produced Koheleth. Why some should read the situation through cynical abdication, and why some through determined anticipation, is not known. Partly the text invites such a second reading, partly the second readers cling to a radically revised form of the old ideology that has now become passionate hope. And partly, we do not know why faith is given as a convinced way in which to read life and text.

The second reading lives very close to the first reading in its theological premise concerning Yahweh's powerful resolve for social reality. The intention, result and effect of this second reading, however, are quite the opposite of the first. The first reading, with self-satisfaction and self-sufficiency, celebrates a reliable present tense. The second subverts the present in its passionate embrace of a revolutionary future, a future as revolutionary as the Jubilee when the land will be given to those who have lost it.[65]

V

It is not surprising that the same text permits more than one reading. The text is open enough to permit more than one reading. Given our common critical propensity, we may prefer

64. Walter Brueggemann, 'Psalms and the Life of Faith: A Suggested Typology of Function', *JSOT* 17 (1980), pp. 3-32.

65. On the radicality of the Jubilee, see Ringe, *Jesus, Liberation, and the Biblical Jubilee*. But see the insistence of Itumelang T. Mosala, *Biblical Hermeneutics and Black Theology in South Africa* (Grand Rapids: Eerdmans, 1989), pp. 154-89, that even in the Gospel of Luke (of all places), that radical claim has been reduced to accommodate the ruling class. Erhard S. Gerstenberger, *Psalms, Part I. With an Introduction to Cultic Poetry* (FOTL, 14; Grand Rapids: Eerdmans, 1988), p. 160, almost inadvertently voices the double reading: 'The intention is a double one: to admonish the faithful to keep on the right path...and to revive and sustain hope for a fundamental change for the better...'

to adjudicate these competing readings in order to settle on a 'true reading'. All of our adjudication, however, is also context-laden. We are left to probe experientially the deeds–consequence claim of the text, whether it pertains either to present-tense possession of the land or to anticipated, promised possession of the land. Even our experiential probes, however, will be context- and interest-laden.

In our own context, an ideological-descriptive, celebrative reading might be given the Psalm, as those in the 'economic West' celebrate the collapse of communist regimes in the East. Such celebration could conclude that we have 'been doing something right', i.e. capitalism, which makes us 'righteous' and has led to our legitimate success.[66]

Conversely, in the United States, the massive power of agri-business continues to occupy and possess more and more land to the disadvantage of smaller farmers. An anticipatory criticism of agri-business, as voiced for example by Wendell Berry,[67] will conclude that such indifferent, absent ownership of the land is in the long run not viable.[68] It is an exploitative practice that does damage not only to the dwellers in the land, but to the land itself. Eventually the land will be regiven to the small owner, for such large-scale acquisitiveness and greed will, soon or late, be 'cut off'. This anticipation is of course a refusal to accept current 'economic realities', and in some sense is a hope-filled reassertion of faith that links land

66. This case in all its triumphalist shamelessness has been made by Francis Fukuyama, 'The End of History?', *The National Interest* (Summer, 1989), pp. 3-18, and more fully, Francis Fukuyama, *The End of History and the Last Man* (New York: The Free Press, 1991).

67. Wendell Berry, *The Gift of Good Land: Further Essays Cultural and Agricultural* (San Francisco: North Point Press, 1981); *Home Economics: Fourteen Essays* (San Francisco: North Point Press, 1987); *The Unsettling of America: Culture and Agriculture* (New York: Avon Books, 1977).

68. The point has been most trenchantly made by J. Steinbeck, *The Grapes of Wrath* (New York: Penguin Books, 1967), pp. 298-99, and *passim*. For a critical analysis of the pertinent issues in the Old Testament, see John Andrew Dearman, *Property Rights in the Eighth-Century Prophets: The Conflict and its Background* (SBLDS, 106; Atlanta: Scholars Press, 1988), and D.N. Premnath, 'Latifundialization and Isaiah 5.8-10', *JSOT* 40 (1988), pp. 49-60.

to virtue. In this context, an assertion of deeds–consequences performs only critical and anticipatory functions, and does not consolidate the *status quo*.

The maddening and inescapable reality is that these alternative readings of the same Psalm continue in our own time to live in lively tension with each other, a tension that is theologically demanding and politically urgent. In contemporaneous readings, stable wealth is justified, peasant yearning is legitimated. There is no contextless reading. Various readings may reassure or threaten. How one reads depends upon where righteousness (and therefore wisdom) are thought to be.

INTERTEXTUALITY:
ALLUSION AND VERTICAL CONTEXT SYSTEMS
IN SOME JOB PASSAGES[*]

Tryggve N.D. Mettinger

All literature participates in the discursive space of the culture to which it belongs. This is an insight that we owe to the recent increase of interest in intertextuality[1] on the part of present-day literary critics. A new text can only be fully appreciated in terms of a prior body of discourse which it implicitly or explicitly takes up, cites, prolongs, refutes or transmutes. We may indeed speak of 'the intertextual nature of any verbal construct' (Culler)[2] and of the act of reading as experiencing a series of *déjà lues* (Barthes).[3] This participation may manifest itself in various ways. In the introduction to her analysis of T.S. Eliot's work, Marianne Thormählen puts forward the following list of key concepts which she uses to analyse the work of Eliot: quotation, source, influence, allusion, association, reminiscence, echo, suggestion and reference.[4] The length of the list reveals that we are dealing with an elusive and multifaceted phenomenon indeed. The recognition

[*]   I would like to thank Professor Louise Vinge of the Department of Comparative Literature of the University of Lund, Dr Marianne Thormählen of the Department of English, and Michael S. Cheney, ThM, Görau Eidevall and Dr Fredrik Lindström, all of the Department of Biblical Studies of the University of Lund, for valuable discussions. Mr Cheney checked my English. Unless otherwise indicated translations of biblical quotations follow the NRSV.
    1.   The term seems to have been introduced by Kristeva (1967: esp. 440-41; cf. 1969: 255).
    2.   Culler 1983: 101.
    3.   Barthes 1970: 26.
    4.   Thormählen 1984: 12.

of the central intertexts that lie beneath the surface in poets like Dante, Milton, Eliot and Joyce is the key to the appreciation of these works. *A fortiori* the same holds true of the Book of Job, a work that Norman Whybray aptly describes as belonging to Israel's 'intellectual tradition'.[5] What I want to do in this paper is to argue that our understanding of the Book of Job can be fruitfully informed by the insights and perspectives of the modern study of intertextuality. In order to lay the groundwork for this argument I shall first alert the reader to some of the important contributions made by this new discipline and then discuss some examples in Job.

1. *The Study of Intertextuality*

In his article 'Allusion' in *The Princeton Handbook of Poetic Terms*, Earl Miner defines allusion as 'tacit reference to another literary work, to another art, to history, to contemporary figures, or the like'.[6] Allusion differs from source-borrowing since 'it requires the reader's acquaintance with the original for full understanding and appreciation', says Miner.[7] Literary critics have felt the need to distinguish what Staffan Bergsten in a study of allusion in Eliot called 'allusion proper', which is 'intended by the author and depending on its source for its full meaning', and 'mere reminiscence', 'the source being of no significance to the meaning'.[8] Applying a somewhat different terminology, Laurent Jenny hints at the same distinction: when a text alludes to or redeploys an entire structure, a pattern of form and meaning from an earlier text, he speaks of 'intertextuality proper'; when a text repeats an element from an earlier text, without referring to the original meaning in the original context, he speaks of 'simple allusion or reminiscence'.[9]

    5.   Whybray 1974: 61-67. On Job's place in relation to the various Israelite traditions see Roberts 1977.
    6.   Miner 1986: 10.
    7.   Miner 1986: 11.
    8.   Bergsten 1959: 10-11.
    9.   Jenny 1982: 40. Cf. Di Cesare, who studies Vida's imitations of the Aeneid and distinguishes between three categories of derivative elements:

Major contributions to the issue of intertextuality come from the pens of Bakhtin, Kristeva, Barthes, Riffaterre and Bloom. I shall not here present a conspectus of their work; recent contributions contain good surveys.[10] Instead I would like to call attention to the work of two literary critics whose contributions should be of particular interest to Biblical scholars: Claes Schaar and Gérard Genette.[11]

Claes Schaar prefaces his study of intertextuality in Milton's *Paradise Lost* with a worthwhile discussion of what he calls 'vertical context systems'.[12] What Schaar studies is the functions of various derivative elements, ranging from 'allusions in the proper sense of the term, overt or covert, and all conceivable borderline cases down to reminiscences and faint echoes of various kinds, quite irrespective of authors' awareness'.[13] He describes the vertical context systems 'as made up of a surface context charged with additional meaning by contact with a deep context, an infracontext, bearing some kind of verbal similarity to the surface context...In a great number of cases the additional meaning is of the connotative kind, and the meaning of the surface context is modified, amplified, reinforced or brought into contrast by the infracontext.'[14] On the thorny problem of authorial intention Schaar takes a cautious position, paying due homage to Wimsatt and Beardsley and

(a) the commonplace phrase, which just gives the illusion of the epic style, (b) the echo, which makes clear the relation between Vida's work and Virgil's, and (c) 'the evocative allusion', which Di Cesare defines as 'a correspondence in language which, by recalling a passage, draws on the emotions or meanings attached to that passage' (Di Cesare 1964: 149).

10. See Pfister (1985), Jardin (1986) and Worton and Still (1991: 1-44, esp. 15-33). In addition to the literature mentioned in these surveys I would like to call attention to Espmark (1985: esp. pp. 19-38). Among studies of the general phenomenon of allusion I would like to mention especially Vinge (1973) and Ben Porat (1974). Note also the useful bibliography compiled by Perri *et al.* (1979).

11. Among the studies of intertextuality by exegetes I would like to mention those by Ellen van Wolde (1989, 1990) and Kirsten Nielsen (1990). Note also the various contributions (mostly New Testament studies) in the *Festschrift* for Bas van Iersel; see Draisma (1989).

12. Schaar 1975; 1978; 1982: esp. pp. 11-33.

13. Schaar 1982: 19-20.

14. Schaar 1978: 382.

their exposé of 'the intentional fallacy'.[15] Schaar does not regard the question of whether or not an allusion is intentional as the most significant one since, to him, 'the question, "Is this passage an allusion?" does not always make sense, but the question, "Does this passage suggest some other passage?" always does...'[16] Instead of focusing on author's intentions, Schaar wants to stress the function of allusion.[17] Here the issue of recognition becomes important. An allusion is a kind of coded message that can be decoded only by recipients familiar with the nature of the code. If an allusion is not recognized, the 'absent structure' (Eco) remains hidden, undecoded.[18] When an allusion is recognized the vertical context system becomes operational.[19] Another term that is important in Schaar's repertoire is 'matrix': 'A set of infracontexts constitutes a matrix, a bed or mould which serves as the base for the surface context and at the same time, up to a point, determines its form'.[20]

Though he only vaguely relates his own work to that of the well-known exponents of intertextuality and uses his own terminology, it is nevertheless clear that Schaar is, in fact, discussing nothing other than the phenomenon of intertextuality.[21] Focusing on the role of allusive images in *Paradise Lost,* his study is important both for its theoretical insights and for its erudite observations on a host of details in Milton's vertical context systems. In his 1975 study Schaar notes that 'the study of vertical contexts is in fact text archaeology, and the past becomes the key to the present'.[22]

15. Wimsatt and Beardsley 1954.
16. Schaar 1975: 148. Note the discussion of this position by Vinge (1973: 148-153), and see below.
17. Schaar (esp. 1982: 11-16).
18. Cf. Vinge 1973: 142, referring to Eco 1968.
19. Schaar 1982: 17.
20. Schaar 1982: 26.
21. Note, for example, how close Jenny comes to Schaar in his understanding of intertextuality; see Jenny 1982: 44-45. Jenny points out that intertextuality 'introduces a new way of reading which destroys the linearity of the text' (p. 44) and tends to see the intertextual reference as 'a paradigmatic element' (p. 44).
22. Schaar 1975: 149.

The critical reader would perhaps remark that, in practice, Schaar's investigation has a tendency to develop into a variety of source hunting in which the function of an allusion within the discursive universe of the *new* text does not always receive due attention. But even so, Schaar opens new vistas on vertical context systems that train our sight to recognize and understand a number of important literary phenomena.

If Schaar works like an accomplished archaeologist, Gérard Genette is the Linnaeus of intertextuality. His 'last word' on the subject is the work *Palimpsestes* (1982), with a title that borrows its metaphor from Jorge Luis Borges's story about Pierre Menard who wrote the 'real' *Don Quixote,* which is a verbatim copy of Cervantes's text, but is, nevertheless, infinitely richer. This 'final' *Quixote* is seen by Borges as a 'palimpsest' where traces from previous writing are still visible on the parchment. This way of looking at text is reflected in the title of Genette's work, *Palimpsestes: La littérature au second degré* (1982).[23] *Palimpsestes* is a major attempt to map the various phenomena usually found under the heading of intertextuality. The focus of Genette's insightful and extensive arguments is directed towards late works that contain traces of the *Odyssey,* the *Aeneid* and *Hamlet.*

Genette creates his own terminological repertoire.[24] His overarching category is called 'transtextuality' and includes anything explicit or implicit in a text that links the text to others.[25] Under this umbrella he discerns five main subcategories. (1) The first of these is 'Kristevan' *intertextuality,* which consists of phenomena such as allusion, quotation and plagiarism. Much of both Bloom's and Riffaterre's studies have dealt with this part of the terrain. (2) The second type is *paratextuality,* defined as the relationships between the body of the text and its titles, preface, epigraphs and the like—in brief, that is, to the whole framework of the text. (3) A third category is *metatextuality.* This is the relation of the commentary to the text it comments upon, that is, the critic's

23. Cf. Genette 1982: 451-52.
24. For the following, see Genette 1982: 7-14. Note also his previous work (1979).
25. Genette 1982: 7.

attitude to the text. (4) *Architextuality* takes within its scope
the more comprehensive types of discourse such as novel, epic,
essay, etc. This category takes cognizance of the fact that
when a reader recognizes a particular text as belonging to a
certain genre that text is automatically compared to other
texts from the same genre. (5) The last type is *hypertextuality*,
which comprises every relation that unifies a text B (the
hypertext) with a prior text A (the hypotext), onto which it
has been grafted so that it constitutes something other than a
mere commentary. The relationship of Joyce's *Ulysses* to
Virgil's *Aeneid*, and of both works to their Homeric hypotext
belong in this category. It is mainly this last type that absorbs
Genette's interest in the rest of his book.

After this brief presentation of Schaar's and Genette's views
of intertextuality I must make some further comments of a
more general nature. (1) The main problem in all discussions
of intertextuality is how to find criteria for establishing just
what constitutes an intertext behind a certain text. Kjell
Espmark[26] cogently argues for a distinction between true
'dialogicity' and intertextuality in general.[27] Within the latter,
the broader category, one finds many cases in which echoes of
earlier texts are heard in more recent works without eliciting
an articulate answer, when the past reverberates in the
present text without the present work asserting its own
position. Espmark talks of 'dialogicity' only when a reference
to a prior text can be identified as 'an intended semantic fact'
in the content-structure of the later work. This is his first
criterion. This criterion implies that Espmark's dialogicity is a
variety of intertextuality that is not first created in the mind
of the reader (it is not primarily a concept related to reader-
response criticism) but is a phenomenon 'present in the space
of the text at the moment when the poem is completed'.[28]

26. Espmark 1985: 26-27. Contrast Stierle (1983: 17), who argues for
the view that true dialogue presupposes the autonomy of the participants
in a way that is not found in intertextual relations. Espmark (1985: 25)
insists on the metaphor of dialogue because it highlights the aspect of the
intention of the later poet.
27. Cf. above in the introduction.
28. Espmark 1985: 27. As is well known, the question of authorial

In addition to this criterion Espmark also stresses the necessity of specific similarities[29] between text and intertext. Here he touches upon what many others have discussed using different terminology. Thus Riffaterre speaks of 'connectives' between text and intertext.[30] Vinge speaks of 'markers' that work as signals, a function that is best served by the unusual word, the specific construction, or the evocative, allusive image.[31] Schaar also makes use of the notion of signalling devices: 'Strictly speaking, two stages are involved in the appreciation of a vertical context system. Recognition means that the surface context, operating as a signal, triggers a memory of the infracontext. Then, as recognition turns to understanding, the signal is transformed into a sign... as surface and infracontexts coalesce.'[32]

One aspect of this discussion deserves special attention in

intention is a controversial issue. I would like to formulate my opinion as follows: As part of *a process of communication* any literary work has a structure. This structure is a manifestation of a *Strukturwille*, namely that of the author. Since they participate in the recognizable construction of a literary work, allusions are manifestations of the same *Strukturwille*, and thus express the intentions of the author. I thus sympathize with the position of Vinge (1973: 148-53). A fairly straight line leads from Wimsatt and Beardsley with the 'intentional fallacy' (originally pub. in 1946, repr. 1954) to the 'death of the author' at the hands of Barthes—see Barthes (1984: 61-67; originally published in 1968) and cf. Ljung's survey (1991). Espmark appears to be aware of the problem inherent in a position that implies the abolition of the author. Nevertheless, he does not dare to speak of author's intentions but only of 'the intention of the text' (1985: 133). Cf. Panofsky's essay on *das Kunstwollen* in pictorial art (Panofsky 1964). Others have voiced a more whole-hearted refusal to take the pre-packaged pontifications of deconstructionism as the final word on the matter. Note especially Hirsch (1967); Steiner (1989: esp. 51-134); Backman (1991: 11, 14, 16, 31-33, 44, 46-48). But note also the critiques of Hirsch's position by Lentricchia (1983: 256-80) and Cain (1984: 15-30). It was Lentricchia (1983: 257) who coined the term 'the organic fallacy' to describe the contention that Hirsch wants to excoriate, namely 'the metaphorical doctrine that a text leads a life of its own' (Hirsch 1967: 212). Or the whole issue, cf. Barton (1984: 147-51, 167-70).

29. Espmark (1985: 27) speaks of 'kvalificerad överensstämmelse'.
30. Riffaterre 1991: 58.
31. Vinge 1973: 140.
32. Schaar 1982: 18.

our present context. Riffaterre has stressed that the marker, the trace of the intertext, often or always takes the form of an aberration on one or more levels of communication: lexical, syntactical or semantic. It is in one way or another perceived as a deviation from the norm, as an incompatibility, a 'non-grammaticalité, au sense large du terme'.[33] The markers are distinguished from their context by their dual nature: 'They are both the problem, when seen from the text, and the solution to that problem when their other, intertextual side is revealed', says Riffaterre.[34]

(2) The presence of an allusion creates an interaction between text and intertext in a way that is reminiscent of the way a metaphor works.[35] Whether we classify all allusions as a subclass of metaphors[36] or we take only certain allusions to be metaphorical ones,[37] metaphor and allusion clearly belong together as sense-expanding strategies. The semantic expansion taking place by means of a metaphor could be described as $a = B$ while the one that takes place through an evocative allusion is to be described as $a < A$. The reproduced element serves as a vehicle for the poetic tenor that it acquires in the new text. In the metaphor there is a movement across semantic fields, in the allusion a transfer between literary contexts.

Of a certain interest in this connection is the fact that the allusive signal sometimes triggers a memory of an earlier text that may refer not just to one single point in that text but to one or more of its larger sections as a unit. There are cases when the marker allows a large portion, maybe even the totality of the echoed text, to become part of the semantic structure of the new poem. 'The source text is there, potentially present, bearing all of its meaning without there being any need to utter it', asserts Laurent Jenny.[38] The allusion

33. Riffaterre 1980a: 5-6 (6); also 1980b: 627.
34. Riffaterre 1991: 58.
35. See e.g. Kittang and Aarseth 1985: 97-103; Still and Worton 1991: 10-11.
36. Thus Thornton 1968: 3.
37. Thus Miner 1986: 11.
38. Jenny 1982: 45.

then works as a *pars pro toto*, as a case of synecdoche, as
Louise Vinge pointed out.[39]

(3) The intertextual relations between text and intertext
invite comparison and generally serve to produce either alignment or contrast. In the first case the effect is to provide
reinforcement or validation to the later text. Thus Gautier
writes,

> Les dieux eux-mêmes meurent.
> Mais les vers souverains
> Demeurent
> Plus fort que les airains.

His statement that the gods die but the 'sovereign' verses
remain, stronger than works of bronze, is quite understandable in itself: Masterfully written verses endure longer than
religions, which may last for millennia, and longer than works
of bronze. However, the marker 'airains' clearly makes an
allusion to Horace's classic formulation 'Exegi monumentum
aere perennius'. The tacit reference to this line is more than
an isolated piece of elegance. The allusion made to Horace's
words almost two millennia after their composition provides a
clear case in point for the contention formulated in the
modern poem.[40]

In addition, the allusion serves to produce contrast or
surprise, or to express an attitude of opposition on the part of
the characters in the story or even of the author of the more
recent poem. The allusion to Psalm 8 in Job 7, to which we
shall turn in a moment, is a good example.

2. *Some Notes on Job*

Without relating their enterprise to the discussion of inter-
textuality among the students of comparative literature, some
Old Testament scholars have applied a related perspective to
Job. Claus Westermann, in his book *Der Aufbau des Buches
Hiob* (1956, 3rd edn 1978), called attention to the relations to
the psalms of lament and to hymnic material. Georg Fohrer's

39. Vinge 1973: 142.
40. The example was adduced by Vinge (1973: 144).

essay 'Form und Funktion in der Hiobdichtung' (1959) is also an important contribution to the study of literary techniques in the Book of Job. In this article, Fohrer pays special attention to the use of forms in Job and notes that they frequently have a different function from the one they had in their original setting. Katharine J. Dell, in *The Book of Job as Sceptical Literature* (1991), devotes a chapter specifically to the use of literary forms in Job. Relying heavily on Fohrer's work, she discusses a number of cases of what she calls 'deliberate misuse of forms'.[41] Among studies that touch upon phenomena related to the major issue of intertextuality in Job I would also like to mention Veronika Kubina's excursus on what she calls the 'anthological style'.[42] It is important to note that these varieties of intertextual reference are not Espmark's brand of active dialogue with one's poetic precursors.

Having recourse to the insights of these scholars, I shall now comment on some intertextual relations in the Book of Job, notably in the Job speeches.

a. *Job 7*

The Job speech in Job 7 deals with the futility of human life. This theme is especially visible at three points: v. 8 'I shall be gone [w^e'ênennî]' (cf. 9-10), v. 16 'my days are breath' and v. 21 'I shall not be [w^e'ênennî]'.[43] In its portrayal of God the text uses intertextual relationships to produce an effect of parody and irony. This is certainly true in the well-known case of Job 7.17-18's subversion of the hymnic praise in Ps. 8.5-6:

> *mâ-*^{e}*nôš kî-tizk*^{e}*rennû*
> *ûben-'ādām kî tipq*^{e}*dennû*
> *watt*^{e}*hass*^{e}*rēhû m*$^{e'}$*at mē*^{e}*lōhîm*
> *w*^{e}*kābôd w*^{e}*hādār t*$^{e'}$*att*^{e}*rēhû*

---

41. Dell (1991: 110) makes the distinction between 'reuse' and 'misuse' of a traditional form. By the second term she means 'a traditional form being used with a different content and context'.

42. See Kubina 1979: 110-14, esp. 113-14. Cf. Fishbane 1988: 286-87. The notion of an 'anthological style' was introduced by Robert in a series of studies on Prov. 1–9; see Robert 1934–35. Note also Deissler's work on Ps. 119 (Deissler 1955).

43. See Habel 1985: 153-56.

What are human beings that you are mindful of them,
mortals that you care for them?
Yet you have made them a little lower than God,
and crowned them with glory and honour (Ps. 8.5-6).

mâ-ᵉnôš kî tᵉgaddᵉlennû
wᵉkî-tāšît ᵉlāyw libbekā
wattipqᵉdennû labbᵉqārîm
lirgāᵗîm tibhānennû

What is man that you make so much of him,
fixing your mind upon him,
inspecting him every morning
at every moment testing him? (Job 7.17-18).[44]

The markers or traces of the intertext are unmistakable: the construction *mâ-ᵉnôš kî* and the use of the verb *pāqad*, 'visit in mercy' (Ps. 8), 'visit in anger', 'call to account' (Job 7). Job 7.17-18, just like Ps. 144.3-4, emanates from a sceptical tradition. The proud proclamation of the glory of humanity that is the very point of Ps. 8.5-6 is left out. Ps. 8.6 has no counterpart in the Job passage, nor in Psalm 144. Throughout, the language of the infratext is reapplied ironically in the Job passage.[45] In the psalm the attitude is one of thankful wonder at the grace of God towards insignificant humans. His 'visitation' is a welcome token of divine favour. In psalmic language God's help in the morning is a well-known topos linked with God's retributive justice against evildoers.[46] In the Job speeches, again, God's dealings are directed against Job: God inspects him and tests him every morning. God's visitation has become an unwelcome intrusion. This is emphasized by two formulations framing the allusion in Job 7 to Psalm 8. In v. 16b Job says, 'Let me alone...' In v. 19 he voices his despair with the words: 'Will you not look away from me for a while, let me alone until I swallow my spittle?'
The portrayal of God that results from the subversive use of

44. Translated after Clines 1989: 157.
45. Cf. Fishbane 1988: 285-87; Clines 1989: 192-93; Spieckermann 1989: 237-38; Perdue 1991: 130-31.
46. Ps. 5.4; 46.6; 90.14; 143.8; Lam. 3.23; Mal. 3.20. Cf. Ziegler 1950; Janowski 1989: esp. 180-91. Note the occurrence of this motif in Job 38.12-15.

Psalm 8 is effectively summarized in the participial description of him as 'the Watcher of Humans', *nōṣēr hā'ādām* (Job 7.20). This is a formulation that may well contain an allusive assonance to God as *yōṣēr*, 'Creator', in psalmic language.[47] The surveillance metaphor is indeed central to the passage and seems to be anticipated already in v. 8, with *'ên rō'î*, 'the Seeing Eye', 'the eye of him who beholds me'. This formulation seems to refer to God and to introduce its own irony into the text by recalling the Hagar story of Genesis 16. At the point of Hagar's utter despair El-roi reveals himself to her.[48] If the formulation in Job 7 is an allusion to Genesis 16 (or the tradition found there), the implication is very much the same as that in 7.17-20. The Hagar story presents a God who cares, saves and gives a new future. The associative assonance in Job 7.8 (*'ên / 'ēl*) gives a hint that reminds the reader of the subversive strategies of the text: it presents a God who is engaged in merciless spying on humanity, an image counter to that of the God of Hagar in Genesis 16 and a concept contrary to that of the God of Psalm 8.

The same negative portrayal of God surfaces in an allusion in v. 12: 'Am I the Sea, or the Dragon, that you set a guard over me?'[49] Note that v. 12 is couched as a rhetorical question just like vv. 17-18, and note the formal similarity between vv. 12b and 17b (*kî*-clauses). The hymnic tradition speaks of a God who subdues the Dragon, *tannîn*.[50] Here in Job 7.12 Job finds himself standing in for the Dragon with whom God does battle;[51] Job himself is the target of God's assaults, the *mipgā'* (v. 20), a formulation that points forward to the laments on God as the enemy in chs. 16 and 19 (esp. 16.12).

It is difficult to avoid the conclusion that the allusions in

47. Ps. 33.15; 94.9; Isa. 45.7, 18; 49.5; Jer. 10.16. For *yāṣar* with *'ādām* as the object, see Gen. 2.7.

48. Note the occurrence of a certain 'Baal-roy, son of Zippor, of Gaza' in the Egyptian Pap. Anastasi III (*ANET*, p. 258). This theophoric personal name may well help to explain the religio-historical background of the Hagar story.

49. On Job 7.12, see esp. Diewert (1987) and Janzen (1989).

50. Ps. 74.13; Isa. 27.1; 51.9; Jer. 51.34; Ezek. 29.3.

51. See Mettinger (1992). On the role of the chaos battle motif, especially in the speeches of God, see Mettinger (1988: 189-98, with lit.).

Job 7 are 'intended semantic facts' in the content-structure of the passage, especially in view of their distortions of the images of the original texts/traditions. Furthermore, it is difficult not to see that paying attention to the vertical context systems that include Psalm 8 and Genesis 16 is an investment that yields a richer understanding of the Job passage. It is indeed the intertextual relations between text and intertexts that fill out the structure and content of the Job passage to their true dimensions.

b. *Job 16.7-17 and 19.6-12*
For our purposes, chs. 16 and 19, where God is portrayed by the bold image of the brutal foe who lays Job under siege (ch. 19) and who defeats him in single combat (ch. 16), may be taken together.

The suggestion has recently been made that 16.7-17 parodies passages in Psalms where God gives strength to a person, e.g. Ps. 94.18-19.[52] However, I believe there are more attractive possibilities. It is not easy to find one specific intertext. However, we find in v. 9 a formulation that contains a rather remarkable statement about God: *'appô ṭārap wayyiśṭ'mēnî ḥāraq 'ālay b'šinnāyw*, 'He has torn me in his wrath, and hated me; he has gnashed his teeth at me...' I am inclined to take v. 9 as a marker that signals an allusion, but not an allusion to one individual text but to the conventional metaphors of a whole genre. The formulation in Job about God tearing Job's flesh becomes understandable if we see it against the background of the individual psalms of lament[53] where the enemies are regularly portrayed as wild animals, notably as lions who tear (*ṭārap*) the flesh of their prey (Pss. 7.3; 17.12; 22.14; cf. 10.9).[54] As Riffaterre pointed out, we can see how the marker, the connective between the text and the intertext, is both the problem (when seen from within the

52. Dell 1991: 130.
53. Broyles (1989) recently suggested a new categorization of these into pleas and complaints. For our purposes it does not seem necessary to take a position vis-à-vis this suggestion.
54. In Ps. 50.22 God is the subject of this verb. Note the similarity with the formulation in Ps. 7.3.

text) and the solution to that problem (when seen in the light
of the intertext). The same holds true for God's gnashing his
teeth at Job (16.9). Gnashing teeth is scarcely a main feature
of the Old Testament portrayals of God, but it is a favourite
preoccupation of the enemies in the psalms of lament (Pss.
35.16; 37.12; 112.10; cf. Lam. 2.16). The sudden switch to the
plural in v. 10 of our Job passage is in line with this. Drawing
on the notion of the evildoers from the Psalms, the poet easily
moves from God as the foe to a portrayal of God's entourage
in his hunting and military ventures.[55] The markers in the
text then point to a play on an entire genre. Thus it appears
that this text employs the intertextual device that Genette
called architextuality.

The idea of a divine archer shooting his arrows at Job is a
metaphor specific to Job (see 16.12-13; cf. 6.4; 34.6). It may be
that this as well subtly alludes to the activities of the enemies
in the Psalms.[56] However, it seems that the psalms of lament
utilize an established and conventionalized metaphor of God
as the divine archer who shoots his arrows at evildoers (cf.
Pss. 7.13-14;[57] 64.8).[58] I am inclined to take Job 16.12-13 as a
subversive use of this psalmic metaphor of God.

The nature of intertextual relations between this passage
and the genre of lament, therefore, tend to create contrast by
means of the conventional motifs of the lament genre: in Job,
God behaves in a way parallel to the role of the enemies of the
praying psalmist in the psalms of lament. And, with a particular twist of ambiguity, he treats Job in the same way that he
treats the enemies in these psalms. In Job 7.12, God treats Job
in the same way that he treats the Sea and the Dragon. In a
similar way the verb *pārar* is used in our present passage (Job
16.12a), a verb also found in the Psalms in a chaos battle

---

55. Cf. Habel 1985: 264.

56. Cf. Pss. 11.2; 37.15; 57.5; 64.4.

57. In Ps. 7 God is probably the subject in vv. 12-14; see Ravasi (1988:
165-76, esp. 168-70).

58. Note also the occurrence of the same motif to express the divine
punishment of Israel/Israelites in Deut. 32.23; Ps. 38.3; Lam. 3.12-13. On
YHWH as the divine archer, see Fredriksson (1945: 94-95).

context (Ps. 74.13), albeit not in an individual lament.[59] No wonder then that Job refers to God as his 'foe' (*ṣārî*, 16.9; cf. 19.11 and note also the use of *'ôyēb*, 'enemy', 13.24; 27.7; 33.10).

If Job 16 draws on the lament genre, as so much other material in Job does, we should not overlook an important fact pointed out by Frank Crüsemann: the most central element of the lament genre, namely *petition to God*, is strikingly absent from the book.[60] Never does Job pray for his restoration to his former position, for his salvation from his suffering. While the psalmist prays for God's benign attention, that he should turn to him,[61] Job tells God to leave him alone, a complete reversal of the pattern found in the prayers of the Psalms (Job 7.16, 19; 10.20; 14.6).[62] The psalmists pray that God will vindicate them and restore their rights (*šopṭēnî*).[63] Job never does so.[64] In the psalms of lament the basic conflict is between the praying psalmist and the evildoers, the enemies; God has the role of the supreme judge who will at last vindicate his faithful servant. In Job the basic conflict is between Job and God; God is the enemy and accuser of Job, and so Job is left in the peculiar situation of having no one to vindicate him.

Using Dell's terminology,[65] we can say that Job 16 represents a 'misuse' of the lament genre to formulate a plea against God. Or, with a neutral and therefore preferable term, I would say that cases like Job 16 represent a 'metamorphic' use of a traditional genre. Whatever the terminology, we should not overlook the fact that at one rare but important point in Job there may be a non-inverted use of the psalm of

59. On the meaning of *pārar*, see *HALAT*, p. 917 and BDB, p. 830.

60. Crüsemann 1980: 375. Cf. Westermann 1978: 81-84.

61. With *rā'â* in Pss. 9.14; 59.5; 84.10; with *nābaṭ* hiph. in Pss. 13.4; 74.20; 84.10; with *'al tastēr pānêkā* in Pss. 27.9; 69.18; 143.7. Cf. Aejmelaeus (1986: 26-29, 45-47).

62. Note, however, that the view of Job is very similar to Ps. 39.14: *hāša' mimmennî wā'ablîgâ*, 'Turn your gaze away from me, that I may smile again...' But Ps. 39 may well be later than Job.

63. Pss. 7.9; 26.1; 35.24; 43.1; cf. with the root *ryb* 35.1; 43.1. Cf. Aejmelaeus (1986: 37-39).

64. His desire to initiate litigation with God is something quite different; see Roberts (1973).

65. Dell 1991: 110.

lament genre. When Job formulates his wish to see God (19.26-27, *ûmibb^{e}śārî 'eḥ^{e}zeh ^{e}lôah*), he does indeed hope for something that the psalmists looked forward to (cf. *^{a}nî b^{e}ṣedeq 'eḥ^{e}zeh pānêkā*, 'I shall behold your face in righteousness', Ps. 17.15; cf. Pss. 11.7; 27.4, 13).

From Job 16 we move on to Job 19.6-12. Here the same martial language continues but the siege metaphor now occupies centre stage. This is especially clear from v. 6, *ûm^{e}ṣûdô 'ālay hiqqîp*, 'he has thrown up his siegeworks against me',[66] and from v. 12, 'his troops come on together; they have thrown up siegeworks against me, and encamp around my tent'. Indeed, the same metaphor is also found in Job 16.14: *yipr^{e}ṣēnî pereṣ 'al-p^{e}nê-pāreṣ*, 'He breached me, breach after breach'.[67]

The use of the siege metaphor to describe God's dealings with an individual may seem surprising. In Lamentations 3, however, we find the same siege metaphor,[68] but here it occurs in a context that deals mainly with the sufferings of a city; behind the agony of the individual of this text, of the suffering person, stands suffering Zion.[69] In addition to this, it happens to be the case that there are some striking verbal similarities between Job 19 and Lamentations 3. Job 19.8 reads: *'orḥî gādar w^{e}lō' 'e^{e}bôr w^e'al n^{e}tîbôtay ḥōšek yāśîm*, 'He has walled up my way so that I cannot pass, and he has set darkness upon my paths'. First, a similar use of *gādar* is found in Lam. 3.7, 'he walled (*gādar*) me about so that I cannot escape', and in Lam. 3.9, 'he has blocked (*gādar*) my ways with hewn stones, he has made my paths crooked (*'iwwâ*)' (cf. Job 19.6a). Secondly, the darkness upon Job's paths has a counterpart in Lam. 3.2, 'he has driven and brought me into darkness without any light', and 3.6, 'he has made me sit in darkness'.

What are then the implications of these and other similarities between the two texts?[70] David Clines feels inclined to

---

66. Habel 1985: 289. Cf. Clines 1989: 427.

67. Translated by Habel (1985: 262). Cf. *HALAT*, pp. 914-15, for cases where the verb is used about breaching into a city under siege.

68. Note also Ps. 3.7.

69. Lindström 1983: 214-36, esp. 219.

70. Lévêque (1970: 384) lists a number of other points in common, but the above-mentioned ones are the most striking.

believe that they 'must belong to a conventional stock available to both poets'.[71] Jean Lévêque, on the other hand, holds that the Job author made deliberate use of Lamentations.[72] It is generally overlooked that there are two striking similarities between Lamentations and the first passage we studied in this section, Job 16. In this passage we find the sufferer describing himself as a target for the divine archer: *wayqîmēnî lô lemaṭṭārâ*, 'he set me up as his target' (16.12). Similarly, in Lam. 3.12 we read: 'He bent his bow and set me as a mark (*kammaṭṭārā*') for his arrow'. In Job 16.16 Job says, *pānay homarmerûh*, 'my face glows from weeping'.[73] The only other cases of the verb used in this stem are in Lam. 1.20 and 2.11.

Although we cannot be entirely sure about this, I feel inclined to agree with Lévêque that Job 19 represents a deliberate allusion to Lamentations 3. Once again, the marker has the dual nature of a problem and its solution, to use Riffaterre's expression. The surprising application of the siege metaphor to the predicament of an individual triggers a memory of Lamentations 3. We must therefore ask what function is fulfilled by the allusions to Lamentations in Job 16 and 19. 'An allusion achieves its purpose through inviting a comparison and contrast of the context in which it occurs with the original context', says Weldon Thornton.[74] This is precisely what is happening in the text under examination. By means of a light use of allusion, the poet strikes a note that makes the themes of Lamentations echo in his text. Behind Job the reader discovers the figure of the mystical 'I' who suffers and laments in Lamentations 3, that is, personified Zion.[75] Suffering Job finds his fate an unresolved riddle. Along the same lines, it should be noted that Zion's suffering presented a paradox to any Israelite, when seen in the light of God's previous promises to maintain and protect his city.[76] However,

71. Clines 1989: 442.
72. Lévêque 1970: 385.
73. My translation.
74. Thornton 1968: 3.
75. Lévêque 1970: 385.
76. See Lam. 2.15; 4.12; and cf. Albrektson (1963: 214-39, esp. 219-30); Renkema (1983: 267-323).

the poet of Lamentations sees the ultimate explanation for the suffering of Zion in her former sins.[77] Such explanations, however, are not accepted by Job. Yet another contrast is to be found in the fact that the suffering 'individual' in Lamentations looks forward to deliverance,[78] while Job is completely devoid of hope. Therefore, it should be observed that the allusions to Lamentations 3 in Job 19 serve at one and the same time to produce both alignment and contrast.

Our observations on Job 16.7-17 and 19.6-12 may thus be summarized as follows. We see here how two different but related vertical context systems surface in the Job passages. Drawing on the conventional motifs of the genre of lament, the poet depicts Job as standing in the place of the enemy whom God annihilates, that is, in the position conventionally assigned to evildoers under divine judgment. Furthermore, he speaks of God as acting towards Job in the same way that the enemies do in their attacks on the sufferer in the psalms of lament. Genette's model would place this phenomenon under the heading of architextuality. This could be further qualified by noting that what we have here is a metamorphic use of a conventional genre, which serves to highlight the acute incongruousness of Job's situation. Thus by alluding to the metaphor of Zion as a suffering man in Lamentations 3 the poet presents the metaphor of suffering Job as a city under siege. By means of this intertextual strategy the poet places added emphasis on Job's guiltlessness. His is a suffering that is even more paradoxical than the sufferings of devastated Zion.

3. *Concluding Remarks*

The Book of Job draws on literary material from a very wide range of backgrounds: wisdom, law, cult, psalmody, etc. As Norman Whybray puts it, 'What is surprising about the book of Job is not that its author was familiar with these various forms, which would be part of Israel's literary and cultural heritage, but that he felt free to use them as he chose'.[79] What

77. Lam. 1.18, 20, 22; 3.42; 4.6, 13, 22.
78. Lam. 3.22-25, 31-32, 58-59.
79. Whybray 1974: 63.

I have preferred to call the metamorphic use of a traditional genre is a literary technique that the Job author seems to utilize especially in the speeches of Job.[80] We noticed how Job, in his expostulations against God, refers to a paradoxical change of roles: suddenly God is threatening him as an enemy from the psalms of lament, God is treating him as he treats enemies and monsters in the Psalms—that is, God has adopted the role of the enemy, God himself has become a monster. This ingenious change of roles has a corollary in the second speech of God.[81] In the introduction to this speech (Job 40.6-14), God suggests that Job switch roles with him: 'Have you an arm like God...Look on all who are proud, and bring them low; tread down the wicked where they stand' (40.9, 12). Job is invited to assume God's role—if he is able to do this! This invitation is formulated in a passage that anticipates the body of the speech where God subdues Behemoth and Leviathan. Job's accusation against God for treating him and the world like a criminal (cf. 9.22-24)[82] is countered by God with a speech portraying God as one who subdues the wicked.[83] An awareness of the author's use of intertextual techniques and especially of his metamorphic use of conventional motifs and genres thus helps us to better grasp the great compositional contrasts of the Book of Job. There is a deep truth in the superficially obvious statement that 'the identification of an intertext is an act of interpretation'.[84]

80. Cf. Dell 1991: 136-38.

81. This was pointed out to me by Dr Fredrik Lindström.

82. Note Dion (1987: 189) for the interesting observation of a close similarity between Job 9.22b and what is said in the Erra Epic (5.10) where the Mesopotamian pestilence god Erra says in the first person: 'The righteous and the wicked, I did not distinguish, I felled'.

83. Insufficient attention to the new understanding of the speeches of God in Job is a weakness in the otherwise very fine work by Dell. See Keel (1978); Kubina (1979); Mettinger (1988: 185-200).

84. Frow 1991: 46.

BIBLIOGRAPHY

Aejmelaeus, A.
1986   *The Traditional Prayer in the Psalms* (BZAW, 167; Berlin:
           de Gruyter).
Albrektson, B.
1963   *Studies in the Text and Theology of the Book of Lamentations*
           (Studia Theologica Lundensia, 21; Lund: Gleerup).
Backman, G.
1991   *Meaning by Metaphor* (Acta Universitatis Upsaliensis. Studia
           Anglistica Upsaliensia, 75; Stockholm: Almqvist & Wiksell).
Barthes, R.
1970   *S/Z* (Paris: Seuil).
1984   *Essais critiques. IV. Le bruissement de la langue* (Paris: Seuil).
Barton, J.
1984   *Reading the Old Testament: Method in Biblical Study*
           (Philadelphia: Westminster Press).
Beardsley, M.C.
           See Wimsatt.
Ben Porat, Z.
1974   *The Poetics of Allusion* (PhD dissertation, University of
           California, Berkeley). Not consulted; cited by Perri (1979: 180).
Bergsten, S.
1959   'Illusive Allusions. Some Reflections on the Critical Approach
           to the Poetry of T.S. Eliot', *Orbis Litterarum* 14: 9-18.
Broyles, C.C.
1989   *The Conflict of Faith and Experience in the Psalms* (JSOTSup,
           52; Sheffield: JSOT Press).
Cain, W.E.
1984   *The Crisis in Criticism* (Baltimore: Johns Hopkins University
           Press).
Clines, D.J.A.
1989   *Job 1–20* (WBC, 17; Dallas: Word Books).
Crüsemann, F.
1980   'Hiob und Kohelet', in R. Albertz *et al.* (eds.), *Werden und
           Wirken des Alten Testaments* (Festschrift C. Westermann;
           Göttingen: Vandenhoeck & Ruprecht), pp. 373-93.
Culler, J.
1983   *The Pursuit of Signs: Semiotics, Literature, Deconstruction*
           (London: Routledge & Kegan Paul [1981]).
Deissler, A.
1955   *Psalm 119 (118) und seine Theologie* (Münchener Theo-
           logische Studien, 1/11; München: Karl Zink).
Dell, K.J.
1991   *The Book of Job as Sceptical Literature* (BZAW, 197; Berlin:
           de Gruyter).

Di Cesare, M.A.
1964   *Vida's Christiad and Vergilian Epic* (New York: Columbia University Press).

Diewert, D.A.
1987   'Job 7.12: *Yam, Tannin* and the Surveillance of Job', *JBL* 106: 203-15.

Dion, P.E.
1987   'Formulaic Language in the Book of Job: International Background and Ironical Distortions', *SR* 16: 187-93.

Draisma, S. (ed.)
1989   *Intertextuality in Biblical Writings: Essays in Honour of Bas van Iersel* (Kampen: Kok).

Eco, U.
1968   *La struttura assente* (Milan: Valentino Bompiani).

Eslinger, L.
1992   'Inner-Biblical Exegesis and Inner-Biblical Allusion: The Question of Category', *VT* 42: 47-58.

Espmark, K.
1985   *Dialoger* (Stockholm: Norstedts).

Fishbane, M.
1988   *Biblical Interpretation in Ancient Israel* (Oxford: Clarendon Press [1985], corrected paperback edition).

Fohrer, G.
1959   'Form und Funktion in der Hiobdichtung', *ZDMG* 109: 31-49.

Fredriksson, H.
1945   *Jahwe als Krieger* (Lund: Gleerup).

Frow, J.
1991   'Intertextuality and Ontology', in Worton and Still 1991: 45-55.

Genette, G.
1979   *Introduction à l'architexte* (Paris: Seuil).
1982   *Palimpsestes: La littérature au second degré* (Paris: Seuil).

Habel, N.C.
1985   *The Book of Job: A Commentary* (OTL; London: SCM).

Hirsch, E.D.
1967   *Validity in Interpretation* (New Haven: Yale University Press).

Janowski, B.
1989   *Rettungsgewissheit und Epiphanie des Heils: Das Motiv der Hilfe Gottes 'am Morgen' im Alten Orient und im Alten Testament*, I (WMANT, 59; Neukirchen: Neukirchener Verlag).

Janzen, J.G.
1989   'Another Look at God's Watch over Job (7.12)', *JBL* 108: 109-14.

Jardin, A.
1986   'Intertextuality', in Th. A. Sebeok (ed.), *Encyclopedic Dictionary of Semiotics* (Approaches to Semiotics, 73; Amsterdam: Mouton; Berlin: de Gruyter).

Jenny, L.
1982   'The Strategy of Form', in T. Todorov (ed.), *French Literary Theory Today* (Cambridge: Cambridge University Press [1982]):

34-63; originally published as 'La stratégie de la forme', *Poétique* 27 (1976): 257-81.

Keel, O.
1978   *Jahwes Entgegnung an Ijob* (FRLANT, 121; Göttingen: Vandenhoeck & Ruprecht).

Kittang, A., and A. Aarseth
1985   *Lyriske strukturer* (Oslo: Universitetsforlaget [1968]).

Kristeva, J.
1967   'Bakhtine, le mot, le dialogue et le roman' *Critique* 239: 438-65.
1969   *Sēmeiōtikē: Recherches pour une sémanalyse. Essais* (Paris: Seuil).

Kubina, V.
1979   *Die Gottesreden im Buche Hiob* (Freiburger Theologische Studien, 115; Freiburg: Herder).

Lentricchia, F.
1983   *After the New Criticism* (London: Methuen, paperback edn [1980]).

Lévêque, J.
1970   *Job et son Dieu* (EBib; Paris: Gabalda).

Lindström, F.
1983   *God and the Origin of Evil: A Contextual Analysis of Alleged Monistic Evidence in the Old Testament* (ConBOT, 21; Lund: Gleerup).

Ljung, P.E.
1991   'Vart tog författaren vägen?', *Tidskrift för litteraturvetenskap* 20: 36-60.

Mettinger, T.
1988   *In Search of God: The Meaning and Message of the Everlasting Names* (Philadelphia: Fortress Press).
1992   'The God of Job: Avenger, Tyrant, or Victor?', in L.G. Perdue and W.C. Gilpin (eds.), *The Voice from the Whirlwind: Interpreting the Book of Job* (Nashville: Abingdon Press), pp. 39-49, 233-36.

Miner, E.
1986   'Allusion', in A. Preminger (ed.), *The Princeton Handbook of Poetic Terms* (Princeton, NJ: Princeton University Press): 10-11.

Nielsen, K.
1990   'Intertextuality and Biblical Scholarship', *SJOT* 1990/2: 88-95.

Panofsky, E.
1964   'Der Begriff des Kunstwollens' (originally pub. in 1920), in his *Aufsätze zur Grundlagen der Kunstwissenschaft* (ed. H. Oberer and E. Verheyen; Berlin: Bruno Hessling): 33-47. English Version: 'The Concept of Artistic Volition', *Critical Inquiry* 8 (Autumn, 1981): 17-33.

Perdue, L.G.
1991   *Wisdom in Revolt: Metaphorical Theology in the Book of Job* (JSOTSup, 112; Sheffield: JSOT Press).

Perri, C. *et al.*
1979   'Allusion Studies: An International Annotated Bibliography,
            1921–1977', *Style* 13: 178-225.
Pfister, M.
1985   'Konzepte der Intertextualität', in U. Broich and M. Pfister
            (eds.), *Intertextualität, Formen, Funktionen, anglistische Fall-
            studien* (Tübingen: Max Niemeyer): 1-30.
Pucci, P.
1987   *Odysseus Polutropos: Intertextual Readings in the Odyssey
            and the Iliad* (Ithaca, NY: Cornell University Press).
Ravasi, G.
1988   *Il libro dei Salmi*, I (Bologna: Edizioni Dehoniane).
Renkema, J.
1983   *'Misschien is er hoop...' De theologische vooronderstellingen
            van het boek van Klaagliederen* (Franeker: Wever).
Riffaterre, M.
1978   *The Semiotics of Poetry* (Bloomington: University of Indiana
            Press).
1980a   'La trace de l'intertexte', *La Pensée* 215: 4-18.
1980b   'Syllepsis', *Critical Inquiry* 6: 625-38.
1991   'Compulsory Reader Response: The Intertextual Drive', in
            Worton and Still 1991: 56-78.
Robert, A.
1934–35   'Les attaches littéraires bibliques des Prov. I–IX', *RB* 43 (1934),
            pp. 42-68, 172-204, 374-84 and *RB* 44 (1935), pp. 344-65, 502-25.
Roberts, J.J.M.
1973   'Job's Summons to Yahweh: The Exploitation of a Legal
            Metaphor', *RestQ* 16: 159-65.
1977   'Job and the Israelite Religious Tradition', *ZAW* 89: 107-14.
Schaar, C.
1975   'Vertical Context Systems', in *Style and Text: Studies
            Presented to Nils Erik Enkvist* (Stockholm: Almqvist &
            Wiksell): 146-57.
1978   'Linear Sequence, Spatial Structure, Complex Sign, and
            Vertical Context System', *Poetics* 7: 377-88.
1982   *The Full Voic'd Quire Below: Vertical Context Systems in
            Paradise Lost* (Lund Studies in English, 60; Lund: Gleerup).
Spieckermann, H.
1989   *Heilsgegenwart: Eine Theologie der Psalmen* (FRLANT, 148;
            Göttingen: Vandenhoeck & Ruprecht).
Steiner, G.
1989   *Real Presences: Is There Anything in What we Say?* (London:
            Faber).
Stierle, K.
1983   'Werk und Intertextualität', in W. Schmid and W.-D. Stempel
            (eds.), *Dialog der Texte: Hamburger Kolloquium zur Inter-
            textualität* (Wiener Slawistischer Almanach. Sonderband 11;
            Wien): 7-26.

Still, J., and M. Worton
1991   'Introduction', in Worton and Still (1991): 1-44.
Thormählen, M.
1994   *Eliot's Animals* (Lund Studies in English, 70; Lund: Gleerup).
Thornton, W.
1968   *Allusions in Ulysses* (Chapel Hill: University of North Carolina Press).
Vinge, L.
1973   'Om allusioner', *Tidskrift för litteraturvetenskap* 2: 138-54.
Westermann, C.
1978   *Der Aufbau des Buches Hiob* (Stuttgart: Calwer Verlag, 3rd edn [1956]).
Whybray, R.N.
1974   *The Intellectual Tradition in the Old Testament* (BZAW, 135; Berlin: de Gruyter).
1981   'The Identification and Use of Quotations in Ecclesiastes', *Congress Volume, Vienna 1980* (ed. J.A. Emerton; VTSup, 32; Leiden: Brill): 435-51.
Wimsatt, W.K. and M.C. Beardsley
1954   'The Intentional Fallacy' [1946], repr. in Wimsatt, *The Verbal Icon* (Lexington: University of Kentucky Press): 1-18.
Wolde, E. van
1989   'Trendy Intertextuality?', in Draisma 1989: 43-50.
1990   'Van tekst via tekst naar betekenis. Intertekstualiteit en haar implicaties', *Tijdschrift voor Theologie* 30: 333-61.
Worton, M., and J. Still (eds.)
1991   *Intertextuality: Theories and Practices* (Manchester: Manchester University Press, paperback edn [1990]).
Ziegler, J.
1950   'Die Hilfe Gottes am Morgen', in *Alttestamentliche Studien* (Festschrift Nötscher; BBB, 1; Bonn: Peter Hanstein): 281-88.

JUDAH AND TAMAR (GENESIS 38)

J. Alberto Soggin

1. Within the Story of Joseph, the episode of Judah and Tamar
is obviously an independent literary unit. It does not connect
in any way with the adventures of Joseph, and its relations to
the remaining patriarchal stories are very tenuous. This must
be maintained against E.A. Speiser (1964), who would like to
see a connection with ch. 37. Moreover, the story has clearly
an independent, new beginning: Judah starts a business on
his own with a Canaanite partner, as we shall see; he marries
a Canaanite woman and founds a family outside of his
father's house. Less clear is the conclusion of the story: Tamar
has a son by her father-in-law, but we hear nothing about
the brother-in-law who was supplied to fulfil the obligation of
the levirate. What has happened we are not told; perhaps the
fact that Tamar had a son by her father-in-law was considered to be sufficient. In any case, the chapter does not
debouch into ch. 39 and therefore shows its fundamental
independence. If it must be classified, I would rather consider
it an independent part of the Jacob cycle, something like
ch. 34 (see Westermann 1982 for details).

2. The translation does not present any major difficulty.
    Verse 1: The root *nāṭâ*, used also in vv. 12 and 20, has a
specialized meaning, not the usual one, 'to open a tent'
(figuratively 'heavens' in II Isaiah), but something that has to
do with business. I propose therefore a root *nāṭâ* II, with the
meaning 'to join (in business)' or something similar, against B.
Jacob, who would like to render '...he pitched his tent as far
as Adullam'.
    Verse 2: *šûaʿ* is the name of the father of the bride, not of

the bride herself; cf. v. 12, where she appears as *bat šûa'*, and 1 Chron. 2.3, against the rendering of the LXX.

Verse 6: *tāmār* is the 'date palm'.

Verse 9: The practice followed by the levirate husbands is the one medically defined as *coitus interruptus*; it is condemned here for the lack of consideration it shows for the woman and her rights, not as a practice in itself, an issue about which nothing is being said.

Verse 11: To blame the woman in such cases and attribute everything to her evil powers is done also in Tob. 3.7-9 and 8.9-11.

Verse 14 confronts the reader with the only textual difficulty of the episode. I propose to render, '...she sat down at the cross-road on the way to Timnah', according to the reading of the Vg (followed by the Syr), *in bivio itineris*; it is known also to Jewish mediaeval exegesis (texts in Jacob 1966). The Hebrew 'she sat down at the gate of '*ênayim*...' makes hardly any sense, and a place by that name is unknown. The 'veil' is part of the dress of a married woman (Jdt. 10.2; 16.9), and not of a prostitute, who, on the contrary, is supposed to be looked at; it is only because of the veil that Judah does not recognize his daughter-in-law (so rightly Jacob). *zônâ* is the ordinary harlot.

Verse 18: '*erābôn* in the meaning of 'pawn' or 'earnest money' is a Graecism; cf. ἀρραβών, well known from the New Testament in the Pauline epistles. To derive it from the Akkadian *erub(b)atu(m)* (*AHw*, I, p. 248), a rare word that appears in ancient Assyrian, as suggested by E.A. Speiser (1964), is rather improbable. The 'seal' is not a ring, as many commentaries propose, but a major implement carried at one's belt or neck.

Verse 21: *qᵉdēšâ* is the cultic harlot attached to a temple. Our text seems to confuse the two categories.

Verse 24: In many archaic societies a woman having sex outside wedlock is called a harlot, even if she has not been professionally engaged; here the charge is supported by the fact that she had disguised herself as such; on the other hand it is difficult to say how she would have been recognized, as her father-in-law had been unable to do so. The death sentence at the stake is not prescribed for adultery except in certain cases (Lev. 20.14; 21.8); stoning seems to have been the common penalty (Lev. 20.10; Deut. 22.23-25; cf. Ezek. 16.40; Jn 8.5). Further, Tamar being a widow, one should not speak about adultery at all. The whole conclusion of the story is typical for the fairy tale, in which sometimes extravagant forms of penalties are threatened, but in the end, for some reason, they are never applied.

In vv. 3 and 30 we have a masculine form where a feminine one is expected (so rightly vv. 4 and 5). In v. 14 *watt^{e}kas* is not correct; one ought to read either *wattit^{e}kas* with Sam., TgO and Syr, or the niph'al *wattikās* (Skinner 1930). In v. 24 read *k^{e}miš^{e}lōšet*, and not *k^{e}miš^{e}lōš*. In v. 29 read either *kah^{a}šíbô* with LXX (ὡς δὲ ἐπισυνήγαγεν τὴν χεῖρα), or *k^{e}mô hēšíb*.

3. It seems to be impossible to assign our text to one of the sources of the Pentateuch: attempts to propose J clash both with the fact that none of the characteristic elements of J can be found and with the interest in genealogies (vv. 1-2 and 27-30).

3.1. Other proposals have been made to explain the origin and the scope of our text. G. von Rad (1972) thinks of an ancient tribal situation; others believe in oral tradition, originating among the successors of Judah and Tamar (so, for example, Westermann 1982); but all this ought to be proved before being proclaimed as obvious; in the next lines I shall present some elements that I think prove exactly the contrary (see §4).

3.2. C. Westermann is on the right track when he observes that our chapter reminds the reader of the book of Ruth; in both cases the reader is confronted with a family story, not a tribal story, in which the author speaks to his people about ancestry. As in Ruth (where there is one of the rare cases in which reference is made to another biblical episode), relations with the Canaanite population are friendly—not only is there good neighbourliness and commerce, but also intermarriage— a difference between Ruth and our chapter lies in the lack of a conversion by Judah's wife, something hinted at in Ruth 1.16. On these bases most authors have been thinking of an ancient tradition coming from a time in which Israelites and

Canaanites were living peaceably side by side, in any case before Deuteronomy and later texts.

3.3. In the context of this family story the text treats the problem of levirate marriage. About it little is known, not even if and how far it was ever practised. Its task was evidently to solve the problem of widows who had become such without having borne a child to their deceased husbands (see further §4). And the widow of the story is presented in the act of using a ruse, in order to bring about the application of the law in her situation, something that had not been the case; and such a ruse was not without danger, as one can see.

3.4. Interesting is the notice that Judah separates himself from his family and starts a business on his own with a Canaanite partner—if this is the way we should render the verb—and marries a Canaanite woman, something that happens later also to his eldest son.

4. To ask the question, whether the story originated in Israel or in Canaan (so, if I understand him rightly, Emorton [1979]) does not, as it seems to me, do justice to the very point the narrator is trying to make; it would be like asking whether the book of Ruth originated in Judah or in Moab. Our text does not draw a sharp distinction between the two ethnic groups. It does not even consider the possibility that there may have been a difference in religion, something that Ruth 1.16 acknowledges. No doubt, in any case our text reflects a situation later than the Israelite settlement, as Emerton (1975) has proved.

4.1. But there are some other, interesting clues that suggest a much later date:

1.   First of all, the generally accepted analogies with the book of Ruth, which must be maintained by all differences in some details (see further §5.2-3).
2.   Analogies with the deuteronocanonical books of Tobit in vv. 11 and 14, and Judith in v. 14.
3.   The not always correct and precise use of Hebrew forms in vv. 3, 5, 14, 24 and 29, something that could be a sign that Hebrew was no longer currently spoken where the text originated.

4. A Graecism in vv. 18 and 20.
5. The imprecise use of *zônâ* and *qᵉdēšâ*.
6. These elements, if taken one by one, would hardly be sufficient, but their quantity is at least impressive.

5. Similar considerations can be made about the institution of levirate marriage, a practice attested also among other peoples.

5.1. The word comes from the Latin *levir*, 'brother-in-law'. Apart from our text, the institution is mentioned in Ruth 4, while Deut. 24.5-10 gives the legal formulation of the principle. There is no other evidence in the Hebrew Bible. An intentionally paradoxical formulation is found in the New Testament (Mt. 22.23-33 and parallels).

5.2. Levirate marriage consisted of the obligation to the surviving brother to produce children with the sister-in-law, the first-born of which was considered a son of the deceased (Gunkel 1910). The institution aims first of all, therefore, at securing for the deceased the son he had not been able to father during his life (Deut. 25.6b); later, a provision was made that the son thus born would also inherit the wealth of the deceased. Different seems to be the situation in Ruth 4: here the law applies to the next of kin, whose task it was to ransom the possessions of a debtor; with these possessions he received also the widow.

5.3. It is not stated that the brother of the deceased had the obligation to marry the widow. The widow's only right was to receive a child from him (Coats 1979). Their union was therefore a precarious one, which ceased after reaching its aim. With Ruth the situation is again different.

5.4. The brother-in-law of Tamar resists the institution that he evidently considers repugnant, but not openly, and simulates a fulfilment that has not taken place; and for this he is chastised. That people should resist the practice is anticipated by Deut. 25.7, but no enforcement of the law is foreseen. There is, further, no question of the consent of the widow, probably because it was supposed that she would agree in any case. In Lev. 18.16 and 20.21 there are, further, norms which seem to forbid the practice altogether!

5.5. But it is difficult to consider our text, as B. Jacob puts it, as anterior to this norm; it is, rather, a text which aims at illustrating how the institution worked (or, better, did not work) in practice, without any pretence to legal clarity.

6. At the end we should ask: What is the aim of this chapter? The analogies with the book of Ruth show it rather clearly: Perez is in both texts (cf. Ruth 4.18, an ancestor of David, and 1 Chron. 2.3-5), so that the two texts aim at providing a genealogy for King David, both stressing the Canaanite element in the mothers. But there are also differences between the two books: in Ruth something like a conversion to Judaism by the Moabite partner takes place, an element completely absent from our text. Ruth appears therefore as the theologically more mature work, part of the missionary effort that distinguished later Judaism and especially the Pharisees. Both writings belong, in any case, to those texts that appear to be fundamentally friendly towards the Canaanites and the non-Israelites in general; to the same group one may assign also the book of Jonah, albeit without a Davidic genealogy.

BIBLIOGRAPHY

Aharoni, Y.
1963   'Tamar and the Roads to Elath', *IEJ* 19: 30-42.
Astour, M.C.
1966   'Tamar and the Hierodule', *JBL* 85: 185-86.
Blum, E.
1984   *Die Komposition der Vätergeschichte* (WMANT, 57; Neukirchen–Vluyn: Neukirchener Verlag).
Carmichael, C.M.
1977   'A Ceremonial Crux: Removing a Man's Sandals as a Female Gesture of Contempt', *JBL* 96: 321-36.
Cassuto, U.
1973   'The Story of Tamar and Judah', in *Biblical and Oriental Studies*, I (Jerusalem: Magnes): 108-17 (original, 1929).
Coats, G.W.
1972   'Widow's Rights: A Crux in the Structure of Gen. 38', *CBQ* 34: 461-66.
Emerton, J.A.
1975   'Some Problems in Genesis xxxviii', *VT* 25: 338-61.

1976   'An Examination of a Recent Structuralist Interpretation of
            Gen. xxxviii', *VT* 26: 79-98.
1979   'Judah and Tamar', *VT* 29: 403-15.
Goldin, J.
1977   'The Youngest Son, or Where does Genesis 38 Belong?', *JBL*
            96: 27-44.
Gunkel, H.
1910   *Genesis* (HKAT, I/1; Göttingen: Vandenhoeck & Ruprecht, 3rd
            edn).
Jacob, B.
1934   *Genesis* (Berlin: Schocken; repr. New York: Ktav, 1966).
Lipiński, E.
1973   'L'étymologie de "Juda"', *VT* 23: 380.
Luther, B.
1906   'Die Novelle von Juda und Tamar und andere israelitische
            Novellen', in E. Meyer and B. Luther, *Die Israeliten und ihre
            Nachbarstämme* (Halle: M. Niemeyer): 173-206.
Niditch, S.
1979   'The Wronged Woman Righted: An Analysis of Gen. 38', *HTR*
            72: 143-48.
Puukko, A.F.
1949   'Die Leviratsehe in den altorientalischen Gesetzen', *ArOr* 17:
            296-99.
Rad, G. von
1972   *Das erste Buch Mose: Genesis* (3 vols.; ATD, 2-4; Göttingen:
            Vandenhoeck & Ruprecht, 9th edn).
Rendsburg, G.A.
1986   'David and his Circle in Genesis xxxviii', *VT* 36: 438-46.
Ridout, G.
1974   'The Rape of Tamar', in *Rhetorical Criticism: Essays in Honor
            of James Muilenburg* (ed. J.J. Jackson and M. Kessler;
            Pittsburgh: Pickwick Press): 75-84.
Ska, J.-L.
1988   'L'ironie de Tamar (Gen. 38)', *ZAW* 100: 261-63.
Skinner, J.
1930   *Genesis* (ICC; Edinburgh: T. & T. Clark, 2nd edn).
Speiser, E.A.
1964   *Genesis* (AB, 1; Garden City, NY: Doubleday).
Westermann, C.
1982   *Genesis* (BKAT, I/3; Neukirchen–Vluyn: Neukirchener Verlag).

LES MILIEUX DU DEUTÉRONOME

Henri Cazelles

Decrivant récemment un milieu qu'il connait bien,[1] R.N.
Whybray nous avertissait qu'il ne fallait pas identifier sans
plus les 'sages' (*ḥakâmîm*) de la Bible hébraïque avec une
classe professionnelle de scribes. Il notait toute une série de
passages bibliques où *ḥâkâm* désigne essentiellement des
personnes 'intelligemment bien douées...ou avant acquis un
savoir-faire'.[2] Il admettait que ces personnes puissent avoir été
en rapports avec la cour du roi, mais sans en faire une
exclusivité. Des changements ont pu se produire tout au long
de la monarchie.

Cette observation est d'importance à un moment où
l'actualité exégétique est fortement concernée par le problème
des milieux d'où est issu le mouvement deutéronomique. Le
milieu des 'sages' n'est pas seul en cause. On a pu faire appel
au milieu prophétique, au milieu lévitique, au milieu des
juges, au milieu des 'anciens', au milieu agraire, au milieu de
l'administration, aux responsables des traités internationaux
...comme étant à l'origine de la composition du Deutéronome

1. R.N. Whybray, *The Intellectual Tradition in the Old Testament*
(BZAW, 135; Berlin: de Gruyter, 1974).
2. 'The Sages in the Israelite Royal Court', dans *The Sage in Israel
and the Ancient Near East* (éd. J.L. Gammie et L.G. Perdue; Winona Lake,
IN: Eisenbrauns, 1990), pp. 133-39: 'natural intelligence...acquired skill';
'Prophecy and Wisdom', dans *Israel's Prophetic Tradition: Essays in Honour
of Peter R. Ackroyd* (éd. R.J. Coggins, A. Phillips et M.A. Knibb; Cambridge:
Cambridge University Press), pp. 181-99 (sp. 194 sur l'évolution de la
notion de *ḥokmah*). Voir aussi R. Murphy, 'shared approach to reality'
('Wisdom: Theses and Hypotheses', dans *Israelite Wisdom: Theological
and Literary Essays in Honor of Samuel Terrien* [Missoula, MT: Scholars
Press, 1978], p. 39).

en fonction de ce que les uns appellent son idéologie, et d'autres sa théologie. Il est certain que ces milieux n'étaient pas étanches. Administration, sages, rédacteurs, des traités étaient naturellement liés à la cour royale.

S. Loersch,[3] P. Buis–J. Leclercq,[4] A.D.H. Mayes[5] et H.J. Preuss[6] ont donné des aperçus synthétiques sur les solutions proposées dans l'exégèse contemporaine. Mais le travail a continué et fait l'objet de monographies qui compléteront les références données par les auteurs précédents.

Une origine du Deutéronome dans un milieu *Lévitique* a été préconisée par Baudissin, Horst, Buis–Leclercq, Bentzen, Lindblom, de Vaux et particulièrement développée par von Rad.[7] Alors qu'Ezéchiel et le code sacerdotal donnent aux Lévites un statut inférieur aux *kôhanîm*, le Dtn parait les assimiler dans les expressions *hakôhanîm halewiyyîm* (17,9.18; 18,1.8; 24,8; 27,9) ou *kôhanîm beney lewy* (21,5; 31,9). Par ailleurs, dans le Dtn, les fonctions sacerdotales sont exercées indifféremment par des prêtres (10,6; 17,12; 18,3; 20,2; 26,3-4) ou par des lévites (10,8; 18,6-7; 31,25; 33,8-11 et

---

3. S. Loersch, *Das Deuteronomium und seine Deutungen* (Stuttgart, 1962).

4. P. Buis et J. Leclercq, *Le Deutéronome* (Paris: Gabalda, 1963), pp. 12-18.

5. A.D.H. Mayes, *Deuteronomy* (NCB; Grand Rapids: Eerdmans, 1979), sp. pp. 103-108.

6. H.J. Preuss, *Deuteronomium* (Erträge der Forschung, 164; Darmstadt: Wissenschaftliche Buchgesellschaft, 1982), sp. pp. 26-44 avec une bibliographie exhaustive pour l'époque, bien classée, et des résumés clairs.

7. G. von Rad, *Das Gottesvolk im Deuteronomium* (Stuttgart: Kohlhammer, 1929); *idem, Das formgeschichtliche Problem des Hexateuch* (repris dans *Gesammelte Studien* [München: Kaiser, 1958], I, pp. 9-86); *idem, Studies in Deuteronomy* (SBT, 9; London: SCM Press, 1953); *idem, Der heilige Krieg im alten Israel* (Göttingen, 1958); 'Deuteronomy', *IDB*, I, pp. 831-38; *idem, Das fünfte Buch Moses: Deuteronomium* (ATD, 5; Göttingen: Vandenhoeck & Ruprecht, 1964). Dans sa dissertation dactylographiée (aux pp. 43-77), L. Hoppe (*The Origins of Deuteronomy* [diss. Northwestern University, Evanston, IL, 1978]) a exposé avec clarté les positions de von Rad dans ses publications successives. Il a résumé ses propres conclusions dans son article, 'The Levitical Origins of Deuteronomy Reconsidered', *BR* 28 (1983), pp. 27-36.

probablement 27,14). Mais von Rad a lié ces considérations à une prédication lévitique, à une célébration cultuelle de renouvellement de l'alliance, à un renouveau d'esprit guerrier, et à l'existence d'une amphictyonie prémonarchique.[8] L.J. Hoppe, après un exposé soigneux[9] a critiqué cette position en observant que dans la plupart des cas les Lévites ne sont pas les bénéficiaires mais les victimes de la centralisation du culte; elle en faisait des personnes 'misérables' à l'instar de la veuve et de l'orphelin.

Le milieu *prophétique* a été proposé par Wellhausen, K. Budde, A. Alt, S.R. Driver, H.E. Ryle, R.H. Kennett, C.F. Burney, G. Dahl, K.J. Zobel, E.W. Nicholson,[10] sur certains points de vue par W.F. Albright. Cette origine explique le souci de la purification du culte et surtout les connexions maintes fois signalées entre Dtn et Osée. L.J. Hoppe a critiqué cette position en observant que les prophètes ne sont pas spécialement bien vus de Dtn (13,2-6; 18,9-22).[11]

C'est au milieu de la *cour* et de ses '*sages*' que se sont attachés M. Weinfeld,[12] N. Lohfink[13] et W. McKane[14] avec

8.   L'hypothèse amphictyonique est maintenant abandonnée (voir les critiques de G.W. Anderson, 'Israel: Amphictyony, '*am, qâhâl, 'edah*', dans *Translating and Understanding the Old Testament: Essays in Honour of Herbert Gordon May* (éd. H.T. Thomas et W.L. Reed; Nashville: Abingdon Press, 1970), et de R. de Vaux, *Histoire ancienne d'Israël* (Paris: Gabalda, 1973), II, pp. 19-36. La structure amphictyonique n'est bien attestée qu'avec le fonctionnement des 12 préfectures de Salomon (1 R 4,8-13 avec retouches Dtr). Auparavant les tribus, encore autonomes, s'unissent en '*am* ou en *qehal YHWH*. Le livre des Juges s'efforcera de regrouper les victoires tribales ou conféderées dans la cadre amphictyonique, comme l'avaient fait J et P par défiance de la monarchie sacrale.
9.   Hoppe, *Origins of Deuteronomy*, pp. 155-211.
10.   K. Zobel, *Prophetie und Deuteronomium* (BZAW, 199; Berlin: de Gruyter, 1992); E.W. Nicholson, *Deuteronomy and Tradition* (Oxford: Blackwell, 1967), pp. 65-79. Voir aussi le dialogue Stuehlmüller–Viviano sur 'prophétie et mystique' où est souligné le 'complex subject of prophetic origins' (*BR* 36 [1991], p. 63).
11.   Hoppe, *Origins of Deuteronomy*, pp. 118-54.
12.   M. Weinfeld, *Deuteronomy and the Deuteronomic School* (Oxford: Clarendon Press, 1972); *idem*, 'The Origin of Humanism in Deuteronomy', *JBL* 80 (1961), pp. 241-47; *idem*, 'The Dependence of Deuteronomy upon Wisdom Literature', in *Yehezkel Kaufmann Jubilee Volume* (ed. M. Haran;

abondance de preuves dans le fonctionnement des cours royales à l'époque du Deutéronome. On signale en particulier que, en Jer 18,18, les 'sages' (*ḥakâmîm*) sont une classe professionnelle dépositaire d'une parole faisant autorité, le 'conseil', à egalité avec l'"oracle' (*tôrah*) du prêtre, et la 'parole' du prophète. L'insertion de la Loi dans un discours parénétique relève non de la prédication lévitique, mais des 'enseignements' de sagesse donnés dans les écoles aux apprentis scribes. Ce sont eux qui, rédacteurs professionnels des traités d'alliance, ont donné au Deutéronome sa structure. La sagesse religieuse envers 'le dieu', et 'humaniste' envers le prochain (surtout le pauvre) de la sagesse d'Amenemope (18,26...) se retrouve dans le Deutéronome, et cette Sagesse a été utilisée par le livre des Proverbes (22,17–24,11). L.J. Hoppe rejoint ici R.N. Whybray dans sa critique de l'existence d'une 'classe professionnelle' de sages dans le Deutéronome. Les 'chefs' de Dt 1 sont des chefs de tribus et non des juges sages (*šôfeṭîm/ḥakâmîm*). Huit fois seulement sont mentionnés des gens *ḥakâmîm*. Rédacteurs du Deutéronome, pourquoi auraient-ils ainsi 'camouflé'[15] leur présence?

L.J. Hoppe préfère chercher l'origine du mouvement deutéronomique dans le milieu des *'anciens'* (*zeqénim*) d'Israël.[16] Mentionnés cinq fois dans le code comme autorités

Jerusalem, 1960), pp. 89-105; *idem*, 'Traces of Assyrian Formulae in Deuteronomy', *Bib* 46 (1965), pp. 417-27; *idem*, 'The Emergence of the Deuteronomic Movement', dans N. Lohfink (éd.), *Das Deuteronomium: Entstehung, Gestalt und Botschaft/Deuteronomy: Origin, Form and Message* (BETL, 48; Leuven: Leuven University Press, 1985), pp. 76-98. Voir aussi W.L. Humphreys, *The Motif of the Wise Courtier in the Old Testament* (diss. Union Theological Seminary, New York, 1970).

13. N. Lohfink, 'Die Wandlung des Bundesbegriffes im Buche Deuteronomium', dans *Festgabe Rahner* (Freiburg, 1964), pp. 423-44 (voir aussi H. Cazelles, 'Autour de l'Exode', dans *Les structures successives de l'alliance dans l'A.T.* [Paris, 1987], pp. 143-56); *idem*, 'Die Bundesurkunde des Königs Josias', *Bib* 44 (1963), pp. 261-88, 461-98.

14. W. McKane, *Prophets and Wise Men* (Naperville, IL: Allenson, 1965).

15. Hoppe, *Origins of Deuteronomy*, p. 256.

16. Hoppe, *Origins of Deuteronomy*, pp. 257-356; cf. J. van der Ploeg, 'Les anciens d'Israël', dans *Lex Tua Veritas: Festschrift für H. Junker* (éd.

locales (19,12; 21,2.19; 22,15; 25,9), ils auraient une position
supérieure dans le cadre du code (5,23; 27,1; 31,9) et dans
l'Histoire deutéronomique, postexilique. Héritiers d'anciennes
traditions, même prébibliques, ce sont les 'Anciens' qui auraient rédigé le Deutéronome après l'exil en vue de garder les
anciennes traditions lors de la disparition des institutions
politiques d'Israël.

Mais si, dans le code deutéronomique, ces anciens sont des
autorités locales, n'est-ce pas dans le terroir même de Juda ou
d'Israël qu'il faut chercher le milieu d'origine du Deutéronome? Ce milieu serait préexilique et non le milieu postexilique dominé par le clergé aaronide, celui des sédentaires
préexiliques et non des rapatriés postexiliques. Ce milieu, le
'peuple du pays' (*'am ha'areṣ*) s'est opposé à la cour, en
particulier lors du meurtre d'Amon père de Josias. N'est-ce pas
à lui, paysan aisé possédant serviteurs et servantes, que
s'adresse en fait le Moïse du Deutéronome dans ses rituels
agricoles (ch. 26), ses fêtes saisonnières agraires (ch. 16), et
dans nombre de ses bénédictions et malédictions? Le calen-
drier liturgique du code sacerdotal (Lév 23; cf. Nb 28–29) aura
une base toute différente. G.H. Wittenberg[17] et Patricia
Dutcher-Walls[18] se sont posé la question.

Pour la résoudre, cette dernière fait une judicieuse remarque:
'To choose only one group is to overlook the social reality of
political structures and factional struggles in agrarian
societies in antiquity'.[19] Cette interrogation sur les 'structures
politiques' est celle que préconise R.N. Whybray. Tout en

H. Gross et F. Mussner; Trier: Paulinus Verlag, 1961), pp. 175-92; J.L.
McKenzie, 'The Elders in the Old Testament', *Bib* 40 (1959), pp. 527-40;
J. Conrad, '*zqn*', *THAT*, p. 647; M. Weinfeld, 'Elders', *EncJud*, VI, pp. 579-
80.

17. G.H. Wittenberg, 'Job the Farmer: The Judaean *'am ha'arets* and
the Wisdom Movement', *Old Testament Essays* (Pretoria, 1991), pp. 151-
70.

18. P. Dutcher-Walls, 'The Social Location of the Deuteronomists: A
Sociological Study of Factional Politics in Late Preexilic Judah', *JSOT* 52
(1991), pp. 77-94. Ce problème sociologique s'étend d'ailleurs à la Phénicie
(Y.B. Tsirkin, *Vestnik* [1991, 4], pp. 3-13).

19. Dutcher-Walls, 'Social Location of the Deuteronomists', p. 93.

contestant l'existence d'écoles de scribes en Israël, il écrit: 'in Israel as elsewhere in the ancient Near East the courts were the intellectual centers of the two kingdoms', et ailleurs il mentionne... 'the deuteronomistic movement, in which it is probable that royal scribes played a part'.[20] Tout en mettant l'accent sur le 'social world of the wisdom writers'[21] de l'époque postexilique à laquelle nous devons les livres dits de Sagesse, il n'exclut pas une sagesse de haute qualité littéraire chez les scribes royaux professionnels préexiliques. Il attend des études plus poussées. Les auteurs que nous venons de résumer trop brièvement ont su mettre en relief des données que l'on ne peut contester. Il y a là six milieux (lévites, prophètes, sages de cour, sages religieux postexiliques, anciens, paysans aisés) qui ont eu leur impact sur la rédaction du Deutéronome et le mouvement qui l'a produit; il ne faut pas non plus oublier les juges, les *šôfeṭîm* associés aux *ḥakâmîm* par Weinfeld. Ils sont mis en tête des institutions en 16,18-20 et 17,8-13, avant rois, prêtres-Lévites et prophètes. Un Deutéronomiste a placé leur installation par Moïse comme prologue à toute l'Histoire deutéronomique (1.9-18).

La question du milieu dépend donc d'une question de politique, ou plus exactement de sociologie politique. Quelle est l'importance relative des différents milieux en fonction desquels sont rédigés le Deutéronome et la littérature deutéronomique? Dans la société israélite ces milieux ne sont pas indépendants les uns des autres; ils interfèrent les uns avec les autres, mais pas de la même manière à toutes les époques.[22]

Qui dit politique dit gouvernement. Quelle a été l'influence des différents milieux sociologiques dans l'organisation de la société israélite, tant à l'intérieur (oppositions internes) qu'à l'extérieur (pressions exercées par les Etats et Empires voisins)? De l'histoire tourmentée de l'Israël biblique, il est résulté une évolution dans ses institutions et dans l'influence des milieux sociologiques dont elles doivent satisfaire les responsabilités et

20. Whybray, 'The Sages in the Israelite Royal Court', pp. 137, 139.
21. R.N. Whybray, dans R.E. Clements (éd.), *The World of Ancient Israel: Sociological, Anthropological and Political Perspectives* (Cambridge: Cambridge University Press, 1989), pp. 227-50.
22. C'est un des thèmes de l'*Intellectual Tradition*.

les besoins. Cela peut être fait au nom d'une idéologie ou d'une théologie, mais celle-ci n'agit sur les institutions et les lois qu'en fonction des réalités sociales vécues.

La clé de voûte des institutions gouvernementales dans l'ancien Orient est la *royauté*. Fondée à l'instar des pays étrangers (1 S 8,5.20), la monarchie israélite fut sacrale.[23] Au nom du Dieu national YHWH, le roi régit le culte, nomme les prêtres, bénit le peuple, lui commande, et intercède pour lui près de Dieu. Solidaire de son peuple c'est lui, le chef, qui exerce la fonction de salut (*yš'*). Mais les prophètes du 8ème s. BC ont une autre conception de la fonction de salut, surtout Osée (13,10-11). L'histoire de salut, dite élohiste, est centrée, non plus sur l'élection familiale et dynastique, mais sur le prophétisme (Gn 20,7; Nb 11,26-30; 12,6-8; cf. 1 S 10,9-12). Elle ne tient plus compte de la royauté (comparer Nb 23,7-10, 18-24 E, à 24,7.17 J): seul YHWH est roi (Nb 23,21; Mi 4,6-9; Is 6). Avec Ezéchiel et les écrits postexiliques, le 'roi' fait place au 'prince' (qui peut être un étranger), soigneusement distingué du 'prêtre', même le David d'Ez 34,24 et 37,25, même Sheshbasar (Esd 1,8) et Zorobabel n'est qu'un *péha'*. Les Psaumes 'royaux' ne sont repris que comme Psaumes 'Messianiques'. Les Chroniques ne s'intéressent à la royauté qu'en fonction du Temple, des ses restaurations, de l'établissement de juges (2 Chr 19,4-19), et du respect qu'elle doit au 'prêtres' (2 Chr 24,22; 26,20). Où se place la loi royale du Dtn dans ces contextes historiques?

Pour gouverner en *mishpaṭ* et *ṣedâqah*, les rois sont assistés de fonctionnaires (2 S 8,15-18). Ils donnent des 'conseils' au roi selon Jér 18,18 qui les appelle *ḥakâmîm*.Ces conseillers politiques (Is 30,1-2; 31,1-2) sont appelés *ḥakâmîm* par Isaïe (29,14; cf. 5,21), Jérémie (9,11; cf. 8,9) et Ezéchiel (28,3-4). Ces prophètes leur sont hostiles, de même que les textes préprophétiques étaient très défiants de cette *ḥokmah* politique;[24]

23. H. Cazelles, *Le Messie de la Bible: Christologie de l'Ancien Testament* (Paris: Desclée, 1978), pp. 60-76, avec bibliographie. Héritage des *ḥakâmîm* politiques, Pr 16,10.12-15, Lam 4,20 en témoignent encore.
24. H. Cazelles, 'A propos d'une phrase de H.H. Rowley', dans *Wisdom in Israel and in the Ancient Near East* (Festschrift Rowley; éd. M. Noth et D. Winton Thomas; VTSup, 3; Leiden: Brill, 1955), pp. 26-32: Salomon

en effet Phéniciens, Araméens, et Judéens du temps de Salomon la reconnaissaient en leurs souverains; n'était-elle pas l'apanage du dieu suprême El qui pouvait la faire partager par d'autres dieux et dont les 'avis' (*thm*) étaient censés donner la vie? Cette *hokmah* était celle par laquelle la Pharaon voulait détruire Israël (Ex 1,10) et qui compromit la vieillesse de David (2 S 13,3; 14,2.20; 16,23; 20,16). Les textes 'prophétiques' sont au contraire favorables à la *hokmah* (Os 13,13), surtout pour Joseph (Gn 41,33.39). Dans l'Histoire deutéronomique ni les bons rois ni les bons conseillers ne sont dits *hakâmîm*. Après l'exil ce n'est plus une sagesse politique de gouvernement, mais une sagesse morale personnelle, 'l'arbre de vie' de Pr 3,18-20, dont Dieu seul connait les secrets (Job 11,6). Où situer la sagesse du Dtn? Est-elle celle de la politique, celle de la morale de la 'crainte de Dieu', ou encore la sagesse populaire du terroir, celle des villages loin de la cour?

Précisément dans le Dtn, l'autorité dans les bourgades et villages est aux mains des Anciens (*ziqney hâ'îr*, 19,12; 21,3.4. 6.19; 22,15.17.18; 25,8). Mais l'institution des *zeqénîm* a un contenu vague et changeant; souvent le terme signifie simplement la 'vieillesse' par opposition à la 'jeunesse' (1 R 12,6-8; Esd 3,12; Zach 8,4). A Mari les anciens (*šibutu*) sont les chefs de tribus Benjaminites non sédentarisées.[25] Il en est de même dans les textes de l'Exode qui appartiennent vraisemblablement tous à la strate Elohiste, qu'ils s'agisse des 70 anciens étroitement associés à Moïse ou des anciens en général.[26] Exilés en Babylonie, les Anciens de Juda se groupent auprès d'Ezéchiel (8,1; 14,1; 20,1); en Ez 7,26 ils prennent la place des *hakâmîm* de Jer 18,18. Au retour de l'exil, il y a des 'Anciens de ville' qui dépendent des *sârîm*. Mais Néhémie les ignore. Ce n'est plus une institution vivante; elle n'est citée

---

(1 R 3,28; 5,10), Azitawadda, le roi phénicien (*KAI*, 26 A I 13), et Panammu araméen (*KAI*, 215, 11). Elle est équivoque en 1 R 2,9; 3,12.

25. Hoppe, *Origins of Deuteronomy*, p. 260 n. 3; H. Klengel, 'Zu den šibutum in altbabylonischen Zeit', *Or* 29 (1960), pp. 357-75. Pour Israël voir *supra* n. 16.

26. H. Cazelles, *Autour de l'Exode (Etudes)* (Paris: Gabalda, 1987), pp. 250-51.

qu'à titre d'archaïsme. A toutes les époques les Anciens sont liés aux tribus ou aux lieux; ce n'est donc pas une institution homogène en Israël. Le Dtn ne connait des 'Anciens d'Israel' qu'en 31,9 pour le rassemblement de toutes les tribus (cf. 31,28). Ce n'est pas là une institution politique de gouvernement. Reste que, lorsque le Dtn s'adresse à Israël, c'est le propriétaire aisé qu'il a en vue, avec serviteurs et servantes (12,18); il doit avoir le souci du pauvre et la charge du lévite (12,19; 14,27.29...).

Qu'en est-il du milieu *lévitique*? Ici encore le terme recouvre des acceptions diverses.[27] En Gn 34 et Ex 32,27, c'est une tribu combattante, quoique divisée (Ex 32,28) et dispersée (Gn 49,5-7). Selon Jd 17–18 (mais pas 19–21) et 1 R 12,31 un Lévite peut aller de tribu en tribu, étant spécialement lié aux sanctuaires locaux, même si Jéroboam affecte à ce culte des non-lévites. Ils ont en particulier la charge du sacerdoce de Dan (Jd 18,31), un des deux sanctuaires royaux du Nord (1 R 12,29). Il est également possible que les sacerdoces de Bethel[28] et de Silo[29] aient été lévitiques. En Dt 33,8-11, texte prédtn avec complément Dtr (9b-10a) qui connait la tradition combattante d'Ex 32, ils ont des adversaires, mais sont chargés du culte (Urim et Tummim, holocauste, encens).

Dans le Dtn, ils restent chargés du culte et sont prêtres/lévites (18,1-8). Mais ils sont dépossédés de leurs revenus au sanctuaire local et doivent être aidés par le propriétaire terrien. C'est à la littérature Dtr qu'il convient d'attribuer leur

27. A. Cody, *A History of Old Testament Priesthood* (AnBib, 35; Rome: Pontifical Biblical Institute, 1969), avec ses importantes remarques sur le sacerdoce des Elides à Silo et sur les noms égyptiens de ce clergé (pp. 69-70). Sur les Lévites de Dt 33,8-11, voir pp. 115-16.

28. Ce serait par Eléazar, curieusement enterré dans la 'ville de son fils Pinhas' à Gibea en Ephraïm. Ex 18,4 est le seul texte qui mentionne un second fils de Moïse du nom d'Eliezer (mêmes consonnes qu'Eleazar). Ce serait dans ce texte élohiste le sacerdoce de Bethel, sanctuaire royal, parallèle à celui de Gershom à Dan.

29. Voir Cody, *Priesthood*, p. 108. Selon 1 S 2,35-36, ce sacerdoce (Abiathar) a été supplanté par un autre (Sadoc) de même que les Lévites de 2 R 23,9 n'avaient pas égalité de droits avec les prêtres du sanctuaire central, et que Jérémie 'des prêtres d'Anatot' se heurta aux prêtres de Jérusalem (Jér 19–20; 26,8,11; 28,16-17).

relation spéciale à l'Arche d'Alliance et à la lecture de la Torah, ainsi que le refus de leur attribuer part égale aux prêtres de Jérusalem (2 R 23,9). Ezéchiel parle encore de prêtres-Lévites (43,19; 44,15) mais il les identifie aux Sadocites. Partout ailleurs (44,10; 45,5; 48,11-13.22), il distingue prêtres et Lévites et donne à ceux-ci un statut inférieur, non sacerdotal, car 'ils ont été loin de moi'; dans la perspective de ce prêtre de Jérusalem, ces Lévites étaient 'loin' de Jérusalem le sanctuaire où résidait la gloire de Dieu. Ce statut lévitique d'Ezéchiel va être appliqué par le Code sacerdotal et par la littérature postexilique, quitte à ce que Malachie accuse les prêtres de Jérusalem d'avoir 'violé' l'alliance de Lévi (2,8) qui devait être perpétuelle grâce à Pinehas (Nb 25,13; cf. Je 33,22 TM). En tout cas, pas plus que les Anciens des villes et les propriétaires terriens, les Lévites locaux du Dtn ne peuvent avoir été les promoteurs de la centralisation du culte à Jérusalem, tout en avant été profondément concernés par elle.

Et les *Prophètes* ? Ce milieu, lui aussi, paraît très complexe dans le Bible et l'Ancien Orient (Mari, Byblos, Hazrak...). Il y a les prophètes indépendants comme Eldad et Medad de Nb 11,27, les bandes de 'fils de prophètes' autour de Samuel et d'Elisée. Mais il y a aussi des prophètes royaux qui interviennent à la cour en fonction des problèmes politiques. Nous avons vu le nombre et l'importance des spécialistes qui voient dans le milieu prophétique l'origine du Dtn. Ils ont été contestés par L.J. Hoppe pour lequel le Dtn souligne surtout les défaillances des prophètes (13,2-6; 18,9-20). Il est certain que la formule globale 'mes serviteurs les prophètes' est Dtr et non Dtn[30] (2 R 9,7; 17,13; Jér 29,19; Am 3,7...). Le Dtn distingue entre les prophètes 'comme Moïse' (18,15) et les autres. Il est embarrassé pour donner un critère antérieur à la réalisation de la prédiction (18,21s). C'est au Lévite dépositaire de la Torah et non au prophète qu'est subordonné le roi. On voit ainsi que ces milieux ont été modifiés au cours de

30. Même en Am 3,7. Voir cependant les réserves de S. Paul, *Amos: A Commentary on the Book of Amos* (Minneapolis: Fortress Press, 1991), p. 112, à l'égard de l'opinion commune.

l'histoire, et que la terminologie est ambigüe. Peut-on préciser quelle époque et quel milieu le code deutéronomique concerne?

Pour determiner le milieu d'origine du Dtn et de la littérature Dtn il faut trouver une époque où:

1°. L'institution royale nationale est affaiblie (un 'frère') mais existe encore, quoique non sacrale selon le Deutéronome, même si, en fait, elle l'était encore à Jérusalem.

2°. Elle est assistée de Juges (qui même la précédent), et d'institutions de gouvernement qui sont *hakâmîm*, non pas au sens moral et religieux, mais au sens politique: aptes à donner des solutions prudentes.

3°. Ces institutions gouvernent des propriétaires terriens aisés, qui disposent de produits agraires, et des Anciens de bourgades locales; ils peuvent avoir une sagesse populaire rurale,[31] mais non pas de cette sagesse intellectuelle de cour acquise très probablement dans des écoles préparant à leurs tâches les fonctionnaires royaux.[32]

4°. Au culte central du seul sanctuaire où 'YHWH fait demeurer (mettre) son Nom', sont associés des Lévites qui peuvent rester dans leurs bourgades, mais sont alors sans ressources, comme la veuve, l'orphelin, l'étranger. Leur statut n'est ni celui des Lévites d'avant la centralisation du culte, ni

31. S. Terrien, 'Amos and Wisdom', dans B.W. Anderson et W. Harrelson (éds.), *Israel's Prophetic Heritage: Essays in Honour of James Muilenburg* (London: SCM Press, 1962), pp. 108-15, tout en admettant un 'common sense' dans la sagesse d'Amos, montre à quel point elle reflète la sagesse orientale.

32. A. Lemaire, *Les écoles et la formation de la Bible dans l'ancien Israël* (OBO, 39; Fribourg [Suisse]: Editions Universitaires, 1981). Les abécédaires témoignent d'exercices d'école. Or, pour former des fonctionnaires d'Etat, il fallait non seulement apprendre à écrire et compter (selon la graphie égyptienne, voir les ostraca de Cadès Barnéa et d'Arad), mais aussi a rédiger un jugement, faire un rapport et juger équitablement pour ne pas être lapidé comme un Adoram. Cela ne relève pas d'une éducation paternelle. Un scribe était nécessaire pour inscrire les noms des témoins (Jér 32,25; c'est le même ductus pour tous les noms, aussi bien dans la liste de Sichem (*ZDPV* 59 [1926], pl. 45) que dans un acte d'Elephantine (Cowley, §18; E. Sachau, *Aramäische Papyrus* [Leipzig: J.C. Hinrichs, 1911], pl. 33).

celui des Lévites postexiliques sans droits sacerdotaux, même
si le Chroniste cherchera à leur en rendre quelques uns
(2 Chr 29,5; 30,22; 31,14; 35,11.14).

5°. Les prophètes ne sont pas encore les prophètes 'canoni-
ques' que reconnaîtront le Dtr et les prophètes postexiliques
comme Zach 1,8. Quand on parle de l'influence du milieu prophétique sur le Dtn, sa théodicée et sa morale, on pense surtout aux quatre prophètes du 8ème s. BC: Amos, Osée, Michée
et Isaïe. Or aucun des quatre ne se présente comme *nābî'*.
Amos le dénie (7,14), et les trois autres prennent leur distance
vis à vis des *nebî'îm* (Os 4,5; Mi 3,5.11; Is 28,7). Le *nâbî'* est
encore à cette époque soit celui qui, à la cour, désigne l'élu de
YHWH ou annonce la victoire, soit l'un des *beney nebî'îm*
extatiques proches d'Elisée. Les suscriptions tardives d'Amos
(1,1), de Michée (1,1), et d'Isaïe (1,1; 2,1) les considèrent plu-
tôt comme des visionnaires, même quand elles leur attribuent
le *dābār*, et nous savons par 1 S 9,9 que le *nâbî'* fut d'abord
considéré comme un 'voyant'. Ces quatre 'prophètes' ne con-
stituent pas un milieu, mais ce sont des figures lucides dont
les disciples rassembleront les oracles après avoir reconnu leur
véracité. Contestés de leur vivant, ils témoignent (comme le
Dtn) de la division entre les prophètes, surtout de cour, et cela
depuis Michée ben Yimla (1 R 22) jusqu'à Jérémie (ch. 28).

Dans les premiers temps de leur activité, ces quatre
'prophètes' sont surtout préoccupés des problèmes du royaume
du Nord, celui qu'on appelle Israël, distingué de Juda. Osée
est du Nord, Amos quitte Jérusalem pour vaticiner à Bethel,
Michée s'en prend d'abord à Samarie (1,5aba'.6). C'est le cas
aussi d'Isaïe dans son grand poème à refrain (9,7-10) comme
en 28,1-4; à mon avis, l'endurcissement d'Israël dans la vision
inaugurale au début de la guerre syro-ephraïmite ne
s'explique bien qu'en fonction du refus du Nord d'accepter le
successeur de David à la mort d'Ozias.[33]

33. J'ai étudié cette difficile question à propos du nom de Shear-Yashub
(*Eighth World Congress of Jewish Studies [1981]* [éd. J. Kaplan;
Jérusalem: World Union of Jewish Studies, 1985], pp. 47-50), des
premiers destinataires d'Isaïe 2,2-5 (*VT* 30 [1980], pp. 409-20), des
aspects royaux de la vision d'Isaïe (*SEÅ* 39 [1974], pp. 38-58). En Is 5,3

C'est toutefois a Jérusalem que se forment leurs livres et que s'achève leur activité (Os 1,7; 3,5; Am 1,2; 2,4-6; 9,11). Qu'en est-il du Deutéronome dont on ne peut nier les connexions avec les traditions du Nord, ce que reconnait même L.J. Hoppe?[34] Nicholson a rassemblé les arguments et les a développés;[35] il termine en se posant la question: 'How did it [Deuteronomy] find its way to Judah?' C'est en effet de Jérusalem que part la réforme de Josias[36] comme l'avait démontré de Wette. Pour la littérature deutéronomique Jérusalem/Sion est le lieu choisi par YHWH pour centraliser le culte.

Or certaines des dispositions du Dtn sont apparues comme peu adaptées à l'epoque de Josias. Les critiques formulées par Hölscher,[37] bien que réfutées par Budde et beaucoup d'autres, ont eu un grand écho et conduit des auteurs de poids à faire du Dtn un programme postexilique. Pour Würthwein la réforme de Josias en 2 R 23 serait une composition artificielle

c'est Jérusalem qui est appelée comme témoin contre la 'vigne' donc le Nord. L'étude très soignée de D. Vieweger sur Is (8,23ab'b), 9,1-6 (*BZ* NF 36 [1991], pp. 77-86, rend vraisemblable l'attribution de 9,6bb' à un disciple, mais l'oracle d'intronisation royale se place mieux lors de l'élévation d'Ezéchias à la corégence (dans la troisième année d'Osée d'Israël (circa 728; cf. 2 R 18,1) qu'à une époque où Josias était roi depuis huit ans.

34. Hoppe, *Origins of Deuteronomy*, p. 257; cf. p. 121. C'est l'opinion de Welch, Gressmann, Alt *et al.* (liste dans Preuss, *Deuteronomium*, pp. 30-31), même de R. Smend, *Die Entstehung des Alten Testaments* (Theologische Wissenschaft, 1; Stuttgart: Kohlhammer, 1978), pp. 78-81; et, quoiqu'on en ait dit, de F.R. McCurley, Jr, 'The Home of Deuteronomy Revisited: A Methodological Analysis of the Northern Theory', in *A Light unto My Path: Old Testament Studies in Honour of Jacob M. Myers* (Gettysburg Theological Studies, 4; éd. H.N. Bream, R.D. Heim, C.A. Moore; Philadelphia: Temple University Press, 1974), pp. 295-318 (311). Cf. H. Cazelles, 'Sur l'origine du mouvement deutéronomique', dans *Festschrift A. Malamat* (sous presse).

35. Nicholson, *Deuteronomy and Tradition*, ch. 4, pp. 58-82.

36. Sans admettre avec Bächli et Lindblom que le Dt soit produit des Lévites du Sud.

37. G. Hölscher, 'Komposition und Ursprung des Deuteronomium', *ZAW* 40 (1922), pp. 161-255, qui a impressionné d'éminents auteurs comme S. Mowinckel, O. Kaiser, R. Smend, H.J. Preuss, E. Würthwein.

visant à donner de l'importance au Dtn.[38]

La difficulté, c'est qu'on ne voit pas quel serait à cette époque postexilique le milieu qui aurait produit ce texte et sa réforme. Il n'y a plus ni roi ni cour. Le roi est un étranger, non un 'frère'; c'est d'un *nâśî*', même David, qu'on attend une restauration. Il n'est pas fait mention d'Anciens dans les listes de rapatriés installés dans les villages. Le paysan n'est plus le riche propriétaire terrien, mais un fellah endetté opprimé par des nobles (*ḥôrîm*) et des officiers (*segânîm, sârîm*, Esd 9.2) en relations avec les autorités étrangères (Né 7,5) et habitant Jérusalem (Né 11,1). Les Lévites, qu'Esdras eut du mal à recruter (Esd 8,15), ont le statut diminué d'Ezéchiel et de P; ils n'ont place dans le culte que comme chantres ou portiers. Les Psaumes qui doivent beaucoup au milieu lévitique ne connaissent le roi que comme futur Messie. L'école d'Isaïe (40–66) ne s'appuie pas sur les institutions deutéronomiques, même quand il s'agit de pratiques idolâtres (65,3-8; 66,3). Jérémie est exclu de l'Histoire deutéronomique, alors même qu'un éditeur Dtr a utilisé son livre. Le prophétisme post-exilique connait le Dtn, mais il ne le promeut pas. Quant aux Ecoles de sagesse, elles ont une conception d'une *ḥokmah* fondée sur la 'crainte de Dieu' et non sur une sagesse politique humaniste.

On pourrait penser que le 'peuple du pays' (Esd 4,4) auquel se sont heurtés les rapatriés ait pu être le porteur du mouvement Dtr. C'est en fonction du culte à Sion que viennent les gens de Samarie en Jér 41,5, qu'ont été chantées les Lamentations, et que ces 'gens du pays' proposent de participer à la reconstruction du Temple. Mais ils dépendent des autorités perses de Samarie et ne peuvent songer à une loi royale en faveur d'un roi 'frère'. Il y a certainement une édition postexilique du Dtn et de l'Histoire deutéronomique. Mais ces Dtr ne font nullement oeuvre créatrice. Ils sont des éditeurs de traditions du passé pour assurer l'unité d'Israël.

---

38. E. Würthwein, 'Das josianische Reform und das Deuteronomium', ZTK 73 (1976), pp. 395-423 et son commentaire de l'ATD (1984), p. 455. Mais voir les positions et arguments de Eichrodt, Gressmann, H. Schmidt, J.A. Bewer, J.B. Paton, W. Baumgartner, et, avec nuances, de G. Nebeling, G. Seitz et M. Rose.

On ne voit pas qu'ils songent à promouvoir une idéologie
religieuse qui s'opposerait à celle des rapatriés qui sont
soutenus politiquement par les autorités perses.

P. Dutcher-Walls a judicieusement observé qu'à l'époque
qu'elle étudie, celle du Dtr préexilique,[39] les différents milieux
sont mêlés dans les différentes factions qui s'opposent politiquement. Les prises de position de ces factions dépendent non
d'une idéologie, mais de la situation internationale.[40] N'en ser-
ait-il pas de même à l'époque du Dtn, préalable à celle du Dtr?

La seule vraie spécificité de la littérature Dtn/Dtr est celle de
l'existence de 'scribes' dans le gouvernement. A côté des scribes
intellectuels, formés à lire et à écrire, et qui parviennent à de
hautes fonctions dans l'Etat, ces *hâkâmîm* ministres ou juges,
il y a des *šôṭerîm*[41] qui assistent ces hauts fonctionnaires. Ce
terme juridique, d'origine araméenne, désigne ceux qui met-
tent par écrit les décisions, les listes de recrutement, et les
témoignages dans les contrats. Or ils apparaissent, selon toute
vraisemblance, dans l'histoire Elohiste;[42] ils disparaîtront au
profit du *sôpher*, spécialiste de la Torah dans les textes postexiliques, et n'interviennent plus dans l'administration civile,

39. Dutcher-Walls, 'The Social Location of the Deuteronomists', p. 91.
Il me paraît impossible de ne pas admettre une rédaction Dtr préexilique;
cf. N. Lohfink, 'Kerygmata des deuteronomischen Geschichtswerks', dans
*Die Botschaft und die Boten: Festschrift für Hans Walter Wolff zum 70.
Geburtstag* (ed. J. Jeremias et L. Perlitt; Neukirchen–Vluyn: Neukirchener
Verlag, 1981), pp. 87-100; R.D. Nelson, *The Double Redaction of the
Deuteronomistic History* (JSOTSup, 18; Sheffield: JSOT Press, 1981),
M.A. O'Brien, *The Deuteronomic History Hypothesis: A Reassessment*
(OBO, 92; Fribourg [Suisse]: Universitätsverlag, 1989). Je reste
impressionné par les analyses de H. Weippert en faveur d'une première
rédaction antérieure aux deux autres ('Die deuteronomistischen
Beurteilungen der Könige von Israel und Juda und das Problem der
Redaktion der Königsbücher', *Bib* 53 [1972], pp. 301-39).
40. Dutcher-Walls, 'The Social Location of the Deuteronomists', p. 84.
41. J. van der Ploeg, 'Les šôṭerîm d'Israël', *OTS* 10 (1954), pp. 185-96;
H. Cazelles, 'Institutions et terminologie en Deutéronome i 6-17', in
Volume du Congrès, Genève 1965 (éd. P.A.H. de Boer; VTSup, 15; Leiden,
1966), pp. 97-112 (104-107).
42. Il faut distinguer dans ce texte les šôṭerîm d'Israël frappés avec les
Israélites (E, Ex 5,14) et les šôṭerîm de Pharaon, assistant les
fonctionnaires *nôgesîm* (5,6), scribes qui enregistrent les normes.

sauf commission donnée par le roi perse.

Nous sommes ainsi renvoyés à une époque où Israël a encore un gouvernement avec des administrateurs *ḥakâmîm*. Nous avons ici un lien de plus entre le Deutéronome et l'Israël du Nord. Ce n'est pas le lieu de réétudier les contacts entre le Dtn et Osée. Il est utile toutefois de souligner que les quatre 'prophètes' du 8ème s. ont été provoqués dans leur activité par les problèmes politiques de l'Israël du Nord: problèmes de l'administration royale et de ses abus, problèmes de politique internationale (Am 1–2; 5,27; Os 7,11; 9,3; Mi 1; 5,4-14; Is 7).

Puisque le Dtn est avant tout un code, il conviendrait davantage de mettre en relief les rapports de ce Dtn avec les textes normatifs de la strate E du Pentateuque: le Décalogue de l'Horeb, les malédictions de Sichem,[43] le code d'Ex 20,22–23,19, déduction faite des ajouts Dtr.[44] Retenons qu'Osée (8,12) connait les collections d'oracles[45] en même temps qu'il est très préoccupé par les déviations de ceux qu'il appelle 'prêtres' et que le Dtn appellera 'lévites'. Il y a donc une activité de scribes aux sanctuaires locaux; on doit donc admettre un lien entre milieu lévitique et milieu scribal. De plus, l'Elohiste considère Josué non comme un guerrier, mais comme un serviteur de Moïse (Ex 24,11; Nb 11,28), un gardien de la Tente (Ex 33,11b). Enfin l'Elohiste considère Abraham

---

43. Ce texte a été repris par le Dtr qui refuse un autel sur le mont Ebal (cp. 27,5-6 et 2-3). De même 27,1, qui associe à Moïse les Anciens, appartient à ce texte prédt (cf. Nb 11).

44. H. Cazelles, 'Histoire et institutions dans la place et la composition d'Ex 20,22–23,19', dans *Prophetie und geschichtliche Wirklichkeit im alten Israel: Festschrift für Siegfried Herrmann* (éd. R. Liwak et S. Wagner; Stuttgart: Kohlhammer, 1991), pp. 52-64.

45. Le TM parle de mise par écrit de *rubby* (Q) ou *rubbw* (K) (cf. LXX *nomima kai*) de 'ma torah'. Toutes les versions ont lu le pluriel 'mes tôrôt' plus rare, donc *lectio difficilior*. En tout cas, chez Osée (4,6), une *torah* est à la charge du prêtre, donc d'un sanctuaire local. Voir les commentaires: W.R. Harper, *A Critical and Exegetical Commentary on Amos and Hosea* (ICC, 24; Edinburgh: T. & T. Clark, 1905), p. 320; H.W. Wolff, *Dodekapropheton*. II. *Joel und Amos* (BKAT, 14/2; Neukirchen–Vluyn: Neukirchener Verlag, 1969), pp. 170, 185; W. Rudolph, *Joel—Amos—Obadja—Jona* (KAT 13/2; Gütersloh: Mohn, 1971), p. 167; J.L. Mays, *Amos: A Commentary* (OTL; London: SCM Press, 1969), *ad loc.*

(Gn 20,7) et Moïse (Nb 12,7) comme *nebî'îm*, pensant plus aux prophètes itinérants tel un Elisée, qu'aux prophètes de cour. Mais Moïse est plus qu'un prophète car il 'est fidèle dans toute ma maison', tente ou sanctuaire.

Il y a donc des relations, non entre milieux, mais entre personnalités appartenant aux différents milieux d'Israël, l'influence la plus grande étant celle de Lévites. Toutefois, ce ou ces Lévites, responsables de l'histoire de salut Elohiste (sur la base d'une *berît* et de son formulaire), ne paraissent pas appartenir a un 'sanctuaire royal' comme Bethel (Am 7,13); ils partagent la grande défiance d'Osée vis à vis de la royauté, de son clergé, de ses prophètes (sauf Moïse) et de ses chefs (*śârîm*).

Or le Dtn va reprendre les traditions normatives ou historiques de l'Elohiste, non seulement du Code dit de l'Alliance,[46] mais de l'Horeb (Décalogue) et du désert (Ex 18). Il les reprend, mais dans de nouvelles perspectives. Il a une attention toute particulière pour les scribes auxquels on emprunte leur mode d'enseignement. En Ex 18 les juges associés à Moïse sont des militaires; ils sont maintenant des *ḥakâmîm* (Dt 1,15; 16,19). L'institution royale n'est pas supprimée mais maintenue sous condition. Elle est précédée de l'institution de juges, locaux ou centraux, et contrôlée par des prêtres/lévites et des prophètes comme Moïse. L'innovation principale est la centralisation du culte en 'un seul lieu choisi par YHWH dans l'une de tes tribus' (12,14), en contradiction avec le code Elohiste (Ex 22,24).

Ces transformations des institutions sont-elles le fruit d'une 'théologie' qui veut purifier le culte en fonction d'idées sur Dieu? Ou est-ce l'écho de la volonté de milieux Elohistes qui veulent rester fidèles a YHWH Dieu national trônant encore dans la seule Jérusalem, sans se soumettre politiquement aux dieux de l'étranger?[47] Chez l'Elohiste, Dieu est déjà au ciel

---

46. Cf. G.E. Wright, 'Deuteronomy', *IB*, II, pp. 323-25; H. Cazelles, *Etudes sur le Code de l'Alliance* (Paris: Letouzey et Ané, 1936), pp. 104-106; *idem*, 'Sur l'origine du mouvement deutéronomique', dans *Festschrift A. Malamat* (cf. n. 34 supra). Excellent tableau des parallèles dans Preuss, *Deuteronomium*, pp. 104-106.

47. Ce sont des *'elohey nakèkar* dans la littérature élohiste (Gn 35,2.4; Jos 24,23; Jud 10,16; 1 S 7,3), et des *'elohim 'aḥérîm* dans la littérature

(Gn 21,17; 28,12) et le culte épure: tout autel est lié à une manifestation divine (Ex 22,24-25; cf. Dt 27,5-6a, 15-25). Mais, selon l'Elohiste, ce sont encore douze tribus qui sont unies dans l'alliance de l'Horeb et de Gilgal (Ex 24). Or, en 722 BC *dix ou onze tribus* ne sont plus soumises à l'obedience (cf. Hoppe) de YHWH, Dieu d'Israël, mais aux 'dieux de l'étranger' (E), aux 'autres dieux' (D). Dans le Dtn Israël est regroupé en un 'peuple' consacré, réuni en un *qehal YHWH*, en un seul lieu d'*une seule tribu* où règne un roi 'frère' et un juge suprême. Le plus vraisemblable est d'admettre avec Clements, Nicholson, Bächli,[48] et d'autres, que le Dtn est rédigé par des 'Elohistes' qui ont vécu l'agonie de Samarie avec Osée. Ils proposent un regroupement de 'tout Israël' autour de YHWH et du Temple construit par le fils de David.

Or la monarchie de Juda était encore sacrale: ce sont Ezéchias et Josias qui règlent le culte. La loi royale ne pouvait convenir à cette cour, critiquée par Isaïe. Beaucoup d'indices suggèrent qu'Ezéchias, soutenu par Michée,[49] tenta une réforme appuyée sur le Dtn. C'est alors que le projet Dtn se montra inapplicable, tant à cause de la situation internationale (pression de l'Assyrie triomphante), que de la répugnance de la cour et du clergé de Jérusalem vis à vis de ces traditions du

Dtr (5,7; 6,14; 7,4...).

48. O. Bächli me parait avoir bien montré (*Israel und die Völker: Eine Studie zum Deuteronomium* [Zürich: Zwingli, 1962]) que le Dtn était plus conditionné par 'l'existence du peuple' menacée (pp. 32-33) et la fonction du roi 'porteur du pouvoir' (pp. 192-200) que par une théologie centralisatrice. Mais je ne crois pas que le roi ait pu être l'initiateur de la loi royale, ni d'une théologie, si dépendante de E, et si différente de celles de J et de P. Les vues de Nicholson (*Deuteronomy and Tradition*, pp. 91-101) me paraissent très fondées, quoique je placerais la première rédaction de Dtn entre 722 et 716/715: Ezéchias est devenue seul roi et, avec l'appui de Michée, tente une réforme politico/religieuse qui sera vite mise en échec.

49. Il se présente comme le prophète vaillant (Mi 3,8), entre deux réquisitoires contre les 'chefs de Jacob et d'Israël' (seul le second mentionne Jérusalem). La réforme est attestée non seulement par 2 R 18,4.21, mais par Jér 26,18-19. Comme la racine de *'tq* implique toujours un transfert, un mouvement, il est probable que les 'gens d'Ezéchias' de Pr 25,1 sont des *ḥakâmîm* du Nord qui ont apporté avec eux, près d'Ezéchias, des proverbes du Nord. Enfin la découverte par Avigad du 'mur d'Ezéchias' témoigne de l'extension de Jérusalem en un nouveau quartier, le Mishneh.

Nord. On sait qu'il en fut de même à la mort de Josias. Mais le Deutéronome avait été promulgué comme Loi d'Etat, même à Samarie, Sichem et Silo (Jér 41,5). Le Dtr le conservera dans son histoire; les 'gens du pays' (Samaritains) y resteront attachés et, dans la Torah, il fut incorporé dans le cadre du code sacerdotal.

Auparavant, le milieu qui, à Jérusalem, tenta d'adapter les traditions du Nord à la monarchie et aux institutions de Juda, ne peut être que le milieu Elohiste établi dans le Mishneh, un nouveau quartier de Jérusalem; c'est là qu'on ira consulter la prophétesse Huldah, femme d'un gardien de vêtements du Temple, donc un lévite selon Ezéchiel. Pour lui, les Lévites sont portiers et 'font le service du Temple' (44,11); ils gardent donc les vêtements liturgiques réservés au *kôhanîm* (42,12.14). Ce fils du prêtre Buzi connaissait les coutumes du Temple. C'est ce groupe de réfugiés du Nord, composé de milieux sociologiques différents qui, unis aux Helkias, aux Shaphanides et à Jérémie, allait se heurter aux prêtres, aux prophètes (Jér 26,11.16) et aux *ḥakâmîm* de R.N. Whybray.

RUTH: A HOMILY ON DEUTERONOMY 22–25?

Michael D. Goulder

The legal problems of the book of Ruth should be treated as
Bertrand Russell treated the question of life after death: with
a noble and unyielding despair. For the charming tale repeatedly confronts the readers with dissonances. Legal customs
are presupposed by the story that are in contradiction to the
provisions they read in the Law books; and commentators
then undertake the thankless task of reconciliation.[1] Such
reconciliations are a mistake.[2] They may rest upon

1. So for example H.H. Rowley, 'The Marriage of Ruth', *The Servant of
the Lord and Other Essays on the Old Testament* (Oxford: Basil Blackwell,
2nd edn, 1965); D.H. Weiss, 'The Use of *qnh* in Connection with Marriage',
HTR 57 (1964), pp. 244-48; D.R. Ap-Thomas, 'The Book of Ruth', *ExpTim*
79 (1967–68), pp. 369-73; T. and D. Thompson, 'Some Legal Problems in
the Book of Ruth', *VT* 18 (1968), pp. 79-99; D.R.G. Beattie, 'Kethibh and
Qere in Ruth iv 5', *VT* 21 (1971), pp. 490-94; *idem*, 'The Book of Ruth as
Evidence of Israelite Legal Practice', *VT* 24 (1974), pp. 252-67; E.F.
Campbell, Jr, *Ruth* (AB; New York: Doubleday, 1975); J.M. Sasson, *Ruth:
A New Translation with a Philological Commentary and a Formalist–
Folklorist Interpretation* (Baltimore: Johns Hopkins University Press,
1979; repr. The Biblical Seminar; Sheffield: JSOT Press, 1989); E.W.
Davies, 'Inheritance Rights and the Hebrew Levirate Marriage', *VT* 31
(1981), pp. 138-44, 257-68; *idem*, 'Ruth iv 5 and the Duties of the *gōʾēl*',
VT 33 (1983), pp. 231-34; H.-F. Richter, 'Zum Levirat im Buch Rut', *ZAW*
95 (1983), pp. 123-26.
2. K. Nielsen, in a bold and imaginative article, 'Le choix contre le droit
dans le livre de Ruth' (*VT* 35 [1985], pp. 201-12), correctly despairs of
legal solutions and suggests that Ruth offers herself to Boaz much as
Tamar did to Judah. She was wearing *only* her mantle, and she uncovered
herself by his *margᵉlōt*. Dr Nielsen does not comment on the last verses of
ch. 3, where Boaz fills Ruth's mantle with six measures of barley and 'laid
it upon her'—it would appear that on this hypothesis she had a chilly
journey home.

hypothetical earlier, or later, forms of law and custom; or upon parallels alleged from other countries; or upon an alleged difference between actual local practice and notional national law-codes.[3] All these attempts to resolve the 'difficulties' are misguided, because, as I hope to show, the wording of Ruth is in many cases so close to that of the laws it contravenes, especially Deut. 25.5-10.

Chapter 4 is the most obvious minefield for legal explanations. Num. 27.8-11 provides that on death a man's property goes to his sons, and if no sons to his daughters, and if no daughters to his brothers. The widow is by-passed[4] (along with the sons' widows), and Elimelech's land would belong to his family, not to Naomi. In fact it would already belong to the near kinsman, and he would not have to buy it from the hand of anyone. In Deut. 25.5-6 the levirate is laid down as incumbent upon a brother living with the family, not upon a next-of-kin: so the *gōʾēl* would have no duty to sire a child of Ruth.[5] Further, Naomi tells her daughters-in-law that it is no use

3.   G.E. Mendenhall (*The Tenth Generation* [Baltimore: Johns Hopkins University Press, 1973], ch. 7) argues plausibly that Israelite law as administered in the village was not likely to have corresponded exactly to the laws preserved in our (defective) biblical codes, but will have been based on local tradition and accepted principle. Campbell uses this proposal to account for the disparities between Ruth and the Torah codes (*Ruth*, pp. 133-38), as do T. and D. Thompson and Beattie. Beattie argues that the legal settings cannot be impossible or the audience would not have accepted them; but the audience was as distant as the author from the former times when the judges judged.

4.   Rowley says, 'we are nowhere told of the wife's title to inherit in Israel, though in 2 Kgs 8.1-6 we find a widow in possession—presumably in trust for her son' ('Marriage of Ruth', p. 184 n. 2). 2 Kgs 8.5 actually speaks of '*her* house and *her* land'; she was the 'great woman' of 2 Kgs 4.8, and it would be better to presume that the property was hers as heiress.

5.   There are two ways of avoiding this difficulty. One is to assert that the levirate applied more widely in earlier times; so Rowley, 'Marriage of Ruth', pp. 174-81, comparing laws for blood feuds. But whereas the levirate law is said to have become *less* strict by the time of Deuteronomy, the disapprobation for not observing it has become markedly stricter with the 'introduction' of spitting in the face. The other is the less common line of denying that the levirate is involved (so Sasson, above). This faces the problem of the extent of the language in common with Deut. 25.5-10.

staying with her, for they could not wait till she bore and reared sons for them to marry; but such sons would not be of the 'seed' of Elimelech and Mahlon, and descent through the mother was irrelevant.[6]

Ruth 4.5 is a famous aporia. The Hebrew (K) reads, 'What day thou buyest the field of the hand of Naomi and from (*wm't*) Ruth the Moabitess, the wife of the dead, I have bought (*qnyty*) to raise up the name of the dead upon his inheritance'. The sense of this is opaque.[7] The *q^ere* gives *qnyth, qanita*, which gives some (if obscure) meaning: 'thou hast bought [also] [the duty] to raise up the name...' A common proposal is to emend *wm't* to [*w*]*gm 't*[8] (and no doubt this is correct). One can then translate, '...of Naomi, you have also bought Ruth the Moabitess...' However, not only would this be invalid, since the levirate was not incumbent outside the nuclear family; it was also no more customary to buy one's wife in Israel than it is in England.[9] Nor is this an accident; at

---

6. Rowley ('Marriage of Ruth', pp. 190-91) says that this is to press the passage too far. Naomi is merely 'stressing the complete impossibility of her providing them with fathers for their children'. But this would seem a rather pointless stress unless levirate husbands were in mind; they might quite easily have got themselves husbands otherwise by 'following the young men, whether poor or rich', as is said at 3.10. Cf. Campbell, *Ruth*, pp. 83-84: 'we encounter real difficulties... some form of levirate marriage practice'. The matter is 'nailed down' by the introduction of *y^ebimtēk* at 1.15, since the *ybm* root is found elsewhere only in the levirate passages in Gen. 38 and Deut. 25.

7. Beattie ('Ketibh') defends K, translating, 'I am acquiring Ruth...' But *qnh* (of humans) nearly always means to acquire by purchase, and in any case the near kinsman would have prior rights. Sasson (*Ruth*, pp. 120-36) denies that levirate marriage is in question, and suggests that Boaz is buying *Ruth's services* from Naomi. No evidence is alleged for such payment.

8. 'Most editors recognize that the Hebrew text needs to be corrected by the change of a single letter, to yield "Also Ruth the Moabitess thou must acquire"' (Rowley, 'Marriage of Ruth', p. 193 n. 1). He is followed by Sasson (*Ruth*, p. 122); Campbell (*Ruth*, p. 146) thinks the *mem* is enclitic.

9. Campbell comments sensibly, 'What does the verb "to buy" come to mean when applied to Ruth? Is there portrayed here a concept of marriage by purchase? If so, to whom would be paid a bride-price?' (pp. 146-47). He escapes the problem through the theory of D.H. Weiss,

4.10 Boaz says, 'Moreover Ruth...have I bought to be my wife'.[10] RV's translation of 4.5, 'thou must buy it also of Ruth', ignores 4.10, and is hardly defensible.

There is further trouble over the shoe. The plain sense of the law in Deuteronomy 25 is that the brother who will not undertake the levirate is *disgraced in public*. The widow pulls off (*ḥlṣ*) his shoe before the elders and spits in his face. But according to 4.7-8 the 'custom in former time' was in such matters for the one declining the obligation to draw off (*šlp*) his shoe and give it to the one accepting as 'the manner of attestation'.[11] This is very much nicer, especially if there is no spitting. Not that Ruth is in a position to do such a thing, since she is not present, although according to the law it is she who is required to lodge the complaint to the elders.

There is a final muddle in that the whole purpose of the book has been to 'raise up a name' for *Mahlon*, but once Ruth is married to Boaz he is totally forgotten, and Obed is said to be the son of *Boaz*. Even those who excise the last five verses[12]

'The Use of *qnh* in Connection with Marriage', *HTR* 57 (1964), pp. 244-48. Weiss argued that whereas *qdš* and *'rs* were the normal words for 'marry' in the Mishnah, *qnh* was used when goods were also involved; but Sasson objects (*Ruth*, p. 123) that the contexts are reminiscent of Ruth, and may have been influenced by it.

10. The author thought that whoever redeemed the land had to buy Ruth as part of the bargain. He is likely to have taken the idea that one bought one's wife 'in the days when the judges judged' from the story of Samson, who says to his father, 'now therefore get (*qḥw*) her for me to wife' (Judg. 14.2) and 'pays' thirty changes of raiment; or from the story of David who 'paid' two hundred foreskins of the Philistines for the hand of Michal (1 Sam. 18.27).

11. Rowley ('Marriage of Ruth', pp. 182-83) and Campbell (*Ruth*, p. 150) agree that in Ruth the shoe symbolizes the transfer of a right. They do not feel obliged to explain how this early custom (as both of them believe it to be) became a symbol of disgrace in Deuteronomy 25. One might have thought that the disgrace would have been sharper in earlier times, in line with other forms of social pressure.

12. It is the ousting of Mahlon by Boaz that has led to the widespread treatment of 4.17c-22 as an appendix (Campbell, *Ruth*, p. 15). But the logic is poor—the whole book is full of 'difficulties'. If the original author did not have David's ancestry in mind, why is the story set in Bethlehem? Why are Elimelech's family said to be 'Ephrathites of Bethlehem-Judah'?

have to explain why Mahlon is not mentioned in the narrative; the women say merely, 'There is a son born to *Naomi*'.

The paradox is that although the *story* is in such dissonance with the law, especially the law in Deut. 25.5-10, the *wording* is extremely close; the impression given is rather like a first-rate sermon on Isaiah 53 by a country vicar who has unfortunately missed the point of the passage by not reading Norman Whybray[13]—the preacher is expounding his text phrase by phrase, but has totally misunderstood its force. We may see this in the case of Ruth from the following points:

1. Deut. 25.5: If brethren dwell together, and one of them die, and have no son, *the wife of the dead* ('*ēšet-hammēt*) shall not marry without unto a stranger...

This is exactly the situation in Ruth. Mahlon and Chilion are brethren dwelling together, and Mahlon dies; Orpah stays in Moab to find a second husband, but Ruth declines to do that, nor does she 'follow young men' in Israel (3.10). She is called *the wife of the dead* ('*ēšet-hammēt)* at 4.5.

2. Deut. 25.5: ...her husband's brother shall go *in unto her and take her to him to wife* (yābō' 'āleyhâ ûl°qāḥāh lô l°'iššâ).

The phrase occurs elsewhere only at 1 Sam. 17.12: 'Now *David* was the son of that Ephrathite of Bethlehem-Judah, whose name was Jesse'. Why 4.12, 'And let thy house be like the house of Perez, whom Tamar bare unto Judah'? Of course the levirate marriage recalls Tamar; but we might have expected 'Perez and Zerah', as we have 'Rachel and Leah', unless Perez's house was in mind for a reason. And then the name Obed becomes pointless, and has to be replaced with a hypothetical earlier Ben-noam (O. Eissfeldt, *The Old Testament: An Introduction* [ET; Oxford: Basil Blackwell, 1966], p. 479; A. Brenner, 'Naomi and Ruth', *VT* 33 [1983], pp. 385-97 [386]). Cf. also the carrying of an ephah of barley/parched grain to one's family (Ruth 2.17-18; 1 Sam. 17.17); and Moab as a place of refuge for David's father and mother in time of trouble (1 Sam. 22.3-4).

13. It is a great pleasure to be invited to take part in a volume to honour Norman Whybray, whose robust friendliness and incisive scholarship have made him so widely loved and admired.

In Ruth 4.13, Boaz *took* Ruth and she became *his wife; and he went in* to *her* (*wayyiqqaḥ...lô lᵉ'iššâ wayyābō' 'ēleyhâ*). The preposition *'el* is more delicate.

3.   Deut. 25.6:... and it shall be, that the firstborn which *she beareth* (*tēlēd*) shall *succeed in the name of his brother that died* (*yāqûm 'al-šēm 'āḥîw hammēt*), that his *name* be not blotted out of Israel.

In Ruth 4.13 Yahweh gave Ruth conception, and *she bore* (*wattēled*) a son, but unfortunately the author fails to mention his 'succeeding in the name' of his mother's first husband. This may be because of his human warmth, which goes out to the hitherto 'bitter' Naomi; or, if we accept the final form of the text, because the hidden agenda of the story has an interest in King David's ancestry. In 4.5 and 4.10 the duty of the *gō'ēl* is said to be *to raise up the name of the dead* (*lᵉhāqîm šēm-hammēt*) on his inheritance, and in the latter *the name of the dead* will not be cut off from among *his brethren* (*'eḥāyw*). It should be noted that in Gen. 38.8 Judah tells Onan to raise up *seed* to his brother (*hāqēm zeraʿ*); Ruth 4.5, 10 has retained the noun *šēm* from Deut. 25.6, but has adopted the hiphil of *qûm* as in Genesis 38, and accordingly dropped the *'al*. The similar *lᵉ'āḥîw* comes in Deut. 25.7.

4.   Deut. 25.7: And if the man like not to take his brother's wife, then his brother's wife shall *go up to the gate unto the elders* (*wᵉʿālᵉtâ haššaʿᵉrâ 'el-hazzᵉqēnîm*).

In Ruth 4.1-2 it is Boaz who *goes up to the gate* (*ʿālâ haššaʿar*) and takes ten men of the *elders*; this is in line with the kindly spirit of the whole book. It is embarrassing for a foreign girl to claim her rights against the local Israelite of some substance, and Boaz, as throughout, behaves like a gentleman.

5.   Deut. 25.9:... [she shall] loose *his shoe* (*naʿᵃlô*) from off his foot, and spit in his face...

In Ruth 4.7 the former custom is said to have been that a man drew off *his shoe* (*šālap ʾiš naʿᵃlô*), and gave it to his neighbour (that is the actual *gō'ēl*) as 'a manner of attestation'. The kindly author has no wish to drag the near kinsman in the mud; he wishes in any case to exalt Boaz's good-heartedness, and this is best done by removing all reproach from the kinsman, whose only fault becomes his limited capital. So Ruth is kept off stage, and with her any suggestion of spitting. The kinsman 'draws off' his own shoe, where in Deuteronomy 25 the widow pulls it off (*ḥlṣ*) with contempt and roughness.[14] The whole symbolic action is said to have been normal in business matters of bargain and redemption for 'attestation'. The world is close to the vision of Dr Pangloss.

6.   Deut. 25.9:...and she shall answer and say, 'So shall it be done unto the man that doth not *build up* his brother's house' (*lō'-yibneh 'et-bêt 'āḥîw*).

In Ruth 4.11 the people and the elders bless Boaz and pray that Yahweh will make Ruth like Rachel and Leah, 'which two did *build the house of Israel*' (*bānû šᵉtêhem 'et-bêt Yisrā'ēl*).

So many verbal contacts with Deut. 25.5-10 cannot be accidental; and yet the narrative is riddled with what seem to be misunderstandings. How are we to explain this? If, as is often thought, Ruth is a late book,[15] say, of the fourth century, then we might think that the Deuteronomic laws have become

---

14. There is no evidence of the force involved in the qal of *ḥlṣ*; but the piel is commonly used of God 'rescuing' his people from trouble, pulling them out firmly, and in Lev. 14.40, 43 of pulling or tearing out (BDB) stones from a house.

15. A list of scholars' opinions down to 1963 is given by Rowley, 'Marriage of Ruth', p. 172 n. 1, of whom about half give post-exilic dates. More recently an early date is given by Campbell and Sasson; a late one is given by J.-L. Vesco ('La date du livre de Ruth', *RB* 74 [1967], pp. 235-47) and J. Gray (*Joshua, Judges and Ruth* [Century Bible; Cambridge: Cambridge University Press, 1967]). The issue has often turned on the claimed Aramaisms, but other arguments are more telling. Ruth is a *family Novelle*, like Tobit or Susanna or Joseph and Aseneth; it is about a *woman*, like Esther, Judith and Susanna; it is an *edifying tale* in which faithfulness to God in time of trial comes to a happy ending, like Esther and Job; it was classed with the *Writings* despite its belonging by subject with the Former Prophets. All these associations suggest a late date.

obsolete, and so no longer understood,[16] and the author has made use of them to provide part of the plot of his story, to give a 'period' feel to it. In the same way he writes 'And it came to pass in the days when the judges judged', of Orpah going back 'unto her gods' (cf. Judg. 11.24), of 'the custom in former time' (cf. 1 Sam. 9.9), and many other period touches. But then where has the rest of the plot come from?

The theme of ch. 2 is reminiscent of Deut. 24.19:

> When thou *reapest* thine *harvest in* thy *field* (*kî tiqṣōr qᵉṣîrᵉkā bᵉśādekā*), and hast forgot a *sheaf* (*'ōmer*) in the *field*, thou shalt not go again to fetch it: it shall be for *the stranger* (*laggēr*), for the fatherless and for the widow: that the LORD thy God *may bless thee* (*yᵉbārekᵉkā YHWH ᵉlōheykā*) in all the work of thy hands.

Naomi and Ruth come to Bethlehem in the beginning of the barley *harvest* (*qᵉṣîr*), and Ruth goes and gleans in the *field* (*śādeh*) after the *reapers* (*haqqōṣᵉrîm*). It is the portion of *the field* belonging to Boaz, who comes, and his *reapers* say to him, *The LORD bless thee* (*yᵉbārekᵉkā YHWH*). Ruth had asked to glean after *the reapers* among the sheaves (*bāᵃmārîm*). Boaz is kind to her, and tells the young men to let her glean even among the *sheaves*. So Ruth gathers plentifully, for herself and for Naomi. The story is particularly close to the Deuteronomy 24 law in that Naomi is a widow, and Ruth is both a widow and a stranger—this is the only time when we see this law in operation in the Bible. As in ch. 4, the narrative is marked by an even kindlier spirit than the law requires. It is not that Boaz's reapers have forgotten a sheaf, but they are told by him deliberately to let Ruth glean among them, and even to pull some corn for her out of the bundles. There are similar laws on gleaning for *gērîm* in Lev. 19.9 and 23.22, with the provision not to harvest the corners of the field rather than the forgotten *sheaf*, but they do use the verb to glean (*tᵉlaqqēṭ*).

A contrast is often also felt to be intended between Ruth and Deut. 23.3-6.[17] The law provides:

16. Vesco, 'La date', p. 242.

17. So Eissfeldt, *Old Testament Introduction*, p. 483; Vesco, 'La date', pp. 242-43; Ap-Thomas, 'Ruth', pp. 369-73. Vesco points to the frequent repetition of 'Ruth the *Moabitess*'. The suggestion is discarded by Rowley

> An Ammonite or a *Moabite* shall not enter into the assembly of
> the LORD: even to the tenth generation shall none belonging to
> them enter into the assembly of the LORD for ever: because
> they met you not with bread and water in the way, when you
> came forth out of Egypt; and because they hired against thee
> Balaam... Thou shalt not seek their peace nor their prosperity
> all thy days for ever.

The law is the more strikingly hostile against Ammonites and
Moabites because of the contrast in the following verses with
the Edomites and Egyptians, Israel's two traditional enemies:
these are not to be 'abhorred', and the children of the third
generation born to them—i.e. the grandchildren of a mixed
marriage—may enter the Israelite assembly. Of the two, the
Moabites are held in the greater abhorrence because their
king Balak was responsible for hiring Balaam to curse Israel.[18]

Now this passage is expressly cited in Neh. 13.1-3, and is
said to have been read in the audience of all the people; and
in consequence (it appears) Nehemiah persecuted those Jews
who had married women 'of Ashdod, of Ammon, of Moab'
(13.23), when he saw that their children did not speak
Hebrew. He merely contended with them, reviled them, beat
them and pulled out their hair, forcing them to swear to
marry their children only to Israelites; but in Ezra 10, in similar circumstances, there were compulsory divorces. It would be
easy to understand that liberals (especially any with foreign
marital connections) might wish to influence public opinion in
an opposite direction.

The contrast of Ruth with Deuteronomy 23 is therefore
probably intentional despite the lack of verbal correspondence.
Elimelech and his family are in need of food and drink, like
Israel in the desert, and it is to Moab that they go; the
Moabites not only receive them, but supply two extraordin-
arily nice daughters-in-law, one of whom becomes a pattern
proselyte, and the great-grandmother of King David. The

('Marriage of Ruth', p. 173), Campbell (*Ruth*, p. 27) and (with feeling)
Sasson (*Ruth*, pp. 246-47), on the ground that Ruth is 'a tale utterly
devoid of factious discord'. But so is Jonah—that may be their art.

18. A more probable reason for the law is the incursions of Ammonite
and Moabite bands into Israel mentioned in 2 Kgs 24.2.

famine in the land of Israel shows that the Moabites have been a good support to Israel this time; and there seems no question that one born from a Moabitess in the *fourth* generation was quite welcome in the assembly of Israel. A plausible setting in life is thus suggested for the book. Deut. 23.3-6 is (from whatever date) a function of the defensive movement in Israel, the strain most obviously in evidence in the rulings of Nehemiah and Ezra that Israelites should not have foreign wives.[19] Ruth is a highly skilled counterblast to this. If Moabites are so decent to famine-struck Israelites, and make such delightful wives, surely marriages with them should be acceptable.

In this way it would seem as if the author of Ruth had derived the plot of his idyll from certain laws in Deuteronomy 23–25; and this impression is strengthened by Deut. 22.30 (Heb. 23.1):

> A man shall not take his father's wife, and shall not *uncover* his father's *skirt* (*lō' yᵉgalleh kᵉnap 'ābîw*).

The two cola are in parallel: the man who marries his dead father's wife is felt to be infringing a tabu and, so to speak, exposing his father's genitals—cf. Lev. 18.7, 'The nakedness of thy father, even the nakedness of thy mother thou shalt not uncover: she is thy mother'.

This somewhat obscure expression will then provide an explanation for the puzzling scene in Ruth 3. Naomi instructs Ruth to go down to the threshing floor, and when Boaz has done eating and drinking and lies down to sleep, she is to *uncover* his 'leg-areas' (*wᵉgillît margᵉlōtāyw*, 3.4), and lie down. Boaz comes, merry at heart, and lies down in a conveniently private place, 'at the end of the heap of corn', and Ruth *uncovers* him as directed, and lies down; he awakes at midnight and is startled to find a woman lying by his *margᵉlōt*. She tells him her identity, and says to him, 'spread therefore thy *skirt* (*kᵉnāpekā*) over thine handmaid' (3.9).

---

19. It should be noted that the liberals had the whip-hand over Ezra and Nehemiah in this matter; so far from foreign wives being forbidden, they were expressly permitted, and their rights defended, in Deut. 21.10-14. The paragraph begins *kî tēṣē'*, 'When you go forth (to war)'.

Boaz accepts her request, and tells her to lie there till morning; and she lies by his *marg^{e}lōt* till dawn approaches.

This controverted[20] incident seems understandable in the light of what has been said above. The author of Ruth is drawing on the corpus of laws in Deuteronomy 22–25, many of which are obsolete, and not understood. Deut. 22.30 says that one must not uncover one's father's skirt; and this can be naturally read to mean that one must not expose his genitals, literally—a thing that no decent Israelite would wish to do (cf. Gen. 9.20-27). But the law associates the uncovering of the skirt with *marriage* ('A man shall not take his father's wife'), and the author of Ruth has misunderstood the words to imply that under certain circumstances it would be proper to uncover a man's skirt as a preliminary to marriage. The idea is taken to be sheerly symbolic; no hanky-panky is implied, and the whole atmosphere is pure as the driven snow. At 2.12 Boaz prays a blessing on Ruth from 'the LORD, the God of Israel, under whose *wings (k^{e}nāpāyw)* thou art come to take refuge'. In the same way at 3.9 Ruth asks Boaz to 'spread thy wing *(k^{e}nāpekā)*' over her; and here the author may be drawing on Ezek. 16.8, where Yahweh finds the naked, nubile Jerusalem by the way and *spreads his skirt/wing over* her. For an Israelite man to spread his wings over a Moabite girl would be on a human level what Yahweh is doing by spreading his wings over her on a divine level: providing for her, defending her, being served by her—in other words, marriage. Deut. 22.30 had puzzlingly combined the notions of *uncovering* and *skirt/wings* in a single phrase; Ruth's interpretation requires their separation, *uncovering the* marg^{e}lōt, and *spreading* the *skirt/wings*.

We have reached what might seem to be a surprising conclusion. The author of Ruth is writing some centuries after

---

20. Campbell *(Ruth,* pp. 130-31) stresses the ambiguity of the language, and the common use of sexual verbs *škb, yd', bw',* but concludes that there was no sexual intercourse (p. 138). Sasson *(Ruth,* pp. 76-77) leaves the question open. Beattie ('Ketibh', p. 493) thinks it is obvious that they slept together, as do Nielsen ('Le choix', pp. 205-206) and Brenner ('Naomi and Ruth', p. 387).

Deuteronomy, so that a number of its laws are misunderstood (22.30; 25.5-10), and one (23.3-6) is being covertly challenged. But for some reason it is drawing on a small concentration of laws in Deut. 22.30–25.10, and forming from them the plot of its story. The *motive* for doing this may be thought to be the current pressure against marriage with foreign wives that I have noted. But it would be satisfying if a reason could be suggested for the author's exploitation of such a series of Deuteronomic texts.

Two scenarios may occur to us. On a literary hypothesis, the author might be a learned man who had access to a copy of the Torah. He read the prohibition on Moabites in Deuteronomy 23, and carefully read through the surrounding text. As he meditated on it, he began to weave the masterpiece that we now have, and wrote it down. He circulated copies, and it became sufficiently popular that in time it came to be honoured, and its scroll was eventually adopted for liturgical reading at Pentecost. Such a view is not absurd. It assumes a leisured and literate public, and the habit of writing and circulating politico-religious tracts, which we may suspect of being anachronistic; but of course such assumptions are made to explain many of our biblical texts.

An alternative might be a liturgical theory from the beginning. Luke tells us that 'Moses from generations of old hath in every city them that preach him, being read in the synagogues every sabbath' (Acts 15.21). We do not know how many generations of old; but Deuteronomy itself suggests an original liturgical setting—'At the end of every seven years... in the feast of tabernacles, when all Israel is come to appear before the LORD thy God in the place that he shall choose, thou shalt read this law before all Israel in their hearing' (Deut. 31.10-11); and Deuteronomy 23 was being read liturgically in Neh. 13.1-3. People always needed to be taught the Law, and a continuous history of liturgical reading and exposition is a likely hypothesis. If so, we may return to our image of the vicar's moving but ill-instructed sermon on Isaiah 53. Perhaps a fourth-century country preacher was called upon to read and expound Deuteronomy 22–25, and had the genius to do so in the form of a story. Perhaps, indeed, he told the same story each year in progressively more detailed form, working in law after law. These laws are read in a single section in the Jewish cycle to this day; it runs from Deut. 21.10, the law covering foreign wives, to 25.19, and is known as *kî tēṣē'*, 'When thou goest forth'.

INDEX OF REFERENCES

OLD TESTAMENT

NEW TESTAMENT

INDEX OF AUTHORS